POWER JAPAN

HOW AND WHY THE JAPANESE ECONOMY WORKS

WILLIAM T. ZIEMBA
SANDRA L. SCHWARTZ

PROBUS PUBLISHING COMPANY
Chicago, Illinois
Cambridge, England

ISBN 1-55738-275-1

Printed in the United States of America

BB

1 2 3 4 5 6 7 8 9 0

This book is dedicated to our daughter Rachel
who lived the Japanese experience with us.

CONTENTS

All that working, living in small houses, traveling in crowded trains, saving all the time, not having any parks and not taking any holiday. It must be awful.

There is talk of Japan everywhere you look these days. The great wealth acquired in the 1980s by the Japanese and their giant companies has given the country vast economic clout. Many of the largest financial institutions and richest individuals in the world are Japanese. Land prices have risen to astronomical levels with Japanese land valued in 1990 at over 20 percent of the world's assets and over four times the value of U.S. land.

Japan has become the world's largest creditor nation but time will judge how it fills this role. The previous modern occupants of the position, Britain and the United States, did not handle it well. After attaining the position of creditor they each then entered a decline in competitive advantage. At the same time they overextended military obligations. Eventually they each, in turn, lost the title.

The apparent carefulness that the Japanese used in planning their moves meshed with their consensus decision. Their sense of vulnerability to natural disaster, meshed with their long planning horizons and respect for social cohesion, gives us hope that this period will be navigated successfully for Japan and the rest of the world. However, the 1990-92 turmoil in the stock and land markets and in the administration, banking and derivative markets is not encouraging.

Japan is a complex country. It is a land of paradox which makes it hard for North Americans to comprehend it. On the one hand they can produce the most sophisticated electronics, yet most houses do not have enough electricity to run several appliances (TVs, air conditioners and clothes dryers) at the same time. The banks are modern and world class but no one uses checks and credit cards are rare. In North America, there is praise and admiration as well as fear and hostility towards Japan. Atlanta has openly asked Japanese corporations to please buy their trophy buildings. They need investment money and the jobs that will follow. If the Japanese overpay, then this excess profit will spill over into the economy. With their huge wealth, large balance of trade, and vast holdings of U.S. and other foreign currencies, a natural way to reinvest this money is to buy all or parts corporations, land, and resorts around the world. Many of the resort areas

of Hawaii and Australia's Gold Coast are already in Japanese hands. They
have bought many of the major hotels in Whistler, Canada's top skiing
resort. They have bought Rockefeller Center and Pebble Beach. Moreover,
many of these resorts are close to being operated as fully integrated travel
companies. Japanese tourists travel on Japanese airplanes, stay in Japanese
hotels, eat Japanese food, and the yen they spend essentially stays in Japan.
In some resort areas, particularly in Hawaii and Australia, there is
considerable resentment toward the Japanese. The price of land and
housing and the general cost of living ostensibly contributed to the high
prices the Japanese are willing to pay, yet this has made these places un-
affordable to the locals. In some areas, the resentment is extremely deep.
Indeed some people believe the conspiracy theory that things are kept so
expensive at home precisely to enable Japan to buy up the world cheap.
Others greatly admire Japan's investment moves and its stability. Property
is usually purchased after considerable and careful study with the aim to
hold it essentially forever. Yet there are many exceptions such as some
panic cash crunch selling in 1991 and early 1992. Having one foot in the
high-tech future and one in the traditions of the past makes Japan an
especially interesting and complex society.

In this book we take a broad view of the variables necessary to deal
intelligently with Japan so we also provide background on how Japan
works, how they got what seems to be so far ahead of North America
economically, and what the future might hold. Many management gurus
have come before us to learn from Japan and have given us descriptions
and prescriptions of what to do to beat the Japanese. It is as if there were
time for only one observation and then a rush home: just-in-time inventory,
lifetime employment, quality control circles, bonus system. But each one is
only an aspect of Japan. A snapshot frozen in time and not a hologram.
Japan is all of these and more.

We discuss a number of aspects of Japan concentrating on the accumulation and use of its wealth. From 1949 to 1989, land values and stock prices
in Japan went up over 500 times in U.S. dollars. Why did these prices get so
high? Why were 1988 and 1989 such strong years for the Japanese stock and
land markets and 1990 and 1991 such weak years and what does the future
look like? Will there be a banking crisis if stock and land prices do not rise
substantially? Why are the Japanese so naive in derivative securities trading
and willing to leave so much easy picking money for foreign security firms?
Will the high-tech finance and takeover activity of the U.S. which brings so
little productive activity to the country spread to Japan and how will it
affect things? What was the impact in Japan and the U.S. of the Boone
Pickens' purchase of nearly a quarter of the shares of Koito Manufacturing?
Will the Japanese, who were the world leaders in productive export output
in the 1980s, be the world leaders in finance in the 1990s? Where are they

investing their money? Who has the money they have made and how is it spread around in the economy? What will be the impact of the 1989 Recruit and sex scandals on the economy, people and financial markets? What will be the consequences of the 1991 stock market scandals which led to the resignation of Finance Minister Hasimoto and to a large extent the withdrawal of support for Prime Minister Kaifu? We address these and related questions to provide an up-to-date look at Japan's economy and financial assets. We also discuss the 1990-92 stock and speculative land market crises and their impact on the economy and particularly the financially sensitive banks. Our companion books, *Invest Japan* and *Japanese Futures, Options and Warrants Markets*, deal with the workings of the Japanese stock markets and discuss the derivative security markets, respectively.

Without implicating them we thank our colleagues at the Yamaichi Research Institute and the University of Tsukuba for their helpful information and discussions on various aspects of Japanese culture, institutions, and investment strategies. It was Professor Keizo Nagatani of the University of British Columbia who, while visiting the University of Tsukuba on his sabbatical, suggested to Professor Rinya Shibikawa that he bring WTZ to Japan on the Yamaichi visiting professor chair program to help develop western-style financial research and teaching in Japan. At the same time SLS served as visiting Associate Professor of Economics and taught classes on comparing U.S. and Japan management for the information age and world debt. This allowed us to live the Japanese experience in daily life and in the financial markets. This book is dedicated to our daughter Rachel who not only puts up with her father's academic globe-trotting but thrives. In this case making friends, learning Japanese and about Japanese culture through the extraordinarily pleasant experience in Japanese public school, Teshirogi Minami in Tsukuba. We shall always treasure the wonderful treatment our family received during our stay in Japan in 1988-89. Every effort was made to make us feel comfortable and welcome as foreign guests. Our hosts did more for us than one would ever expect in a North American or European visit. The help through the maze of regulations and rules associated with university and business life was especially gratifying. Without their help it would have been hard to function. Atsuko Asano and Satoshi Nojiri were particularly helpful in this regard. We hope that this unique experience will be reflected positively in this book. Special thanks go to Yukio Okada, formerly vice chairman of the Yamaichi Research Institute, the organizer of the Tsukuba professorships for his exceptionally kind and generous help during our visit. Shizuya Kurata of Nihon Keizai Shimbun, Inc. and Kazuhiko Fujiki of the Japan Real Estate Institute supplied the golf course and overall land price data, respectively. Special thanks also go to Warren Bailey, Sean Elrington, David Myers, John Mulvey, Masao Nakamura, Steve Neville, John Ries, Julian Shaw, Emily Sion, Douglas Stone, Edward O. Thorp, Andy Turner, Ilan Vertinsky and Peter Williamson for helpful discussions and comments on earlier drafts of the book. Special thanks go to Atsuko Asano, Kar Miu and Nancy Thompson for outstanding research assistance. Kevin Thornton and Pamela Sourelis made many helpful suggestions in their editing of the book.

Continuing involvement with consulting and research activities related to Japanese financial markets with Buchanan Partners, the Frank Russell Company, Edward O. Thorp and Associates and the Gordon Capital Corporation has been very beneficial to this book. Some chapters have also benefited from seminar and conference presentations at Cornell University, Dartmouth College, New York University, the Vancouver ORSA/TIMS, the Osaka International TIMS, the Athens IFORS, the DAIS Group client conference, the Frank Russell client conference, the Operations Research Society of Japan, Tokyo and Nagoya branches, the Berkeley program in finance in Asia and in the U.S., the Swiss Institute of Banking and Finance, the Mexican Bolza (Stock Exchange) and the Pacific Basin Finance conferences organized by the University of Rhode Island and the Taipex Foundation. Partial support of research activities on the Japanese economy and its financial markets by the Social Sciences and Humanities Research Council of Canada and the Center for International Business Research at the University of British Columbia is also gratefully acknowledged.

William T. Ziemba and Sandra L. Schwartz
Vancouver, June 1992

Japan has one foot in the present looking to the future while the other foot is steeped in tradition. In everyday Japanese life, the past and the present mesh to create a complex society, at least for the *gaijin*—foreigner—to understand. An intense loyalty and camaraderie is found amongst the Japanese in both social and workplace life. Yet there is much competition among firms. The West sees Japan as a unified nation of middle class workaholics, living in rabbit hutches, spending hours commuting to work, taking no vacations, and living a dull existence in order to pile up mountains of money, for the benefit of big corporations, from the sale of state-of-the-art electronics, automobiles, and other products. Japan is seen as efficiency plus. Everything appears to work smoothly.

Less is known in the West about the other side of Japan. To its residents, Japan is not a straightforward, simple, efficient place. Bureaucratic red tape is high by Western standards. Rigid roles control many aspects of activity and behavioral expectations are very strictly held. The penalties for non-conformity can be severe. For all the apparent rigidity, the workers are flexible and adaptive and the society is responsive to changes in the global environment.

The Japanese are very proud people. Though as individuals the Japanese are extremely kind and generous to foreign visitors and workers, their institutions are nationalistic.

The Japanese have developed a cooperative, group-consensus style of decision making, *ringi*. Reflective of their Buddhist roots, they believe that the best decisions are made through harmonious rather than adversarial modes. Little can get accomplished until the group agrees that the plan is sound. As even the ordinary workers are well educated, Japanese managers can empower their workers and trust in the group process. The ringi process improves planning and eases implementation of strategies and also makes it easier to adapt their plans.

The cooperative Japanese system imparts a different attitude toward creativity. It does not reward, nor does it encourage, individual creativity as in the West. Taking credit for one's ideas goes counter to *ringi*. The Japanese truly see the whole as more than the sum of its parts, and the contribution

1

of any one part is recognized as having been nourished by the contributions of all. Even research scientists are expected to show humility in recognizing that their ideas depend on researchers who worked before and on the contribution of staff and custodial workers, without whose help the work would not have been possible. This is the true meaning of the term *middle class society*.

The Japanese are duly famous for developing other people's ideas to their full potential. They have done this in the auto, steel, shipbuilding, and electronics industries. Many of Japan's greatest successes are extensions of basic and developmental research done in the U.S. or elsewhere. They do not have a not-invented-here mentality and are enthusiastic to improve on all ideas. Once the Japanese have a vision of new product concepts, they are patient in developing them. They will invest what effort, money and time it takes to make a product a commercial success. In this they reflect a craft or hands-on approach to a strategy of continual improvement of both process and product.

Often the Japanese have seen practical applications where others see only theory or frivolity. They invested where others saw only pain, aggravation or disruption of the status quo as was the case with the U.S. steel industry. In the 1960s and 1970s, the Japanese firms built modern plants and used the new technologies of continuous casting and the basic oxygen furnace. U.S. steel industry lagged in implementing these though, with the funds invested, the industry could have revamped their plants. They were rightly left behind for ignoring the latest technology. That the U.S. industry lagged is not the fault of the Japanese, who did only what needed to be done, but lies with the U.S. firms which could not be bothered implementing the new technologies (Schwartz, 1989).

The Japanese have been criticized far too much for being imitators. All innovations are creative adaptations of prior work. The U.S. industry also started as an imitator. Americans *stole* factory layouts and machinery plans from the British and called it Yankee ingenuity. The British before them borrowed from the Dutch. Drucker (1985) in fact suggests the strategy of *creative imitation*.

The Japanese are not overly greedy and do not usually go for the immediate gain. Hostile takeovers and programmed trading, two darlings of the U.S. stock market, are still largely taboo for Japanese companies.[1] The Japanese stock market drop in 1990 was exacerbated by various types of

---

[1]While programmed trading is taboo by Japanese firms *in Japan*, it is a good way for them to make money in foreign markets. For example, in 1991 and 1992, Nomura was one of the largest index arbitrage program traders in the S&P 500 cash and futures markets in the U.S. Some profit is also made through foreign subsidiaries partly owned by large Japanese brokerage firms involved in Japanese derivative securities trading.

program trading. Much of this was associated with hedging activities of foreign firms that backed numerous Nikkei put warrants traded in Toronto, New York, and London. Although the big Japanese brokerage firms could make a lot of money with arbitrage and other forms of programmed trading, they have done little of it, leaving this business, at least for now, to the purview of the foreign brokerage firms, such as Baring, Jardine Fleming, First Boston, Goldman Sachs, Morgan Stanley, Merrill Lynch, Shearson Lehman Hutton, and especially Salomon Brothers. Working to the advantage of the foreign firms, arbitrage and derivative trading have become the main areas where they make money in Japan.

The Japanese firms have been content to deal with high volume but moderate margin markets.

The 1980s were a time of Japanese superiority in export marketing of manufactured goods. The thrust has always been to sell competitively at home and then overseas by responding to what customers value and then to manufacture the product so well that they can dominate the market. Do American firms do that? Well, the quiet successful ones do but there are a number of vocal ones who are busy lobbying for help and who are not willing to. They think it is almost un-American.[2] Japanese firms have been masters of providing what the customer wants. The Four Tigers— Singapore, Hong Kong, Taiwan and Korea—are also good at it.[3] This, after all, is what management is about—seeking market niches and providing what the customer wants.[4]

Once a market is established and the product is accepted, it is assumed that large profits will follow. They are concerned with quality. Witness Toyota cars in North America. At first they were cheap, then they were cheap and of good quality, then they were superior and well priced, then they were the best and high priced—always responding adaptively to the market. When quotas were placed on Toyota, the company moved upscale and built on product loyalty as well as quality, and earned the most economic rent. Now the public is so convinced of their superiority that

---

[2]Lest the reader think this too strong, we share credit for this statement with many commentators including Lester Thurow (1988). While obviously not strictly true the point is well taken. American firms produce products in the main for their own market which is big. If others want the products, fine, but there has not been an emphasis on asking what foreign markets might want and learning how U.S. companies can supply that need. Classic examples include trying to sell large refrigerators for small Japanese kitchens or marketing left-hand drive cars.

[3]These up-and-comers, called Newly Industrializing Economies (NIEs), deserve much study on their own; their development patterns exhibit both similarities and differences..

[4]Another telling example is the controversy concerning American hormone fed beef that was banned from the European Community. When the head of the Texas Department of Agriculture said they would be happy to sell hormone-free beef, he was labeled disloyal.

Toyota cars sell easily even at high prices, as with the Lexus. The pattern has been used successfully time after time.

In the 1980s, Japan emerged as the leader in manufacturing productivity. In the 1990s, Japan will be challenged by its role as a major creditor nation and will try its hand at financial engineering. These are both difficult tasks for long-term growth and success. The 1989–92 period has shown that despite their great wealth and power, the big Japanese brokerage firms have not excelled as the financial markets have become more deregulated. Indeed, to help them and the weak stock market in 1992, there is talk of regulatory constraints on derivative securities trading.

A combination of cultural and institutional constraints has led to poor economic performance in this period relative to the past and relative to the best foreign firms despite substantial in-house knowledge and products. The Japanese firms have been especially weak, relative to their strength in other areas, in their use of derivative securities, that is, securities whose price depends upon one or more underlying assets. The main problem seems to be cultural since these firms have strong in-house talents for sophisticated trading methods. They simply do not implement modern derivative securities trading techniques.

So far, Japanese financial firms have had only modest success in foreign markets. The foreign offices of the major brokerage firms, such as Nomura, Daiwa, Nikko and Yamaichi, and the major banks, such as Sumitomo, Fuji and Dai-Ichi, have not been very profitable. Except for those in London, where the Japanese securities firms got in early on profitable business resulting from the *big bang* (the expansion of the market through extensive use of derivative securities) many of these offices are losing money and are of the caretaker variety. Costs are high, including expensive hotels for Tokyo-based visitors who stay for long periods, and that cuts deeply into profits. However, the Japanese are patient. It is market presence, then market share and later profitability that they are after. They are gaining the presence now and tending their growing financial assets. Once the institutions move toward retail operations, have name recognition, and develop all the U.S. high-tech financial theories to their best use, they may be able to compete in finance the way they have competed in production.

Although they have been behind in many areas, such as modern portfolio theory, options,[5] futures, and the like, they are quickly catching up to the best U.S. firms in terms of in-house technical and execution knowledge. (Some say this may be the first sign of their demise, many have warned the Japanese to stick to production.) They are already much more

---

[5]Indeed they have their own type of options called *loyalty* that allows firms a free hand in developing their strategies. See for example the discussion of Koito in Chapter 10.

sophisticated than even the best Canadian financial firms, and they are catching the U.S. firms with their usual patient methods and substantial assistance from top U.S. financial experts.

Many firms, such as large insurance companies with vast resources to invest, are utilizing the talents of the best western consulting firms to develop sophisticated investment strategies. Star U.S. professors are teaching the Japanese what they know. The Japanese are listening and reading, planning and buying into small U.S. financial boutiques of high quality, such as market makers and futures traders. What they lack now is a commitment to *aggressiveness* in derivative security markets. So far they have been content letting the foreign firms lead in the actual trading of these instruments. The main U.S. financial journals and economic, political, and social periodicals and books are regularly translated into Japanese so that the results of research are quickly embedded into their store of knowledge. The speed of access to foreign language information is demonstrated by the example of an article by Fallows, "Containing Japan." It appeared in the *Atlantic Monthly* in May 1989 and, by June, was in a Japanese periodical along with a commentary and a number of other articles on the topic. The Japanese have Japanese translating the research so they can understand it from their point of view. One suspects that if any reverse translation (Japanese to English) is being done, it is by bilingual Japanese.[6] There are also, on a regular basis, many high-level interviews of top Western and Japanese business and economic experts on the NHK (the national network) and other TV channels. The Japanese are serious about their information.

There is a friendly competition between individual Japanese firms. Nikko bought into the factor analysis firm Barra, formed by Berkeley professors to form NIBA (Nikko-Barra). Its affiliation with Wells Fargo investment advisors, pioneers in index funds, and Leland, Obrien and Rubinstein, the U.S. portfolio insurance and super share firm, enhances this. Yamaichi is at the forefront in high-technology computerized financial models. Its technology computer room is heavily stocked with the latest high-tech devices, including an NEC supercomputer. They and others have computer models to pick and trade stocks based on fuzzy logic[7] using theories devised by Berkeley professor Lofti Zadeh. To date, the results have been less than stellar.

---

[6]Kanter (1989) takes this a step further in suggesting that one explanation of the apparent asymmetric benefit gained by the Japanese in joint ventures is that Japanese managers learn English but few U.S. managers learn Japanese.

[7]Fuzzy logic can deal with imprecise data sets and can handle concepts like *near* and *small*. Normally decision models are based on precise 0-1 Boolean logic.

Yamaichi has used foreign consultants, such as NYU's Thomas Ho and Steven Brown, to help construct state-of-the-art models to beat the market. Daiwa has the services of the distinguished academic team of Richard Roll and Stephen Ross, who have developed a Japanese arbitrage pricing (APT) model, as well as Nobel Laureate Harry Markowitz who is its U.S. research director. Meiji insurance has worked with Stanford's Nobel Laureate Bill Sharpe. The Frank Russell Company, with some help from WTZ, has built a very sophisticated asset allocation decision model for Yasuda Fire and Marine. But Nomura, the world's most powerful securities firm, is working fast to recover its top position and no doubt will do so. Its joint venture with Barr Rosenberg's international investment management firm is a step in this direction. The recent dismantling of some of the large computer networks by major U.S. firms may give the Japanese with their long-run thinking an open door to catch up and possibly move ahead of the U.S. competition.[8]

Much criticism has been directed at Japan for having grown at the expense of the U.S., we seek to explain Japan's rise to riches as an organic process in which they have creatively adapted to their environment. Japan has not sought to defeat the U.S. economically. Indeed, both Japan and the U.S. are advanced, powerful and rich countries operating in the modern global economy that need each other to remain economically vital and adaptive. Jacobs (1984) stresses the need to have trading partners at a similar level of development so it is not too difficult to imitate their goods. Trade is the best window on the world of new ideas and innovations that can keep an economy vital.

SOME JAPANESE DEMOGRAPHICS

Japan's society and economy have undergone tremendous changes in the last 50 years. Tables 1.1-1.4 show some social and demographic character-istics of Japan. Life expectancy has been steadily increasing. Japan now ranks first in life expectancy at birth. For children born in 1986, life expectancy reached 75.2 for males and 80.9 for females, an improvement of 10 years over 1960. With the exception of Korea, Japan has the lowest differential between the life expectancy of women and men. The reasons for the high life expectancy include the traditional low fat diet of fish and vegetables and a happier work environment with better treatment by managers.

---

[8]See van Slyke (1989) on the dismantling of the computer networks of the major U.S. firms.

Table 1.1
Life Expectancy at Birth

	Year or Period	Male (Years)	Female (Years)
Japan	1960	65.32	70.19
	1970	69.31	74.66
	1986	75.23	80.93
Iceland	1983-84	73.96	80.20
Sweden	1984	73.84	79.89
Norway	1982-83	72.69	79.54
Australia	1984	72.59	79.09
U.S.A.*	1983	71.60	78.80
France	1982	70.73	78.85
U.K.**	1982-84	71.60	77.60
Germany	1982-84	70.84	77.47
U.S.S.R.	1975-80	65.00	74.30

* White only; ** England and Wales only.

Korea, Rep. of	1980-85	62.70	66.60

Source: Ministry of Health and Welfare, Japan; U.N., *Demographic Yearbook*, 1986.

Table 1.2
Deaths per 100,000 in Five Major Countries, 1985

	Heart Disease	Strokes	Cancer Lung	Cancer Stomach	Suicide*	Total
Japan	45.0	123.6	25.0	42.9	19.6	256.1
U.S.A.	229.8	62.8	52.0	6.1	12.2	362.9
Britain	243.3	104.3	57.7	16.0	8.5	429.8
France	74.4	79.8	31.7	11.6	21.3	218.8
Germany	167.0	104.5	34.6	18.8	18.6	343.5

*These data are often unreliable given cultural taboos against suicide.

Source: World Health Organization

Lifestyle factors also contribute to different patterns of disease. The Japanese are more likely to have strokes than heart attacks and are very vulnerable to stomach cancer. The latter is probably a result of eating many raw but often chemically washed foods, as well as drinking excessively to hold down the stress levels, and attending the numerous company *meetings* in restaurants and bars. The leading cause of death in Japan in 1985 was cancer with 168.8 per 100,000, followed by various forms of heart disease, 128.6, and cerebral strokes, 106.5. These deaths amounted to 205,000, 158,000, and 129,000, respectively.

Japan has a very safe environment as shown in Table 1.3. Starting in the first grade, children walk to and from school without adult supervision. The rate of violent crime is so low that at first one suspects a typographical mistake or a misplaced decimal point. The low crime rate keeps home security sales down. Electronic firms like Toshiba, Matsushita Electric Industrial, Sharp, Sanyo Electric, and Fujitsu Electric all hope to provide security systems to Japan's 38 million households but find little market even though Japanese consumers are typically quick to buy the latest electronic gadget.

Table 1.4 compares the vital statistics in Japan with the U.S. and other major countries. Low infant mortality, death and divorce rates point to the safety and stability in Japan.

Table 1.3
Violent Crimes per 100,000, Five Major Countries, 1985

	Murder	Rape	Robbery	Total Violent	Larceny/ Theft
Japan	1.4	1.4	1.6	4.4	1130.2
U.S.A.	8.6	37.5	225.1	271.2	4862.6
Britain	4.3	10.4	60.1	74.8	5796.9
France	4.4	5.3	91.8	101.5	3692.7
Germany	4.5	9.2	46.8	60.5	4456.7

Source: JETRO

Table 1.4
Vital Statistics in Several Countries up to 1987 per 1,000

	Births	Deaths	Infant Mortality	Marriage	Divorce
Japan	11.1	6.2	5.5	5.7	1.16
Korea	30.5	6.1	29.7	8.9	0.64
U.S.	15.5	8.7	10.3	10.0	4.80
U.K.	13.6	11.2	9.4	7.0	3.20
Sweden	12.5	11.1	5.9	4.9	2.27
Germany	10.5	11.2	9.2	8.5	3.14

Source: UN Statistics

The birth rate has been steadily declining since 1974. In 1988, 1.3 million babies were born, for a rate of 10.8 per 1,000 (down 0.3 from the previous year). The average number of babies born to each woman declined to 1.66. The number of deaths increased to 793,000, for a rate of 6.5 per 1,000 (up 0.3 from 1987). The rise in the death rate was attributed to a severe outbreak of influenza claiming the lives of many old people. Marriages increased for the first time in six years, reaching 158,000, while the number of divorces continued to decline, reaching 154,000. Japan continues to have the lowest death rate and divorce rate compared with the U.S., Britain, France, Germany, the Netherlands, and Sweden.

As Figure 1.1 shows, these statistics mean there will be many more old age pensioners and relatively fewer workers in Japan's future. As with the European and North American countries, the population is graying. Japan's population distribution is aging faster than in most other countries, including the U.S. and Canada. The problem will be severe past the year 2000 when 17% of the population will be over 65. By 2025, this figure will be 22%.

Starting in 1990, the number of those under 25 years old will decline by 2% per year (the same as in France and Britain, while in West Germany it will fall by 3.6%). The proportion of pensioners will rise from 11% to 15%. One reason for the investment boom now is an awareness of the future need to replace workers with machines. More than 60% of Japanese men over 55 work, compared with 40% in the U.S. Japanese women over 55 lead the world in labor force participation at 30%.

Figure 1.1
Percent of Population 65 Years Old and Over, by Country, 1850-2040 (Based on U.N. Demographic Indicators Estimated in 1980)

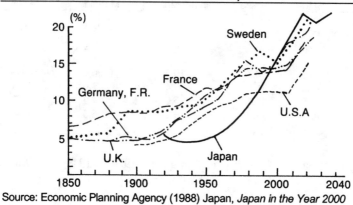

Source: Economic Planning Agency (1988) Japan, *Japan in the Year 2000*

Table 1.5
Japan's Social Expenditure Projections, Percent of GNP

	1980	2000	2010	2025
Medical Care	4.8	6.2	7.2	8.4
Pensions	4.2	10.4	14.3	15.3
Education	5.1	4.0	4.3	3.8
Unemployment	3.0	0.3	0.3	0.3
Family benefits	1.0	1.0	1.0	1.0
Total	15.4	21.9	27.1	28.8

By the year 2000, the cost of government services is projected to require heavy taxes or borrowing. This will put upward pressure on interest rates or, at the least, keep any extra savings at home. Table 1.5 shows Japan's social expenditure as a percent of GNP and its projections into the future. Large increases in the early part of the 21st century are expected. This may contribute toward solving Japan's long-standing over-savings problem.

Japan is self-sufficient in rice, the nation's staple, but it produces only an estimated 14% of the wheat, 75% of the fruit, 78% of the milk and dairy products, 76% of meat, and 34% of the sugar it consumes, according to the Ministry of Agriculture, Forestry and Fisheries for FY (fiscal year) 1987. Japan's rate of self-sufficiency in agricultural products was 71% in terms of market value in that year. However, this is an overestimate, as rice, live-stock, and vegetables produced domestically are priced extremely high. When one adjusts for the food value, such as by calories supplied, the rate of self-sufficiency drops to 49%. This is quite low compared to countries such as Great Britain at 77% and the 100% complete self-sufficiency of countries such as France and the U.S.

Japan is the only industrialized country that still has its primitive religion.

The saying goes that the Japanese is born Shinto, marries Christian and dies Buddhist. More than 90% of the population is Shinto and 75% are Buddhist. Shinto, the way of the gods, is the native religion of Japan and it dates back to prehistoric times. Shintoists revere nature. Until the Meiji era (1868), the Japanese used a Chinese lunar calendar and some rural and farming people still use it. Even today, many of the festivals in Japan are related to the traditional calendar. The solstices are national holidays, and a number of other holidays relate to star stories and lunar conjunctions. It is incredible to experience the attention paid in modern industrial Japan to the phases and cycles of nature as embodied in picnics under the cherry blossoms and walks among the falling maple leaves. Along with the weather reports are details of the blossoming plum trees and later the cherry trees as spring moves up the Japanese archipelago. The rice fields are planted during the major spring holiday when many Japanese are traveling about the countryside and can observe it first hand. Japan, one of the most urban, industrialized societies, is still very close to nature. Its rituals bridge the gap between technology and nature and, along with frequent earthquakes, keep the Japanese grounded in nature. Thus, the many paradoxes of Japan open to us.

THE PLAN OF THIS BOOK

In this book we investigate how Japan became a world economic leader. We will look into its economy and where it differs from the U.S. market: at its firms and their management, and at its people. Then we will look at some of the transitions occurring in Japan that are the result of more open markets and globalization and will peer into the future role of Japan as a creditor nation.

CHAPTER 2

THE GROWTH OF THE ECONOMY

Japan's economy grew strong and wealthy in the post-war decades. Many believe this was deliberately at the expense of the United States, which had lost its competitive edge. However, we argue that Japan developed naturally and moved into a vacuum created by the decline of the U.S.

In this chapter we investigate the growth of the Japanese economy, its strong savings and compare that with the twin deficits in the U.S.

JAPAN'S RECENT ECONOMIC PAST: WWII TO ITS RISE AS CREDITOR

The Japanese had much rebuilding and catching up to do after WWII, and the people worked hard. A policy decision was made to ensure that sufficient investment would come from domestic sources. They fostered high savings to meet their high investment needs. As an additional source of savings, the government ran surpluses. The excess of taxing overspending, created a high level of forced saving. The tight monetary fiscal policy was complemented with expansionary monetary policies, such as low interest rates to increase investment. The surplus or sometimes balanced budget meant that there was little crowding out of investment needs as the government did not compete for funds. Public works supported business rather than social objectives. Import barriers were erected both to protect industry and to avoid too high an import imbalance because the exchange rate was fixed. During the Korean War mobilization, the Japanese economy received a boost from U.S. wartime demand.

Japan's macroeconomic balances explain its rise to creditor status as shown in Table 2.1. Japan has had an excess savings *problem* since the early 1970s. In the period of reconstruction and growth, Japanese policy had wisely emphasized domestic saving to provide needed capital (both real and financial). However, when the investment requirements slowed, the savings did not.

Table 2.1
Recent Macroeconomic History of Japan, 1950–92

Period	Savings/ Investment	Taxes/ Government Spending	Exports/ Imports	Exchange Rate
High growth 1950–73>10%				
	deficit	surplus	zero	fixed till 1971
Lower growth 1974 and beyond				floating
based on trade to counter oil imports				
1974–79	surplus	rising deficit	small surplus	
1980–85	surplus	falling deficit	rising surplus	
based on domestic demand to respond to high yen				
1986–87	surplus	~ zero	falling surplus	
1988 (about 6%)	less surplus	rising deficit	rising surplus	
1989–90 (about 6%)	less surplus	falling deficit	falling surplus	
based on rising domestic consumption				
1991–92 (est. 2.5%)	less surplus	rising deficit	variable surplus	
based on falling domestic consumption and trade				

Source: adapted from Lincoln (1988) and updated

The world economic environment was supportive of stable growth, including factors such as falling raw material prices and stable exchange rates. The Japanese valued education, hard work, and loyalty seeing these as routes to economic improvement. Labor-management relations were nonconfrontational, as most of the militant unions had been wiped out by the early 1960s. The postwar occupation had brought in a number of structural changes, including land reform that helped increase agricultural production.

By the early 1970s, Japan had met its driving needs. Investment slackened, but the custom of sacrifice and saving was deeply ingrained in the people and savings remained high. At this point, Japan's economy began undergoing shifts and it was set for changes. The technological gap was closed, investment requirements slowed, excess labor had been absorbed from agriculture, and the retirement age increased. Then followed a number of economic shocks:

• Stock market crash in 1965.

- Revaluation of the yen from its fixed value of 360 yen per dollar where it stood since 1949, brought a 16% appreciation in 1971, causing a recession followed by rising prices. The U.S. imposed an import surcharge.

- Collapse of the Smithsonian agreement and institution of floating exchange rates with further appreciation of the yen in 1973.

- A soybean embargo from the U.S. With only 6% of soybeans domestically produced, this created a scare even though there were no interruptions in the supply.

- Oil embargo and two oil price shocks in 1973–74 and 1977–79.

- Growth sustained by public expenditures in the late 1970s.

- U.S. trade deficit and shocks of yen appreciation (endaka) from 1985 to 1988.

- Stock market collapse and weak speculative land markets with a weak yen, high interest rates, and relatively high inflation in 1990.

The surplus of savings could have led to a recession if it had not been redirected. In part, the first oil crisis helped redirect and perhaps reduce the surplus through vastly higher costs of imports. Later, the government ran deficits to mop up some of the excess. At the time, Japan's public debt rose to 58% of GNP versus 55% for the U.S. This was a period of extensive road building. By the 1980s, the growing trade surplus was large enough to absorb the excess production. Japan had a current account deficit of $136 million in 1973 and a trade deficit that grew to $13 billion in the 70s. By 1985 it had a current account surplus of $49.2 billion. It reached $87 billion in 1987 and fell to $38 billion in 1990. It is expected to hover at about this rate through 1992.

Wage demands were kept moderate. Good labor-management relations are not an intrinsic factor of Japanese society but have been cultivated to avoid crisis and in recognition of the effectiveness of a non-adversarial approach. In 1974, workers in Japan negotiated very high wage increases, but after the reality of the recession hit, they quickly moderated their demands the next year as shown in Figure 2.1. At this time a new social contract was forged that recognized a commitment of firms to maintain long-term employment. The wage structure was changed to incorporate semi- or tri-annual bonuses which gave firms flexibility in recessions.

The two oil crises created in Japanese management an ongoing commitment to the reduction of energy use. The cost of imported fossil fuels is a continuing vulnerability for the Japanese.

By 1980, the Japanese were confident of continued economic growth and the high quality of their manufactured goods. The reputation for high quality, often specialty goods, has enabled export and other forms of growth despite the rise in the value of the yen.

Figure 2.1
Negotiated Spring Wage Increases, 1965–91

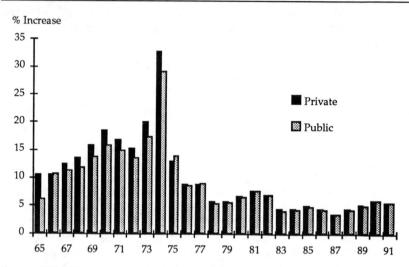

Source: Nikkei NEEDS

The next crisis was that of *endaka* or the high-valued yen. Japanese firms adapted to the high-valued yen by process improvements in manufacturing and new product designs. They lowered their manufacturing breakeven points, aided by the lower costs of imported raw materials. Exporters came to be able to retain their strong competitiveness at high values for the yen. The average in January 1989 reported competitiveness at 128.1 ¥/$, an improvement from ¥140.1 in 1987. Meanwhile 44% of the respondents felt they could compete with an exchange rate 120–130 ¥/$ and half of these (22% of the total) could still compete at ¥110–120. In February 1989, Japan's trade surplus increased 37.8% over the previous year for the sixth straight monthly increase. From 1989 to 1991, the trade surpluses fell, in part because of increased offshore manufacturing. During the Persian Gulf war, oil costs again increased and the trade surplus took a dramatic decline. However, with the return of lower oil prices in 1992, the surplus with the U.S. widened again.

Figure 2.2
Sources of Japan's Real GNP Growth (1981–89)

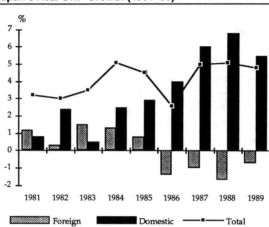

Foreign Demand   Domestic Demand   ──■── Total

Source: EPA, Japan

Since the fall of 1986 when the yen began its rapid climb, growth has depended more and more upon domestic consumption. From 1985 to 1989, the economy grew at a 4.9% rate per year and all that and more has come from *domestic demand*. In the first half of the 80s, the growth rate was 4.0% with 1.6 percentage points of that from foreign trade, see Figure 2.2. While Japan's rate of growth has dropped during the 1990–91 recession, it is still the highest among the major economies. Smaller companies, which always depended less on exports, have continued to thrive.

Official policy began to encourage more domestic consumption and leisure to deal with the structural oversavings. The policy seems to be working, but it is not clear how much domestic consumption can rise. There is little space to add appliances and trinkets, but the Japanese continue to buy newer higher technology goods. They just throw away the obsolete ones.

There are limits to the growth of domestic consumption. Japan cannot build growth on increasing sales of large consumer items like cars. Heavy consumption of large durables takes space. Parking is limited, so two-car families are rare. Just to buy and register a car, one must have a guaranteed parking space. Electrical capacity is limited, and not many appliances can be used at the same time.

Family friends of ours who live in a relatively spacious apartment in Tsukuba remarked: "We probably will be moving within the next ten years when I change jobs, so we do not need to buy any more furniture since our new apartment probably will be smaller."

Even increasing leisure activities will require more space. Resort facilities are crowded, this has encouraged travel abroad. However airport runways are limited. Overcrowded Narita, Tokyo's International Airport, has only one runway and it is closed from 11 p.m. to 6 a.m.

In the end, the true savings balancer may be the aging population. The growth in the elderly population and their need to draw down savings is often written about in the negative, showing that this demographic change is not understood. It should not be feared because it could solve the structural problem of over savings.

EXCHANGE HISTORY

In 1871, with the opening of external trade, the yen was set at par with the dollar.[1] At the reopening of trade following WWII the yen was arbitrarily set at 360 to the dollar in ritual acknowledgment of one meaning of the word yen—circle, a circle having 360 degrees. From 1949 to 1971, the yen traded at this fixed rate of 360 to the dollar.

The yen has risen dramatically from the Bretton Woods value of 360 set in 1949 to its March 1992 rate of about 135 ¥/$. The yen peaked at nearly 120 ¥/$ on two occasions in 1987 and 1988 after which it fell as low as about 160 during March and April 1990. By August 1988, the dollar had recovered to the 135 range but it fell back into the 120s in October and November before the U.S. presidential election. The close on November 17, 1988, triggered by higher European interest rates and *news* that high-ranking U.S. officials favored a further decline in the dollar to trim the trade deficit dropped to an all time low close of 121.52 ¥/$. The dollar rose in December partly because of very high, short-term U.S. interest rates as well as a high demand for dollars to repatriate foreign subsidiary earnings to U.S. parent companies. The dollar closed 1988 at 124.95¥/$ but there was a sharp rise in the first half of 1989 to the ¥150 range. It fell back to the ¥123 range in 1991 and then has risen to the ¥130–135 range in early 1992. Figure 2.3 shows the historical value of the yen from January 1, 1973, to March 27, 1992. The historic low of the U.S. dollar in the post-World War II era was 120.25 ¥/$ on January 4, 1988.

---

[1] A beautiful antique book of prints the authors have, dating from the 1880s originally cost 2¥.

Figure 2.3
Yen/U.S. Dollar Exchange Rate, 1973–92 (March 27)

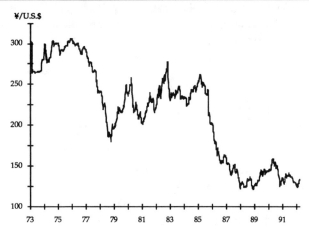

Source: Nikkei NEEDS

It is hard to predict future exchange rates, but it is likely that the U.S. dollar's woes will not be over for some time, unless considerable progress is made on the trade deficits with Japan and Germany. The moving average of the trade deficit with Japan was fairly constant during the second half of 1988, at about $11 billion per month. At the end of 1988, the Japanese and German trade deficits were widening. Only a U.S. recession would reduce these trade deficits and, at the end of 1988, this did not seem likely soon. During 1989 and 1990, these deficits did fall somewhat; however, they have begun rising again in 1991. Consumer spending, even with the higher interest rates, remained steady at an excessive level. Despite the U.S. recession in 1991–92, demand for Japanese products has been high.

The broad bands that are acceptable to the G-7 are not publicly known but are believed to be 120 to 140 ¥/$. Many analysts had expected 120 to be broken in 1989 with 110 to 115 possible, particularly in the second half of the year before the China turmoil moved the dollar up. This turmoil led to flight to the dollar, which was also strengthened by a lower U.S. trade deficit in April, the continuing aftermath of the Recruit scandal (see Chapter 9) and rising confidence in President Bush. Part of the rise represented Japanese on both sides of the market, the insurance companies and other speculators and investors were buying and the Bank of Japan was selling. The exchange rate on speculation hit 151.35 and closed at 151.30 on Thursday June 8, 1989. One dealer said the dollar could go up to ¥170 by mid August. The Bank of Japan announced it was prepared to spend $1 billion per day to support the yen. Within hours a panic set in, and the dollar was quickly in the ¥145 range. With the sudden mood change, it drifted into the high ¥130s in the next two weeks. Rumor had it that some Japanese speculators were asked to moderate their dollar purchases. Such is the substance of currency trends.

THE CURRENT ECONOMIC TRENDS

Table 2.2 gives the official 1991 economic forecast of the Japanese cabinet. Nominal and real GNP were expected to increase by 7.2% and 5.2%, respectively in 1990, and they were forecast to increase 5.5% and 3.8%, respectively, in 1991.

In 1989 the Japanese GNP reached ¥4.06 trillion or about 15% of the world GNP. Per capita GNP was $27,000, 30% higher than the U.S., and the foreign assets balance was $367 billion. Some predict the Japanese economy will reach ¥10 trillion, matching the U.S., by the year 2000.

Capital spending increased by 15% in 1990. Companies in basic industries, including petroleum, pulp and paper, and food, are expanding capacity, while those in vehicle, textiles, and electronics industries are focusing on product development. Computer and telecommunications equipment are major areas receiving funding, and many firms are continuing to turn their attention toward the domestic market.

Table 2.2
Official Economic Forecast for Fiscal Year 1991

	FY89 Actual	FY90 Expected	FY91 Forecast
GNP, ¥1,000 billion	406.2	435.4	459.6
Work force, 10,000 people	6302.0	6415.0	6495.0
Completely unemployed, %	2.2	2.2	2.2
Prices—rate of increase			
Wholesale, %	3.5	2.0	0.1
Consumer, %	2.9	3.1	2.4
Balance of Payments			
Current balance, U.S. $100 mil	534.0	320.0	300.0
Trade balance, U.S. $100 mil	700.0	570.0	560.0

The consumption tax created a short-term set back to the GNP, causing a 3% decline in the second quarter of 1989. It then rebounded to an annual real rate of 4.5%.

Japan's economy has averaged 3.7% growth in the seven years from 1983 to 89, compared with a 2.6% average in the United States.

Tokyo itself accounts for half of Japan's GNP and about 7% of the world's. Though people are moving out of Tokyo, companies are still moving in. Companies awash with cash and no place to put it have parked it in land and stocks, thus funding their dramatic increase. Wages have not kept pace with the changes: consumption from self-employment and farming increased five times faster than consumption by wage earners (wealth effect). The Japanese are traveling abroad more and buying foreign designer items. Resort areas are growing. Yuzawa, a spa town of 8,000 near Tokyo, recently built 20,000 apartments. These have been sold to the Tokyo rich for weekend use. Narita has a bigger fish market than Tsukiji (Tokyo's famed central fish market) because so much fish is now *flown* in at high prices.[2]

In 1989, the major Japanese companies were flush with cash and other liquid assets as a result of the support of the U.S. dollar from 1985 to 88. In order to meet G-7 (the group of seven industrialized nations—the U.S., Japan, West Germany, France, Britain, Italy and Canada) agreements and keep the dollar from falling further, the Bank of Japan bought up surplus dollars. It did this by printing more yen, creating extra liquidity. The extra liquidity went into stocks and more property, see the discussion in Chapter 7.

Meanwhile the land and stock market booms have made thousands of people instant millionaires with huge assets both paper and real. Yet the Japanese do not act as though they are rich. They have continued a high savings rate. Those who do not own property have to save even more if they want to buy, while those who owned property worry about paying the property sales tax if they were to sell.

The economy continues strong. Bankruptcy, a measure of the strength of an economy, was low in the late 1980s because of the easy domestic credit conditions. Corporate bankruptcies fell 19.1% in April 1989 to 786 cases, the lowest level in 15 years. An excess of loanable funds made it easy to stave off bankruptcy. This in turn is indirectly a result of the trade surplus, as the accumulation of dollars contributed to an increased domestic money supply and low interest rates. Firms in the service sector were the most vulnerable, however the total debt left behind was the lowest

---

[2]Some fish goes the other way. The delicacy fugu that must be specially cut by an expert to avoid its deadly poisonous parts is flown to Japanese restaurants in New York to be sold at $150 per serving. Some 100 to 200 amateur cutters die each year from improperly preparing fugu.

since 1975. Also notable was a decline in construction bankruptcies because of increased demand before the new 3% consumption tax began in April 1989. With the fall in the Nikkei stock average (NSA), higher interest rates and a number of fraudulent stock and bank cases, bankruptcies are increasing in Japan. Voluntary personal bankruptcy filings numbered 23,287 in 1990. Analysts again expect in excess of 20,000 for the fiscal year (FY) ending March 31, 1992. Credit card companies have been expanding card use; Visa International holders increased from 5 million in 1987 to 37 million in 1992. This is also contributing to the increased bankruptcy rate.

One disturbing trend is the increase in the bankruptcy rate of small firms because of the lack of available labor.

Japan has proved itself very adaptable to its economic environment. Not only has it met external shocks, it is also now coping with the ability to loosen its domestic control. The number of transformations in the decades since the war has been dramatic. The yen is beginning to attain the status of an international currency with its attendant responsibilities as well as benefits. The U.S. began to understand its fall from sole dominance when some states began to borrow in yen. The yen now accounts for 8% of world reserves (up from 4% ten years ago). The West German mark accounts for 12%, and the U.S. dollar 80%. Japan is looking to lend more in yen. Perhaps the question is how it can do this without taking over devalued dollar loans.

THE SAVINGS RATE: $1.8 BILLION PILING UP EVERY DAY

Mrs. Sato is back doing what she likes best — squirreling away spare household cash in all sorts of savings and investments.

The Economist, June 17, 1989

In Japan, women's place has traditionally been in the home with the children. The number of women in executive positions is a scant 3%. But it was a tenth of one percent in 1985. The myth is that most women are not working outside the home. Yet, 40% of women with children *are* working. The presence of women in the workplace is only now growing significant. However women have had power over savings and investment decisions of the family for a long time.

Certainly, Japan is a male-dominated society. However, in Japan, women's status in the household includes important power over economic decisions. In most families, virtually all important financial decisions are made by the wife, so their actual economic power is great. In junior high and high school, girls take courses in household *management* while boys take physical education. Girls are taught about saving and credit management. Boys are taught cooking and simple sewing so they are not helpless in the home.

Husbands are sent to work with an allowance for the day's expenses including the night's entertainment. Decisions about when to buy a house or a new car, where to put the money and other important financial decisions are made by the wives. They like to save. The couple puts the husband's savings into bank deposits, postal savings accounts, investment trusts, life insurance policies, and stock shares. The bulk is in cash or near cash instruments which though safe, have had low returns in the 4 to 6% range until 1990, when they increased to the 7 to 8% range. In May 1992 they were back in the 4 to 6% range.

Figure 2.4 shows the savings rates from 1979 to 1989 for the five largest world economies. The household savings rate is the total household savings divided by the household's disposable income. The savings rates in Japan as a percent of disposable income are much higher than in other major countries such as France, Germany, and the United Kingdom, all of which dwarf the low U.S. savings rate. A comparative study in 1990 showed that

Figure 2.4
Trends in Household Savings Rates, 1979–89

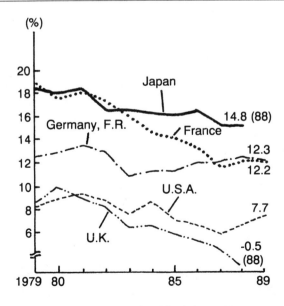

Source: Bank of Japan, Comparative International Statistics, 1990

the Japanese had the highest total savings per capita (in U.S. dollars): Japan, 45,118, Switzerland, 19,971, Canada, 6,531, and the U.S., 4,201.

Table 2.3 shows how the average Japanese family earns and spends its income each month. The husband earns most of the family's money from

Table 2.3
Monthly Income and Expenditure for the Average Worker's Household in Japan in Yen, 1986–90

	1986	1987	1988	1989	1990	1986–90
Number per household	3.78	3.77	3.74	3.72	3.7	average
Total Income	452,942	460,613	481,250	495,849	521,757	
Current Income						% total
Head of household						Income
Regular	291,751	296,587	306,904	318,898	332,026	64.1
Temporary & bonus	81,571	79,655	88,052	91,219	98,644	18.2
Spouse (wife)	37,393	38,302	43,195	40,862	44,101	8.4
Other members	16,450	16,871	15,170	15,555	15,854	3.3
Business & homework	6,014	6,468	5,589	5,600	5,216	1.2
Other	10,198	11,956	11,608	12,567	14,886	2.5
Non-current	9,620	10,774	10733	11,118	11,030	2.2
Expenditures	367,052	369,214	382,517	390,904	412,813	79.7
Living	293,630	295,915	307,204	316,489	331,595	64.1
Food	74,889	73,431	74,827	76,794	79,990	15.8
Housing	14,215	15,170	15,722	15,846	16,475	3.2
Fuel, light and water	16,912	15,655	15,701	15,887	16,797	3.4
Furniture & household items	11,888	12,632	12,235	12,388	13,103	2.6
Clothing & footwear	20,554	20,834	21,715	22,577	23,902	4.5
Medical care	6,985	7,255	7,753	8,092	8,670	1.6
Transport & communication	28,819	30,069	31,210	32,217	33,499	6.5
Education	13,118	13,570	14,522	15,349	16,827	3.0
Reading & recreation	26,142	26,072	28,109	29,585	31,761	5.9
Other	80,109	81,127	85,410	87,753	90,569	17.6
Surplus	85,890	91,399	98,733	104,946	108,944	20.3
Net Savings	51,241	54,683	60,676	69,978	74,528	12.8
Disposable income	379,520	387,314	405,908	421,435	440,539	84.3

Source: JETRO

his regular job and from additional income and bonuses. Savings amount to about 12% of total income, piling up in 1988 at over ¥60,000 per month. In 1989 total savings was up 15.3% over 1988 to some $86,250 per family. In 1990 there was a further 16.6% increase in total savings or about 14% of income. Bonus income typically has been almost 30% of the regular income of the head of the household. The wife's income has been only about 8% of total family income. The low housing expense reflects the availability of subsidized housing. Transportation and communication at 10% is almost equivalent to the total for housing and fuel, light, and water.

Despite the extreme interest in owning land, which is quite expensive, the main reasons Japanese save, according to the Central Council of

Table 2.4
Reasons for Savings, % Responding

	1988	1990
To provide for illness and disasters	77.1	74.3
For retirement	50.2	52.4
To pay for their children's education	45.3	40.0
To buy land and buildings	19.2	18.3
To pay for weddings of their children	19.1	NA
No specific purpose but feel more secure with savings	NA	25.7

Source: Central Council of Communications for Savings

Communications for Savings in 1988 and 1990, are for security reasons as shown in Table 2.4.

Part of the reason for this saving is fear that there is a gap between Japan's economic power and that of the individual family. Fully 81.6% of those that have high economic power believe there is this gap, and only 12.2% think they are keeping up, according to a December 1987 survey by the Office of the Prime Minister as reported in the White Paper on National Life. Of those who actually have a high standard of living according to statistical measures, fully 58.9% feel there is this gap and only 36.8% feel they are keeping up. Figure 2.5 shows that most people are not satisfied with their current standard of living and are saving for a better one.

In mid-1989, a survey was undertaken to determine what Japanese wanted and what they would do with extra money. Twenty percent immediately answered with one thing or another, and another 20% responded with a trip, to acquire some skill, or take up a hobby, or get

Figure 2.5
The Degree of Satisfaction with Current Standard of Living of Living, 1978–87

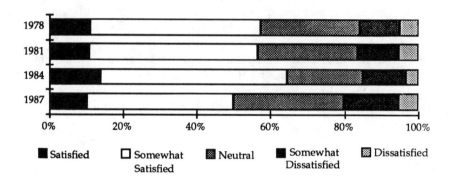

Source: Japan White Paper on National Life, 1989

In another survey of middle management, wage earners in their 40s were shown cards with ¥50,000, ¥200,000, ¥1 million, ¥10 million, ¥100 million and asked what they would do if they received each amount. Again over 60% said they would save it. When shown ¥50,000 and ¥200,000, they responded that as the amount was not large, they would save it. Most men shown ¥100 million would invest it in stocks or mutual funds or invest in land or apartments, all seen as forms of savings. Basically, the Japanese appear to lack a desire for more material goods. Except for a few extravagant rich, the typical Japanese simply prefers to save money rather than to spend it.

As of June 1989, the average amount of savings per household was about 1.91 times the yearly net income. Table 2.5 details this. The average household held about ¥10.13 million in savings and its annual net income was ¥5.31 million. By June 1990 there was ¥11.81 million in savings and ¥5.77 million in annual net income. Salaried workers had the least savings, in total and as a percentage of their net income. Farmers, forest workers, and fishermen save the most. Also, lower income and older workers have higher savings rates.

Table 2.5
Savings by Occupation, Income and Age in Japan, 1989 and 1990

	Total Savings (¥10,000)		Disposable Income (¥10,000)		Total savings as a multiple of DI	
	1989	1990	1989	1990	1989	1990
Total	1013	1181	531	577	1.91	2.05
By occupation						
Farmers, etc.	1044	1145	484	599	2.16	1.91
Self-employed	1039	1285	557	628	1.87	2.05
Salaried	924	843	556	525	1.66	1.61
Freelance	1074	1610	582	641	1.85	2.51
Others	1241	1486	444	465	2.80	3.20
By Income						
<¥2 mil	509	478	164	123	3.10	3.90
¥2–3 mil	659	820	253	238	2.60	3.40
¥3–4 mil	687	727	352	327	1.95	2.20
¥4–5 mil	633	870	451	423	1.85	2.10
¥5–6 mil	1103	1138	600	556	1.84	2.00
¥6–7 mil	1794	1825	1047	991	1.71	1.80
Age of household head						
20–29	348	413	328	362	1.06	1.10
30–39	625	645	434	481	1.44	1.30
40–49	858	967	567	588	1.51	1.60
50–59	1181	1436	630	709	1.87	2.00
60–69	1555	1752	507	539	3.07	3.30
70+	1149	1669	419	496	2.74	3.40

Source: Central Council of Communication for Savings

Total personal savings have piled up at huge rates. They reached ¥746.48 trillion at the end of March 1989, up 11.4% from the previous fiscal year and equivalent to ¥2.01 million for every household. Using an exchange rate of 140 ¥/$ this is a staggering $5,332 billion. The savings for the year were ¥93.88 trillion, which is ¥257.21 billion, or $1.837 billion in U.S. dollars, *every day!* This does not count corporation profits that add to net cash flow. For the third consecutive year in 1989, personal savings grew by more than 10% from the previous year. Most of the savings, some ¥641.14 trillion are held in bank and postal deposits and in the form of bonds and insurance. Some ¥105.34 trillion is held in the stock market and other assets. Figure 2.6 and Table 2.6 show where the savings were allocated. Postal savings and the banks have the bulk of the money at low rates of interest, which were in the 4 to 6% range except for a rise to about two percent

higher in 1991. Total personal and corporate assets in mid 1992 exceeded
¥1.50 quadrillion.

Figure 2.6
Personal Savings in Japan (¥ billion, except %)

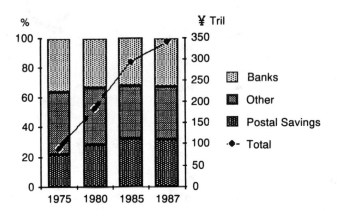

Source: Bank of Japan

Table 2.6
Savings Per Household by Category, 1991 and 1990

	June 1991		June 1990	
	¥ mil	share	¥ mil	share
Fixed term deposits	2.30	19.5	1.86	18.4
Deposits and savings	4.00	33.9	3.46	34.2
Loan and money trusts	0.65	5.5	0.58	5.7
Life and accident insurance	2.50	21.2	2.25	22.2
Stocks and shares	1.25	10.6	1.16	11.5
Securities	1.58	13.4	1.82	18.0
Workers property accumulated savings	0.44	4.3	0.44	4.3

Source: Central Council of Communication for Savings

Personal savings at the end of March 1988 had risen 10.2% over the
previous year. Bank and postal savings accounts had lower growth as
funds were moved to higher yields such as provided by insurance firms,
money market certificates and high yield savings deposits. Postal savings

increased only 33%, but investment trusts increased three times; direct stock investment rose 250% and funds in life policies doubled.

To regain savings, in 1989 banks introduced money market certificates (MMCs) in smaller denominations of ¥30 million to ¥3 million and even ¥1 million making them accessible to most households. On these, the rates are fixed monthly beginning at 4.14% on a 12-month MMC. On the first day, close to 110,000 were sold for ¥427 billion. Not to be left behind, the postal savings agency also introduced small lot MMCs and they received deposits totaling ¥208 billion. The savings rate is high and these storage places are safe, but the yearly return has been well below that in the stock market, which has averaged about 19% from 1952 to 1989. A novel savings account is the 250-year term deposit. At 3.96% per year it turns ¥50,000 into ¥60 billion. One can sell the term, and the rate fluctuates annually. The example does show the power of compound interest, even at the low rates available in Japan.

Table 2.7 compares household savings allocation patterns in Japan with those in the U.S. There has been a switch from banks and postal savings to brokerages and a deregulation of interest rates and tax policy, particularly the elimination of *Maruyu*, the tax break for postal savings. Postal savings have historically accounted for 20% of all personal savings and have grown steadily (see Figure 2.7).

The vast majority of the wealth of Japanese households is contained in their land and buildings. This constitutes nearly two-thirds of their assets.

Table 2.7
Portfolio Shares of Japanese and U.S. Households,
Average for 1974–83

	Japan	U.S.
Cash	0.8	na
Demand deposits	1.2	3.4
Time deposits	7.9	23.2
Postal saving	4.9	–
Trust	1.8	–
Insurance and pensions	3.8	13.1
Securities	3.1	19.7
Residential structures	11.6	23.4
Land	53.4	7.1
Consumer durables	4.0	11.9
Non corporate structures, equipment & inventories	7.3	6.1

Source: Noland (1988)

Figure 2.7
Postal Savings, 1955–92 (February)

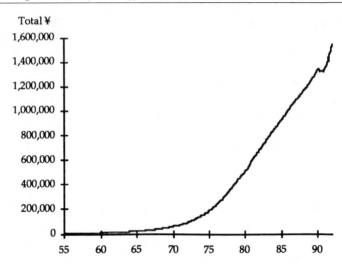

Source: Nikkei NEEDS

Various savings deposits amount to about 14%. Until 1990, rates of return on these savings accounts were regulated, low and changed infrequently, but this income was usually not taxed. Securities, insurance, and pension assets are only about 6.9% of the Japanese wealth, and an astonishingly low proportion of this is corporate stock, some 0.3%. Government bonds and bank debentures each account for 0.9%, so the bulk of the savings goes into cash savings instruments. This is partially explained by the practice of financing Japanese corporate needs with bank loans and retained earnings rather than with equity. Household assets are growing at about $1.8 billion U.S. per day, and the excess is going mostly into savings deposits, much of which is then made available to corporations for loans to purchase assets in the stock market, land, bonds, and overseas investments.

U.S. households, in contrast, have their assets concentrated in time deposits (i.e., savings accounts) (23.2%), insurance and pension funds (13.1%), and securities (19.7%) along with residential housing (23.4%), with land comprising only 7.1% of total assets. Table 2.7 details the differences in the household shares in Japan and the U.S. using averages for 1974 to 1983.

The Japanese high rate of savings has made their financial institutions strong as discussed in Chapter 6.

HOW THE U.S. LOST ITS POSITION OF DOMINANCE

Last night Sidney had the Great American Dream. Now he's going to try to arrange some Japanese financing.

Cartoon in *The Wall Street Journal*

Wealth is a relative thing. One feels wealthy when others are poor. Japan is often described as wealthy because it has the highest per capita income and high savings. The assumption is made that it has gained at the expense of the U.S. This is not true, but let's see how the U.S. has lost its economic vitality as compared with Japan.

It is difficult to make simple comparisons. The cultural and economic contexts among countries differ and impose varying costs and benefits. Consider, for example, income inequalities where the average ratio of the top to the bottom incomes in the U.S. is 14:1 compared with 6:1 in Germany, and only 5:1 in Japan. Wealth disparities are wider in all countries and these are growing in Japan as well (see Chapter 4). In addition, there are some real economic costs from expanding the economy through continued deregulation which is eating away at the social linkages and expectations. The U.S. economy must bear the costs of 602,000 private security guards and an extremely high labor force turnover of 4% per month (Thurow, 1985). These extra costs count as increased GNP.

In the post war period, the U.S. economy was the only one intact, and it could and did benefit from free trade. Other countries needed so much. So why did the U.S. lose its position of dominance? To answer this question, we can investigate several factors as they compare with Japan to give us insight into why Japan has succeeded.

SUPPLY -SIDE REFORMS: GIVING AWAY THE U.S. WEALTH

Ronald Reagan speaks:

We are in the worst economic mess since the Great Depression.

February 5, 1981

The deficit is Public Enemy Number One.

1981–1982

A large trade deficit could be a sign of economic strength rather than weakness.[3]

January 1988

Ronald Reagan retired as one of the most popular presidents in American history. Throughout his presidency, from January 1981 to January 1989, he was confident under fire, and, when a crisis was at hand, he gave a strong speech. The stock market reacted very positively to the president's speeches. The economy had a strong expansion during the later Reagan years (after a strong contraction in the first few). The GNP was $2.73 trillion in 1980; by 1987, it was $4.49 trillion, an increase of 64.5%. In real inflation-adjusted terms, from 1982 to 1989, the GNP went from $3.19 to $3.82 trillion, an increase of 19.75%. Table 2.8 and Figures 2.8–2.11 provide the background data.

Excess social security receipts have contributed to a lower budget deficit, though this is a short-run gain because social security is unfunded. Much of the talk of getting the budget in line involves similar *creative* accounting such as keeping the more than $50 billion cost of the savings and loan bailout off the budget. For example $56 billion was added back in fiscal 1989 for the Graham-Rudman deficit reduction law. Figure 2.8 shows the effect with projections into the 21st century.

---

[3]This opinion is shared by other conservatives such as the economist Paul Craig Roberts, a *Newsweek* columnist. The argument is that the U.S. gets to spend the foreigners' money on goods and then gets the money back as well since the foreigners want to keep it in the U.S. We argue that this is a time bomb.

Table 2.8
U.S. Federal Budget Receipts, Outlays and Deficit (FY 1970–91)

			Budget Outlays					Deficit	Debt
	Receipts	Total	Defense	Inter-natl.	Social Security & Medicare	Health & Income Security	Interest	Total	Total
	(A)	(B)	(C)	(D)	(E)	(F)	(G)	(A–B)	
1970	193.7	196.6	78.6	4.3		56.1	18.3	-2.9	2,382.6
1975	279.1	332.3	86.5	7.1	77.5	63.0	23.2	-53.2	544.1
1980	517.1	590.9	134.0	12.7	150.6	109.7	52.5	-73.8	994.3
1984	666.5	851.8	227.4	15.9	235.7	143.1	111.1	-185.3	1,564.1
1985	734.1	946.3	252.7	16.2	254.4	161.7	129.4	-212.2	1,817.0
1986	769.1	990.3	273.4	14.2	269.0	155.7	136.0	-221.2	2,120.1
1987	854.1	1003.8	282.0	11.6	282.5	163.3	138.6	-149.7	2,345.6
1988	909.0	1064.0	290.4	10.5	298.2	173.8	151.7	-155.0	2,600.8
1989	990.7	1142.6	303.6	9.6	317.5	184.4	169.1	-151.9	2,866.2
1990e	1073.5	1197.2	296.3	14.6	345.1	204.4	175.6	-123.7	3,113.3
1991e	1170.2	1233.3	303.3	18.2	363.4	217.4	173.0	-63.1	3,319.2

Categories as % of Total Budget

	(C/B)	(D/B)	(E/B)	(F/B)	(G/B)
1970	40.0	2.2	0.0	28.5	9.3
1975	26.0	2.1	23.3	19.0	7.0
1980	22.7	2.1	25.5	18.6	8.9
1984	26.7	1.9	27.7	16.8	13.0
1985	26.7	1.7	26.9	17.1	13.7
1986	27.6	1.4	27.2	15.7	13.7
1987	28.1	1.2	28.1	16.3	13.8
1988	27.3	1.0	28.0	16.3	14.3
1989	26.6	0.8	27.8	16.1	14.8
1990e	24.7	1.2	28.8	17.1	14.7
1991e	24.6	1.5	29.5	17.6	14.0

Source: U.S. Government Printing Office, Economic Indicators, June 1990, quoted in JETRO

Americans enjoy very high living standards, the best in the world by some accounts. This is a reflection of **past** productivity improvements. From World War II to 1973, productivity increased about 2% per year. Since then it has been only 0.8%. But Americans are still consuming more and more. How do they do it? There are a number of reasons: the labor participation of women has increased, investment has fallen, and there has been huge borrowing from abroad.

Figure 2.8
Social Security and the U.S. Budget Deficit

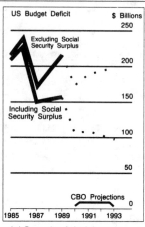 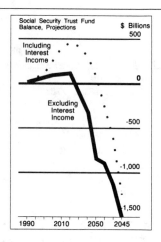

Source: Social Security Administration

Foreigners may not be willing to finance an ever-expanding consumption binge. They have been taking dollars in debt instead of goods and have suppressed and postponed their own consumption. Eventually they will want to call in their chips. That is, eventually they will want to enjoy the postponed consumption. The U.S. even asks that Japan increase its consumption. The Japanese are beginning to understand that working hard and saving is not all there is to life and are expanding their consumption and leisure time. The Japanese government is encouraging more leisure time and consumption by shortening the work week and taking other measures to increase individual spending. There is hope to cut the huge trade deficits, but the increase in spending has been slow. When this happens, the U.S. will need to forgo enjoying some of the domestically produced goods in order to turn them over to others who have dollars. Paying back the debt will mean working hard and consuming relatively less, in fact living like the Japanese do now. In the end, for sustainability, consumption and living standards will be brought in line with productivity growth and real production.

Figure 2.9
The U.S. Trade and Current Account Deficits, 1950–88

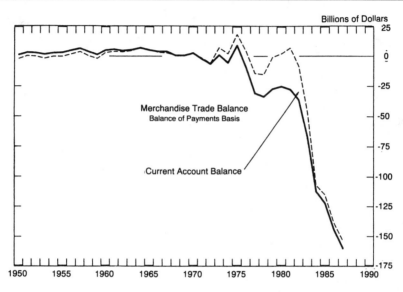

Source: Federal Reserve System

Figure 2.10
Net U.S. Government Debt, 1953–88

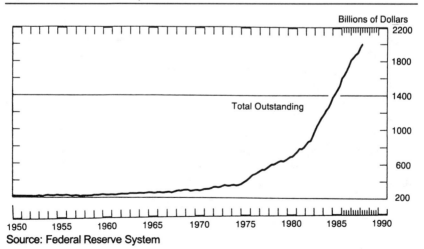

Source: Federal Reserve System

Figure 2.11
U.S. Government Receipts, Outlays and Deficit, 1950–88

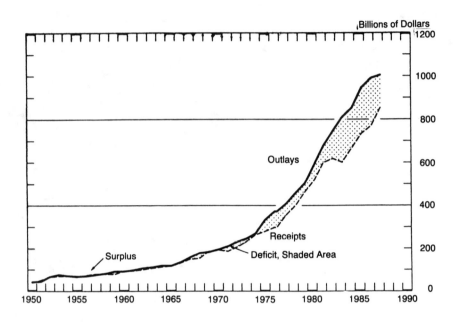

Source: Federal Reserve System

Figures 2.12 and 2.13 from Mann and Schultze (1988) show the extent of the drop in U.S. savings, the rise in U.S. government debt, and the growing percentage of overseas borrowing needed to pay for domestic investment. Government and private savings combine to yield national savings. From 8% of net national product during 1951–80, U.S. national savings dropped to 3.1% during 1984–86 and to 2.4% in 1987–88. The 8% during 1951–80 was enough to cover all the domestic investment as well as some U.S. investment abroad. But during 1984–86 only half of the 6.2% GNP devoted to domestic investment was financed by national savings. The other half was borrowed. During 1987–88 it was even worse, with only 40% financed domestically.[4]

---

[4]These numbers might be laudable for an underdeveloped economy, but it is shameful for the wealthiest nation in the world to rely on savings from abroad to meet its minimal investment needs.

Figure 2.12
U.S. Net National Savings, % of Net National Product, 1951–88

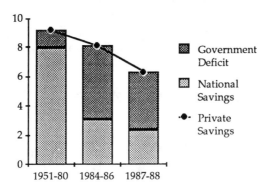

Figure 2.13
Source of U.S. Real Investment, Percent of Net National Product, 1951–88

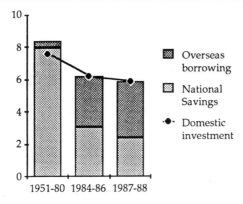

With the amount of borrowing escalating and the national savings rate falling, there is less and less total investment in the U.S. and more and more of the total that is foreign owned. Figure 2.14 shows the trade deficit with various parts of the world to compare the 1980 and 1990 situations. Figure 2.15 shows the growth rates in real gross domestic product, population, real personal income and consumption per capita and real government spending in Japan, the U.S., Germany and Britain from 1928 to 1988.

While Europe has maintained and increased its relative share, there has been a vast transfer of the *relative* stock market capitalization from the U.S. and the rest of the world to Japan. Table 2.9 documents this. Japan's share of the world's stock market rose from 15% in December 1980 to 42% in September 1988, while the U.S. share fell from 53%—more than triple

Japan's—to 31%, a quarter less. In dollars, the U.S.'s share has not fallen, but it has not grown fast enough to keep pace with Japan's and Europe's. The steep Japanese stock market decline in 1990 has dropped Japan's share below the U.S.'s: 31% versus 36% as of March 1991. The U.S. share is considerably higher than the Japanese after adjustments for cross holding, the fall in the Japanese market and the rise in the U.S. market.

Figure 2.14
U.S. Trade Deficit, 1980 and 1990 in Billions of Dollars

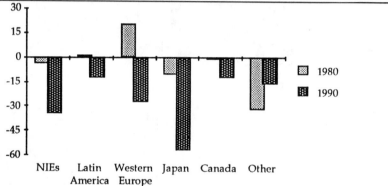

Source: U.S. Department of Commerce

Figure 2.15
Growth Rates in Real Gross Domestic Product, Population, Real Personal Income and Consumption per Capita, and Real Government Spending in Japan, the U.S., West Germany and Britain, 1928–88

	Japan 1930-88	United States 1928-88	W. Germany 1928-88*	Britain 1928-88
Real GDP	17.8	6.0	7.1	3.4
Population	2.0	2.0	1.7	1.2
Real Personal Income per Head	9.4	2.9	4.2	2.4
Real Consumption per Head	10.9		8.8	5.2
Real Government Spending	5.8	2.9		
Real Consumer-Durables Spending		10.4		
Real Federal-Government Spending		19.6		

1988 level as a multiple of 1930 level (Japan); 1988 level as a multiple of 1928 level (others)
*Share in 1928 estimated
Source: Official Statistics

Source: *The Economist*, December 24, 1988

Table 2.9
Stock Market Capitalizations, as a Percentage of World Total —20 Main Markets

	Dec 1980	Sept 1988	March 1991
Japan	15	42	31
United States	53	31	36
Europe	20	21	27
Rest of World	12	6	6

Source: Morgan Stanley Capital International.

THE COSTS OF DEFENSE SPENDING

The Cold War is over and Japan has won.

Hazel Henderson

The U.S. contends that it is doing more than its share of defense spending. A comparison of U.S. and Japanese spending on defense shows a vast discrepancy. However, the U.S., which has built more capacity for destruction than could ever be used, can now cut back and reallocate its revenues to more productive uses. The disintegration of the Communist world in the U.S.S.R. and Eastern Europe will hasten this reallocation. Defense spending is a large drain on economic vitality, as both Kennedy (1989) and Jacobs (1984) demonstrate. Excessive defense spending is another explanation of why Japan is on the ascent economically. Japan has been saved by U.S.-written law which limits it to spend at most 1% of GNP on defense. This is in contrast to about 7% in the U.S. and over 20% in the former U.S.S.R. Figure 2.16 provides a comparison among a number of countries.

Figure 2.17 shows defense spending, foreign aid, and GNP growth for the U.S. as of the end of 1987. The U.S. spent about 12 times as much in total and six times as much per person as Japan did—7% of U.S. GNP versus 1.3% in Japan. In 1988, Japan's expenditures were about 1.5% of an expanded GNP, placing it third behind the U.S. and the Soviet Union.

Figure 2.16
Defense Spending in 1986 in Total, Per Capita and as a Percent of GNP

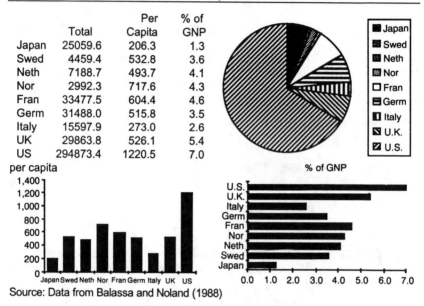

	Total	Per Capita	% of GNP
Japan	25059.6	206.3	1.3
Swed	4459.4	532.8	3.6
Neth	7188.7	493.7	4.1
Nor	2992.3	717.6	4.3
Fran	33477.5	604.4	4.6
Germ	31488.0	515.8	3.5
Italy	15597.9	273.0	2.6
UK	29863.8	526.1	5.4
US	294873.4	1220.5	7.0

Source: Data from Balassa and Noland (1988)

Japan consistently understates its military budget. If it used standard NATO accounting, it would be larger than any other ally of the U.S.[5] NATO accounting includes six categories: personnel and materiel, R&D, military assistance, paramilitary forces (coast guard, gendarmerie), funds for military purposes by agencies other than defense, and retirement allowances and pensions. Japan's budget includes only personnel and materiel, R&D, and some pensions. If military pensions were included, defense would be 1.5–2% of the GNP versus the official 1%. Japan's defense budget has been growing at 5% per year in real terms.

---

[5]There are many measurement differences in the functioning of the two economies. Differences in capital depreciation rules and categorization of government expenditures make U.S. and Japanese savings rates as percent of net national product more similar at 7% instead of 20% versus 4.2%. Though this accounting is interesting, it would be better to look at savings as a percent of the gross output and measure gross investment as well as depreciation. Depreciation is in itself an accounting artifact. Their success is even harder to explain if the Japanese are *not* saving more!

The U.S. is making an effort to better account for service trade, for example, including trade in accounting and advertising services and spending by foreign students. These give a net improvement of $10 billion and another gain is made by a revision of profit flows to parent firms. Again all this is fine except that Japan is owning more of the U.S. and the U.S. net foreign assets have declined in a time of overall growth.

Figure 2.17
The Military, Foreign Aid and U.S. Growth

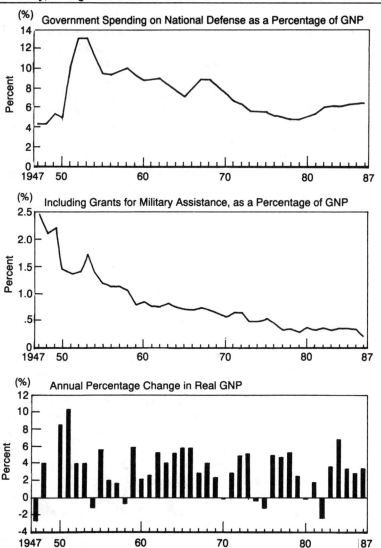

Source: Bureau of Economic Analysis

Japan pays about 45% or $2.8 billion of the annual $6 billion cost of keeping 45,000 U.S. troops in Japan, and the U.S. is asking it to increase this amount.

The Japanese are planning new defense spending including a missile to replace the U.S.-designed Hawk, an airborne warning and control system (AWAC), and an aircraft carrier. Though the U.S has been trying to get Japan to increase its defense spending, it is not enthusiastic about Japan building its own systems. Japan is increasing the share of its defense budget that goes to R&D from 1.5% (1984) to 2.35% (1989) and to a proposed level of 2.5% for 1990 (compared with 5 to 10% in the U.S. and Europe). Japan buys about $1 billion in military hardware each year from the U.S. Unfortunately the FSX dispute may make it harder for the U.S. to strike more joint ventures. The debate over the development of the FSX is interesting because it brings together a number of political and trade and technology issues. The technology to be used for the jet's wings and the radar system for the FSX have all been primarily the result of civilian R&D.[6]

THE U.S. TWIN DEFICITS — BUDGET AND TRADE

Supply side tax cuts were initiated ostensibly to improve the 6% savings rate in the U.S. It was believed by the Reagan administration that 70% of the tax cut would be saved and available for investment. Instead, the savings rate *fell* to 5% in 1983 and rose to only 6.1% in 1984. The tax cuts and increases in defense spending opened a domestic deficit. In a closed economy, this extra demand for goods and services would have resulted in inflation. But the U.S. is not a closed economy, and its currency serves as the main international medium of exchange and reserves. So Japan and others were willing to help the U.S. cover its deficit by selling it more goods and holding onto extra dollars. Much was put into Treasury bonds to take care of the domestic budgetary accounting.

The supply-side policy was turned into a demand-side policy. A real supply-side policy would work by increasing investment and thus expanding future supply, hence the name. Though it had taken the U.S. since the end of World War I to accumulate $152 billion of net foreign assets, under this policy it took only two years to lose them.

---

[6]The Japanese people were generally opposed to the Persian Gulf war. The government was in a bind; on the one hand they wanted to cooperate with the international embargo and pay their share, but it was a tough fight in the Diet. In the end they contributed around $11 billion although the exact amount was in dispute because the Japanese made the pledge in yen. When the yen strengthened, the Japanese wanted to pay in dollars.

The stage is set for the recognition of the strong interdependence between the U.S. and Japan that began with Reaganomics, and the U.S. budget deficit that gave rise to a trade deficit mostly to the advantage of Japan. In the symbiosis that evolved, Japan was saved from an over savings recession by the high demand in the U.S. In the late 1980s, the yen was strong and the U.S. dollar weak. Japan's trade surplus grew naturally out of the excess demand in the U.S. Both U.S. and Japan have structural problems. In 1989 and 1990 this was reversed with a weak yen and strong dollar.

The U.S. problem is one of overconsumption, while in Japan the problem is oversaving. Economic basics require that what is produced be sold for that level of income to be maintained. The balances from the basic circular flow help show what is needed. What is not spent is represented by savings, imports, and taxes; in a sense, these are hoarded from income, and, if not balanced by spending like investments, exports, and government spending (like defense) would be contractionary.

Savings + Imports + Taxes = Investment + Exports + Government

	Savings	Imports	Taxes	Investment	Exports	Government
U.S.	low	??	low	low	low	high
Japan	very high	low	low	falling	??	low

What about imports and exports? In Japan, with high savings, a small government deficit, and falling investment, the hoarded goods (represented by the excess savings) would be a potential for recession except that Japan found its mirror. In the U.S., the imbalance is met by high imports. The U.S., with low savings and a government deficit, could use the extra goods to avoid inflation. If the U.S. had not been vulnerable, Japan would have needed to deal with its oversavings. Japan's much maligned inefficient distribution and services sectors are another way of dealing with overproduction by redistributing the income and maintaining employment. Often being inefficient is effective.

Table 2.10, computed by Modigliani (1988), gives another view of this balance problem, showing the separate effects that led to the change in the budget deficit from 1981 to 86. The series of supply-side economics left the budget with a deficit of 2.6% of GNP. Defense and interest amount to 2.2 of the 2.6% of GNP deficit. The revolution in tax receipts was responsible for 1.7%. Government expenditures increased by a net of 0.9%, but most of this was interest and defense. Other expenditures actually fell 1.2%.

Table 2.10
Change in the Deficit, 1981–86

	Percent of GNP	
Total increase	2.6	
Reduction in tax receipts	1.7	Supply-side economics
Increase in expenditures	0.9	More government
Defense	1.1	
All other non defense plus cuts	-1.2	
Interest	1.1	

Source: Modigliani (1988)

When one looks at a graph like that in Figure 2.18 showing that more than 20% of the nation's children are living below the poverty level, one wonders about all that military spending at the expense of the nation's poor.

Figure 2.18
Changing Places

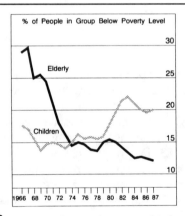

Source: Urban Institute

GOLD AND FOREIGN EXCHANGE RESERVES

Japanese gold and foreign exchange reserves peaked in April 1989 at some $101 billion. Nearly $17 billion was used to support the yen in May, June, and July 1989, and much more in late 1989 and early 1990. Table 2.11 shows these reserves from 1984 to the end of January, 1992 (see also Table 2.14). Taiwan, Japan, the U.S., Spain, Germany and Italy have the most in the world. Spain and Italy also had reserves in excess of $50 billion. The U.K.

had $36 billion; West Germany, $61 billion; France, $37 billion, and Canada, $18 billion. Per capita, Singapore has the most reserves followed by Switzerland and Taiwan. Although its reserves, at $17 billion, are far below those in Japan, Singapore's per capita rate is over $6,000. By this measure, Japan, with less than $1,000 per capita, is not even in the top 20 (see Table 2.12). Taiwan, which is not an IMF member, has the most reserves. Table 2.13 shows the trade, exchange rates, and reserves for March 1992. Table 2.14 shows U.S. trade with Japan by category from 1980 to 1989.

Table 2.11
Gold and Foreign Exchange Reserves end of Years 1984–1992, Millions of U.S. Dollars

	Japan	U.S.	U.K.	Germany	France	Canada
1984	26,313	32,354	10,093	43,406	23,748	
1985	26,510	42,193	13,951	48,406	29,735	3,275
1986	42,239	48,671	19,236	55,809	34,958	4,095
1987	81,479	47,748	42,681	83,482	37,114	8,203
1988	97,662	49,079	44,079	63,002	29,219	15,392
1989	84,895	75,597	35,641	65,086	28,109	16,750
1990	79,707	83,340	35,850	77,065	28,400	15,300
1991 (Jul)	70,400	63,800	39,300	59,500	33,300	16,700
1992 (Jan)	71,700	64,800	36,100	60,800	36,800	18,100

Table 2.12
Per Capita International Reserves Including Gold, U.S. Dollars at the end of 1988

Singapore	6,459	Finland	1,393
Switzerland	4,881	Iceland	1,125
Taiwan	4,012	Italy	1,100
Norway	3,096	France	1,099
U. Arab Emirates	3,000	Germany	1,084
Bahrain	2,790	Belgium	1,083
Denmark	2,233	Kuwait	1,041
Netherlands	2,027	Sweden	1,033
Saudi Arabia	1,465	Australia	1,023
Austria	1,400		

Source: IMF

Table 2.13
Trade, Exchange Rates and Reserves, March 1992, Billions of Dollars

	Trade		Current Account	Trade Weighted Exchange, 1985=100		Currency per $		Foreign Reserves	
	Latest Month	12 month	Latest 12 month	Latest	Year ago	Latest	Year ago	Jan	Year ago
Australia	0.38	3.7	-10.2	85.4	87.1	1.3	1.3	14.7	16.1
Belgium	-0.17	-2.8	4.7	111.6	111.2	34.1	34.0	11.1	12.1
Canada	0.56	6.4	-23.4	100.4	104.0	1.2	1.2	16.1	18.1
France	0.68	-3.7	-5.5	103.5	102.7	5.6	5.6	31.3	36.8
Germany	3.12	12.9	-22.7	118.6	118.1	1.7	1.7	60.8	68.2
Holland	0.87	7.7	9.8	114.6	114.1	1.9	1.9	126.8	17.9
Italy	-0.10	-11.5	-19.7	98.7	99.4	1242	1234	45.1	62.5
Japan	10.30	105.8	75.6	138.7	133.1	133.0	138.0	71.7	79.1
Spain	-3.70	-32.9	-15.8	107.3	108.9	104.0	103.0	64.0	52.9
Sweden	0.73	6.5	-2.2	95.4	93.5	6.0	6.0	18.3	18.0
Switzerland	-0.40	5.4	9.0	106.6	111.4	1.5	1.4	26.9	26.0
U.K.	-1.81	-17.1	-9.6	90.2	92.0	0.6	0.6	41.2	36.1
U.S.	-5.94	-66.2	-8.6	65.0	64.8	-	-	64.8	74.0

Source: *The Economist*, April 1992.

THE ROLE OF TRADE IN THE GROWTH OF JAPAN'S ECONOMY

Net exports became important to Japan's growth beginning in the early 1970s, but most especially in the early 1980s. Figure 2.19 shows the overall trade balances of the U.S. and those with Japan from 1960 to 1990. Figure 2.20 shows Japan's trade surplus with the U.S. and Japan's current account surplus from 1975 to 1989. Figure 2.21 shows Japan's trade and current account surpluses from 1984 to 1990. Finally, Figure 2.22 has the trend in current account balance from 1982 to 1990. This shows a peak in 1986 and a steady decline to $35.6 billion. Japan had a negligible surplus in the early 1980s. From 1981 onward, the U.S. trade balance first declined and then plunged into deficit. Trade balances that are sustained over time end up as a wealth transfer and reflect long-term structural changes. The U.S. had positive trade balances for 80 years, during this time it did not register any complaints nor admit to the status of unfair trader. This coincided with a rise in the power of the U.S. economy and growth in relative income.

Figure 2.19
The U.S. Merchandise Trade Balance: Decades of Red Ink

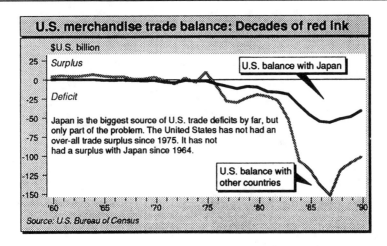

Source: U.S. Bureau of Census

Figure 2.20
Japan's Trade Surplus in Total and the Portion that is with the U.S. in Billions of U.S. Dollars, 1975–89

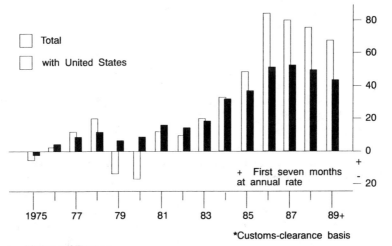

Source: Ministry of Finance

Figure 2.21
Japan's Trade Surplus with the U.S. and its Current Account Surplus, 1984–90

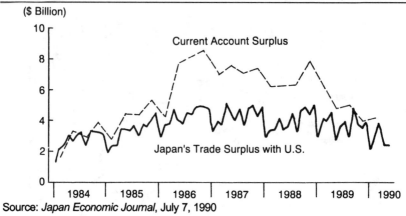

Source: *Japan Economic Journal*, July 7, 1990

Figure 2.22
Current Account Balance in Billions of U.S. Dollars, 1982–90

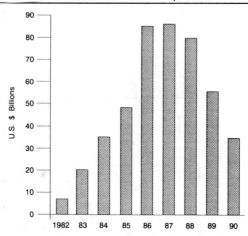

Source: JETRO

Japan's bilateral trade account with the U.S. had been in balance until 1976 when there emerged a $7 billion surplus. This grew yearly except in 1979, 1989 and 1990. Lincoln (1988) notes an asymmetric U.S.-Japan relationship: U.S. exports to Japan have been fairly constant at about 11% of total U.S. exports, while Japanese exports to the U.S. have risen from 26 to 37% of Japan's exports. This is further confirmation of the importance of the ballooning of the U.S. budget deficit and its effects on the balance of trade.

Table 2.14 shows the U.S. trade with Japan broken down by categories in 1980 and from 1985 to 1989. The deficit on the balance of trade had grown also 5 fold from 1980 to 1985. This was the result of a huge growth in the imports of automotive products, capital goods and consumer goods. Total exports increased about 10% but imports more than doubled. (Note that the balance of trade neglects services.)

Figure 2.23 shows the Japanese commodity trade, from 1969 to 1989. The petroleum import share increased steeply in 1973. Motor vehicle exports increased steadily throughout the 1980s. Petroleum reached almost 40% of the imports while motor vehicle exports reached 20%. Petroleum imports dropped precipitously in the early 1980s, opening the gap in the

Table 2.14

U.S. Trade with Japan, Millions of Dollars, 1980–89

	1980	1985	1986	1987	1988	1989
Total Exports	20,790	22,631	26,882	28,249	37,725	44,584
Food, feed, and beverages	5,393	5,001	5,043	5,555	7,892	8,443
Industrial supplies	9,501	8,680	8,752	10,156	12,989	15,372
Capital goods	4,148	5,694	6,428	7,388	9,874	11,331
Automotive products	192	245	300	382	754	1,034
Consumer goods	1,154	1,416	1,690	2,551	3,564	4,987
Other exports	403	1,596	4,670	2,218	2,652	3,418
Total Imports	30,701	68,763	81,911	84,575	89,519	93,586
Food, feed, and beverages	297	500	504	451	394	344
Industrial supplies	5,926	7,035	6,949	7,281	8,471	8,464
Capital goods	6,555	21,516	25,334	28,947	33,853	37,015
Automotive products	11,436	24,980	32,849	33,695	31,978	33,734
Consumer goods	6,198	14,017	15,451	13,385	14,083	12,961
Other exports	289	734	824	817	740	1,068
Net Exports (Imports)	-9,911	-46,132	-55,029	-56,326	-51,794	-49,002
Food, feed, and beverages	5,096	4,501	4,539	5,104	7,498	8,099
Industrial supplies	3,575	1,645	1,803	2,875	4,518	6,908
Capital goods	-2,407	-15,822	-18,906	-21,559	-23,979	-25,684
Automotive products	-11,244	-24,735	-32,549	-33,313	-31,224	-32,700
Consumer goods	-5,044	-12,601	-13,761	-10,834	-10,519	-7,974
Other exports	114	862	3,846	1,401	1,912	2,350

Source: U.S. Commerce Department

trade balance. Automobiles were a large share (value) of exports emphasizing the poor competition in the U.S. As more and more Japanese cars are produced in the U.S., the decline in exports could cure much of the trade imbalance. The total imports and exports to and from Japan in 1990 for various major countries including the U.S. appear in Table 2.15.

The volume of merchandise imports rose 39% and of manufactured imports by 78% from 1985 to 1988. Manufacturing imports rose to 50% of imports from 25%. Manufactured goods as percent of imports into Japan has risen from 24% in early 1980s to about 49% in 1988. Imports from the U.S. increased 45% in 1989. Total inter-Asian trade grew twice as fast as Asia-North America trade (Mansfield 1989). Imports from Southeast Asia went from 23.8% in 1987 to 25.6% in 1988.

Japan's trade surplus was $100 billion in 1986 and $95.3 billion in 1988. It is predicted to fall below $60 billion in 1994 while the return from earnings abroad will increase to $40 to $50 billion a year. The current account surplus will not fall as fast but should reach $48.4 billion by 1994 (*Economic Journal*, December 30, 1989).

Figure 2.23
Commodity Trade in Japan, 1969–89

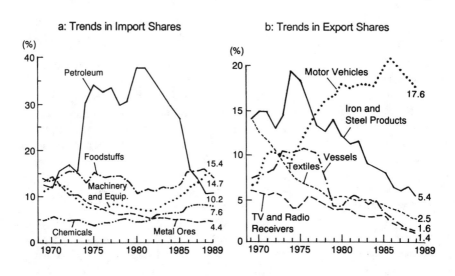

a: Trends in Import Shares   b: Trends in Export Shares

Table 2.15
Japanese Exports and Imports and Balance of Trade in 1990 by Region and Country in Millions of U.S. Dollars

	Exports	% Change	% Share	Imports	% Change	% Share	Balance of Trade
Total	286,965	4.3	100	234,565	11.2	100	52,400
Advanced countries	169,948	1.5	59.2	119,185	11.1	50.8	50,763
U.S.A.	90,315	-3.1	31.5	52,287	8.4	22.3	38,028
EC	53,510	11.7	18.6	35,063	24.6	14.9	18,447
Australia	6,903	-11.6	2.4	12,320	6.2	5.3	-5,417
Developing countries	113,280	9.3	39.5	110,448	11.5	47.1	2,832
Latin America	10,283	9.6	3.6	9,826	10.8	4.2	457
Asia	88,814	8.3	30.9	66,586	4.0	28.4	22,228
NIES in Asia	56,664	7.4	19.7	25,936	-4.5	11.1	30,728
Middle East	9,919	15.9	3.5	31,335	35.9	13.4	-21,416
Africa	3,409	17.9	1.2	1,875	-8.2	0.8	1,534
Communist Bloc	9,864	-22.2	3.4	16,945	8.7	7.2	-7,081
USSR	2,564	-16.8	0.9	3,354	11.6	1.4	-790
China	6,128	-28.0	2.1	12,018	7.8	5.1	-5,890

Source: JETRO

Japan's trade imbalance continued to increase in April 1989 by 7.7% and was up to $7.3 billion following a monthly decline of 9.7% in March, which may indicate a seasonality problem. The balance was calculated at the rate of ¥132.12 compared to ¥125.70 in April 1988. Exports of computer chips increased 39.7% to $731.64 million, car exports rose 0.8% to 570,392 units and gained 3.5% in value, to $4.59 billion. Meat imports increased 19.1% to 99,131 tons, and crude oil rose 5.7% to $1.8 billion. Auto imports also rose 29% to 16,525 units. Imports of textiles rose 19.1% to $1.03 billion. Japan's trade surplus with the U.S. rose 10.4% to $45.61 billion, for a third consecutive gain. Exports to the U.S. rose 7.7% fed by computer chips.

In January 1990, Japan ran its first current account deficit in six years. The current account was $636 million in deficit compared with a $2.51 billion surplus a year earlier. The previous deficit was $562 million in January 1984. The yearly surplus fell from $79.63 billion to $56.98 billion in 1989. January is a weak time with a typical fall in exports and an increase in imports, especially foreign travel and energy. Long-term capital flows were also in deficit by $2.87 billion after a surplus of $3.39 billion in the previous month. The trade account itself remained in surplus at $340 million down for $3.25 million in January 1989. Exports fell 3.8%; demand was off in the U.S. and Europe. Imports increased 13.4%. The trade gap with the U.S. is still high at $2.97 billion versus $2.20 billion a year ago, in large part due to increased machine tool exports for Japanese factories in the U.S. Oil prices were up 40.7% from the previous year and these products account for 20% of all imports.

In terms of investment, Japan holds about 3 to 4% of U.S. investment. Japanese investment in the U.S. represents about 33% of all Japanese accumulated investment abroad. Three quarters of Japan's trade surplus is with the U.S. and 40% of the U.S. deficit is with Japan. In 1989, the trade account was out of balance by about $50 billion a year.

Japan's profits began to grow as the U.S. and other countries placed quotas on Japanese products, shifting the economic rent to Japanese producers and pushing up the excess savings gap. In 1977, a quota was placed on televisions and, in 1982, on autos. In general, the quotas raised the U.S. prices above the Japanese price. So now money made in North America subsidized domestic sales. Earlier, U.S.-Japan trigger prices on steel had made the U.S. more vulnerable to European steel while not gaining any positive response from the major U.S. steel producers.

Robert Lawrence of the Brookings Institution reported that barriers to U.S. goods have been falling (*Japan Economic Journal*, January 13, 1990). He found that the high yen both increased imports and at the same time loosened the control by the large trading groups.[7] American firms increased shipments to affiliates in Japan from 11% of exports in 1983 to 17% in 1987. From 1985 to 1988, imports of U.S. manufactured goods rose 80% to $22 billion. Measured in 1980 yen, the import share of Japan's manufactured goods rose from 6% in 1980 to 8.2% in 1987 (the U.S. ratio is 14%). Per capita, the Japanese buy more U.S. goods than Americans buy from them. Only Canada buys more U.S. goods than Japan.

SELF-CONTAINMENT AND CONTENTMENT

It has been said that U.S. companies have been content to produce for their own domestic market and have not been willing, nor have they needed, to design for other markets. Table 2.16 reflects Americans' lack of interest in Japan compared with the Japanese interest in the U.S. Recall that the U.S. population is nearly twice that of Japan.

The *Asahi Shimbun* estimated that the number of visiting Japanese doing business in the U.S. on any day is ten times that of Americans doing business in Japan (say 5,000 to 500).

---

[7]Studies using 1970-86 data predicted a 1% rise in volume for every 1% increase in the value of the yen for no impact on the total value of trade! New data suggest the volume increased 1.1%.

Table 2.16
Japanese Interest in the U.S. versus American Interest in Japan

	Japanese in U.S.	Americans in Japan	Number of Americans if at same rate as Japanese
Visits	2.1 mil	0.55 mil	4.1 mil
University students	20,000	1,800	40,000
Residents	102,000	70,000	202,000
Government offices	12 (prefectures)	4 (states)	

Classic examples of U.S. self-containment include: the company that thought it did not need to translate its manual into Japanese nor convert to metric to meet Japanese standards, or the firm that tried to market large refrigerators for small Japanese kitchens.

There are many factors behind the U.S. balance of payments deficit and the trade deficits with Japan, Germany, and other countries. One of them is that the U.S. is simply not making enough products that can be sold to pay for the goods consumed. The country's spending habits have grown beyond its income. Throughout most of its existence, U.S. incomes in real, inflation-adjusted terms continued to increase and, on average, doubled during each 20-year generation until the mid-1980s. This growth is no longer being realized.

The U.S. has always been complacent, producing for its own use, and if any foreigners bought the products, that was fine. Little attention has been paid to what other countries might want. There are many cries now that the Japanese should buy more American products, but America produces little that the Japanese might want. While the U.S. was relatively complacent, other countries were developing products for sale in the U.S. that customers wanted. In the 1980s, Greece and possibly Australia were the only major countries that had lower productivity growth than the U.S. In addition to the normal high productivity in Japan, Germany, Taiwan, Hong Kong, Singapore, and Korea, countries such Canada, France, and Great Britain had higher productivity growth than the U.S.

THE PROBLEM WITH QUOTAS,
OR HOW THE U.S. TRANSFERRED PROFITS TO JAPAN

Japan's profits began to grow as the U.S. and other countries began to place quotas on Japanese products, shifting the economic rent to Japanese producers and pushing up the excess savings gap. In 1977, a quota was placed on TVs and in 1981, on autos. The quota raised the U.S. prices above the Japanese price. Money made in North America now subsidized domestic sales. Earlier, U.S.-Japan trigger prices on steel had made the U.S. more vulnerable to European steel while not gaining any positive response from the major U.S. steel producers. Figure 2.24 gives a chronology of U.S.-Japan trade friction.

Figure 2.24
Chronology of U.S.-Japan Trade Friction

Textiles	Oct 1974	Agreements signed on the basis of the multi-fiber
	Jan 1986	agreement (MFA)
Steel Products	Jun 1966 Dec 1974	Japan enforces controls on steel exports to the U.S.
	Feb 1978	U.S. introduces trigger price system for foreign steel
	Jul 1983	U.S. introduces an import control system for foreign specialty steels
	Oct 1984	Japan introduces an export market share system
TVs	July 1977	Japan enforces export controls on TV to the U.S.
Machine Tools	Mar 1978 Jan 1987	Japan introduces a minimum export price system
	Dec 1986	Japan introduces an export control system
Automobiles	May 1981	Japan introduces an export control system with total shipments to the U.S. limited to 1.68 million cars per year; raised to 1.85 million in FY1984 and 2.3 million in FY1985.
Semi-conductors	Jun 1985	U.S. charges Japan with violation of Section 301 of the Trade Act of 1974
	Sept 1987	Japan-U.S. semiconductor agreement signed
	Apr 1987	U.S. adds surcharges on Japanese personal computers, color TVs and electric tools because of violation of the SC agreement
	Nov 1987	U.S. lifts surcharges but the problem of U.S. manufacturers' access to the Japanese market continues
Agricultural Products	Sept 1986	U.S. Rice Millers Association (RMA) files a petition with the U.S. Trade Representative (USTR) demanding access to the Japanese rice market on the Basis of Section 301
	Oct 1986	USTR turns down the petition
		GATT creates a special panel on petition from the U.S. to discuss 12 product categories on Japan's import restrictions list

	Feb 1988	GATT finds 10 of the 12 product categories violating its principles and urges Japan to liberalize the domestic market for such categories
	Jun 1988	Japan and the U.S. agree on staged liberalization for oranges and beef
	Sept 1988	RMA files another petition with the USTR re rice access
Public Works	May 1986	U.S. demands that Japan allow foreign companies to participate in bidding for construction for the new Kansai International Airport
	Mar 1988	agreement reached
Tariffs	Sept 1985	U.S. demands lower tariffs on tobacco (rates lowered in Apr 1987)
	Dec 1985	U.S. demands lower tariffs on aluminum (in Jan 1988)

Source: Tokyo Business Today

Voluntary restraint agreements didn't stop Americans from buying Japanese goods. Indeed Americans began to buy more expensive Japanese products. The quota limits expressed in quantities encouraged the Japanese to export higher quality and higher priced products.

Though the U.S. imposed import quotas on many Japanese products, one of the most talked about examples was that on automobiles first imposed in 1981. *The Economist* estimated that the agreement on cars enabled Japanese manufacturers to raise their prices by $2,000 and domestic manufacturers by $500 per car. Another result has been the building of a number of Japanese-owned or joint-venture auto plants in the U.S., such as the Nissan plant in Tennessee, the Toyota plant in Kentucky, and the Toyota-GM plant in California. These, in effect, jump the quota barrier and provide protection against more stringent quotas in the future. Though there have been some employment-creating benefits, design and engineering jobs often remain in Japan, and profits, when they accrue, will be paid to Japanese owners.

Were quotas a good idea? There are many aspects to this question and we will focus on an important and often overlooked aspect: quotas generate a profit or an unearned income, that is, a windfall. Who gets the profit realized because of the higher prices paid due to the artificial shortage of goods in high demand? You guessed it: Japanese auto producers!

Let's compare the quota with a tariff that would have created the same level of sales. Figure 2.25 shows how this works in simplified fashion. Assume a quota limit is set at the previous year's quantity, but over time the demand increases. No more cars can be sold because the quota has been placed on imports. With the new demand (people have learned that Japanese cars are reliable and trouble-free), and the quota, the price increases. Yet the producers would have been willing to sell at the old price (that's what the supply curve tells us, and the old quantity and price cleared the market free of restrictions the previous year). Thus, any increase in price represents a per unit profit on each car sold. The shaded area, equaling the change in price times the quantity sold, represents the extra revenue the seller receives. So the seller, the Japanese firm, gets *all the extra revenue*. This extra revenue also represents *an increase in the trade deficit* because the same number of cars now cost more.

Figure 2.25
Where Does the Profit Go with Quotas?

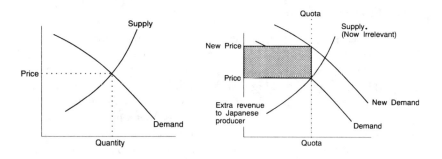

Theoretically, a tariff could have been set—in this case equal to the price increase, and then the U.S. government would have collected all of this extra revenue. The benefits would have accrued in a number of directions: the trade deficit would have been less (the total spent on imported cars would be reduced), the budget deficit would have been less (tariff revenues collected), and the Japanese firms would have had less of a profit (and less ability to buy U.S. investments). This analysis does not consider the political consequences of a tariff, especially the ramification on the General Agreement on Tariffs and Trade that has been in operation to lower tariffs since the end of World War II. The point is that, with quotas, *all* the extra revenue goes to the Japanese firms.

Protected behind the quota wall, the Japanese firms do not have to compete with each other. Behind the quota barriers, the Japanese have used profits generated in the U.S. and Canadian markets to enable them to lower prices in Japan. As a consequence of the quotas, the Japanese have moved upscale. Meanwhile, U.S. car manufacturers are still attempting to beat the

Japanese where they *were* — small fuel-efficient cars—while the Japanese have moved into the luxury market. A short-term benefit of the quotas to the U.S. firms was that they were able to raise prices and become slack on quality, since the competition had been contained. Now, with increased Japanese production in the U.S. (making the Japanese firms into U.S. firms), they can no longer avoid competing.

Europe has also used quotas, but in preparing for 1992, it appears to be searching for other means to deal with trade imbalances, such as content rules and focusing on strategic content.

COMPUTER CHIPS, A CASE STUDY: BEWARE, YOUR WISH MAY COME TRUE

Japanese companies such as NEC, Hitachi, and Toshiba now account for 80 to 90% of worldwide *sales* of memory chips. This does not include chips made for in-house production; IBM is still the largest producer by this accounting. Cray Research Inc. relies on Japanese chips, while attempting to compete with Japanese supercomputer manufacturers. How did this come about given the U.S. lead in computers?

By 1986, D-RAMs were in oversupply. The U.S. merchant companies complained and imports were limited. Other factors limited supply, including an earthquake at a Hitachi factory, the withdrawal of AT&T from production, and an increase in demand in 1987. MITI oversaw a cut in production of 32% while demand increased 30% as the computer industry turned around. The trade agreement had a good impact on the Japanese industry. In the mid-1980s, Japanese manufacturers lost $4 billion as production overexpanded and they sold at low prices, but now they are making large margins and funding R&D into state of the art chips and design tools.

The U.S. policy to protect its domestic chip manufacturers has, surprisingly, had a negative impact on the major computer firms. The policy created a shortage, so firms such as Sun, Apple, and Compaq were forced to cut production. This may threaten entry of Japanese computers into the U.S. market. Small U.S. firms must pay two to three times more for the vital D-RAMs than Japanese firms or IBM. A better policy would guarantee availability and low cost of these vital memory chips. Though the cost of producing these chips has dropped dramatically, the price to manufacturers has increased and the price of memory add-ons is increasing. This has given an edge to IBM, which is a major in-house producer of chips. The major Japanese firms produce both in house and sell outside in competition with U.S. merchant chip companies like Texas Instruments and Motorola.

The U.S.-Japan trade agreement gave a structure to the Japanese industry that otherwise was in disarray and in which the U.S. firms had been making inroads, the growing information sector in areas of computer, software, and telecommunications.

ECONOMIC STRENGTH?

Japan has announced what the U.S. must do to improve its trade deficit: cut the budget deficit, increase savings, increase investment, improve quality, give up short-term decision making, spend more on education and training, increase incentives for exports, increase R&D, end the ban on foreign sales of Alaska oil, and tax gasoline.

Many of the suggestions for improvement of the U.S. economy refer to better structures that already exist in the Japanese economy and management—for example, less adversarial labor-management relations, fewer mergers and acquisitions, more hands-on, engineering-based management versus financial management, higher savings, shifting some of the risk of recession toward management, developing loyalty in the work force with a bonus system giving both security and incentives for productivity improvements. For the remainder of this book we explore how these differences have worked their way into the manufacturing and financial markets of Japan and the ramifications for the future.

CHAPTER 3

THE FIRMS: EFFECTIVENESS IN MANUFACTURING THROUGH A CRAFT APPROACH TO MANAGEMENT

Number of Japanese Cars manufactured in the U.S.
in 1978: 0   *in 1988: 695,000*
Number of fax machines sold in the U.S.
in 1983: 70,000   *in 1988: 1.5 million*

In 1969 U.S. manufacturers produced:

82% of televisions for the U.S. market but hardly any in 1988

88% of cars and only 70% in 1988

90% of machine tools and only 50% in 1988

In semiconductors, the share went from 95% in 1980 to 15% in 1988.

Japan's success from 1949 to the present has been remarkable. In this chapter we investigate the role of Japanese firms and their management in this dramatic economic success. Japanese firms are resilient and rebound from trouble with the help of patient bankers and stockholders and some government help.

DIFFERING ECONOMIC FOCUS

In the elementary school the students walk to school with their red hats and leather book bags. They clean up the school and do many things as a group. When the teacher is sick they go on with their work. This cooperative spirit and group camaraderie learned in the first grade stays with them throughout their lives.

Japan practices the old economics of household management. The schools and factories and other institutions come together to build an economy concerned with sustainability and survival. Many firms provide lifetime

59

employment and rewards seniority but there is restricted mobility of labor. Unions are company-wide recognizing a commitment to the firm above ones profession. Boards of directors are composed of insiders and retirees who recognize the firm's long-term interests as well as representatives of the major lenders and major shareholders. Directors have responsibility for a general staff area relating to the company as a whole, for example, finance, personnel, R&D, licensing, government and community relations. In Japan, there is no director in charge of all manufacturing or specific operating functions. Corporations are linked through share cross holdings. Mergers are infrequent as there are ways other than ownership and control for stabilizing the environment.

The Japanese economy is built on commitment and mutual responsibility. While North Americans like to keep their options open, the Japanese enter long-term commitments.

Many of the qualities now perceived as *Japanese* are new, and have been evolving as the Japanese learn how to improve their institutions. For example, Japanese workers rarely go on strike now, but they did until the early 1970s. The workers traded lower wages for long-term job security and benefits.

The Japanese work more hours than workers in other major industrialized countries. Their 44-hour weeks are 10 to 20% longer, and their wages relative to their high output are lower than those of other countries. They have very high savings rates helped along by low income taxes and company fringe benefits such as subsidized housing.

Their cash economy, until 1989 virtually free of credit cards and checks, discourages unnecessary spending and hence increases the savings rate. They are even willing to buy prepaid cards for telephone and other services which are highly appreciated for their convenience.

Japanese companies make large profits based on excellent products and effectively designed production. Corporate tax rates are high, but investment is tax deductible, so the country, via the major corporations, accumulates huge wealth. The savings of individual workers as well as company profits are stored in Japanese securities, bonds, and banks. The system has worked remarkably well. It has led to high stock prices, tremendous confidence in Japan and its products, and low inflation within the country.

Japan has been very successful in the economic sphere. It is competitive but it is not an *economic* society. Students learn the same economics as students in the U.S. If asked what is the role of the firm, they respond—*to maximize profits*. Yet we observe in Japan that most firms are interested in survival and continuity. The same unreality happens in discussing the production possibility frontier, the concept used to define in neoclassical economics how resource limits impose product scarcities, trade-offs, diminishing returns and the need for choice. The Japanese take a very different approach, not really treating the question of what to produce as a choice from a set of alternatives but as a primary choice and commitment.

The Japanese do not think in the economic terms of options, trade-offs, and decisions; however, once they choose to do something, they craft it so it is done effectively. They understand economics as a design problem while neoclassical economics in the tradition of Ricardo is most concerned with static, auction markets. The classic explanation of international trade is based on fixed resource endowments. It focuses on land and other natural resources in recommending that specialization and trade will improve the standard of living of the trading partners. That held true when economies were based primarily on primary activities like agriculture and mining.

In the modern economy, at least half the jobs relate to service industries. Primary activities account for from 5 to 10% of employment and output. Reich (1991) summarizes the importance of the service sector: steel is a service industry where the crafting of alloys to specific weight and tolerances helps customers become more effective. Less than half of IBM's employees are production workers and only 10% of the output reflects physical manufacturing. More than 85% of the value of a computer chip is for design and engineering services, patents, etc., and only 15% is for physical materials, plant and equipment and routine labor.

Japan understands this transformation. Perhaps it is easier for Japan to break with the traditional economic model because it has such a poor natural resource endowment and they have learned to appreciate that production possibilities and effectiveness are created by the research and learning of business firms. It is impossible to argue comparative advantage relative to the super computer. The production of super computers is not limited by an endowment of natural resources but by attention and skills. To Japan it is not a question of fixed endowment but a question of desirability and then design. In a similar way, the tradition of customer-supplier relations is also justified on a learning basis.

It is hard to understand the web of differences and transformations that accrue with the introduction of Japanese management systems. It involves not just one system but an approach to designing systems. On plant tours in Japan, U.S. managers typically ask about just-in-time inventory and quality circles as if understanding these is all that is necessary. The polite Japanese hosts smile. If pressed for a one-concept summary of the secret of Japanese success, we suggest the *Clean Up the Classroom Theory*. It is during classroom *suji* that Japanese young people learn caring, attention to detail and participation and responsibility, skills that can be applied for success anywhere (Schwartz, 1989).

The Japanese understand the role of rituals such as classroom cleanup. Rituals can create a structure within which one can adapt and meet whatever challenge arises. They do not create structure for specific problems but structures that are problem finding as well as problem solving. Herein is the secret and what makes the *salaryman* the modern samurai. Because of this pervasive and hard to define quality, the results of learning and joint venturing with the Japanese are often unpredictable. They have created an economic structure that enables them to adapt. We investigate the lessons of Japanese management from a variety of perspectives: the role of corporate objectives, craft production for effectiveness, the role of education combined with investment in workers, the importance of information, the managerial revolution and how it helped Japan adapt to the high-valued yen. The chapter ends with some examples of effective Japanese industries.

CORPORATE OBJECTIVES AND BEHAVIOR

To a degree that Americans would find astonishing, big Japanese companies are run for the benefit of employees rather than stockholders. That this leads to high productivity should not be surprising.

Alan Blinder *(Business Week* Nov 11, 1991)

Japanese firms have different objectives than U.S. firms. One key to this, as well as the riddle regarding the high stock market values, is found in the growing importance of synergy and symbiosis for strategy decisions. Japanese managers seek opportunities to make the whole worth more than the sum of its parts. Japanese firms are usually worth less broken up and cut off from their relationships. U.S. management has attempted to create profit centers and units that can stand independently. As a result, overhead is often considerable and the firm is indeed worth more dismembered than whole. Koito stock fell on the announcement of T. Boone Pickens' large purchase of stock which could have led to greenmail or possibly a hostile takeover; in the U.S., stock prices typically rise in such a circumstance.

Stated simply, Japanese firms derive value from associations. They seek and grant long-term commitment to effective suppliers. A firm like Toyota remains effective and lean by relying on suppliers; suppliers remain effective by being flexible and working with Toyota on needed innovations. Break the tie with Toyota, and Koito is likely to stagnate technologically and be less effective in the future. The market knows this. One defense against takeovers is an employee profit-sharing plan to formally give labor a long-term stake in the firm. Related to this is the observation that earnings per share may not be an appropriate measure for Japanese firms. Valuation measures are discussed in Chapter 5 of Ziemba and Schwartz (1991b).

Japanese firms seem to do what Drucker advocated many years ago. He suggested the goal of a firm is survival/sustainability, and a number of subsidiary objectives are important to this. He suggested five subobjectives: (1) product or service; (2) profitability, including productivity, financial resources, and profit; (3) human resources, including managerial development, and worker performance and attitudes; (4) innovation and technology; and (5) social responsibility and the role in the community. Neglect of any area gives rise to failure, so focusing on only one (profit) also is a prescription for failure. Recently, he even suggested that profit is an anachronism.

The Japanese firm acts as if it is not maximizing profit but ensuring survival in terms of long-term employment, dedication to quality and innovation, meeting customer needs, close supplier relationships, and spin outs of new firms.

The Japanese manager's primary objective is survival, with return on investment and new product development the next most important goals. Quality of products is also emphasized, and this results in low breakdown rates and excellent after sale service. Social image, improving working conditions, and increasing stock prices are less important considerations. Employees may have lifetime employment, but they are exploited for the company's gain.

U.S. managers, on the other hand, emphasize return on investment and stock price increases. New products, social image, and working conditions are the least important; see Table 3.1.

Table 3.1
Ranking of Corporate Objectives in the U.S. and Japan

	U.S.	Japan
Rate of return on investment	2.43	1.24
Increase in stock prices	1.14	0.02
Market share	0.73	1.43
Improving product portfolio	0.50	0.68
Rationalization of production and physical distribution systems	0.46	0.71
Net worth ratio	0.38	0.59
Improving the social image of the company	0.05	0.20
Improving working conditions	0.04	0.09

*Values are the average scores given to various attributes on a 0 to 3 scale

Source: Kagono (1986)

Large foreign companies in Japan are making more money than Japanese counterparts abroad because they are profit-oriented, according to the Ministry of International Trade and Industry (MITI). MITI compared two surveys of 2,729 foreign companies in Japan and 3,708 Japanese companies abroad as of the end of March 1988. The response rates were 50% for foreign and 79% for Japanese. Foreign respondents had pre-tax profits to sales of 6.1% versus 0.9% for Japanese firms. Japanese companies use profits for capital outlays and corporate reserves, while foreign firms use the profits for dividends.

In 1989 and 1990, the *Japan Economic Journal* reported that U.S. firms began to sell assets in Japan to improve their profit profile. For example, General Motors, which had paid ¥71 per share for a stake in Isuzu Motors in 1971, sold 20 million shares in late 1989 for ¥986 for a pretax profit of about $125 million U.S. Its stake was reduced to 38% from 40.2%. Chrysler sold 44% of its stake in Mitsubishi Motors raising $600 million and an after-tax profit of $309 million. In this way it was able to maintain its profit level, which otherwise would have fallen 80%! Honeywell sold 25% of its half ownership of Yamatake-Honeywell to realize the capital gains. Shaklee sold controlling interest in its subsidiary Shaklee Japan KK to Yamanouchi Pharmaceutical for $350 million to increase its dividend and discourage a takeover. Three months later, it sold the remainder of its stake for $395 million.

Other firms, including Levi Strauss and Getz Bros. & Co, made stock offerings on the Tokyo market. The Bank of America sold the Tokyo residence of its Asia representative in 1987 to cover losses in the U.S. In 1988, IBM Japan sold its building in Kawasaki to support its parent's earnings.

In focusing on short-term profits, U.S. firms historically turned to foreign suppliers (Asian and European) to gain better quality, faster delivery, and lower prices. Now they need them for more advanced technology. U.S. firms seem not to understand that short-term costs might not be costs at all but an investment in providing future supply and new technology. More and more, Japanese suppliers are forging joint ventures in North America to continue to be suppliers to Japanese firms now operating there.

The Koito Case (discussed in Chapter 8) illuminates the different perceptions and rules about corporate rights in Japan and the U.S. The debate was as follows: Boone Pickens as an exemplar of unregulated markets believes companies are private property and shareholders, as owners, have the right to manage companies as they wish. Share prices should reflect true value, including hidden assets such as land and other stocks that are undervalued. In Japan, companies are considered to be social organisms, like extended families. Owners' rights are not exclusive of those of a variety of stakeholders. In fact shareholders' rights come after those of employees, customers, suppliers, and society. Japanese firms use the term *sha-in*, or member, rather than employee. Japanese companies are essentially people. They see the company as a living organism that grows over time (they may want to extend the analogy and understand that living things grow rapidly only when young!)

Martin Bronfenbrenner writing in the *Japan Times* discussed the differences in ownership and control. In the U.S., stock ownership is so diffused that a 26% block would constitute control; in Japan, firms are held by stakeholders such as financial institutions, suppliers, customers, and sometimes even competitors who together hold more than 50%. This ownership of each other is a good compromise between control by management and recurrent threats of raids.

Another perspective suggests that the Japanese concern with the modern economy and its social connectedness and commitment, rather than focusing on just the market economy, is more advanced than in Europe and the U.S.

Historically, in the U.S., raided firms, by incurring debt, have been hamstrung regarding innovation and development. Alternatively, assets are sold, dividends are increased, and stock prices rise in the short run.

SCHOOLS

Schools form the foundation in which children learn not only specific technical skills but in which they also learn social skills including cooperation, responsibility, and accountability as well as how to learn and create new things.

The school is very important in Japanese life. As the houses are small, without gardens, the school yard provides the space for children to play. Even during the summer—and their summer vacation is only about five weeks—there are activities at the schools: a sports day, swim days, weeding days. If one is serious about the community, it is difficult to plan a holiday.

It not easy to sort out the mythologies about Japan from the realities. It is in the midst of change, so it's difficult to predict which aspects are lasting. This is compounded by the difficulty of Westerners comprehending that social goals can be fostered without harsh repression; it is hard for us to understand that people can *enjoy* contributing to the common good. The concept of *Wa* helps capture the idea. Wa is team spirit, loyalty, unity, absolute dedication to all aspects of the Bushido or samurai code. In Japan, everything is done according to ritual, in form and as part of a discipline.

Like the martial arts, baseball in Japan is seen as a moral discipline rather than pure entertainment (Whiting, 1987, in a book contrasting baseball in Japan and the U.S.). Schools help pass on the important rituals.

Social concern and cooperation is encouraged from the beginning. Children clean up after lunch and serve their own meals and weed and clean up the grounds. The schools do not need janitors, gardeners, or substitute teachers. Recognition is given daily to students who do a particularly good deed as judged by the two class leaders.

Once cooperation is established, it continues through life. At university, someone always erases the blackboard and moves the tables back to their places. At a party we attended to welcome all the new faculty, refreshments were served. At the announced time for the party to end, everyone cleaned up together (perhaps one must even not leave early or be seen as shirking one's duty). There was no distinction between chairman and secretary. In a few minutes the room was clean.

Because of training in classroom *shuji*, everyone accepts responsibility for what needs to be done. It is this that later shows up as everyone's concern for quality control. Even if the mistake was made elsewhere, each worker accepts the responsibility for catching and correcting mistakes.[1]

At our daughter's school, the students set goals for themselves at the beginning of each term. Like new year's resolutions, these are displayed on the bulletin board, so they are very public. They include things like not being late, practicing the recorder, not missing school.

Ritual space is created by acknowledging the finish to each lesson. The students stand up, say something and bow before changing to the next lesson.

The Japanese students are treated very responsibly. When the teacher is absent, they do not have a substitute; the class assignments are written on the board and the students do the work. One day the teacher was absent and the students took exams on their own with the neighboring teacher checking on them periodically. It's really another interesting paradox of Japan.

Before each major sports event—the marathon, swimming, rope jumping—one fills in a health report attesting that the student had eaten dinner the night before, what their temperature was, and that their stomach was all right. This helps teach them to reflect on their bodies and their sense of being as part of the process and in context. For the marathon, everyone received a certificate with their finishing place.

---

[1]Because they do not avoid responsibility for fixing mistakes that were made elsewhere, they are probably less susceptible to the not-invented-here syndrome that prevents adoption of new technology that is not produced in-house.

Science class is focused around experiments and hands-on learning. They walk around searching for signs of winter life, looking for buds and insects. They grow, tend and harvest potatoes and care for the school gardens. For the experiments the children each have their own kits. Each costs less than $10 and they buy three or four a year. For example, when they work on pressure, the kit contains a simple plastic tube and a variety of stoppers. For learning about electricity they build a simple working flashlight and the kit has all the things required; on the way they experiment with sequential and parallel placement of batteries. They have field trips for example to a local open market where they observe the produce and fish, learning the names and sketching what they saw. There is considerable hands-on learning in a class of 39. And this is in the third and fourth grades.

Their approach to art teaches observation. One day was for sketching. The children had a special art kit and drawing board and they took a walk to a building and spent the day sketching it. The next few art sessions were spent coloring. The sketches are on display at the school. The pictures all are different as one would expect from art, but they are strongly reflective of the discipline of sketching, that is of putting down what one sees.

In one open classroom, the lesson was Japanese literature. The children were learning how to read poetry with feeling and to discuss it. They seemed happy to volunteer, and the teacher patiently waited for their responses. When called on the student would stand, and after contributing, the whole class would applaud. They do get used to participating and it was warm and friendly.

In May, we had a home visit from the teacher. For one week school finishes at 1:45 and the teacher visits each house for 15-20 minutes seeing the environment and giving the mother a chance to raise questions.

On Father's Day, there was a special open class day especially for fathers who usually are not available. We observed a physical education class. The children were practicing routines that were being developed for sports day in the fall. Each group had created its own routine and one would be chosen from among grades four to six. They were all very good. The children had created the dance and gymnastics routines themselves. Contrary to our expectations of rigidity and control in Japan, we found a vital, participatory and enriching approach to education,

The first day of school for the first graders is a very important event. Girls come in nice dresses and the boys wear jackets, shorts and ties; some of the mothers are in kimono. Families stand in front of a special board announcing the first day of school for picture taking. The first graders wear yellow caps going to and from school instead of the red of the older children (though they wear the red caps at school) and their backpacks are covered with a yellow cloth. Again the Japanese sense of ritual combines a mass event with individual meaning and aids the children in the transition.

Just learning the *kanji*, the Chinese characters, takes a lot of effort and time. A set number is taught each year and it takes until about age 16 to be able to read the newspaper. But it may well be worth it. They learn to understand things from context. The characters build thinking in analogies and metaphors (as well as the obvious thinking in pictures). No new characters have been invented since about 600 CE but they can express new ideas. For example, *typewriter* is formed by the kanji for machine and writing (a writing machine), and *computer* is a calculating machine. This synthetic writing gives them a different approach to innovation. They do not approach R&D from the analytical but from analogies and the metaphoric.

The characters lend themselves to a variety of forms of writing text. Children from an early age learn that books may go back to front (our view) with the text written in columns and the columns going right to left, or they may go front to back with the text in lines from left to right. There is an early built in flexibility and adaptability.

AMERICA'S UNEDUCATED WORKFORCE

Vice President Dan Quayle on a visit to Latin America is said to have remarked "I wish I had studied Latin more in high school so I could speak with you."

A major reason the U.S. is not competitive in world export markets, or even in its home market, is the astonishingly poor preparedness of its work force. At the top end, researchers trained at the Massachusetts Institute of Technology and Berkeley can compete with the best in the world in high-level research and development (R&D), but increasingly these are *foreign* researchers. The best U.S. graduate schools are full of Asian Ph.D. candidates, particularly in science and engineering where 50% of the graduate students are Asian and approximately 20% of foreign student MBAs in the U.S. are Japanese. Many top U.S. schools have informal quotas on the number of Asian students. In part this is a reflection of the U.S. decline in relative wealth, in part to lack of preparation. A Stanford University engineering department head commented that foreigners are practically the only ones who can afford the nearly $20,000 tuition at the graduate level. Top U.S. students continue to receive scholarships, but there are not enough to go around.

The big problem is at the *low* end of the educational scale. The bottom half of the U.S. labor force has woefully inadequate training compared to that in Japan and Germany and almost all industrial countries.[2] According to Thurow (1988), *The Economist* (1988), and other sources, the U.S. can be described by the following startling facts:

- 13% of the U.S. population, some 27 million people, is functionally illiterate versus 0.5% in Japan; a 26:1 advantage for Japan. 20 to 27 million U.S. adults lack the basic reading, writing and math skills to perform in today's complex job market.[3]

- 28% of the U.S. population does not graduate from high school versus 8% in Germany and 2.2% in Japan; a 7:2 advantage for Germany and a 13:1 advantage for Japan. Fully 75% of the minority students in New York City are dropouts.

- In 1972, 47% of students taking the SAT college entrance exams scored 750 or better in their combined verbal and mathematics scores. In 1982, only 23% scored this well. In 1991, SAT scores were the lowest since 1983 and 7% below the 1976 scores.

- Every student in Japan takes calculus. In the U.S. only one of three high schools even teaches calculus and only 10% of the students take it; a 10:1 advantage for Japan. Figure 3.1 shows the Japanese lead over the U.S., measured in standard deviations. Since two standard deviations equals about 95%, at 15 years of age 95% of the Japanese are better than Americans in mathematics. At three standard deviations, 99% are better and so on. The 5.8 standard deviation edge at 18 is truly astounding! This may be an exaggeration, but the point is well taken.

- More than half the mathematics Ph.D. candidates in the U.S. are foreign.

- A poll of more than 2,000 adults conducted in 1988 by Jon Miller of the Public Opinion Lab at Northern Illinois University found that 95% of these were ignorant of basic scientific facts. Fully 21% believed the sun revolved around the earth and 7% didn't know. Asimov reminds us that scientific illiteracy is not a new problem. The U.S. had not been renowned in science but gained in the 1930s with the influx of scientists fleeing Nazi persecution.

---

[2]President Bush attempted to address this problem in his 1990 State of the Union Address and again in 1991, but he did not back up his concern with any funding.

[3]Because many employees are functionally illiterate, one-third of Canadian companies have trouble introducing new technology, maintaining product quality, and improving productivity.

Figure 3.1
Japanese Lead Over U.S. in Mathematics

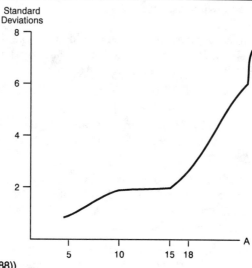

Source: Lynn (1988))

- 25% of teenagers drop out of high school. A quarter of the graduates have the equivalent of an eighth grade education.

- 10% of the high school graduates in the U.S. cannot read their diplomas.

- When Matsushita opened a semiconductor assembly facility in North Carolina, it could not find a single high school or college graduate who could learn the technology necessary to monitor the statistical quality control. The company had to hire someone with graduate work to do what a high school graduate does in Japan.

- 50% of junior college students in California cannot locate Japan on a map. All of the students in junior high school in Japan can locate the U.S.

- A reflection of the growing problems of social disharmony and ineffectiveness is found in the statistics on the five most common discipline problems in U.S. high schools and how these have changed (Marcus, 1985): in 1940—talking, chewing gum, making noise, running in the halls, getting out of turn in line; in 1982—robbery, rape, assault, burglary, arson.

- In a typical day in the U.S., 125,000 students go to school with guns.

- Americans are unaware of how poor their schools are. In a 1982 poll, 91% of parents in Minneapolis, a city with a well-known standard of high educational achievement, said their children's schools were doing a good job. Only 39% of parents in the Japanese city of Sendai said theirs were. Mathematics tests then showed that the worst school in Sendai had a higher average score than the best school in Minneapolis.

- U.S. corporations are aware of the problem and spend at least $300 million for remedial training such as:

Company	City	Number of Employees	Subject	Cost
Polaroid	Cambridge, Ma.	1,000	English and math	$700,000
Planters Nuts	Suffolk, Va.	48	Reading and writing skills	$40,000
Unisys	Mission Viejo, Ca.	125	Reading, writing & speaking	$150,000
Hewlett Packard	Spokane, Wa.	30	High school math (to production supervisors)	$22,000

Source: *Time*, December 19, 1988

More than half the Fortune 500 companies have become educators of last resort.

- U.S. children go to school 180 days a year and are absent 22 of these, so they actually go 158 days, versus 220 in Europe, 240 in Japan (with only two misses per year), and 250 in Korea. Our ten-year-old daughter was in a Japanese public school, and even in the fourth grade the students are about a year ahead of Canadian and U.S. schools. With the longer hours and Saturday morning classes, Japanese students will be two years ahead by high school. Even during the short six-week summer vacation, the students have homework. There is little time to forget the material learned in the first term, which started in April.

The concern is raised that Japanese education is narrowly directed toward taking college entry exams.[4] This may be a problem but at least

---

[4] In 1988 there were six suicides among school children in late August, just before the second term began. The students apparently fear returning to school with uncompleted summer vacation homework. The examination pressure is not unique to Japan and can be seen in the context of development and striving for betterment. The same pressure is now reported in Korea, where special boarding schools are run in a military style for those who have failed university entrance. In Korea, 85% of parents wanted their sons and 70% wanted daughters to have a university education, but there are spaces for only 27% of high school graduates. The students see first class college education as the only way to get ahead in the society. It is a very serious concern. Nearly half of the members of the Korean National Assembly are graduates of the top three schools, while half the cabinet has graduated from one, the Seoul National University. This was a familiar story in Japan, but now this pressure is on

Japanese students can pass exams. We have seen how the Japanese elementary school education forms a solid foundation in skills as well as creativity. The competition for university places starts in junior high school and appears to change this, but mostly because of the very high prestige of a few schools (Tokyo, Kyoto, Keio, and Waseda) and the relatively limited space.

The North Americans who go to college may catch up there. In college they work at least as hard as the Japanese (who think of college as a vacation in preparation for the hard work they will have to do when they start their regular jobs), other Asians and Europeans. But the handicap of the weak bottom half of the work force is too difficult to overcome. These workers do not have the opportunity to catch up later. Even if U.S. R&D were vastly superior, which it is not, it could not compensate for its work force. The Japanese and Germans each have an educated, adaptable workforce, a true competitive advantage. In our stay in Japan, we were constantly amazed at how sharp the rank and file are. They are disciplined.

The main areas where Japanese fall short is in individual initiative where they are held back by strong cultural beliefs in company loyalty and rigid rules against individual achievement. This structure is being altered, particularly in finance and financial engineering. There the creative and high producers want to be rewarded like their U.S. counterparts since their contribution can be clearly measured. Firms are being forced to grant separate rewards of achievement. Still, it will be a long time before the extra economic benefits that the firms receive from these stars go to the U.S. limits. The Japanese are masters at extracting the best work out of their employees and consultants and then embedding it into their own knowledge. Where the ideas originated is immaterial. What is important is scrutinizing new ideas to sift out those with advantage, and after extraordinarily careful research using them to their full potential. It is in this way the Japanese utilize to good advantage the *gaijin* consultants and professors.

The Japanese are improving on a variety of measures of creativity. According to Roth (1989) the top ten companies registering patents in the U.S. were Canon (847), Hitachi (845), Toshiba (823), General Electric (779), Phillips (687), Westinghouse (652), IBM (591), Siemens (539), Mitsubishi Electric (518), and RCA (504). Even in the U.S., the Japanese are very strong in this measure of creativity. Roth also relates that using a citation measure as an estimate of quality indicates Japanese patents are cited more than U.S. ones and this gap is growing.

---

the wane as opportunities are expanded both in the number of schools and positions for students and in the availability of career paths that do not require degrees from the three prestigious schools.

It is impossible to overstate the differences in educational preparedness for the age of design and information.[5]

INVESTMENT IN WORKERS

In a country with few natural resources, skilled, committed workers have been treated as an important resource. Japanese firms pay considerable attention to training after recruitment. Often new recruits are sent to Zen Buddhist retreats where they meditate and write Buddhist *sutras* in a group. This brings them together with their colleagues and makes them respectful of their superiors, but, most importantly, begins building the association of one's own interests with those of the firm.

Being inducted into the firm is like being adopted into a family. Mitsubishi Trust & Banking Co. hands out a list of do's and don'ts which include the following: respond with a quick yes when a superior calls; stand up immediately to receive instructions; never scratch your head or cross your legs or arms in front of customers or superiors, never smoke while talking with a superior, and never criticize the company or its management. At Columbus Co., a maker of shoe polish, the top officers shine the shoes of young recruits, who then reciprocate. Also, a new comic book for the company worker introduces the new recruit to work, it includes instructions for being on time, how to bow, etc. Some companies assign big brothers to help mentor the new recruits in their acculturation process.[6]

INFORMATION IS TAKEN SERIOUSLY

It is impressive how quickly the Japanese translate and discuss books and articles from the West, particularly those about Japan, economics and politics. One could trace the important authors through the course of the year by the conversations overheard. First, there was Paul Kennedy and the *Rise of Great Powers* and the Japanese were concerned that they should not be considered a great power as they are not militarily strong (Kennedy defines great powers by military might). Then van Wolferen, *The Enigma of Japanese Power*, was read and everyone was concerned that Japan had no transcendent values, no absolute values (or as some would say, no values

---

[5]Already in 1986, 25 Japanese manufacturing companies were among the top 108 of Fortune's top ranking manufacturing companies outside the U.S. At that time GM, Ford, IBM and GE were higher ranked than any of the Japanese companies.

[6]Margaret Shapiro of *The Washington Post*.

worth *dying* for). James Fallows' book, *More Like Us* and an article for the *Atlantic Monthly* which appeared in May 1989 had already appeared in Japanese in the following month's issue of an important magazine along with other articles and commentary.

NHK (Japan's CBC or BBC) Satellite Channel shows their thirst for information. They broadcast ABC news, MacNeil-Lehrer, BBC, French, German, and Russian news live daily (and sometimes Italian, or Spanish). These are all transmitted bilingually using the stereo facility of the TV/video so that you can hear them in the original or the simultaneous translation. With both you do get subtitles as well. They spend a lot on receiving the news. The *Super Seminar* series was a series of in-depth interviews (for over an hour in most cases) of top U.S. academics and important business leaders, again with both translation and subtitles. Those interviewed have included Tom Peters, John Young, the CEO of Hewlett-Packard, Michael Porter of Harvard on competition, John Kenneth Galbraith, Paul Kennedy, and Michael Boskin, head of the U.S. Council of Economic Advisors. As a *gaijin* it was easy to forget that the seminars were designed for a Japanese audience, so it was disappointing not to have access to the commentary of the Japanese who did the interviewing and to the seminar of Kenichi Ohmae of McKinsey Japan.

CRAFT PRODUCTION

The craftsperson is involved in the product and process and leaves neither the quality control nor clean up and maintenance to others.

Historically the U.S. and Japan represented two approaches to the lack of skilled labor. Japan, lacking other resources as well, invested in labor making it flexible, skilled and adaptable. Then to profit they needed to find ways to make labor relatively immobile. In the U.S., otherwise resource rich, management deskilled labor by controlling tasks and mechanizing making it easy to substitute one worker for another. This fostered a non-trusting environment. Japanese management has a commitment to labor that makes it a fixed input whereas in the U.S. the only fixed input is the plant and equipment. Though a small difference it has a very significant impact on accounting and pricing by lowering the operating break even costs.

The craft method thrives on and promotes constant innovation. It fosters skills and adaptability. Mass production deskills labor decreasing the ability to innovate. In the 19th century, skilled workers used general purpose machinery to turn out a changing variety of goods as opposed to the 20th-century deskilled workers with special purpose machines who could only turn out one good (or with costly setup for other goods). For craft production to succeed, cooperation as well as contained competition are required. Cooperation among firms to establish conditions that foster innovation, cooperation among owners, managers and workers, cooperation between firms and community, along with competition to innovate. This is also a picture of Japanese industry.

Piore and Sabel (1984) call craft management communitarian or familial production. It is capitalism without an emphasis on financial markets. Craft production tends to be rooted in the community. It cannot be moved because the links to the community, suppliers and customers are important. It is not like a branch plant that is specialized, with a frozen technology and independent of location.

For the craft approach to work, there must be flexibility in employment and in resource use including land. High land prices work in the same way as mass production machinery to limit flexibility. This is supported by the observation that a major problem facing small manufacturing in Tokyo is high land costs. Japanese firms are trying to adapt. One story is that of the Subaru plant in Ota, a company town. The factory is surrounded by layers of suppliers. The fourth and fifth layer suppliers were having trouble getting labor and the system was stretched to its limits. Orders did not arrive on time, a real problem in just-in-time inventory systems. Finally, the town decided to hire immigrant workers. These show up only in the outer layer suppliers but are important to the flow of the system. Subaru itself and the inner echelon of suppliers also do not hire the migrant workers. It is a phenomenon of the small firms.

In Japan, firms limit their activities to a part of the process and sub-contract the rest. If a large firm wants to enter a new market, it sets up a subsidiary or if it does make a new product on its own it separates the division as soon as possible. A subsidiary so formed grows increasingly independent.

Mass production combined with cost minimization have led to the attempt to unbundle a variety of costs of doing business and impose them on others. Mass production is cost efficient only in that it creates externalities including lengthening commutes that are not paid for by the organization.

The average age of the owners is high. The biggest problem facing one workshop owner was the lack of a successor: his son did not want it. Not land, not money, not the high-valued yen, not wage rates, but no successor. Japan is changing. In a sense this is the big *survival* question.

Until recently Japan has been able to support a large, inefficient service sector. Young workers now want to have clean office or service jobs. There is less emphasis on craft jobs. Those who are not good students are being left out. Those who do not make it into a good high school, mark time in a vocational school but do not get a craft. Students in good high schools who do not get into college also mark time studying for exams to try again. These two types reflect the deskilling that is occurring. Eventually they find service sector jobs. These are likely to be affected strongly by open markets as they lack effective skills.

Zaibatsu are family groupings of firms, where each associated firm retains operating independence. They combined provision of capital with relationship via family employees so they could have more trust and independence. Post-WWII Japan evolved a looser type of zaibatsu system. The nurturing model is very important. Firms formed subsidiaries which outgrew the parent company which became a minor stockholder. Here again is the importance of the blurring of conception and execution of tasks.

There are differences in response to the crises of uncertainty and instability in mass versus craft production. Mass production attempted to create areas of stability via control. Craft production learned to withstand uncertainty by developing the ability to respond flexibly and this will serve it well in the future. In the steel industry, for example, Japan pioneered in new products and flexible equipment and production; new shapes and new alloys such as rustproof steel. Specialty steel can cost 30 times more than carbon steel so it is a high value added product. Continuous casting, computer controlled cutting and rolling facilitate rapid changeover among products. Minimills using electric arc furnace first processing scrap did not need to keep blast furnace in continuous operation. They could locate near their markets. Both mini and integrated mills require skilled workers trained as craftspeople. The success of the craft approach leads to a flattening of the hierarchy including the elimination of industrial engineers as distinct group.

Flexible specialization requires some ground rules to nurture small shop production. Because resources are used flexibly, there is the need to create institutions that facilitate cooperation and maintain flexibility. Competition of the wrong kind undermines the necessary coordination; misdirected coordination undermines competition

Various policies are needed to support the craft-based system: work sharing and guaranteed employment provide flexibility, limited entry and mobility fosters loyalty skill acquisition; competition on quality but not on price or wages to be able to maintain a quality focus; a bonus system or other wage method to give flexibility in the wage bill. Most especially, firms must be committed to the larger community. When firms threaten to leave if their demands are not met the system begins to fall apart. Similarly with respect to blue collar workers, firms must recognize a long-term commitment.

When U.S. firms tried *kanban,* or just-in-time system, suppliers were still subjected to haggling over prices so they say saw it as exploitive, a way to pass inventory costs onto them. They prefer mergers and control which creates overhead that makes it hard for them to be flexible.

In Japan, some firms are moving back to rural areas for low land costs and lower labor costs but more importantly for remnants of skills. Some government aid in Japan countered efficiency by keeping people in rural areas. Paradoxically, this may help Japan maintain its competitiveness as the cities become too crowded.

The challenge for Japan will be to move into the global community with its communitarian commitment intact.

THE JAPANESE MANAGERIAL REVOLUTION[7]

The Japanese have created a managerial revolution that is hard to measure because it cuts across categories. The Japanese excel in process-oriented innovation. This type of innovation often goes unrecognized and does not require a separate R&D division. In fact, it cannot occur if there is a separate division. What we have seen in Japan is organic change where ideas are built one upon the other and products can cross industry lines as opposed to organized change where overzealous planning and control misses links and ignores possible changes along the way.

The Japanese understand how things grow because they live in context and process. They can teach the fundamentals of a new management, *enablement,* which is really the old craft management. We will investigate a few management concepts that have disappeared or been transformed in Japan:

Inventory: Just-in-time inventory (JIT) control eliminates the concept of inventories. Just-in-time inventory, as its name suggests, requires suppliers to provide parts as they are needed so the producer need not store inventory. The classic example is Toyota which calls its suppliers two hours before parts are needed. What exists now is a network, not a store house of goods.

The old costs of inventories—interest and storage costs and risk of obsolescence—have been replaced by *relationship costs.* The network must be kept open. There is an option value on its use: goods must be there when needed. To maintain this relationship, this link among firms requires trust, loyalty, and mutual understanding. Expenses to maintain it include lunch and evening meetings, mutual stock holding, gift giving, visiting plants,

---

[7] This section is based on Schwartz (1989).

and sharing plans. The goods themselves are created only as needed. The risks have been shifted from financial costs to relationship costs. The required loans and operating capital of the goods-in-waiting system have been replaced by trust and vulnerability to delay. The ramifications of the change are far reaching. The goods-in-waiting system has been called the just-in-case inventory approach, and by its nature it is untrusting.

Quality Control: The separate function of quality control has also been eliminated when it is embedded in design and the process of production. Now production workers must be trained in caring and attending to the product. They must care enough to fix a fault even if they did not create it. Before quality control experts could measure mistakes, now production workers must repair things without relying upon special measures. *Measuring up* has vanished. Again the risks have been shifted and redefined. Now the risks are not met by hiring more quality controllers to oversee the operation (a thankless, separating act) but by training all workers in caring and participation.

Another approach to the problem provides product and production designs which are more resilient so mistakes are less likely. If products are designed well, production can be smooth and the product popular. Honda's early success in Japan was due to design resiliency not to efficient production techniques. It designed a commercial motorcycle that would be easy to handle with one hand. It was made affordable owing to design with light weight materials.

Interesting advertisements by Hewlett Packard and Motorola focus on quality and demonstrate that these top firms have an understanding of the Japanese approach toward quality. HP's ad says, "All quality control does is catch our mistakes. I want to start avoiding them." It suggests that HP's integrated manufacturing computer systems can help tackle this. Motorola has a series on the power of belief: "When you aim for perfection, you discover it's a moving target." It also mentions that defects once measured in parts per thousand are now measured in parts per million or parts per billion. Motorola's Six Sigma quality is aiming it toward 99.9997% perfection by the end of 1992. The Japanese have a word for it: *kaizen* or constant improvement.

Inventory and quality control have been linked in Japan. Under JIT/TQC (total quality control) the Japanese have set up a positive quality improvement, cost-reduction feedback mechanism. Errors are spotted early. Good work is rewarded by pats on the back by colleagues. Also, the system is fully run by the foreman and workers, saving time and money on data processing, inventory accounting, inspection, and production scheduling, and freeing management for strategic planning.   The whole concept of scarcity has been turned on its head. Not only does added quality not cost anything, but it also is a positive contributor to lower costs. Looking for cost efficiency ignores the quality avenue to savings.

R&D: research and development also disappears as a separate corporate function when change is organic.

Western manufacturers look for major technological breakthroughs, while Japanese companies focus on incremental improvements. NHK even devotes prime time TV news to relating crafty innovations, which motivates everyone.

The Japanese strength has been to involve everyone in the firm in change and interchange. The average time to develop new car models is less than four years in Japan, compared with five in other countries. In the 1980s, Japanese firms have had three times the number of new models as American auto makers and twice that of the Europeans. This is reflected in the average life of a model, according to data reported in *The Economist* in December 1989: 4.6 years in Japan, 8.1 in Europe, and 12.2 in the U.S. Yet Japanese models have more incremental changes in their briefer time due to constant feedback from sales, customers, suppliers, managers, and employees. Key to this is that they do not wait for the perfect design but get something out and continually work to improve it.

Even when a firm does have a breakthrough, it does not then sit back on its laurels. The breakthrough is more like a lucky outcome, and the Japanese know they still must continue with development and change. An example in *Business Week* is that of Sony's Walkman. It had to stay ahead of its competition. The first Walkman had 323 parts, and now it has only 118, thus taking half the time to assemble. It has 20 models and a variety of features. This issue of the role of basic research as opposed to applied research is one aspect of the controversy about patent rights and differing patent laws.

U.S. firms can learn from the Japanese, but first they must believe in the efficacy of process-oriented innovation and the possibility of continual innovation. Ford has reduced development time one third by adopting a team approach, and GM, AT&T, and NCR are also using a team approach.

The traditional ways of analyzing innovation management do not really work. Much innovation is small and process oriented but the hierarchy in most U.S. organizations controls and eliminates variability, the very fertile area for new ideas and added work. Even our tax system obscures this linkage, by defining R&D as a separate category.[8]

---

[8]The measuring-up problem appears in many guises. *BusinessWeek* reported on a few: Differences in capital depreciation rules and the classification of government expenditures when adjusted make the

The Japanese are so attuned to craft-oriented improvements it's almost as if they cannot contain their tinkering and improvement. The Mitsubishi Heavy Industries plant in Nagoya is already making F-15s under co-production agreements. They would likely make the FSX. When the plant manager was asked if they had made improvements he said "I can't say no." Officially, they are not supposed to make any changes as long as the plane is still produced in the U.S. It has been acknowledged that the Japanese have made improvements in the F-4 radar and fire control systems. Is it any wonder they do not want to buy an off-the-shelf U.S. plane?

Some successes in Japan (what *The Economist* calls winning fair and square) have come out of this orientation:[9]

- Canon designed the disposable cartridge for a plain paper copier developed by Xerox and it uses the technology for laser printers.

- New ceramic and composite materials designed for the Pentagon have been used in consumer products such as fishing rods, tennis rackets, and sailing masts.

- Toray Industries, a textile maker, leads in carbon fiber technology.

- Mitsubishi Heavy Industries leads in aircraft wings from carbon fiber.

Japanese firms, even the largest, operate with a craft orientation. They do their own messy work. Japanese firms build their own robots because they best know their needs and processes (and even consider these proprietary). Some have then found they can produce robots for sale. They are even willing to sell them to their own competitors because they understand that they know best how to use them. Some U.S. firms have

---

U.S. and Japanese savings rates as percent of net national product more similar at 7% instead of 20% versus 4.2%. Though this accounting is interesting, it would be better to look at saving as a percent of the gross output and measure gross investment as well as depreciation, in itself an accounting artifact. Their success is even harder to explain if they are *not* saving more!

The U.S. is making an effort to better account for service trade. For example, the trade in accounting and advertising services and spending by foreign students. These give a net improvement of $10 billion and another gain is made by a revision of profit flows to parent firms. Again all this is fine except that Japan is owning more of the U.S. and U.S. net foreign assets have declined in a time of overall growth.

[9] *The Economist* cautions that a ban on licenses to the Japanese would only hurt them in the short term. Rather than a ban, the U.S. should focus on their own product development skills and should spend more time reading technical reports from Japan rather than worrying about defense systems from the Soviet Union.

complained of delays in shipment of new machinery. If you rely upon others to improve your processes, you will always be behind.[10]

Management as enablement can be described in life-imitating metaphors—a renaissance of the origin of the word *economics* as household management. We could talk of parenting companies. Jane Jacobs' (1984) views of the processes of growth and development are echoed by Hawken (1987) and Drucker (1985). They all emphasize that innovation is small and at first does not require resources but instead attention, care, and nurturing. What is at risk with innovation is *not* a given amount of development funds, for these tend to be small. What is at risk is the old established company and technology and all the attendant capitalized values of what already exists. Rather than risk their existing investment, the U.S. steel industry invested in shopping malls and retailers rather than rebuilding their factories. This way they could avoid recognizing that their old plants were obsolete. We suggest *enablement* for sustainability, not management for short-term profit.

The Japanese may have learned that economic theory notwithstanding, some *inefficiency* may be effective and necessary. Inefficiency can be growth promoting.[11] Development work and innovation is messy and cannot be judged on efficiency grounds, as one can do that only when one knows what one is doing. "(B)y its nature development has to be open-ended rather than goal-oriented" (Jacobs, 1984). Indeed, operating efficiency comes later and it is rigidifying. This is supported by a theme in Drucker. Hounshell (1988) reviews the argument that the explanation of U.S. industrial decline is to be found in Taylor's efficiency efforts to boil each task down to the bare essentials and train the worker to do the task as fast as possible. This has deskilled the worker, leading to displacement by machinery, and rigidified the production processes, making process innovation impossible.

The problem is that it is often hard to determine what is truly redundant and can be cut out in the name of efficiency without disturbing the future evolution of the organization. Redundancy is an important part of complex systems. Cutting out redundancy in an effort to gain efficiency is what often reduces effectiveness. The more complex the system, the more the probability of failure, so the more one must build in redundancy. For

---

[10]This relatedness is also seen in the way the Japanese can sustain losses waiting for markets to develop or make a comeback. For example, the memory market was abandoned by U.S. semiconductor companies in the mid-80s after losses of $2 billion. The Japanese had losses of $4 billion but hung on showing a craft approach to something that has value. Later when demand recovered, Japanese firms had first priority on the output as they had sustained the industry.

[11]This is not to be construed as advocating waste, only containing the drive for cost efficiency.

example, if the brain is injured early, the other side can take over the functions performed at the site of the injury. It's also why one double hulls oil tankers even if the apparent probability of failure is low. One double hulls and works at the same time to lower the probability of failure. It explains a paradox of Japan: why they measure quality control in parts per million but also make designs more tolerant. In process, it makes the system more resilient, which we can call more effective. But resiliency does not come free, and we are back to the question of how you measure waste and inefficiency.

ENDAKA: ADAPTABILITY TO THE HIGH YEN

The Japanese industrial response to endaka, the high-valued yen provides an example of the resiliency of their management.

When the yen began to strengthen in the mid-1980s, there was much fear and trepidation concerning the impact on Japan. The worries surrounding the high yen were constellated in the term *endaka*: the high yen crisis. With the resilience that they had shown in previous crises, the Japanese firms adapted to the high yen. They worked and researched and sought ways of lowering the yen/dollar rate to a level at which they could break even. They benefited from the lower costs of materials imports. Now exporters can retain their strong competitiveness even at 130¥/$. The average firm in a survey taken in January 1989 could compete at 128.1/$ which was an improvement from 140.1/$ in 1988. Fully 44% could compete at ¥120 to 130/$ and 21.8% at ¥130 to ¥140. Table 3.2 details the progress made since 1985.

Table 3.2
Break-Even Rates by Specific Machinery Industries, ¥/$

	Ap-Se 85	Ap-Se 86	Ap-Sep 87	Oc 87-Mar 88	1985/89 ¥ Change
All Industries	210	152	131	114	-96
General	204	148	127	101	-103
Electrical	203	148	126	109	-94
Transportation	216	155	133	118	-96
Precision	216	155	137	120	-96
Average exchange rate	245	163	145	132	-113
Margin over exchange rate	+35	+11	+14	+18	

Source: Aron (1988b)

Nikon can operate profitably even if the dollar falls to ¥70 at which it would operate at 20% of its present output. In 1989 and 1990, as the dollar strengthened again, the Japanese firms ran even higher profits and increased their cash flow in yen.

Figure 3.2 shows how dramatically the terms of trade turned in Japan's favor with the rise of the yen. Higher terms of trade increase the value of exports and decrease the cost of imports, generally leading to an increase in import volume spurred by lower real costs and a reduction in exports. In Japan's case, the terms of trade effect has dramatically improved their current balance as its imports tend to be commodities like oil and other resources with a fairly inelastic or fixed demand.

Figure 3.2
Terms of Trade

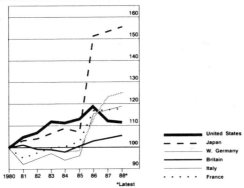

Source: IMF, OECD, National Statistics. Bank of Japan

JAPANESE INDUSTRIES

Capital investment in Japan's smoke stack industries has recently been high, up 30-40% but much of this is not for new capacity but to rejuvenate the industries. The cost of money for investment is low compared with other countries:

Investment type	Japan	Germany	Britain	U.S.
A factory with a 40-year life in the period 1987–89	5.0%	5.4%	8%	10+%
An R&D project with a 10-year payoff	9%	15%	24%	20%

The sharp increase in interest rates in 1989 and 1990 has lessened this advantage, but it is still cheaper to produce in Japan than these other countries. The lower interest rates in 1991 and 1992 point to a Japan in the future that will be more like 1987-89 than 1989-90.

THE AUTOMOBILE INDUSTRY

Absorbing the lessons of NUMMI (New United Motor Manufacturing Inc.) *was more difficult. GM wasn't looking for what it found.*

BusinessWeek, August 14, 1989

A lot of people think America can't cut the mustard anymore, that quality counts for nothing, and hard work for even less, and commitment, that went out with the hula hoop. Well, when you have been kicked in the head like we have, you learn pretty quick to put things first and, in the car business, product comes first, and product is what brought us back to prosperity.

Lee Iacocca, Chairman, Chrysler Corporation

It's just so frustrating. Cars haven't even been invented yet, and I'm already getting millions of ideas on how to improve them.

spoken by kimono-clad Japanese in cartoon by Piraro

The U.S. automobile industry presents an interesting and much-told tale of challenge and loss of market under the onslaught of Japanese production quality. The auto industry, more than any other, best captures the heart of the spirit of U.S. industrial might and vision. It started with Henry Ford and the concepts of an assembly line encompassing all stages from raw materials to final car (the Rouge plant) coupled with his vision of a car for every family made affordable by paying decent wages and offering low prices through efficient mass production. It grew through Sloan's marketing vision to cover the entire range of income and demands as well as his concept of the organization as profit centers, and on to Ralph Nader, who exposed the neglect of social responsiveness pointing to congested highways and urban areas choking with pollution.

The automobile has been central to U.S. industry and its decimation is apparent in employment numbers: auto suppliers had provided 1.4 million jobs in 1979, but by 1983 one-third had disappeared. Hill (1987) provides a look at the worldwide industry: automobile production contributes 5 to 10% of manufacturing output, investment and employment in developed countries, not counting raw materials, distribution, and other services. In the late 1970s, automobiles accounted for 12% of world trade in manufactured goods and 11 to 12% of manufactured exports of producing countries excluding trade in tires.

The auto industry stands for both the best of U.S. industry in its youth and the worst in its arthritic maturity. Set against it is the success of Japanese auto makers in pursuing export markets and now their inroads into becoming domestic producers. The next few years will likely see a major shift in the Japanese-U.S. auto trade.

The high value of the yen has made it profitable and the continuing trade surplus has made it necessary for more Japanese cars to be made outside Japan. Much of this production will be in the U.S., where by 1990 Japan produced an estimated 2 million cars per year. Manufacturing their cars in the U.S. avoids import quotas. They will sell more cars and capture an even larger share of the market. They can produce these cars more cheaply than in Japan (by $600), using superior Japanese production methods with less expensive U.S. labor. Thurow (1985) credits U.S. workers with being efficient but suggests the many layers of management add cost. So Japanese firms working with more direct, involved management could eliminate exorbitant salaries to CEOs and others. They can keep strict control of production, design aspects, and sales.

Japanese firms can also keep all the profits and use them, among other things, to buy more of the U.S. The Japanese can lower their balance of payments surplus with the U.S. further by shipping some of these cars back to Japan, or they may even lower the U.S. deficit by shipping them to Europe and elsewhere. With sufficient U.S content, Japanese import quotas may not apply to these cars, though the European Community is debating the content requirements and has hesitated to admit Japanese cars made in Britain.

Because of its importance, Hill selected the auto industry for an investigation of the global economic restructuring currently underway. In particular, he tries to determine if the impetus of the restructuring is the understanding of the global factory or a version of the company town. The global factory hypothesis suggests that production is being dispersed in search of low-cost resources, while the company town hypothesis stresses the importance of producing in regional areas where all or most of the functions can be near at hand. The changes in the Japanese auto industry production decisions help to clarify the process and indicate a third possibility: the combination of company town located near major market centers. The success of Japanese transplants in high labor cost (relative to the less developed economies) U.S. regions supports this as shown in Table 3.3.

Hill also exposes a number of interesting aspects of Japanese management that are now being verified from other sources.

Table 3.3
The Japanese Auto Transplants in North America, to September 1989

		Start of Production	Planned Output	Planned Workers
NUMMI, Fremont, CA	50-50 Toyota, GM	12/84	300,000	3,400
Cami Automotive, Ingersoll, ON	50-50 Suzuki, GM	4/89	200,000	2,000
Toyota Motor of Cda, Cambridge, ON		11/88	50,000	2,000
Honda of Canada, Alliston, ON		11/86	80,000	850
Mazda Motor of USA		9/87	240,000	3,400
Diamond-Star Motors, Normal, IL	50-50 Mitsubishi, Chrysler	9/88	240,000	2,900
Subaru-Isuzu, Lafayette, IN	51-49 Fuji Heavy, Isuzu Motor	9/89	120,000	1,700
Honda of America, E. Liberty, OH		11/82	440,000	5,100
Nissan Motor of USA, Smyrna, TN		6/83	440,000	5,100
Toyota Motor of USA, Georgetown, KY		7/88	200,000*	3,500

* doubling to 400,000

Source: *BusinessWeek*

The typical U.S. manufactured car is a global product.[12] As Reich (1990) recounts for the Pontiac LeMans, priced at $20,000, only about $8,000 is paid in U.S. salaries and services (strategists in Detroit, lawyers and bankers in NY, lobbyists in Washington, insurance and health care workers and GM shareholders). The rest is accounted for as follows:

---

[12]In February 1992, the U.S. Customs Service ruled that Honda Civics manufactured in Canada fell short of the 50% North American content needed for free importation into the U.S. Honda had claimed that the allowable content was 66%. A number of cost categories were disallowed so that the North American content reached just under 47%. as opposed to the 66% claimed by Honda. Amongst items disallowed were costs for worker safety and an engine manufactured in the U.S. was deemed Japanese. The U.S. has charged Honda with $22 million in back import duties. Engines are produced in a plant in Ohio.

A Ford Motor plant in Wayne, Michigan, began to enforce a parking ban that restricts access to convenient parking to Ford vehicles and those built at UAW plants. But it's proving confusing. A Ford Festiva built in South Korea has the proper label so may park however a Mazda Navajo build beside the Ford Explorer by UAW workers at the Louisville plant may not.

Meanwhile the U.S. has had a very hard time dealing with the patrimony of goods. A company in Greece, N.Y., decided to buy a $55,000 John Deere excavator rather than the less expensive $40,000 Komatsu made in Illinois only to learn that the John Deere machine was assembled in Japan.

$6,000 to South Korea for routine labor and assembly

$3,500 to Japan for advanced components (engines, transaxles and electronics)

$1,500 to Germany for styling and design engineering

$800 to Taiwan, Singapore, and Japan for small components

$500 to Britain for advertising and marketing services

$100 to Ireland and Barbados for data processing

In response to environmental regulations that prohibited domestic gas guzzlers from being averaged in with fuel efficient imports, Ford turned its domestic cars into imports by simply importing more parts and Chrysler cars have high foreign content. Chrysler owns 12% of Mitsubishi Motors and through them a part of Hyundai Motors. Ford owns (1990) 25% of Mazda, and both own shares in South Korea's Kia Motors. GM has 38% of Isuzu and part of Daewoo Motors.

These affiliations directly contribute to the trade imbalance: GM imports 300,000 cars per year just from Isuzu; Chrysler imports Dodge Colts; Chrysler Conquests, Dodge Vistas, Eagle Summits; Ford imports engines for the Taurus.

By 1992, Japanese auto producers in the U.S. planned to have 75% local content, a higher proportion than so-called U.S. producers. Foreign-owned firms in the U.S. are increasing their exports such that they were responsible for more than 25% of the U.S. exports by 1990. They are also responsible for a growing share of the research.

Many in the U.S. welcome the Japanese production because it provides employment, but a backlash is brewing in certain areas. Japanese firms often build *greenfield* plants in areas outside the auto belt. They train their own workers, drawing on skilled workers unassociated with the traditional auto industry. These advantages do not extend to the major U.S. car manufacturers such as Chrysler, Ford and General Motors, except for their joint ventures with the Japanese. Yet this activity is likely to cut dramatically into U.S. auto makers' market share, revenue, profits, and employment.

The activity is just starting. The plant designed to produce American-made Hondas for the Japanese market shipped only 2,630 cars in the first half of 1988. Eventually, they plan to ship about 50,000 American-made Hondas to Japan each year. Exports of other American-made cars during these six months were only 3,527. Meanwhile, in 1987 Japanese auto exports to the U.S. totaled 2,191,797. Figure 3.3 shows how Japanese production overtook U.S. production in the late 1970s. It also shows the cyclical nature of the U.S. industry as compared with the steady growth of that in Japan. More than 60% of the $41 billion trade deficit can be accounted for by autos and parts.

Figure 3.3
Motor Vehicle Production: Japan and the U.S.

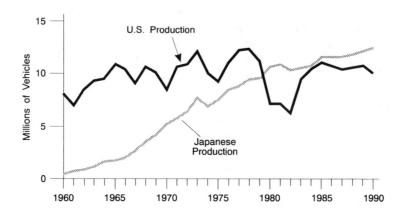

Source: *Automotive News, Japan Automobile Manufacturers Assoc.. Motor Vehicle Manufacturers Assoc. of the U.S.*

Somewhat surprisingly, it is finally becoming clear that the success of the Toyota system, to take one example, is not dependent upon either cheap labor nor sophisticated technology. One study suggested that in 1982 the Toyota cost advantage due to lower labor costs was only $500 per car, which would be offset by shipping and duties, while the overall advantage was $1,500.

This conclusion leaves U.S. management vulnerable because they cannot excuse themselves. They had hoped the advent of Japanese production with U.S. resources (labor) would close the gap and create a level playing field. The Germans' VW Rabbit lost its reputation for high quality when it was produced in North America, but the Japanese appear to be succeeding in the U.S. as well.

For every three transplant cars produced one import and *two* domestic cars are being displaced. The transplants have about a $700 cost advantage on each car. Even on the same field the Japanese rules work better. Transplant production in 1989 was 14.7% of domestic U.S. output versus 8.9% in 1987.[13] Though Japanese imports fell 3.6% in the first six months of 1989, sales of Japanese cars *increased* 5.5%. The weakening yen in 1989 and

---

[13]To emphasize the impact of this, note that almost 15% of U.S. domestic production was from Japanese plants in 1989.

1990 improved the profit figures of the parent firms since the contract prices were in dollars. The transplants have enabled Japanese cars to penetrate into the auto heartland of the U.S.

Hill notes that the Toyota system is a great departure from the mass production assembly line theories of Henry Ford and Frederick Winslow Taylor that are captured in the hypothesis of seeking low-cost resources, but as a company town, the Toyota system captures the vision of Ford's Rouge complex as an integrated production system.[14] Toyota has a vastly different organization, using multiskilled (not deskilled) labor, satellite suppliers with mutuality of responsibility between supplier and Toyota, integrated design, and quality control. Toyota moves from this productive network not to seek lower costs but to maintain access to markets. It moves to other high income centers that support the production, not to low cost areas too poor to afford the output. This too echoes Ford in a new environment; he recognized that one can sell cars only if people can afford to buy them.

NUMMI claims to be 50% more efficient than other U.S. auto plants. Workers at a Toyota line can make 60 cars an hour versus the 43 that GM made before shutting down the plant in 1982. At NUMMI, Toyota is in charge of production using its own management techniques and equipment while GM provides the assembly plant and coordinates output and distribution. The plant makes variants of the Corolla; the Toyota version outsells the GM one. The decision to design and produce two cars may reflect a limited vision of the joint venture. Originally a 50-50 venture, GM cannot sell its cars while Toyota has a backlog of demand so the split is now 60-40. Some have suggested that Toyota will buy out GM after the 12-year term of the agreement. According to Hill, GM took the initiative for a joint venture because they wanted to learn the Toyota system while Toyota wanted to help a competitor, to gain the public relations advantages of becoming a domestic producer, and to learn about GM's global strategy.

The transplants have hired young workers and have lower pension and health care costs. Three of the seven transplants are unionized. These three are all joint ventures. They have all gained concessions from the UAW allowing flexibility of labor utilization and reduced job classifications.[15]

---

[14]Of Toyota's 48,000 workers, 35,000 are employed in Toyota City. There is subsidized housing for the workers—houses for families; dormitories for 20,000 men and 1,500 women, company recreation, hospital, etc. The housing is very cheap: ¥1200 for dorm rooms for singles and ¥12,000 for small apartments for families. Toyota even has a housing subsidiary. The average employee makes 40 suggestions per year for production improvement and 97% are implemented.

[15]There is conflicting evidence about the homogeneity of the transplant workforce. Some suggest that the Japanese producers underemploy minorities; however, the NUMMI plant has a workforce that is 50% black or Hispanic.

They import a large share of components from Japan or buy from transplanted suppliers.

The transplanted system, accustomed to filling its many positions with those who rose through the ranks, may suffer growing pains trying to establish new plants without the pool of in-house trained management. Mazda, in Flat Rock, Michigan, had so much trouble recruiting and retaining Americans in top management positions that they replaced them with Japanese managers. The history of labor problems at Mazda where the UAW has organized workers may reflect the time mismatch between recruiting and training workers and management.

Committed supplier relationships and flexible use of labor both contribute to the success of Japanese transplants. Japanese firms are not content to focus only upon suppliers' costs and quality of output—they inspect the process as well. They are concerned with continual improvements in quality and cost. Whereas the typical U.S. supplier would expect the price to escalate with time, the Japanese assembler expects costs to go down because of improved quality and learning effects. This shift encourages suppliers to increase their research and development. In this way, structure can be created to work with objectives.

Though transplanted Japanese auto makers buy about 70% of their parts from American sources, many of these are also transplants. Honda buys about $1.35 billion in parts and materials from 150 U.S. sources, but at least one-third of these are Japanese. Honda considered 250 potential suppliers before choosing six. Mazda has been contacted by 1,000 suppliers but only 65 have been chosen.

The quality consciousness of the Japanese customers is being felt down the hierarchy of U.S. manufacturing: at each level the firm must rely upon quality inputs from its suppliers. This will help U.S. auto manufacturers that count on the same suppliers. Purchasers of U.S. cars had 59% more problems than those who purchased Japanese cars in 1985; by 1988, this dropped to 37%. Under pressure from Honda, Inland Steel learned to make 0.019-inch thick steel when U.S. customers were settling for 0.028-0.030-inch thick sheets. When smoother steel coating was demanded, Inland had to get better zinc. Now Inland also supplies Toyota.

Once one Japanese customer is satisfied, this often opens the door to other customers. Take the case of Sheldahl, a maker of flexible circuit boards. Honda's supplier required four times the flexibility that had satisfied U.S. producers and refused to compromise. Sheldahl met the requirements, and now its U.S. customers are also as demanding. While in the past U.S. suppliers averaged five defects per 1,000 parts this has been cut to two and Japanese suppliers are down to one (reported in *Forbes* June 26, 1989).

The lessons from NUMMI are not easily grafted onto the existing GM structure. They require a complete redesign of the organization and the concerns of management. To quote from the article referred to in the beginning of the section quote:

> In GM's culture, it was unacceptable to publicly admit having a problem. The first GM executives assigned to NUMMI under Toyota managers took nearly six months to realize that the Japanese wanted problems exposed and fixed, not hidden. Their motto was "No problem is a problem."

The adversarial approach is deeply ingrained in U.S. organizations and decision making. For example, in discussing the Nissan vote on union representation, management there is labeled anti-union. To understand Japanese management success, U.S. management will need to be *pro* something rather than anti.

As an example of differing attitudes and humility, Nissan Executive Vice President Tetsuo Arakawa, was asked by *Business Tokyo* (November 1989) about the UAW vote at the Smyrna plant. Arakawa did not use it as an opportunity to downgrade the UAW. He said that he could not comment on whether a union was good or bad; it was the workers' decision. However, he did note there would be fewer restrictions on management. He commented that though the vote was 7 to 3, management still needed to remember that 30% *had* wanted the union to represent them, and this meant managers needed to step up efforts to communicate with their workers. He predicted the auto market would slump in 1990–91 but Nissan was planning additional capacity for 1992 when he predicted a rebound.

He was also upbeat in talking of U.S. suppliers. Admitting that there are ten Nissan affiliated parts makers with production in the U.S., he still expects 80% of the parts to come from U.S. suppliers. Saying, "American firms have a lot of potential," he suggested their biggest problem is lack of R&D ability. Nissan wants parts suppliers involved in initial stages of design so there will be no problem with parts.

Japanese auto makers moved up scale with the Acura (Honda), Lexus (Toyota), and Infiniti (Nissan) to challenge the Cadillacs and Lincolns, Mercedes, BMWs, and Jaguars. Honda, Nissan, and Toyota are also working on supercars to challenge Ferrari and Porsche. The cars pose a new challenge for the Japanese auto makers. The sexy and fast cars are sold on the prestige of being limited editions, so it may not make sense to compete price via production efficiency. For example, Ferrari produces only 4,000 cars per year.

Honda has already successfully won the Grand Prix and introduced a supercar the Acura NSX in 1991. They are invested ¥10 billion. The car combines racing performance with the capability of crawling along in traffic jams by using a unique variable valve-timing and lift.

Toyota is also imaging a car with a top speed of 180 miles per hour but capable of urban driving and carrying a family of four with their luggage. The Japanese ideal is of a supercar that anyone can drive. This is a contradiction for the current market, but they may create a new niche. Toyota has aerodynamically designed its supercar with a tapered nose and flattened back to avoid the need for fins, giving its car a distinctive look. Its Lexus is retaining customers and drawing off new ones. (Purchasers previously owned BMW, 15%, Mercedes, 14%, Toyota, 14%, Cadillac, 12%, and Lincoln, 6%.)

Mazda is moving from mass production into limited niches with a new sports car the MX-5 Miata. They plan to keep volumes low (60,000 production). The car was designed for the U.S. in Mazda's R&D center in Irvine, California.

GM, in trying to catch up technologically with the Japanese producers, rushed to computerize and modernize its plants without a complete understanding of the full process. Robots, uncontrolled, began welding doors shut!

During the first ten months of 1989, Japanese auto makers sold 4.6 million cars and vans in Japan, an 11% increase over 1988. Meanwhile, the U.S. market has slowed and the Japanese are not expected to sell their full quota of 2.3 million.[16] The Japanese government is considering an export tax on automobiles and has told Mazda to reduce its plans for a 240,000 capacity expansion (over its current 1.06 million). It will add only 150,000 units and import the rest from the U.S. Honda and Nissan each plan 240,000 expansions and Toyota, a 120,000 expansion.

Meanwhile, there is the growing trend toward production in North America where Nissan, Toyota, Mazda, Mitsubishi, Suzuki, Subaru, and Isuzu together will soon be producing 2.4 million units per year. This is occurring despite falling U.S. car sales. Table 3.4 shows the top ten automobiles sold in the U.S. in 1989. The Honda Accord was number one. Also on the list were the Toyota Camry, six, the Honda Civic, seven, and the Nissan Sentra, nine.

---

[16]MITI reallocated the auto quotas in 1989 but they still went unfilled: Nissan lost about 8,000 and Toyota and Honda each lost about 2,000 while the smaller producers gained.

Table 3.4
1989 Largest Sellers in the U.S. Market

1	Honda Accord	362,707
2	Ford Taurus	348,061
3	Ford Escort	333,535
4	Chevrolet Corsica/Baretta	326,006
5	Chevrolet Cavalier	295,715
6	Toyota Camry	257,466
7	Honda Civic	235,452
8	Ford Tempo	238,426
9	Nissan Sentra	221,292
10	Pontiac Gran Am	202,815

Source: Globe & Mail

In 1991, Honda's two plants (Marysville and East Liberty, Ohio) produced 500,000 cars.[17] Honda may soon be the number three auto producer in the U.S. It produced more cars in December 1989 than Chrysler (61,800 to 55,700), and in one week in January 1990, it produced more than GM. [18]

Early 1990 saw a surge in recalls, and the Japanese Transport Ministry called for firms to pay continued attention to quality. Toyota recalled 8,000 Lexus LS400s in the U.S. for defects in the cruise control and the brake light in the rear window. In Japan, recalls included Nissan's Silvia, Bluebird, and 189SX, Daihatsu's Charade and Applause, and eight Toyota models. The Lexus recall was made with excellent treatment of customers. Cars were picked up and returned clean with full gas tanks and a gift. Auto makers in other countries typically experience even more recalls as shown in Table 3.5.

The success of Japanese auto makers will depend on how well they can apply Japanese management techniques abroad. The evidence is not yet in.

---

[17]Honda has designed motorcycles for the U.S. market (R&D engineers attended bikers' rallies, noted how bikers were modifying the bikes and how they were being used) . A new bike, the Gold Wing, is made in the U.S. and exported to 14 countries including Japan. Similarly with autos, Honda expects to export 50,000 to Japan from the U.S. in 1991 and maybe 20,000 to Europe. In Japan, it outsells Ford and GM.

[18]Chrysler is negotiating a tie up with Honda in Japan, to market its popular four-wheel drive vehicles.

Table 3.5
Vehicle Recalls by Manufacturer, 1989

	Car	Country	Number	% Change
1	Volkswagen	W. Germany	34,674	24.1
2	BMW	W. Germany	30,076	23.3
3	Mercedes	W. Germany	31,511	39.3
4	Audi	W. Germany	14,306	47.3
5	Austin Mini	Britain	9,919	47.3
6	Volvo	Sweden	7,122	53.7
7	Accord	U.S./transplant	4,697	-12.9
8	Peugeot	France	4,586	94.0
9	Porsche	W. Germany	4,053	66.5
10	Citroen	France	3,908	61.7

Source: Globe & Mail

THE ELECTRONICS INDUSTRY

The electronics industry presents the image of a vital modern day industry, the king pin of the information age. Here, too, the U.S. industry is threatened by the Japanese. Most of the world's top electronics firms are Japanese; they are ranked by 1988 sales in Table 3.6.

Japanese firms accounted for six of the top ten major suppliers of chips as shown in Table 3.7.

Table 3.6
The Top Ten Electronics Firms in Sales in 1988

Firm	Billions of $U.S.
Matsushita (Japan)	15.6
Phillips/Grundig (Holland)	10.2
Thompson (GE/RCA/Ferguson)	6.7
Sony (Japan)	6.7
Hitachi (Japan)	6.5
Toshiba (Japan)	6.3
Sanyo (Japan)	5.1
JVC (Japan)	4.2
Mitsubishi (Japan)	3.7
Sharp (Japan)	4.0

Table 3.7

The Top Ten Major Suppliers of Chips in 1990

Firm	Sales in $Millions	% Increase
NEC (Japan)	5,547	8.5
Toshiba (Japan)	5,337	8.2
Hitachi (Japan)	4,351	6.7
Intel (U.S.)	4,059	6.3
Motorola (U.S.)	3,915	6.0
Fujitsu (Japan)	3,111	4.8
TI (U.S.)	2,753	4.2
Mitsubishi (Japan)	2,568	4.0
Matsushita (Japan)	2,421	3.7
Phillips (Holland)	2,072	3.2

Source: *Jetro*, 1991

Though the share of the Japanese manufacturers has been dropping slightly and fell to 49.5% in 1990, the first time it was below 50% in eight years; it grew again to 49.5% in 1991. The shares are very sensitive to price changes as the 1990 drop reflects a lower price for the 1 megabyte RAMs. The list has been fairly robots over the last few years.

Ernst (1987) focuses on the semiconductor industry to demonstrate how global restructuring is affecting the electronics industry. His analysis indicates a pulling apart of the market into captive producers (integrated firms that produce chips for their own use); merchant houses (firms producing for the open market and primarily focusing upon cost; these are in the commodity end); and specialty firms that produce for high value added niches. All nine of Japan's leading semiconductor (SC) producers are their own customers: Hitachi, Toshiba, Mitsubishi Electric, NEC, Fujitsu, Matsushita, Oki, Sharp and Sanyo make SC's for their own use. In 1987 they produced ¥3.1 trillion and used ¥2.2 trillion themselves. Many of these are used in consumer products that they produce; only 6% of U.S. chips go into consumer products versus 50% of Japan's. There is a growing trend toward joint ventures as shown in Table 3.8. There are also important ties between Japanese computer manufacturers and Western manufacturers; Fujitsu with Amdahl in the U.S. and with Siemens and ICL in Europe; Hitachi with EDC and with Comparex and Olivetti and NEC with Honeywell and with Bull.

The industry has been plagued by overcapacity as the technology stabilized and more firms entered. Now much of the market responds like perfect competition, pricing at the marginal cost of efficient producers, while in the past, it was operating like an oligopoly, giving reasonable profit to average producers.

Some have blamed transformation on the Japanese, who apparently ignoring their natural comparative *dis*advantage, entered the field and are now the benchmark efficient producers. This, in part, was accomplished through the Japanese management practices previously discussed which have converted normal operating costs into fixed costs via life-time employment and have reduced fixed costs by creating the bonus system. It's not cheating, just different rules. The ones hurting most are the merchant houses.

Another view on the transformation is that before the demand crisis of 1980–81 and the deregulation of the U.S. telephone industry, the semiconductor industry acted much as an oligopoly dominated by a few large firms and a fringe of smaller firms (see Schwartz, 1989). Output by the captive firms has grown at the expense of the merchant firms as the larger firms attempt to gain a competitive edge on design and take advantage of

Table 3. 8

U.S.-Japanese Chip Alliances

Motorola	Toshiba	Manufacturing joint venture and technology exchange	Motorola gains D-RAM technology, Toshiba learns to make microprocessors
Texas Instruments	Hitachi	Joint development	To swap production know-how for 16 megabyte D-RAMs for use in computer and other advanced electronics gear
AT&T	NEC	Technology exchange and joint development	To swap skills for making custom chips and co-develop process technology for advanced memory chips
Advanced Micro Devices	Sony	Joint development and technology exchange	To develop advanced process technology for next generation specialized memory chips
LSI Logic	Kawakaki Steel	Manufacturing joint venture	To make ASICs—custom logic chips for specific applications in a range of electronic equipment
Intel	NMB Semi-conductor	Licensed production	NMB will manufacture flash memory chips using Intel's process, Intel will sell the chip to customers who make notebook PCs

cheap funds (might as well invest them rather than have cash and be a takeover target!) and closeness to customer status as well as distribution networks. Again, this bears witness to the lack of concern for the search for the least-cost producer.

Japanese semiconductor firms are located in Kyushu where wage rates are higher than Texas or California. The Japanese plants are the cleanest in the world and this is important. The new generation of semiconductors is 1 mb D-RAM and Japanese firms produce 95% of these. They have profited because the U.S. requires an artificially high price of ¥2,000 per circuit to prevent charges of dumping. Some fear that too much capacity is being built under the high price. This high price is also hurting U.S. personal computer companies which buy 60% of the 1mb DRAMS produced. The estimated price should be ¥1,000. Japan has agreed not to control the price of D-RAMS exported to third countries.

Japanese companies want to move upscale into microprocessors. Intel and Motorola have dominated this market and have licensed other producers, but now they are refusing. NEC has produced its own full range of similar but more clever microprocessors. Recently a California court ruled that NEC had not violated any patents. NEC has announced a new series of 32 bit mps, outperforming Intel and Motorola.

This is a dynamic sector. Wafer fabrication may be localized in Asia. The Japanese have a 43% share of the U.S. laptop market. In response to a tariff on Japanese laptops, production shifted to the U.S.

Ernst also uncovers a measurement problem: sometimes worldwide production is all attributed to the site of the firm's headquarters, yet trade figures are based upon geography. For example, some suggest that U.S. penetration of the Japanese integrated circuit market is 11% while others estimate it at 20%. The higher figure includes chips produced by U.S. subsidiaries in Japan as well as those produced in other countries.

SUPERCOMPUTERS

In a last minute effort to avoid trade sanctions, the Japanese government agreed to buy eight U.S. supercomputers. The main producers are Cray, Hitachi, NEC, and Fujitsu. Cray sold three times as many supercomputers as any other company worldwide. The Japanese began production only four years ago. Of 101 supercomputers in Japan in 1990, 13 are Crays. There are only three Japanese supercomputers in the U.S. M.I.T. was offered a NEC at about one third the going price but declined under Department of Commerce pressure.

Large academic discounts have been blamed for the lack of U.S. sales to the Japanese government. Japanese firms claim that Apple Computer started deep discounting to schools in the U.S. and has announced discounts to Japanese students. Japanese firms would benefit if the government were willing to pay full price.

The three Japanese firms are each spending $100 million per year from their profits on other products to develop faster supercomputers. All three Japanese supercomputer makers also make semiconductors, including memory chips that account for up to half the value of a supercomputer. Cray relies on Fujitsu (in 1986 on Hitachi) chips to build its machines, a fact that is often forgotten. No wonder Cray computers are more expensive and may soon be behind the Japanese.

NEC introduced the SX-X in 1991 with peak speed of 22 billion floating point operations per second (gigaflops) which surpassed Cray's C-90 (marketed with 15 gigaflops). Fujitsu is expected to have a 16 ggf four processor supercomputer.

There are three times as many supercomputers in the U.S. as Japan, but they are mostly used for defense; though the Japanese have almost as many at universities, they have only one-sixth the number. The supercomputers cost $5-25 million each. Cray has been focusing on the near-term reliable technology of the C-90 in the face of lower stock prices brought on by lowered sales growth (10%). They had a 21% profit margin and had spent 15% on R&D.[19] This market is changing dramatically; some suggest parallel processing will be the way to go for the next breakthroughs.

The supercomputer is essential for a variety of military technologies: for anti-sub warfare, the development of secret codes and their decryption, and control of nuclear weapon detonation systems as well as product design testing applications including modeling car crashes.

NEW PRODUCTS AND HOW THEY CATCH ON: HDTV AND THE FAX

HIGH DEFINITION TELEVISION

HDTV could be a $15 to $25 billion industry by the year 2000 and has implications for defense as well as consumer electronics. Japan began developing HDTV around 1968. Toshiba, Sony, and about 30 other companies have spent approximately $700 million in the past decade on

---

[19] A new accounting system should allow a firm to treat R&D as a cost of business and not consider it coming out of profits.

research. European consumer electronics firms are expected to spend $20 million in the next few years.

Japan and Europe are taking two different routes to adoption. Japan is selling equipment to program makers (video and cinema). HDTV film is cheaper to make than celluloid because it is easy to use and the electronics provide for lower wage and production costs. To introduce the new technology, Sony persuaded CBS to lobby for HDTV use in Hollywood productions. With the purchase of Columbia Pictures, Sony is in the position to encourage the growth of HDTV technologies. The Japanese assume that once HDTV becomes the standard for production, broadcasting will follow. They know that establishing the structure often sets other changes in motion.

Europe, on the other hand, is going for audience by introducing HDTV compatible with existing TV reception. European manufacturers are trying for a smooth transition at the consumer, or final demand, end. They are counting on satellite and cable transmission to incorporate the HDTV signal within the conventional signal. They are relying on selling only on the basis of quality of picture rather than production cost reduction as the Japanese are pushing. Producer groups usually effect change faster than consumer groups.

In both Europe and Japan, the industry receives government support. U.S. government money is being spent as well under DARPA (Defense Advanced Research Projects Agency) which spent $30 million on HDTV in 1989. Unfortunately because this is defense related, it has little impact on consumers. Secret research does not get dispersed. The American Electronics Association has estimated that $1.3 billion is needed to move ahead of Japan in HDTV.

The U.S. has already adopted the Japanese standard. Sony placed a bid for a $30 million grant from DARPA to develop HDTV displays and processors. There were 80 bids, two came from subsidiaries of European companies.

German Post and Telecommunications had asked the U.S. to join in EC research to overcome the Japanese lead.

Japanese, Dutch, and French manufacturers with market presence in the U.S. are making funding commitments to HDTV technology, while U.S. companies are not financing the necessary R&D. The U.S. is a poor third behind Japan and Europe. Only Zenith is left in TV production, holding 13% of the U.S. market.

Zenith and AT&T plan to jointly develop a system for HDTV. They announced a $21.5 million project of which they expect to get $13 million in government grants.

The technology for HDTV is known and easy to distribute via cable and this is part of the problem. The issue in North America is income redistribution from the TV station owners who now get 50% return on investment to cable owners who do even better. This type of argument slows down the introduction of new technology in the U.S. where the old guard does not see the changing market soon enough to change. This, too, is different from Japan where the firms are willing to adapt because they have enough commitment to markets to define themselves broadly.

FAX

The facsimile machine exploded onto the Japanese scene. In 1987, within two years of ministerial approval of fax documents as legally binding, 50,000 fax machines were in place. East Japan Railway began a coin fax service in 1987, and by 1988, 85 stations in and around Tokyo were so equipped. Nikomart, a convenience store chain, equipped all 131 of its Tokyo branches with fax machines by 1989. An added advantage is that a customer ordering a taxi can fax a map of the location! McDonald's installed their first fax in Osaka in September 1987. Customers can place their orders without waiting via fax, and clerks are freed from the need to answer the phone.

Many services sprang up around the fax. Dial Service has a fax service for the handicapped. Those with hearing or speaking problems can receive fax messages and communicate with third parties by phone. One service for the blind reads fax messages on the phone. *Jukes* (cram schools) have students send and receive answer sheets. Salespeople can use the fax for their daily reporting.

Annual production reached 2.8 million worldwide in 1987, and the price and ease of use keep improving. More than 90% of the large organizations are already equipped with the fax.

Japan is the world's leading user of the fax, with 52% of the 4.25 million faxes in use as of March 1988.

HIGHLIGHTING THE ISSUES: THE SOFTWARE INDUSTRY[20]

Many consider that Japan is behind in innovativeness. This perception is especially true in the software industry, which is dominated by Microsoft, Lotus, and other U.S. suppliers. Japan is paying more attention to software,

---

[20]Thanks to Manuel Ceva for information on this example.

but the approach is different. The Japanese are now attempting to increase productivity through automation, and most importantly they are attempting to make software compatible across hardware. Project Sigma, coordinated by MITI and intended to boost production, will cost $205 million.

Computers and electronics are at the very heart of the information economy, and Japanese firms are leaders in RAMs and computer hardware. The Japanese superiority in many industries, such as steel, shipbuilding, cars, optics, is a reflection of a mastery of software as well as hardware technologies. The Shinkansen, the bullet train, and the leadership in robots (70% of the world's robot population is in Japan) would be impossible without software.

This is another reflection of the craft approach. We see success in an embedded technology at the high quality, high profit end rather than the mass production, cost efficient end. Japan is good at making embedded chips with special functions while the U.S. is good at developing commodity software. The U.S. must control pirating and protect patents, while Japan relies on the strengths of meeting customer needs.

The entire organization, structure, and approach to the industry differs in Japan. Basic software is mainly developed by mainframe makers and application software is produced mostly by users rather than independent software firms. Many of the largest users of software have created their own subsidiaries to develop it, and hardware companies offer development of application software as a free service. NEC employs 3,000 people in its company and an equal number in subsidiaries working on software, while 4,000 programmers work in 250 subcompanies. At Fujitsu 6,000 people, or one-sixth of its employees, are engaged in software design; they have developed an advanced operating system, MSP-EX, for general purpose computers that is likely to compete with IBM. Hitachi Software Engineering, a subsidiary of Hitachi, is the largest dedicated software house in Japan. The 2,000 software firms in Japan are supported 40% by users' revenue. Fully 90% of the firms employ fewer than 30 persons. This, too, follows the general pattern of Japanese industry as we discussed earlier.

The Japanese are also making great strides in fuzzy logic, though few in the U.S. are interested in its commercial applications. In the U.S., it is just considered to be a special case of probability theory with little application. Berkeley Professor Lofti Zadeh, the father of this approach, received the Honda prize for his research. Fuzzy logic is now used by at least two major brokerage houses in systems that attempt to beat the market. Hitachi-developed fuzzy logic computerized controls run the subways in Sendai and operate cargo cranes. Mitsubishi air conditioners use fuzzy logic to stabilize temperatures. Nissan has an automatic transmission that uses fuzzy logic. Canon, Sanyo, and Sony make cameras and video equipment that focus automatically using fuzzy logic. This is a good area for the Japanese because they have a strength in combining structure and flexibility and not taking measures too seriously.

Software is a vibrant sector of the Japanese economy. In many ways, it is at the forefront of change. Because it is easy to establish oneself, one need not work for a major company nor graduate from the best schools. The industry developed much like Silicon Valley with breakaways and mavericks. Yet in many ways it is just a continuation of the Japanese way of combining large firms with small craft businesses as they did with bicycles and automobiles before.

CONCLUSION

Much has been written about Japanese management and society. Many management gurus have made their careers on the helpful hints to be learned from the Japanese success. Japanese management is different from Western management just as Japanese economics is also different. But we in the West attempt to get cook book type lessons from Japan. We bring an either/or way of thinking and look with these lenses at Japan. Japan is paradoxical. We find that we cannot make any observation about Japan without also wanting to say *and the opposite is also true*. Paradoxically, it is both more rigid and softer. It is more vulnerable, less in control with group decision making, and a recognition of relationships with suppliers and bankers. But it is also hierarchical and traditional. While management in the West attempts to be independent, the Japanese recognize their interdependence. The myth of the market without personal relationships means that though relationships are there, they are under cover.

Consensus decision making may really be consensus implementation, and it is implementation that has been the real trap in American management.

CHAPTER 4

WHO HAS AND EARNS THE MONEY:
INCOME DISTRIBUTION, THE TAX SYSTEM, AND EXPENSES

In March 1989, I was speaking with the manager of the Remy Nicolas wine shop at the Marco Polo Hotel in Hong Kong:
I see you have Romanee Conti (the burgundy that is perhaps the world's best red wine). Who do you sell it to (at over HK$5,000 per bottle)?

He replied: *The Japanese, of course. They drink it like Perrier!*

In the previous chapter we discussed how the Japanese produce national income; in this chapter, we investigate the distribution of that income, the tax system, and some of the spending habits of the Japanese.

THE INCOME DISTRIBUTION IN JAPAN

Japan has a very desirable income distribution; it is more equal than in most other countries. Most Japanese think of themselves as middle class. However, Japan's growing wealth is creating a gulf between rich and poor. The rich have land, stocks, and other assets that increased sharply in value in the 1980s, yet the consumption tax hurts the poor more than the rich. Taxes take 36.6% of the average income (only slightly more than the 35.8% in the U.S.).

In 1984, when median income in both the U.S. and Japan were similar, the median U.S. household spent 98% of its net income, while the Japanese household spent only 67% (see Wood, 1987). The Japanese spent more on food, education, entertainment and personal care but less on cars, home furnishings, appliances, and utilities. Education represented about 12% of the household budget of Japanese parents in their 40s in 1985. They spent about ¥41,819 or $290/month compared with $114 in the U.S.

The average Japanese worker in 1988 was 43.5 years old with a monthly income of ¥460,613. The average starting pay for male high school graduates

103

in 1989 was ¥125,600, up 4.4% from the previous year. Those with university degrees received ¥160,900, up 5.1%. Women received only ¥155,600, up 4.4%. Not only was their pay less than the men's, but it was also the first year in seven that women's salaries increased at a lower rate. However, the gender gap is much smaller than in the U.S.

The distribution of wages is tighter in Japan than in the U.S. The average ratio of the top to the bottom incomes in the U.S. is 14:1, while in Germany it's 6:1 and in Japan 5:1. Wealth disparities are wider than income disparities and these are growing both in the U.S. and Japan. Relatively few people in Japan earn salaries over $100,000. The difference in wages between entry level and the top executives is much smaller than in the U.S., Britain, Switzerland, and most other countries.

The consumer price index (CPI) hardly moves each year. When the rate of growth of CPI reached 3.5% in early 1990, the reaction was a steep increase in interest rates to control this excessive (for Japan) inflation.

Household spending increased 3.6% (3.1% in real terms) in 1988, averaging ¥291,122 per month. The average monthly spending of salaried families (63% of all families)[1] rose 3.3% reaching ¥307,204. Their income grew 4% in real terms to ¥481,250, the largest gain since 1982. Expenditures for TVs, cameras, packaged tours and cars had high growth. Income for salaried families rose 6.7% in December 1988 from a year earlier, and reached ¥1.03 million. This increase was largely because of high bonuses and income from working wives. Spending in that month averaged ¥434,416.

Yet life is hard for the middle class. Typical workers in Tokyo commute about three hours a day, and those without subsidized housing spend nearly half their take-home pay on rent and utilities for their small apartments. To save on electricity they use their appliances and heating sparingly. Buying a home, no matter how small and far away from work, is the workers' dream, and it is difficult to achieve. To be in the land-house game one must have already purchased property or receive a bequest. With company help, workers may achieve home ownership, but the quality of housing is not high, especially using North American space and heating standards.

Three factors have begun to separate Japan's haves from its have-nots. These include land ownership, stock ownership, and independent income that is not subject to tax withholding. These divisions are splintering what was once a predominantly middle class country into a country of new poor and new rich. These divisions are beginning to affect Japanese attitudes to economic, social, and political life and could eventually undermine the

---

[1]The percentage of salaried families is high compared to the U.S.

social harmony, loyalty, and high savings that have all contributed to the Japanese economic miracle. The changes will likely slowly affect the fabric of the society until a realignment of interest and concerns is achieved. The greatest distortion for wealth distribution is land and stock prices. We will return to this in Chapter 5.

JAPANESE HOUSEHOLD: SAVING AND SPENDING

The vast majority of the wealth of Japanese households, nearly two-thirds of their assets, is contained in land and buildings. Various savings deposits amount to about 14% of total assets. Rates of return on these accounts are regulated, change infrequently and have been low—about 4 to 5% for the best investments. But this income is usually not taxed (see the tax section below). The steep increase in interest rates starting in mid-1989 and the deregulation starting in April 1988 have led to much higher interest rates available for investors with small accounts. Rates of 6 to 7% and even 8% were available on various accounts in 1990 and early 1991. However, this income is taxable. Rates in early 1992 have fallen to the 4 to 5% range.

Securities, and insurance and pension assets constitute 6.9% of assets, and the proportion that is corporate stock is astonishingly low, some 0.3%. Government bonds and bank debentures each account for 0.9%, so the bulk of household savings goes into cash savings instruments. Part of this is accounted for by the practice of financing Japanese corporate needs with bank loans and bonds rather than equity.

In the 1980s, high rates of saving increased household assets about $1.8 billion U.S. per day, most of which excess went into savings deposits. This money was then made available for loans to purchase assets in the stock market, land, bonds, and overseas, investments made largely by corporations. Investment in the stock and land markets through bank loans decreased dramatically in 1990–91 in response to the weak stock and land markets and the general slowing of the economy.

U.S. households, in contrast, have their assets concentrated in time deposits (23.2%), insurance and pension funds (13.1%) and securities (19.7%) along with residential structures (23.4%), with land comprising only 7.1% of total assets. (See Table 2.7 for the differences in the household shares in Japan and the U.S. in the period 1974–83.)

Consumer durables are one-third as widespread in Japan as in the U.S., which is not surprising considering the high levels of consumption in the U.S. Space is a major factor. In Japan, there simply is little space to store things in the house, so much less is purchased. Moreover, when new items are purchased, old ones are discarded or moved elsewhere. Since 1983, the Japanese have started purchasing more consumer durables, postal savings have lost their exemption from taxes and tax reform has changed the relative attractiveness of various assets.

DO THE JAPANESE BELIEVE THEY ARE AFFLUENT?

Seven out of ten say *NO*, they are not affluent. They cite heavy tax burdens, social security premiums, long working hours, unsatisfactory housing conditions, and high costs of commodities, according to a Central Research Services study of 3,000 Japanese adults. Farmers and fishermen like their housing most, while company employees in their 30s, particularly those in Tokyo, liked it the least. Still, over 60% are satisfied with their housing.

Some analysts suggest that the average Japanese does not live as well as the average North American or European. This is hard to judge simply on the the basis of goods consumed and although their consumption bundles contain less, they may be more content with what they have.

The experience of the authors, who consumed less in their stay in Japan than in stays in many other parts of the world, verify the observation of generally lower consumption levels. (One claims to have lived like a graduate student.) Two hour commutes to Tokyo certainly do not add to the fun. According to a *Business Week* article on August 29, 1988:

> Some Japanese are feeling significantly poorer than others and thinking of themselves as lower-middle-class . . . These divisions are contributing to an undercurrent of frustration that's starting to affect basic Japanese attitudes. Dissatisfaction with the quality of life and creeping changes in economic strata . . . could eventually undermine the social harmony and dedication to work that have helped make Japan successful economically . . . The change likely will be a gradual increase of apathy among students and the work force.

COMPANIES VERSUS WORKERS: HOW DO THEY SPLIT THE PROFITS?

Figure 4.1 illustrates how companies partition their profits. There has been a steady but slow increase in wages, about 3 to 4% per year since 1980. This has exceeded the official inflation rate, which does not properly evaluate housing costs. From a base of 100 in 1980, industrial workers were paid about 131 in 1988. Meanwhile, corporate profits were at 184, a rise of 7 to 8% each year.

Figure 4.1
Corporate Profits and Industrial Workers' Earnings, 1980–88

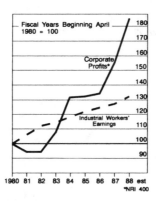

Source: Nomura Research Institute

In 1988, unemployment was at its lowest in five years. Union membership was only 26% of Japan's 45 million workers, according to *The Economist*. A 5 to 5.5% raise in union workers' wages plus a modest reduction in working hours was the typical 1989 contract settlement. Japanese management simply will not pay high wages. Working with the company's benefit as the main goal is ingrained in the society. Individual gains and self-gratification are discouraged.

Management is expected to adequately take care of its workers, and this attitude extends even to marriage. In many firms, single young women are given menial jobs serving coffee and photocopying for the young male professionals. The jobs are so demanding that there is little time for socializing outside of work. The work relationships substitute for arranged marriages. This cradle-to-grave company practice works well for many. It is more difficult to arrange marriages for the young female professionals. The practice is now beginning to slowly change and this will be accelerated as the work week shortens.

UNION DEMANDS IN 1989

Unions sought shorter working hours and more paid holidays. Interest in reduced working hours has been growing, 69.3% in 1989, versus only 13% in 1983. Other negotiating requests included increased wages, desired by 73.4% up from 71.1% in 1983, and improvements in retirement (46.3%, down from 51.1%). The survey was conducted at the end of June 1988 and covered 4,985 of 37,085 unions with membership of 30 or more in eight major sectors. Respondents could choose up to four items. The response rate was 81%.

Japan has less than 5% as many days lost in labor disputes as the U.S. and much fewer than other major countries except for Germany, as detailed in Table 4.1.

Table 4.1
Days Lost in Labor Disputes (1976–86) (1,000 Worker-Days)

	U.S.	Italy	U.K.	France	Japan	Germany
1976	37,859	25,378	3,284	5,011	3,224	534
1977	21,258	16,566	10,142	3,666	1,498	24
1978	23,774	10,177	9,405	2,200	1,353	4,281
1979	20,409	27,530	29,474	3,172	919	483
1980	20,844	16,457	11,964	1,511	998	128
1981	16,908	10,527	4,266	1,442	543	58
1982	9,061	18,563	5,313	2,257	535	15
1983	17,461	14,003	3,754	1,321	504	41
1984	8,499	8.703	27,135	1,318	364	5,618
1985	7,079	3,831	6,402	727	257	35
1986	12,140	–	1,879	568	252	–

Source: Bank of Japan.

With so few days lost to strikes and the generally cooperative spirit, labor and management productivity are both high.

EMPLOYEE PERKS

Many people live in company subsidized housing until retirement, at which time they must fend for themselves. The housing often reflects the status of the person. There are many cases where a family was quite comfortable in the assigned housing yet was forced to move up upon promotion. Often the company or government agency would postpone a move until a break occurred in the family's pattern, such as the youngest child entering high school.

Some firms give low-cost loans for apartment and house purchases for 60 to 70% of the price and then guarantee the rest, which is borrowed at low rates from banks. There is competition for such deals and a waiting list. However, firms prefer to provide company-owned housing and dormitories rather than the loans and loan guarantees. Only 17% provide low-interest loans and this is down from 25% in 1986. Some 26% provide company housing, up 6 percentage points.

At the brokerage firm, discounts on shares of the company are available. Employees can purchase shares at about a 10 to 20% discount. The shares are issued when the cost is covered for the entire purchase. Employees are free to sell the shares, but this is unusual because stock ownership is important for camaraderie. There is strong pressure not to buy stock of other companies because of conflicts of interest, even for people in research and others far removed from the public.

BUSINESS ENTERTAINMENT

Business entertainment is a way of life in Japan and provides a non-discretionary supplement to income. Entertainment takes many forms and, like gift giving, is used to cement and maintain business relationships. Given the regularity and extent of such entertainment, many establishments and businesses can capture economic rents with rather high prices for these sought-after services.

A day at the golf course with green fees, caddie service, snacks, lunch, transportation and miscellaneous equipment expenses can run several thousand dollars for a group of four. The expense is justified as providing good exercise, an escape to a less crowded, green atmosphere with fresh air, and the camaraderie of one's colleagues and business associates. Lavish dinners can run $5,000 to $10,000 for a medium-sized party. It is common for the Japanese to get their guests drunk to bring out their true feelings. Our own experiences with golf and dinner outings were most pleasant. Our hosts practiced exceptional courtesy and graciousness, and the experiences form very pleasant memories of our stay in Japan.

Dinner for four at a *ryotei* with geisha can cost $7,000. In 1987, Japanese corporations spent a record ¥4.186 trillion ($33.6 billion U.S.) or about ¥11.47 billion per day on business entertainment expenses. This was up 6.1% from 1986, according to a survey by the National Tax Administration. In 1989, entertainment rose another 8.7%, despite a call for restraint in the midst of the Recruit stock scandal. For small companies, entertainment can be 20 to 30% of the project budget.

In Japan, entertainment is often considered an activity in which everyone can participate. When we attended the rice planting, we were expected to sing and perform. At a cherry blossom viewing, everyone appeared to take a turn singing. A combination of group and individual talent is at play here. Even at business dinners, everyone makes a contribution.

A related report in 1989 by the Japanese branch of American Express was based on a survey of Japanese companies in the Tokyo and Osaka areas. An estimated ¥11.4 trillion, the equivalent of one-fifth of the national budget, was spent on entertainment and business trips for Japanese employees in 1987 according to the report. This compares to ¥12.4 trillion and ¥3.8 trillion for U.S. and British corporations, respectively.

Entertainment expenses alone amount to 38% of the total entertainment and business trip expenses, or about ¥4.3 trillion. This amount is much higher than the 11% and 8% in the U.S. and Britain, respectively. But Japanese business travel expenses are also rising sharply. Survey respondents indicated they spent about ¥150 million per year on overseas business travel, an increase of 23% over the previous two years.

CEO COMPARISON

The average Japanese CEO earned $317,000 in 1988 ranking third behind the U.S. at $508,000 and Switzerland, which was marginally higher at $322,000. However, after adjusting for the cost of living, the Japanese salary is worth 33¢ on the dollar versus the Americans, and it is worth 54¢ compared with the Swiss. Except for Australia, Korea, and Sweden, CEOs in Japan earn less in real terms than anywhere else in the world, as displayed in Figure 4.2. However, a lot is left out of the accounting metric here. In Japan, for example, the CEO receives country club memberships and other amenities, safety from ransom attempts, the pleasure of being able to provide innumerable company gifts to one's employees, and general social benefits that come with a more narrow income distribution.

Figure 4.2

Comparisons of Salaries and Purchasing Power of CEOs

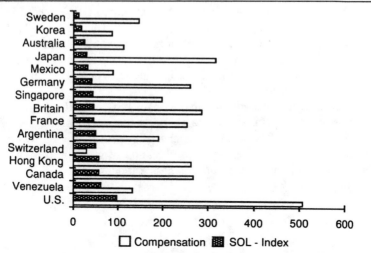

Salaries (cash, benefits and perks) are complemented by large long-term incentives in the total compensation package in the U.S. Figure 4.3 shows how the long-term incentives contribute to the relatively high compensation of U.S. CEOs.

Figure 4.3
International Comparison of CEOs of Companies with $250 million in Sales

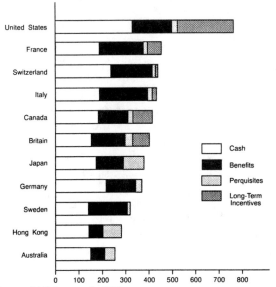

Source: *The Economist* February 1, 1992

The CEO salaries are intricately tied with the different management system in the country. Sanyo Electric President Satoshi Iue, interviewed in *Business Week*, pointed out the jobs of CEOs are different: in the U.S. the chief executive often carries 90% of the responsibility for decision making as opposed to Japan which uses concensus decision-making. The other side of this is reflected in W. Edwards Deming's comment in the *Economist* that the compensation for CEOs in the U.S. has destroyed teamwork and has set worker against worker, manager against manager and worker against manager.

In total compensation, Japanese executives are closer to their workers than U.S. counterparts. In the largest companies, U.S. CEOs receive 85 times the pay of the average factory worker as compared with the Japanese CEO at about 20 times (*Economist*, 1992). The after-tax income of the U.S. CEOs is about 70 times the average worker's versus 12 times in 1960.

Japanese corporate culture prevents CEOs from receiving huge raises and bonuses especially when economic performance does not justify them. In the 1992 recession, CEO compensation was the first to fall. The December 1991 visit to Japan by President Bush and his entourage of U.S. corporate executives illustrates the difference. Many of the U.S. executives had multimillion dollar salaries and bonuses in a period when the company had significant losses and there were worker cutbacks and layoffs.

DOCTOR'S EARNINGS

The average doctor in Japan earns 6.8 times as much as the average worker. This provides the doctor with an income before taxes of about ¥27.48 million per year (about $219,840 U.S.) according to a survey by the Central Social Insurance Medical Council of 3,105 randomly selected general clinics, hospitals, and dental clinics for the month of November 1987. In the U.S., the gap is 5.1:1, in West Germany 4.9:1, and it's 3.3:1 in France. Since Japanese physicians also sell the medications that they prescribe, they may have even higher incomes. This practice provides an incentive to over-prescribe medications.

Specialists received even higher incomes. For example doctors operating mental hospitals had an average income of ¥66.6 million per year (about $532,800 U.S). Relatively few staff and low costs explain the very high earnings of the mental hospital operators. Doctors in remote areas also receive high salaries, up to ¥4 million a month, and all from the public coffers. The salaries in rural Hokkaido are particularly high. Dentists, however, are not paid as well, averaging about ¥16.08 million per year, or about $128,640 U.S.

The council conducts the survey every three years before revising the nation's medical insurance system, under which doctors and dentists claim payment for treating patients.

JAPAN'S BILLIONAIRES AND LARGE ESTATES

Japan, despite a relatively flat income distribution, has many rich people. The majority of the very richest accumulated the bulk of their fortunes in the past 20 years. Some built major businesses from original family cottage industries, but many were self-made. Huge increases in economic activity, stock prices, and land values provided the vast increase in their personal fortunes. Leveraging in land at depressed post-WWII prices was a common ingredient of many of the fortunes. Table 4.2 shows the seven largest estates in Japan.

Table 4.2
The Seven Largest Estates in Japan as of October 1989

Deceased	Value of Estate ¥ bils	Former Position of Deceased
Konosuke Matsushita	244.9	Founder of Matsushita Electric Industrial
Shokichi Uehara	66.9	Honorary Chairman of Taisho Pharmaceutical Co.
Monbe Akiyama	59.5	President of a real estate company
Nobuo Machida	44.8	Chairman of Machida Pharmaceutical Co.
Kentaro Hattori	35.8	Chairman of Hattori Seiko Co.
Ichiro Hattori	35.5	President of Seiko Epson Corp.
Noboru Gotoh	28.7	Head of the Tokyu Group

Source: *The Japan Times*

The largest estate by far was that of Konosuke Matsushita who founded Matsushita Electric Industrial Co. in 1918. He died in April 1989 at 94 and left an estate worth ¥244.9 billion. Some ¥85.4 billion in inheritance tax is owed. The previous record was ¥67 billion left by Shokichi Uehara, who died in 1983.

Nearly 97% of the Matsushita estate was in the form of shares in Matsushita group firms. The group, one of Japan's largest with 148 companies, had sales of ¥5.45 trillion in fiscal year 1988. Half the estate, some ¥122.5 billion, was given tax-free to his 93-year-old widow, Mumeno. The rest of the estate, which will be taxed at about ¥85.4 billion (about 70% of its value), went to his daughter and her husband, ¥44.8 and ¥44.6 billion, respectively, and to four children born outside the marriage. The oldest son received ¥9 billion and the other two sons and the daughter, ¥8 billion. All three sons work for Matsushita group companies.

Konosuke Matsushita, called the god of management, developed the company from a 4.5-tatami-room factory producing light-bulb sockets to a multinational enterprise employing 190,000 worldwide. He invented the two-way socket in 1918, getting his real start, and founded the predecessor of Matsushita Electric Industrial Co. that year. The company survived the financial panic of 1927 without laying off any employees. In 1932, he stated: "the mission of industrialists is to create a paradise in this world."

Noboru Gotoh, whose estate was settled in October 1989, left ¥28.7 billion, of which ¥22 billion was in stock in the Tokyu Group, including 5.3

million shares of Tokyu Corp. and 1.2 million shares of Tokyu Land Corp. The rest of his estate was centered in real estate. The estate was levied taxes of ¥11.6 billion on the ¥17.1 billion not inherited by his wife who received a tax-exempt ¥11.6 billion.

According to a *Fortune* magazine story as of September 9, 1991, there were 12 Japanese billionaires, see Table 4.3.

Table 4.3
The Japanese Billionaires as of July 1991

Name	Age	Home	Wealth in $ Bils	Principle Holdings
Taikichiro Mori	87	Tokyo	10.0	Mori Building Co., the third largest building leasing company in Japan plus other real estate
Kenkichi Nakajima	70	Kiryu	5.6	83.3% of Heiwa Co., sales $360 mil, the world's largest maker of pachinko machines
Kichinosuke Sasaki	59	Tokyo	3.4	Togensha, a real estate firm
Rinji Shino	82	Waka-yama	3.0	Bus, shipping and real estate companies, gas stations, restaurants, Japanese pints, European antiques, a forest near Paris, and a winery in Médoc
Genshiro Kawamoto	59	Tokyo	2.2	Marugen Co. which has hundreds of buildings, residential houses and small pubs in Japan, Hawaii and California
Yoshiaki Tsutsmui	57	Tokyo	2.1	40% of Kokudo Keikaku which owns 48.6% of land rich Seibu Railway,Seibu Lions baseball team, Prince Hotels
Tamasaburo Furukawa	101	Nagoya	1.8	Nippon Herald Films which distribues foreign films and owns a chain of movie theaters in Japan, the Herald Group of some 50 entertainment-related companies including golf courses, ski resorts and restaurants
Shoji Uehara and family	63	Tokyo	1.7	36% of Taisho Pharmaceutical Co. which among other things produces Lipovitan, a popular vitamin health drink for 30 years
Hiroshi Yamauchi	63	Kyoto	1.5	15% of Nintendo
Hiroshi Teramachi	67	Tokyo	1.5	31.3% of THK Co. maker of ball-bearing related products. He personally holds 800 patents nd the firm has 70% of its market
Katsumi Tada and family	46	Tokyo	1.1	48% of Daito Trust Construction, one of Japan's largest construction and leasing companies
Takemitsu Takizaki and family	46	Osaka	1.1	29.8% of Keyence a maker of detection devices and meassuring control equipment

Source: Fortune, September 9, 1991.

The stock held was valued at the July 16, 1991 closing price, and estimates were made of the value net of debt of other assets. For some individuals, the holdings of the immediate family (husband, wife and siblings) are included. Brothers' and cousins' wealth are separated. Absent from this list is Seiji Tsutsumi, the half brother of Yoshiaki and head of the Seibu/Saison group. Other reports list him and others such as Yoshiaki at much higher wealth levels. It is extremely difficult to measure the wealth of the richest people. Estimates are most likely to under represent the true wealth, because their widespread holdings are not generally made public. The *Fortune* study does document specific assets so it is in most cases a conservative estimate of total wealth.[2]

AMERICA'S SWEETHEARTS: WHO GETS THE REWARDS?

As ye sow, so shall ye reap. A recent survey of 16 to 65 year olds in Oregon . . . found that only 12% . . . could estimate the cost per ounce of peanut butter at $1.59 a pound. Only 18% could use a bus schedule to determine the right bus to take from origin to destination at a prescribed time. But 97% could locate information in a sports article.

Think about this when next you sit by your TV watching great American athletes sandwiched between clever American-made commercials selling high-quality Japanese cars.

Alan S. Blinder, *Business Week*, July 22, 1991

Who the country's heroes are provides contrasts among cultures. In the U.S., it is sports, movie, and other entertainment stars. In Japan, it is the major business leaders. Entertainers are important and revered, but even they do not consider themselves the nation's heroes. They view themselves as providing entertainment services when people are not working. In Japan, revered craftspersons are declared national treasures (as are the endangered cranes).

---

[2]According *Forbes* in 1989, there were about 41 billionaires in Japan compared with 55 in the U.S. and 20 in Germany. Japan had the most per capita: 1 in 2.9 million compared with 1 in 3.3 million in Germany and 4.5 million in the U.S. But in 1991 after the steep 1990 stock market decline, there were only 12 Japanese billionaires, fewer than 6% of the world's 202 billionaires. Yoshiaki's holdings in Seibu Railway fell 57% with his wealth declining $5.2 billion in the past year to a modest $2.1 billion, a far cry from the approximately $25 billion attributed to him in some press reports in 1989. Several other 1989 billionaires are no longer on the list, including Kanichiro Ishibashi, 71, of Tokyo, who owns 16% of Bridgestone Corporation; Masatoshi Ito, 67, and family, of Tokyo, who owns 12.4% of Ito-Yokado stores including majority ownership of 7-Eleven Japan and Denny's Japan; Isao Nakauchi, 68, of Kobe, who owns 14.9% of Daiei Japan's largest supermarket/discount chain, real estate, drug stores, the Hawks baseball team, and a stadium in Fukuoka; and Taro Iketani, 74, and family, of Tokyo, who owns 34% of Tokyo Steel Mfg., the largest operator of electric furnaces in the world.

Besides solving the productivity problem and reducing consumption, the U.S. has to lower some of the costs associated with the country's non-producers and negative producers. The list of these drains on the economy is long, starting with more than 700,000 lawyers. Many of them serve very useful functions. But Japan can function well with fewer than 10% of this number and there are fewer frivolous law suits. The U.S. also pays a staggering cost for drug and crime-related activities. This huge negative is hardly seen in Japan. Then there is the vast amount of money and time spent on entertainment. According to *Chicago Tribune* columnist Mike Royko, Sylvester Stallone's 1987–88 income of $63 million gives him the pay of 910 Chicago police officers and 1,240 sanitation workers. The average representative enacting U.S. laws (or a Harvard full professor) makes about $89,500 per year, less than one-fourth what a 4-10 pitcher or reserve infielder makes. Even Elvis Presley, who has been dead for 12 years, made some $15 million, the salary of 167 representatives or 75 presidents. As Royko points out, the key to the public pocketbook is entertainment. Besides Michael Jackson, Bill Cosby and Bruce Springsteen, who each earn more than $20 million per year, hundreds of athletes have salaries of more than $1 million. Table 4.4 lists the income of the top 20 stars in 1988–89. The income of the top sports personalities for the first seven months of 1990 appears in Table 4.5 with boxers, golfers and race car drivers dominating.

Table 4.4
Income in 1988 and 1989 of the Top 20 Stars in Millions of Dollars

Michael Jackson	125	Julio Iglesias	46
Steven Spielberg	105	Johnny Carson	45
Bill Cosby	95	Jack Nicholson	44
Mike Tyson	71	Sylvester Stallone	44
Charles M. Schultz	60	Madonna	43
Eddie Murphy	57	Sugar Ray Leonard	42
Pink Floyd	56	Arnold Schwarzenegger	41
The Rolling Stones	55	Bruce Springsteen	40
Oprah Winfrey	55	Bon Jovi	40
George Michael	47	Prince	36

Source: *Forbes*

Table 4.5
Income from Salaries, Winnings and Endorsements of the Top Sports
Personalities in 1990 to August in Millions of Dollars

Mike Tyson	28.6	Jack Nicklaus	8.6
Buster Douglas	26.0	Greg Norman	8.5
Sugar Ray Leonard	13.0	Michael Jordan	8.5
Ayrton Senna	10.0	Arnold Palmer	8.1
Alain Prost	9.0	Evander Holyfield	8.1

Source: *Forbes*

These people earn this much because of their bargaining position in a money-making business. We do not hold that against them. The problem is the country simply cannot afford this. Higher taxes and lower consumption, are needed. Japan too has its super stars who are well paid, but there are fewer of them and they behave differently. Instead of complaining that their $1.5 million salary is less than someone else's $2 million, they show up at the ballpark to practice for six or more hours before a game when the coach requests it with no sign of resentment. It's a question of values and income distribution. The Japanese do not pay lip service to the value of education; they show they really value it by paying teachers well. Teachers earn more than government workers in starting salaries and later. For the respect and salaries they receive teachers must work in poor and country areas in their prefectures for five to seven years before going to big city schools. See Wrey (1988) for information on the relative salaries of teachers in Japan.

TAXES

Japan is a country with fairly high taxes. The total corporate tax is about 50 to 55% on net income, and individual tax rates vary from 15 to 65%. In typical Japanese fashion, a number of compromises are made to make collection of the tax easy and low cost. Individuals with earned income less than ¥15 million per year (the majority) do not need to file tax forms because any adjustments are made automatically at work where the tax has been withheld. Another example of the spirit of compromise inherent in the system is that when there is a dispute with the tax authorities, the investigating agent reviews the case with the claimant and indicates the correct tax and, if payment is made, that's it.

HOW TAX RATES COMPARE

Table 4.5 compares tax rates in Japan, New York and the U.K. From these rates, in effect in 1987, it is clear that the taxes in Japan are much lower until the high-income brackets are reached. Compared with rates in N.Y. as a representative U.S. city, Japanese tax rates are only somewhat higher at $125,000 income and then very much higher. The U.K. is higher throughout the income range. In compensation for the lower personal tax rates, corporate tax rates are high in Japan. Figure 4.3 compares Japan with Germany, France, the U.K. and the U. S.

Table 4.5
Earnings and Income Tax Ratios (1987)

	Marital Status	Japan	U.S. (New York)	UK
¥3,000,000	S	8.0%	15.7%	23.7%
(US$18,868)	2C	1.6	8.1	20.7
¥5,000,000	S	11.5	23.1	26.8
(US$31,447)	2C	6.3	15.0	24.3
¥7,000,000	S	16.9	27.1	32.2
(US$44,025)	2C	11.0	18.2	29.9
¥10,000,000	S	21.7	30.5	38.3
(US$62,893)	2C	16.9	24.1	36.6
¥20,000,000	S	37.5	34.6	49.1
(US$125,786)	2C	34.4	31.0	48.2
¥50,000,000	S	54.1	35.0	55.6
(US$314,465)	2C	58.7	34.9	55.3

Assuming 1 US $ = 159¥, S=single, 2C=married with two children.

Source: Ministry of Finance

Figure 4.4
Corporate Tax Burden in Five Countries

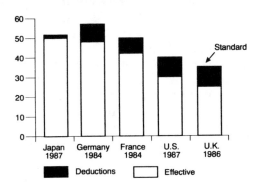

Source: Japan Federation of Economic Organizations

THE TOP TAX PAYERS AND INCOME EARNERS

Some 111,609 people paid income tax of more than ¥10 million in 1988, up 574 from 1987. Seventy-four of these paid more than ¥500 million, compared to 61 in 1987, and 2,207 paid ¥100 million or more up 3.3%. Of the top hundred earners, 70 were real estate owners and 17 others made large profits in stock and other securities transactions.

In terms of current income, the total number of land millionaires in Tokyo in the top 100 earners in Japan fell from 67 to 48, while in the rest of the nation it rose from 7 to 16. Out of the top 100 millionaires, including 6 foreign residents, 70 were made by land sales. The number of stock millionaires increased to 17 from 8. Abdel Habi Debs, a Lebanese, earned the most income in FY1988 after selling land in Tokyo. He earned ¥43 billion (some ¥5 million per square meter) for an 8,600 square meter plot of land in Shibuya, and paid ¥6.354 billion in income tax, the highest paid by an individual. Other big tax payers were Mitsuo Akiyama, owner of a gasoline station who sold a 400 square meter plot in Tokyo for ¥12 billion and paid ¥3.358 billion in tax, and Mitsuhiro Sakaguchi, who sold a 900 square meter plot in Shinjuku and paid ¥9 billion in tax.

Also among the top 100 wage earners: Matsushita, number 38; Shoji Uehara, chairman of Taisho Pharmaceutical, number 42; writer Jiro Akagawa was 52, and Kanichiro Ishibashi, honorary chairman of Bridgestone, was 59. As for other prominent people: 55 (of 512) members of the House of Representatives and 25 (of 252) House of Councillors paid tax of more than ¥10 million, down from 47 from 1987. Eitaro Itoyama, LDP member of lower house, was the top-ranking politician, paying ¥412 million, up from ¥150 million. He owns Shin-Nippon, a tourism group, and is said to have assets of ¥100 billion. Next was Kakuzo Kawamoto, former minister in charge of the National Land Agency, who paid ¥274 million and Tasaburo Kumagai, minister for Science and Technology, was third, paying ¥228 million. The notables in the Recruit scandal, Hiromasa Ezoe, former chairman of Recruit, and former Prime Ministers Noboru Takeshita and Yasuhiro Nakasone, were *not* among the top 100 income earners.

Total tax revenues in 1988 exceeded the ¥50 trillion level. Inheritance taxes, up 31% from 1987, and securities transaction taxes, up 67.8% were the most notable increases. Self-employed workers reported income of ¥40.89 trillion and paid a record tax of ¥4.32 trillion in 1988.

The Showa estate was assessed at ¥2 billion. The Emperor paid ¥460 million in inheritance tax. The Imperial family's private property was restricted to ¥15 million in cash, jewelry and art after the war. The property increased by stock purchases. They receive a ¥200 million annual budget. The Imperial Household Agency is controlling the property to keep its value below ¥2 billion. Most art and craft works given to the late Emperor will be donated to the state.

UNREPORTED INCOME

Unreported corporate income reached a high of ¥1.41 trillion in the year ended June 1988, up 15.4% from the previous year. The Tax Agency investigated 200,000 companies and found that 84% had not reported income. The total was 15.4 times higher than in 1987. Punitive taxes levied on the tax dodgers was ¥570 billion, the highest figure ever. Taxes from both reported and unreported income totaled ¥333.5 billion, up 65% from 1987. About 57,000 companies evaded tax by accounting methods reducing income ¥433.6 billion. The highest rate of evasion was among bars, night clubs and love hotels. Of 2,206 large companies investigated, all but one had failed to report some income, for a total of ¥328.1 billion. Especially common were tax frauds by companies with overseas subsidiaries. Companies were ordered to pay ¥145.6 billion in back taxes.

Mitsui Trust and Banking was penalized ¥270 million for hiding ¥500 million in income it received as an intermediary commission from Oriental Land for a hotel site near Tokyo Disneyland. Oriental Land, which manages Disneyland, sold 8 hectares of land in June 1986 to Dai-Ichi Mutual Life Insurance Co. for ¥21.8 billion.

TAX REFORM

The tax reform debate involves tax equity as well as the role of direct (income) and indirect taxes. Lincoln (1988) refers to *ku-ro-yon* (9-6-4), the distribution of tax burden where wage earners pay tax on 90% of their income, small businesses pay tax on 60% and farmers on 40% and the *to-go-san-pin* (10-5-3-1) where wage earners report 100% of income, small businesses 50%, farmers 30% and politicians 10%. Japan's ratio of indirect taxes is low (7.7%) versus an OECD average of 13.6% (the U.S. is at 8.5% and Spain at 7.1%). In the 1960s, direct taxes represented 50% of taxes collected and had reached 70% before the tax reform. In an attempt to improve equity and to bring the Japanese system in line with tax systems in other countries (a cross between Europe and the U.S.) a number of reforms were implemented in April 1988.

TREATMENT OF SAVINGS AND INVESTMENT INCOME

Under the *Maruyu* system, interest income from savings principal of up to ¥9 million per person with ¥5.5 million per household were tax-exempt. These provisions are subject to widespread abuse. People establish a number of tax-free accounts in different names, or transfer funds to the accounts of family members without paying the gift tax. In addition, certain government bonds are taxed at preferential rates, and capital gains on securities are not taxed under certain conditions. As a result of legal exemptions and illegal evasion, it is estimated that the earnings from 58% to 70% of Japanese personal financial savings were not taxed (for more discussion, see Sato, 1988).

This *Maruyu* system; ended in April 1, 1988, and interest on deposits is now taxed separately from other income at a flat rate of 20% (15% income tax and 5% inhabitant tax). Dividends of less than ¥50,000 from each domestic company are not taxed. Bonuses count as income for tax purposes. Retirement income is treated differently. The taxable retirement income is 50% net of certain deductions depending on years of employment, and is subject to 20% withholding at the source. Kuboi (1989) has a thorough treatment of taxes including capital gains taxes.

For tax purposes there is imputed a return from company subsidized housing (Kuboi, p. 115) either based upon value or space. Also, after December 31, 1990, housing loans will be taxed. One thing that continues to be exempt is golf club and social club memberships held for business purposes.

There is also a new tax on securities transactions. The old tax on capital gains was very low and zero for most investors. Only 200 investors paid tax in 1987. Now investors have a choice: 1% on gross proceeds of sales transactions or 20% tax on capital gains at the time of filing income tax. For unlisted shares, those who sell within a year must pay capital gains tax. For shares held for three years, the capital gains rate falls to 10%. This tax is expected to raise ¥14 billion. The tax does not apply to corporate, institutional or foreign traders, who pay tax on their yearly income. There is also a securities transactions tax which was lowered from 0.55% to 0.3% of the transaction value. This raised ¥1.8 trillion in the fiscal year ending in March 1987.

The new capital gains rules have brought more money up from the underground into Japan's stock markets. Most of the money is from property transactions, not drugs. Though there is tax avoidance, there is a basic honesty in the Japanese that is something Americans might admire: a bag of money worth ¥6 million was found in a remote bamboo forest in a brown paper bag. It attracted interest and a second bag with another ¥8 million was found. The finders turned in the money. It created much interest and many lookers until finally someone claimed it. It had been hidden in the forest until it could be laundered. Now the new tax law on stock transactions provides a way. Ninety percent have chosen the 1% turnover tax because the other option requires revealing all income sources. Some estimate that ¥100 trillion is underground or 20% of the market capitalization or more than 25% of Japan's GNP. Now the market is a washing machine laundering money!

THE CONSUMPTION TAX

The consumption tax, imposed on April 1, 1989, was designed to improve equity in the tax system. It was approved with little debate. It was a compromise tax representing the inability of the Liberal Democratic Party (LDP) government to get constituency agreement on a real value-added tax (VAT).

The consumption tax is not a true VAT. Rather than taxing all transactions equally, it taxes businesses at different rates depending on income. Also invoices are not required, but an accounting method is used.

Business are divided into three categories each with its own tax rate:
≤¥30 million—no tax;
≤¥500 million—assume 20% of total sales is value added without records;
>¥ 500 million—3% of value added.

These departures for a strict value-added tax are compromises under political pressure.

By choosing this route based on sales rather than the invoice method, the consumption tax is riddled with loopholes. Firms with low sales volume can collect the tax on standard goods and maintain the same price plus tax as larger volume stores. As these low volume firms do not need to pay the tax, they are really collecting an extra profit.

The distribution and manufacturing systems will be affected by the design of the tax. Taxing transactions rather than value added may encourage a more efficient distribution system and reduce the number of stages from production to final consumer. As an extra benefit it might improve the access of foreign goods to the Japanese market. It will also affect the production process, likely reducing the number of tiers of suppliers, though this has not been analyzed and it is not clear if this impact is desirable.

The consumption tax replaces a variety of special sales taxes on luxury items and lowers them, including taxes on luxury cars, fine liquor, and upscale items such as golf equipment, watches, furniture, luggage, and appliances. The consumption tax package was a boon to luxury car sales because the tax on these fell. In some cases, there is a multiplier effect, as the 3% tax is added more than once. For example, costs at hotels have two 3% taxes or 6%.

Before the implementation day, everyone stocked up on non-perishables. On the first day of the tax, the stores were like ghost towns. The shops selling prepaid cards were very busy before April 1. Advance purchases were made for *shinkansen* (bullet train) and commuter train and bus tickets. Many bought department store discount coupons with the aim of shopping before the tax, for example, a salaried worker bought coupons worth ¥300,000 for ¥279,000 saving two ways, the discount and the tax. However, some prices on the *shinkansen* and domestic flights actually fell as the consumption tax was lower than the taxes replaced.

The consumption is very unpopular especially with housewives. Most people did not feel any effects of the income tax reduction that was implemented with the consumption tax but were very visibly affected by the tax. Sixty percent of LDP supporters opposed the tax before its implementation and 66% did after it took effect. The tax affects women the most because they control the household spending and do the buying. It is significant that a higher proportion of women vote than men.

The University of Tokyo estimated the new tax would increase the annual costs for students from ¥8,000 to ¥20,000. Students will not have any offsetting effects from the lowered income tax.

On net, there will be a fall in tax revenues of about ¥2.4 trillion (with cuts of ¥3.1 trillion in income tax, ¥1.8 trillion cut in corporate tax, and ¥800 million cut in the inheritance tax). The consumption tax increased overall prices 1.2%. This in turn led to the first of the interest rate hikes that eventually led to the steep stock market and speculative land declines in 1990 and 1991 (see Ziemba and Schwartz, 1991b, for an analysis and also the first section of Chapter 5).

The unpopularity of the consumption tax contributed to political instability in Japan.[3] The LDP promised tax revision during the election of February 1990. One issue is imposition of the tax on food. A compromise supported by the LDP leadership is a reduction to 1.5% on food at the production and wholesale levels and elimination at the retail level.[4] Other items would also be exempt, including childbirth costs, tuition fees, rents, and equipment and services for the disabled. The total cut in taxes would amount to about ¥1.28 trillion, or about ¥1,000 per household per month (the average household with annual income of ¥6 million pays ¥56,000 annually in consumption tax).

THE JAPANESE NONWORK EXPENSES
WHAT THE JAPANESE LIKE TO BUY

Quality! The Japanese have little room in their houses so they focus on quality items. To incorporate a new item, they must discard an old one. Thus, name craftspeople command very high prices. Beautiful earthy but simple tea bowls cost hundreds of dollars. In Vancouver, similar bowls could be produced by dozens of craftspeople and the price would tumble to about $15 to $30.

Companies held in high esteem by Japanese consumers include Mercedes Benz, Sony, Louis Vuitton, Porsche, Rolex, Hattori Seiko, the Imperial Hotel, IBM, Chanel, Toyota, BMW, 3M, Gucci, Cartier and Christian Dior. A survey also rated brands according to the share in

---

[3] All countries that have attempted to balance budgets have met with unpopularity. The government in New Zealand was defeated when a consumption tax was imposed and the government in Canada is also facing unpopularity over a tax similar to a consumption tax.

[4] This is a strange compromise, recognizing the need to tax farmers as well as their more limited ability to pass the tax on if it is not collected at the retail level.

consumer minds in which only three foreign companies appeared: Coca-Cola, Kentucky Fried Chicken and McDonald's.

Family entertainment, such as the circus and ice skating shows, sells well in Japan as in the U.S.

Japanese unmarried office women, paid a modest ¥200,000 per month, live at home, save little, buy ¥600 *obento* (lunches) and spend ¥140,000 per month on leisure, pleasure and designer clothes. They like silk, helping send the price of silk up from ¥8,600 to ¥15,000 per kilogram. The Japan Raw Silk and Sugar Stabilisation Agency has sold silk from its warehouses to attempt to stem the rise. There is some concern about the role of speculators in the market, including Matsumura the boss of the silk exchange and assemblyman of Yokohama who resigned in the face of charges of accepting stock from Recruit Cosmos.

During the 1992 recession as well as in an attempt to be more individualistic, the Japanese are turning to no-brand name goods. Even so they are requiring top quality. The Seibu calls their non-branded goods *Mujirushi ryohin* or no brand/good quality. Seibu/Saison began the trend with foods and now has a separate company Ryohin Keikaku with 201 outlets in Japan and an expanded line of goods. Quality secondhand stores are becoming popular in this country where people used to just throw out last year's model.

GIFT GIVING

Gift giving grew out of offerings of food to the gods which were imbued with spiritual power. The gift giving ritual cements relationships and harks back to the older, less market-oriented economy, the economy of place and belonging and kinship where jobs were passed on from father to son (or son-in-law or adopted son if necessary). Modern gift giving also serves this purpose of social bonding. There are at least two formal gift giving seasons: *ochugen*, the August season when people return to their home towns and *oseibo*, the gift giving during the New Year's season.

More than 90% of Japanese families give *oseibo*. It is slightly more popular than *ochugen*. In 1987, ¥750 billion was spent on *oseibo* (total seasonal gift giving was ¥2,100 billion). The average cost is ¥4,000 to ¥5,000 and the average family sends 5 to 10 *oseibo* gifts per year. These gifts are meant to be conservative and practical because they are thanks for favors or other considerations. Gifts such as food are acceptable. Recipients are often bosses, relatives, and teachers. Companies give *oseibo* to other companies in thanks for good business relations.

Department stores set up special areas and display specially gift-boxed goods including food (traditional and imported gourmet foods). The department store takes orders, wraps, writes cards and delivers the gifts. Concern with brand and store related status has grown over the past ten years. Now that liquor prices on imports have declined, they are no longer considered a good gift, so the number of import brands stocked by some stores has been cut, though total sales are up.

On Valentine's Day, men receive sweets from women. Female clerks spend about ¥6,000 each sending chocolates to about ten men; eight are out of obligation. Men expect to receive two or three gifts. While the average gift is about ¥575, chocolate for someone special costs about ¥1,500. Special packages in top Ginza stores run over ¥6,000. For someone special but married, *Adultry Choco* is the discreet solution. These chocolates have spirit and liqueur centers, but are packaged to look like innocent, run-of-the-mill *Giri Choco*, and can be eaten in front of wives without causing suspicion. Total Valentine's Day gifts of heart-shaped chocolates were estimated to be $380 million in 1991. The Japanese chocolate makers have established a new gift giving day in March when the men can reciprocate.

Wedding gifts now average between $240 and $400 per couple. The custom is for the newlyweds to reciprocate with gifts to those who attend the wedding valued between about $16 and $40. Also at funerals, money is given as a gift (this helps pay the cost of the funeral). In return attendees receive a gift again ranging from $16 to $40 or about half the amount of the money gift given.

We were also the recipients of many gifts. Each time we went on a factory tour, not only were we treated well and made to feel welcome, but we always received something as a memento of the visit. Examples include a sake cup and sample at a sake factory, a key ring at a car factory, a deck of cards commemorating a ship at a ship building factory. Always tea or a juice was offered as well.

Members of the Diet (the Japanese parliament) need at least half a million dollars per year to pay for gift giving obligations to constituents. This has led to trouble and is part of the reason for the Recruit scandal discussed in Chapter 9. In 1989, Japanese corporations donated a record ¥355.6 billion, mostly to political organizations, a 16.2% increase over 1986.

Charitable giving is different in Japan than in the U.S. There is little personal tax incentive for charitable donations, and companies use their charitable allowance for political donations. One channel of charitable donations is the *Keidanren* (business association) which provided ¥4.9 billion domestically and ¥2.4 billion internationally. Funds were used for such things as grants for Japan studies programs at universities in the U.S.

and construction of retirement homes for Japanese-Americans in Los Angeles.

The Japan Shipbuilding Industry Foundation spends more than ¥40 billion a year on public welfare grants and activities financed through revenue from motorboat racing conducted by local governments. It is said to have a budget larger than the Ford or Rockefeller foundations.

The Japanese contribute to the World Health Organization and are becoming more involved in original projects to promote world peace through alleviating disease, poverty and inequality. They have a green revolution project in Ghana called Sasakawa Global 2000. In 1988, 20,000 families participated. They are currently promoting the Ryoichi Sasakawa Young Leaders Fellowship to give $1 million each to 50 selected post-graduate programs throughout the world and the Sasakawa Peace Foundation to establish a network of foundations which will help internationalize Japan.

The Toyota foundation funds translations of Japanese documents into Asian languages, and vice versa. Japanese corporation in the U.S. have established foundations including Hitachi, Honda, and Matsushita, all with assets of more than $10 million. Japanese companies and their employees also donate more than $3 million to the United Way.

LEISURE

Work attitudes are slackening and the time for the shorter work week is at hand. Firms are being encouraged to move toward five-day work weeks and more vacation time. Unlike in the past, 58% of workers now admit they felt like staying home an extra 2.5 days per month; about a third of these actually did not go to work, while two thirds went in late. The most common day taken off was Monday. While 42% of workers in their 50s list work as the thing that makes life worth living; for those in their 20s, this declined to 21%. Children headed the list at 41%—followed by hobbies, spouse, and trips.

The average Japanese works 2,150 hours a year, 200 more than U.S. and British workers, 500 more than West Germans and French but fewer than South Koreans (2,848) and Taiwanese (2,508). Generally there are 15 paid holidays, but the average worker uses only half of them. To increase leisure, some suggest that workers should be required to take the paid vacations and sick leave available to them.

Japanese paid holidays averaged 11.9 days in 1989, but the average worker used only half of them. The government is attempting to reduce annual work hours to 1,800 by 1993 but half the companies surveyed are reluctant to do so. Only 38.2% of those surveyed had five-day work-weeks. Only 41% said they planned to shorten working hours.

MITI has a leisure promoting program. Since 1987, it has been rating companies on their work hours and holidays. MITI proposed a new national holiday *conjugal day* on November 22 (the numbers 11 and 22 can be read as good couple) to promote a husband and wife spending leisure time together. Some firms are expanding their summer vacations, and others are giving managers extended holidays to refresh themselves. For example, one firm gives workers over 40 a three-month holiday which most use for overseas travel.

The Labor Ministry predicted that a five-day work-week with 20 paid holidays would increase domestic demand by ¥8.32 trillion and create 790,000 new jobs. Much of the resort development is to be designed to help areas of declining industry, and tax subsidies and low interest loans are available.

Japan's firms are also helping to build the infrastructure. Mitsui Engineering hopes to turn some of its old yard on the coast of Okayama prefecture, 450 miles west of Tokyo, into recreational facilities, including a golf course and amusement park. Sumitomo Heavy Industries is planning to turn a 30-acre site of an old plant into a 600 boat marina with a hotel and condominium complex. There are already more than 70 resorts on the drawing boards, many of which are joint projects between local governments and developers, such as the Seibu and Tokyu groups. Kajima and Tokyu have joined Naganohara City in Gunma prefecture to develop golf courses, a ski area, and a shopping center (cost ¥30 billion). The Kajima Aquadome will have a capacity of 30,000 and will include a 50-meter pool, a 100-meter surfing pool with automated waves, and a children's pool.

Reflecting the trend toward increased leisure time, more Japanese are buying recreational vehicles. Most popular are the four-wheel drive roofed jeeps with Mitsubishi Motor's Pajaro holding the top share.

And what will the salaryman do with more leisure time? One idea is *My Desk*, a fashionable, new use for rabbit hutches. It began with a 21-unit apartment building in Kyoto originally designed for students, but the owner had second thoughts about renting to noisy students and instead is renting to adults who are looking for a quiet place away from home to work. The rent is ¥39,000 to ¥43,000 per month for the studio units. These will provide a place for small business and also a retreat for the salaryman away from his crowded home on his days off as well as an excuse for leaving work early (on time). He can just say "I'm going to *My Desk*."[5]

---

[5]Stephanie Cook, *Japan Times*.

HOLIDAYS

Golden Week in early May, one of the major vacation times in Japan, is traditionally the start of the new year including the break between graduation and new jobs and the start of the school year. It is a time of fine weather in a country with a rather difficult climate. The number of days off during this period has been increasing. The average number of holidays was set at 6.8 days, an increase from 6.4 in 1988. One in every three firms will offer seven or more days off. Some 10.9% will offer nine consecutive days off; 26.7% seven or more and 30.8% five. The average length of consecutive days off is 5.7 (while 56.1% of manufacturing and 9.7% of service firms will have seven or more which is almost double 1989). Golden Week begins on April 26 with newly created Greenery Day and ends May 10. Though it sounds like a long holiday stretch, the days off are broken up with days of work. For example, the schools had Saturday, April 26, off and then returned to school Monday and Tuesday. These days were often used for class excursions. Though there was no school Wednesday through Friday, students reported back to school for the normal Saturday morning. This makes it hard for families to take vacations. In our case we forgot that there was Saturday school, so we planned an overnight to Tokyo and had to send our regrets to the teacher.

Travel in Golden Week sets records each year. In 1989, 17.7 million traveled for at least one day to rural resorts, and 365,000 left the country. Hawaii, Hong Kong and Europe are the most popular destinations, and each tourist spends on average ¥274,000 per the 5.9-day trip. Airlines requested 524 additional flights for the week, but only 65% of them were approved because Narita has only one runway and cannot process a large number of flights. An estimated 5.41 million rode the rails, up 5% from last year. The *shinkansen* operated at 200% capacity, which means that it is carrying too many people.

Nearly 60 million took advantage of good weather and visited 1,000 tourist sites in Japan, an increase of 12 million over 1988. Hakata Dontaku Festival in Fukuoka was first with 3 million people (double 1988). The Hiroshima Flower Festival had 1.55 million; Ueno Park and Zoo had 1.2 million and Hamamatsu Godenyadai Hikimawashi Festival in Shizuoka Prefecture had more than one million. The Yokohama Exotic Showcase had 970,000 and the Asia Pacific Exhibition in Fukuoka Prefecture had 650,000. As the cherry blossoms had bloomed too early in Aomori Prefecture the Hirosaki Sakura Festival had only 680,000 or half the crowd of the previous year when it was number two.

FOREIGN TRAVEL

World travel is helping cut the Japanese payments surplus. Japanese trips abroad have been increasing at 20% per year. Trade in services includes transport, tourism and patent royalties, interest, profits and dividends. The service deficit peaked in 1981 at $15 billion, after which investment income increased, bringing it down to $6 billion by 1986. Meanwhile, the tourism deficit has been increasing from $5.6 billion in 1986 to $15.7 billion in 1988, reaching $9 billion in the first half of 1989. Thus the balance of payments surplus has fallen from a peak of $87 billion in 1987 to about $70 billion forecast for 1990.[6]

A record 8.43 million Japanese traveled overseas in 1988, an increase of 23% over 1987. Of these, 83.4% were tourists. Japan had a $15.8 billion deficit in travel payments, up $7.1 billion over 1987. This is equal to 16.7% of the trade surplus. For comparison, West Germany has a $15.7 billion deficit, or 22.5% of its trade surplus.

Hawaii was Japan's first travel destination, with 1.37 million visits, followed by Hong Kong with 1.24 million, Korea with 1.11 million and Taiwan with 920,000. Meanwhile, the number of foreigners visiting Japan reached a record 2.36 million, up 9% with only 47% tourists. Americans topped the list with 520,000 but this was a decrease over previous years. Next came visitors from Taiwan, 410,000 up 7%, Korea, 340,000 up 58%, Britain 150,000 up 4% and China, 110,000 up 56%.

In total, about 3.2 million Japanese (one of each 11 foreign visitors) came to the U.S. in 1988, spending about $3.5 billion plus $2.2 billion more to U.S. carriers. The future will bring more Japanese. Among other encouragements is the waiver of visas for visits of fewer than three months.

One in 30 foreign visitors to Britain is Japanese. Fully 40% of the Japanese tourists were women between ages 16 and 35. Women office workers go to Europe to buy clothes and other goods that cost more at home. But in London department stores, nobody speaks Japanese. Mitsukoshi on Regent Street is part of a trend of Japanese buying stores and using Japanese saleswomen to sell British goods at big markups.

The Japanese are beginning to complain about the shortage of space on international flights. It is increasingly difficult to book seats on short notice in and out of Tokyo, especially to San Francisco, Los Angeles, Vancouver, London, New York, Hawaii, Australia and Hong Kong. Also, check-in procedures take a long time. It is ironic that solving some problems, such as

---

[6]The balance of payments provides a more accurate picture than the trade balance.

the high current account surplus and high air fares, exacerbates this shortage of space. The Japanese airlines are responding to the substantial growth in Japanese traveling abroad, which was to reach 10 million in 1989. The total number of seats leaving Japan is about 17 million per year. Japan's three main airlines will spend ¥2 trillion for 140 new planes but deliveries will not be completed until 1995. There will be a new Kansai airport on a constructed island near Osaka in 1993. At Narita, landings and take-offs are restricted to 340 a day between 7 a.m. and 11 p.m. Locals refuse permission for a second runway and landings during the night. Forty airlines have requested more space. To cope with the problem, airlines are starting joint services, for example, JAL with foreign airlines such as Canadian International.

The tours are very profitable. As an example, Japanese tour guides make ¥50,000 per head on a ¥400,000 seven-day European tour.

The flow of investment and tourists is affecting the U.S. service industry. For example, at the Sheraton Hotel in Washington, D.C., half the breakfast clients are Japanese tourists and most enjoy reading a Japanese newspaper. Some hotels provide the option of a Japanese breakfast and newspaper. *Asahi Shimbun, Nihon Keizai (Nikkei),* and *Yomiuri* began printing daily papers in the U.S. via satellite transmission. *Nikkei* charges $90 per month and is making a profit meeting the business demand. *Yomiuri* delivers to households for $48 per month, and *Asahi* tries for both markets at $78 per month and hopes to be profitable in three years. The per copy cost is about $3.

The average Japanese tourist to Hawaii stays a little more than half as long as the average U.S. mainlander but spends about four times as much per day or $400. Japanese, especially honeymooners, take home presents. Americans might buy inexpensive T-shirts and macadamia nuts, while the Japanese buy Chanel dresses and Louis Vuitton luggage.

The Japanese companies are taking advantage of this new demand. Japanese tours are moving up scale. Replacing the whirlwind three-night tours are luxury packages to France with tours of the vineyards and Loire Valley chateaux by jet helicopter ($26,937 U.S. per couple). The three major shipping lines are investing in luxury passenger liners. Mitsui was the first with the Fuki Maru with a capacity of 600 in 163 cabins, which sold out at fares of up to $4,386 for a seven-day trip around Japan and $9,202 for a 26-day trip from Japan to Hong Kong, Singapore and Bangkok. The Showa Line and Nippon Travel Agency are also entering this market.

The Tokyu group has a travel agency and affiliated airline as well as hotels. JAL plans to build a tourist resort near Pearl Harbor, Hawaii, 20 minutes from the airport. The 750,000 square meter resort is part of a 4 million square meter development. The Japanese might succeed where others (UAL, Hertz) have failed. This is another case of the Japanese understanding how to use information to create product and income. Table 4.7 lists some of the major purchases.

Table 4.7
Hotel Groups

Seibu Saison	Inter-Continental Hotels from Britain's Grand Metropolitan	$2.3 billion for 100 unit chain in 45 countries, paying 41 times earnings (it was bought for $500 million in 1981), Saison has travel agency and credit card
Aoki Corp with Robert M. Bass Group	Westin Hotel	$1.4 billion
All Nippon Airways	Meridien Hotel, San Francisco	$100 million
JAL	Manages 23 Nikko International Hotels	Uses reservations network, developing resorts

GETTING MARRIED

Wedding ceremonies cost about ¥1 to ¥2 million on average. Even with that, parties usually have a two- to three-hour limit on the use of the hall. Late autumn is the most popular time for weddings and 90% of honeymooners go abroad. In the fall, more than 70% of those flying out of Narita are newlyweds. It creates a headache for plane seating arrangements. Often *janken*, the scissors-stone-paper game, is played to determine the lucky couples who can sit together. The typical honeymooners spend ¥760,000 on an eight-day holiday. Australia is the most popular honeymoon destination. One flight to Sydney was 90% filled with newlyweds. Hawaii has fallen to third spot behind the mainland U.S. Australia is now the most popular tourist spot for Japanese. About 32% of married couples met through paid or amateur matchmakers, 33.5% met on the job, and 20.8% met through introduction by family and friends. Figure 4.5 shows how the cost of getting married has increased over time.

Ueno no Mori no Rodan no Kai (Named for Rodin's "The Kiss') specializes in helping the elite find a mate. The fee is ¥10 million. When a professional matchmaker is used, the average cost is ¥3.8 million for the wedding and honeymoon plus ¥824,000 for engagement expenses. One telling comparison made by a doctor was that a foreign car cost ¥20-30 million, so finding a good bride at half that is not expensive. The fee includes guidance through the first meeting, a helicopter trip to Karuizawa,

Figure 4.5
The Average Cost of Getting Married

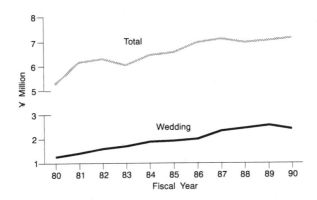

Source: Japan Economic Journal and Sanwa Bank

Nagano prefecture, to play golf or tennis or tour for four days and then a first-class trip to New York City for the marriage proposal (accompanied by a female escort), wedding at the consulate, honeymoon in the Caribbean, and reception back in Tokyo. There have been no divorces, and the success rate is 93% in the first year. Participants must be marrying for the first time. Men must be college graduates and women must have a junior college degree. Most are funded by parents but Rodan no Kai has a loan program. There are also cheaper programs at ¥350,000 to meet potential partners at monthly parties and another program at ¥2 million. The firm has enrolled 165,000 in the three programs.

EDUCATION

The cost of preparing a child for school is rising and is now about ¥160,000 on average. This includes the cost for school supplies, book bags, uniforms, stationery, and a desk and chair for home. Many school supplies are given as gifts from relatives and friends when a child enters primary school.

Tokyo high schools discriminate against girls. taking 10% fewer girls than boys. There are more private schools for girls, but these cost ¥658,800 versus ¥82,800 for the metropolitan schools on average.

There are cram schools (*juku*) for night owls with classes from 10 p.m. to 1:20 a.m. Fees and tuition are ¥200,000 to 250,000 or half that of daytime courses. Some students attend both day and night sessions. American entrepreneurs have set up a cram school, the Princeton Review, to help Japanese pass the standardized Test of English as a Foreign Language (TOEFL) so that they can study in the U.S., as well as the SAT, GRE, LSAT and GMAT. The 39-hour course costs ¥300,000. The Princeton Review gives a money-back guarantee that the scores will improve after the course.

The Ministry of Education has allocated ¥12.3 billion for computers in schools since 1985. Now there is one personal computer for every 2.6 elementary schools, 1.25 for each junior high school, and 18.4 for each high school. Some schools have been designated model schools for computer-aided instruction, for example, Tanaka Kita in Kashiwa has 47 personal computers, and each class has had two lessons per week since 1987. All 18 teachers at Tanaka Kita can program. In fact, they have developed 73 programs of their own because they found the standard software was too easy for the students. They have also bought 60 programs from the Center for Research of Learning Software and suggest that 500 programs are necessary to cover the major fields. They are also marketing their programs. The MOE, MITI and CEC (Center for Educational Computing) are attempting to define a standard.

CHAPTER 5

TRANSITIONS: THE SKYROCKETING PRICE OF LAND AND THE HIGH COST OF LIVING

In this chapter we investigate the high cost of land and housing and look at the high cost of living in Japan.

ASTRONOMICAL LAND PRICES

Land in Japan is the most expensive in the world. Indeed in late 1991, the total land value in Japan was estimated at nearly $20 trillion. This is more than 20% of the world's wealth. Japanese land was then valued at about five times that of the U.S. which is 25 times as large so this works out to about 125 times as much per acre. In downtown Tokyo land in 1989–91 was trading for about $800 million per acre and the Emperor's Palace which is some three-quarters of a square mile, was estimated to be worth about the same as all the land in California or in Canada.

Land is expensive in Japan for a number of reasons. Obviously the actual price reflects the supply-demand relationship. There is much money and many people chasing very few choice properties. Some fundamentals of land use shown in Table 5.1 indicate that population density is 30 times as high and GNP production per acre is 21 times as high as in the U.S. While energy consumption is 12 times as high per acre the high density of production per acre results in almost half the energy consumption per unit GNP as in the U.S.

Other reasons for the extraordinarily high land prices in Japan are:

1. The tax structure which creates low costs for holding land and very high costs of selling land. Agricultural land is especially lightly taxed for holding and heavily taxed for sales.

2. The regulatory framework limits land supply. In particular land sales are discouraged and existing land is underutilized because of regulations on zoning, height restrictions (reflecting earthquake standards), etc. Frequently it is more economical to leave a lot vacant then to build on it.

Table 5.1
Comparison of Fundamentals, Japan and the U.S., 1989

	Japan	U.S.	Japan as % of U.S.
Population, millions	120.00	239.00	50.21
Total area (1,000 sq km)	377.00	9,373.00	4.02
Habitable area (1,000 sq km)	80.00	4,786.00	1.67
Population per habitable area (pop/sq km)	1,500.00	50.00	3,000.00
GNP per habitable area (million $/sq km)	16.90	0.80	2,112.50
Energy consumption (tons oil equivalent/sq km)	4,650.00	390.00	1,92.38

Source: Daiwa Securities America, Inc.

3. The system is organized to protect past land gains by the farmers, large corporations and wealthy individuals. There is no incentive for the LDP government to change this.

4. Until the high interest rate period of 1989–91, no attempt was made to dampen speculative demand. Banks until early 1990 were willing to lend 80 to 95% and even more with land as security.

Despite these astronomical land prices Boone (1989) has shown that such prices can be justified by rational economic models. In particular if the GNP growth of Japan exceeds that of the U.S. by 2% or more per year for an indefinite horizon, then land prices in Japan should be about 100 times as large.

THE ROLE OF THE FARMERS

A major reason for the high land prices is the role of the farmers in Japan. Japanese farmers are regarded almost as national treasures, like pottery masters. Especially valued are rice farmers.[1] Without the rice farmer, the

---

[1] The farm program that maintains the price of farm products has some hidden motives—in addition to the obvious one of maintenance of income and food security there is also the concern for keeping some people on the farm. So many people have been attracted to the cities, it is difficult for farmers, most of whom are men, to find wives. The municipal government of Kurohane, Tochigi prefecture, is investing in matchmaking between its young men and South American women of Japanese descent. The town will spend ¥1.7 million of a ¥100 million subsidy for local community revitalization from the national government. It will invite women from South America and set up matchmaking parties and will provide Japanese language lessons and lectures on Japanese culture for foreign brides. Kurohane has 343 bachelors between 30 and 40, while there are only 200 women between 26 and 40 and most of

Japanese would have to eat primarily imported food because over 95% of the wheat and 99% of the corn is imported. More than 75% of Japanese oppose rice import liberalization though they are willing to have general food imports. Japanese simply will not tolerate dependence on imports of rice, their national staple. Though many think this solely a matter of pride, others (the authors included) see it as a particular recognition by the Japanese of their extreme vulnerability living on a rocky, earthquake prone, typhoon ravaged island. Recalling the soybean embargo under President Nixon in the early 70s, the Japanese do not want to risk any embargo of rice. The line has been drawn at rice.

Rice growing is important to the culture of Japan. Rice agriculture along with metal working came from China and Korea 2,300 years ago. Rice growing fostered cooperation and the development of social institutions.[2] The first public festivals were devoted to rice planting and harvesting. The important Obon Festival mirrors the cycle of rice. Even the rituals around the emperor have always been involved closely with the rice culture.

The role of rice is pervasive; even the word for rice means meal. The rice paddies in and near cities keep everyone aware of nature and the source of their food. The Japanese are made aware of the cyclical nature of the world of agriculture for Golden Week, when the salarymen and their families take vacations, is the time of rice planting and they observe the rice farmers in the fields.

Rice provides up to 28% of calories and accounts for 33% of all farm output in Japan. Under the General Agreement on Tariffs and Trade (GATT), many countries claim exemptions for food programs, and Japan claimed an exemption for rice. Meanwhile, rice plantings are down 28% in two years and the price has fallen 10% reflecting dietary shift toward other grains and meat.

Few imports are allowed, even though the price of Japanese rice is many, many times the cost of what imports would be. Japan consumes about 10.3 million tons of rice a year. It imports only about 20,000 tons, part of which goes to Okinawa where brewers prefer long-grained Southeast Asian rice. Imports are also rising in high value-added prepared rice products, especially from U.S. processors.[3]

---

these wish to marry outside the community.

In response to pressure from the Structural Initiatives talks with the U.S. as well as a reflection of the relative decline in farm population and the growing economic demands of urban Japanese, this is likely to change.

[2]See Visser (1986) for a complete discussion.

[3]The 1992 rice harvest is poor. Rice reserves are expected to decline by October 1992 to 300,000 to 400,000 tons from 1.08 million tons in October 1991. This might facilitate an increase in rice imports.

Since most farms are small, averaging about 2.5 acres, they are inefficient operations. Even at the high prices they receive for rice, farmers barely make enough from farming to support their families. This is not to say that farmers are poor. They are not. Their land is very valuable and they have many other assets. They prefer not to sell their land because they perceive that it would be highly taxed and they would lose out on future land price increases.

The land is classified as farmland and cannot be used for other purposes without losing its tax-exempt status. Farm land is exempt from even the inheritance tax. The economics of land price determination suggests that high rice prices (supported by the government) result in high land values. In fact, these taxes are not really that high and are comparable to tax rates on capital gains in other countries, such as the U.S.

Many farmers have other jobs to provide their major income. Then, when they retire, they farm full-time. Though the returns from the high priced farm land could provide interest and other income to live on in retirement, they prefer to hold onto their land. The government has had to press farmers with very liberal tax breaks before they will consent to selling. A reduction along these lines is the upper limit of tax-exempted income for a farmer giving up farmland for projects that rationalize land ownership and realize large-scale cultivation of the crops. For 1989, the limit rose from ¥5 to ¥8 million. The young are gradually moving away to the cities, but the option is still intact. Much of the farm labor now is migrant workers from the Philippines and other places.

The farm subsidy in Japan is truly incredible. In 1987, the subsidy to farmers, in terms of high prices for their goods, amounted to some $40 billion. In addition, some $20 billion more was put in the pot by the consumers through artificially high prices. Without this double-barreled protection, even without imports, prices would tumble to about one-third of their present levels.

Why does this policy continue to support the 6% of the population who are farmers? Shouldn't the Diet change its policy? The answer is that fully 25% of the Diet members are farmers and they have great influence on the Liberal Democratic Party which rules Japan. Moreover, the farmers' union contributes the equivalent of $100 million to its supporters in the Diet. Steps to remove these subsidies or to change the rules would probably result in the government falling from power. Since farmers pay only an average ¥22,000, or $160, per year according to *The Economist* versus ¥1.6 million in taxes or $11,500 for comparable land, there is no rush to change.

There are 36,000 hectares (about 12%) of farmland in the urban areas of greater Tokyo in the Tokyo, Kanagawa, Saitama, Chiba, and southern Ibaraki prefectures. The area is about 5.7 times larger than that inside Japan

Railways Yamanote circle line. If one-third was used for residential purposes, about 1 million apartments could be built.

If farmers borrowed money and built midsize apartment buildings on their land and rented property out, the construction ministry estimates they would do 11 times as well, after taxes, as by farming with no work at all. The average farmer owns 0.36 hectares of land and produces mostly vegetables. The farmer received ¥886,000 for this produce and paid only ¥22,000 in taxes. By constructing a 40-unit apartment building with each unit having an average floor space of 64 square meters, the annual tax burden would increase about 70 times, but the income would be more than ¥10 million, some eleven times as much.

Some 10,000 hectares could be so developed to provide 700,000 to 1 million apartments over the next ten years according to the Construction Ministry. It argues that such a development not only increases the supply of housing but also benefits the farmer. Obviously many factors are involved, such as the cost of construction, maintenance, environmental changes, and the farmer's inheritance tax burden as well as food security and increased density in and around Tokyo. But from a strictly economic point of view, the construction seems worthwhile.

A TYPICAL STORY OF LAND OWNERSHIP IN JAPAN

Our friend, a university professor in Japan, spent some time in the U.S. in the late 1960s as a visiting post doctoral student. He found California, where he was visiting, to be very expensive. Indeed it was at a time when the weak yen was trading at ¥360 per dollar. (Throughout history one finds that prices are high in countries with strong currencies and cheap in countries with weak currencies.) He returned to teach in Tokyo and in 1970 bought a 60 square meter apartment for about ¥8 million (U.S.$22,222 at the time), and he has continued to live there since.

This tiny four room apartment of about 60 square meters is part of a complex of 64 families that share the buildings and land. His share of the land is about 10m^2 which is a square of slightly more than 10 feet on a side. In December 1988, the apartment was worth about ¥50 million or some U.S.$400,000 at the then ¥125/$ exchange rate. In 1972, as a straight investment, he bought some raw land for ¥1 million in a resort area. This property, which has remained undeveloped, was small, comprising 350 square meters or a square of about 20 feet on a side. Recreational land has not increased in value as much as city land, but still his land was worth about ¥6 million in 1991.

As a professor he has not received a high salary, so he kept his purchases of property and belongings to a minimum. But in 1983, he bought a block of four apartments in central Tokyo for ¥80 million. He paid part of the payment in cash and borrowed the rest. Two of the apartments are tiny single rooms of about 20m^2. Each of these he rents for ¥80,000 (or about U.S.$640) per month. The two larger apartments are about 45m^2 and they rent for ¥140,000 (or about U.S.$1,120) per month. The properties have tripled in value to about ¥240 million, and with the yen increase, give him a profit of ¥160 million, or well over U.S. $1 million as of early 1992. He rents out these properties. The rent of about ¥4 million per year still does not cover his interest of ¥5 million (at the current rate of 6%), but he is gaining on this. Meanwhile, the shortfall is tax-deductible.

Rents increased more slowly than property values, but soon he will be in a positive cash flow position, which is what he wants. He has no intention of selling any of his rental properties. They will provide income in his retirement. His needs and expenses are modest. It is more convenient to travel by train or bus, so he needs neither a car nor many other large consumer goods. Besides his lack of need, he has little space for them. When he retires, he may sell his Tokyo apartment and replace it with a place in his chosen retirement city with a better climate some distance south of Tokyo. More likely he will buy the retirement apartment and continue to rent the Tokyo apartment.

Despite the fact that he has well over U.S. $2 million in property, he does not consider himself rich. He is quite content living on his university salary and saving much of that. He does not spend much at all and is worried about the high prices of many items. Is his lifestyle less good than someone in the U.S. with more material goods and a higher consumption? It's certainly different. He has loans on his property and is concerned about taxes on his land assets. After holding property for ten years, the taxes on his gains will drop to half the current rate (up to about 50% on the top end but see the discussion in Chapter 4 for marginal rates). He will not be rushed into selling.

Where would he invest now? Yokohama, he says. Will there be a crash? He doesn't think so. He thinks the 1991–92 declines will make land prices cheap, so he is thinking of buying more.

COST OF HOUSING IN JAPAN

A 1988 survey by the Japanese Association of Housewives revealed that more than 30% of homemakers who wished to have a house of their own thought it will be difficult to realize their dream. About 70% of homemakers nationwide said they were not satisfied with their present residences. A lack of storage space, including closets, was the main cause of dissatisfaction, followed by poor plumbing, cramped rooms, and too few rooms. Over half the women were not satisfied with the environmental surroundings of their residence, mostly because of long commuting hours to school or work and lack of cultural facilities. This trend was found not only in the Tokyo area but also in other cities, where housing and land problems are considered less severe.

In response to nine questions on ideal housing, 77.5% of homemakers wanted to own a house. Only 30% of those hoping to own their own house believed it would be possible, 31% thought it would be difficult, and 21% didn't know. The hope of home ownership is one more reminder of the huge demand for land which will keep the prices high.

Houses and apartments have small capacity for electrical appliances. Much to the dismay of WTZ (one of the authors) his usual method of working with background videotapes of musicals, adventures and mysteries was thwarted when inadequate electrical power turned colored films into black and white when the dryer and Macintosh were on. It was so tight that turning one light on and off made the difference.

Rents are much cheaper relative to land costs in Japan in comparison with other countries because of the lower interest and inflation rates. Still, office rent in Tokyo is up to 35% higher than in London and 63% higher than Paris, according to a Nagoya-based Tokai Bank report issued in 1988. The report blamed Tokyo's woes on a lack of measures to alleviate urban concentration. Tokyo is also marked by rampant investment in real estate for profit. London requires permission of authorities to develop, repair and construct buildings. Paris also maintains tough restrictions on the use, size, and location of buildings. The Tokai Bank report called for tougher measures to restrict the private use of land and to give priority to public projects to alleviate Tokyo's excessive concentration.

Table 5.2 provides an idea of the relative cost of Japanese office space. Tokyo at 211 is more than double London at 92, which in turn is nearly double the next most expensive cities, Singapore, Paris, Madrid, and Hong Kong.

The private housing situation in Tokyo is even worse. In London and Paris, individuals can buy a house for about three times their average annual income. Tokyo residents must pay about 18 times their income. In 1984, it was six times. This three-fold relative increase is higher than in most other parts of the world.

Table 5.2
Global Office Annual Occupancy Costs per Square Foot in U.S. Dollars in Selected Cities in 1991

Tokyo	211	Vancouver	28
London	92	Los Angeles	28
Singapore	59	Chicago	28
Paris	58	San Francisco	26
Madrid	52	Bangkok	26
Hong Kong	51	Istanbul	24
Glasgow	41	Jakarta	23
Frankfort	40	Boston	22
Birmingham	38	Philadelphia	22
New York	36	Brussels	21
Toronto	35	Wellington	19
Washington, DC	34	Kuala Lumpur	19
Taipei	34	Seattle	19
Montreal	32	Nice	16
Sydney	29	Denver	13

Source: *Colliers*

The high cost of living sends the Japanese on holiday to other parts of the world. In 1987, 2.3 million Japanese visited the United States, while only 440,000 Americans came to Japan. New regulations eliminate visa requirements between the U.S. and Japan for tourists and business travelers staying 90 days or less. Since more than 90% of travelers stay for 90 days or less, this is bound to increase travel, especially from Japan to the U.S. In 1987, some 1.8 million visas were issued to Japanese by the U.S. Embassy in Tokyo. During peak seasons, Japanese travelers have crowded the embassy compound in long lines requiring several hours wait in conveniencing both themselves and those with other embassy business.

One of the visa conditions is a return or onward ticket that must be purchased at about double the North American price. This latter point is especially puzzling: an economy air fare from Montreal-Tokyo-Montreal costs $1,500 Canadian while the reverse trip, Tokyo-Montreal-Tokyo, costs $3,500. These rates are based on old exchange rates (¥296 per Canadian dollar) and could be corrected by using current rates of exchange. However, they do allow package tour groups to price at costs not much exceeding the plane fare. Still, with travel in North America so much cheaper than in Japan and with much more to see and do, the trend of more and more Japanese visitors to North America is likely to accelerate. The acceleration of travel by Japanese and their high duty-free allowance has started a competition among the airlines for in-flight duty-free shops.

Table 5.3 shows the maximum parking fines in Tokyo versus those in Paris, London, New York and Hong Kong. Tokyo with an acute parking problem has fines as high as ¥200,000 for parking in a no-parking zone which is about two weeks pay for an average worker. Parking has been banned on about 95% of the streets in Tokyo. As a result as many as 90% of all parked cars are parked illegally on any given day.

Table 5.3
The Highest Parking Fines for Overnight Violations, in U.S. Dollars, 1991

Tokyo	$1,400
Paris	220
New York	200
London	70
Hong Kong	25

Source: *Japan Times*

JAPANESE LAND HELD BY FOREIGNERS

Many foreign corporations, governments, and other institutions own considerable land in Japan. Some of this land is very valuable if sold on the open market. The garden of the Australian Embassy was sold for over $1 billion to reduce the national debt, but the usual strategy is to hold this land.

More typical is Northwest Airlines, which owns a house where its top executive in Japan lives, a small hotel hear Narita airport, a nine-unit apartment building, and a part interest in an office building. These holdings are valued at $500 million. In 1989, NWA, the parent company of Northwest Airlines, was a takeover target, which came to light when the airline turned down an offer of $200 million for one of the Narita properties. Consider the option of selling versus holding: By holding the property, Northwest uses the apartment building and hotel to house employees, which saves it, say, $6,000 to $10,000 a month for the apartments and $100 to $200 a night for the hotel rooms. These assets are used in running the business; costs would go up considerably without them.

Capital gains taxes depend upon the length of ownership and are structured to encourage land ownership and net sales by being lower the longer the property is held. If Northwest sold the buildings, taxes would be heavy, possibly as much as 60 to 65% of the capital gains if the sale was made by a new company that took over Northwest to break up its assets.

THE RELATIONSHIP BETWEEN LAND AND STOCK PRICES[4]

Land and stock prices have been in a very close, positive relationship since 1955. Figure 5.1 shows that the March 1992 all land index value is nearly identical to that of the stock market, as measured by the Nikkei stock average (NSA). Though stocks have been much more volatile (see Figure 5.2), the net effect over long periods of time is very close total index values. On the whole, in the period 1955 to 1971, land prices increased more than stock prices, with land increasing 100 to 175 times in the largest cities and stocks increasing 109 times. From 1971 to 1989, the stock market increased about 20 times while land only increased about five to ten times in the six largest cities and three to four times in the country as a whole.

Figure 5.1
All Land Prices and NSA, 1955:1–1992:1 (Biannual; March and September), 1955 = 100

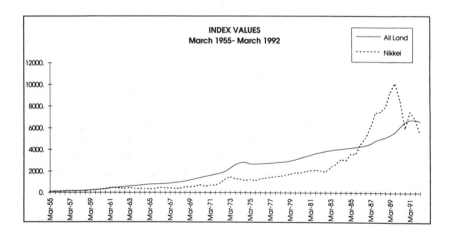

Source: Stone and Ziemba (1992b)

---

[4]This section is an update of the discussion in Ziemba and Schwartz (1991b).

Figure 5.2
Rates of Return All Land and NSA, 1955:2-1992:1 (Biannual; March and September)

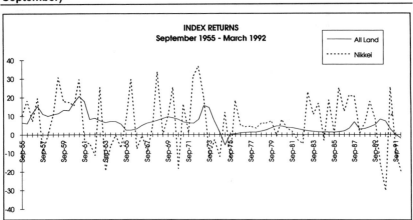

Source: Stone and Ziemba (1992b)

Until 1990–92, land index values had never fallen except in the aftermath of the 1973–74 oil crisis. In the earlier period, land, depending upon the type, fell 5 to 8%. Land prices peaked in September 1990. From then until March 1992, commercial prices fell 16.7%, residential prices, 20.8%, industrial prices, 14.3%, the highest price lots, 14.4% and all land, 17.2%. Meanwhile in the post-war period, stocks have experienced 26 declines of 10% or more, as detailed in Table 5.4.

Land prices fell in 1991 for the first time in 17 years. Residential land nationwide fell an average of 5.6% and commercial property fell 4%. In Osaka prices fell the most at a rate of 22.9% for a total loss of 40% from the peak in the summer of 1990. In greater Tokyo, average prices fell 15.7% in Chiba Prefecture, 10.3% in Tokyo and 9.1% overall. Residential land in Tokyo's 23 wards fell 30% and the decrease was largest in the high-class residential districts. Housing prices are still 2.5 times their level in 1985. Some think they must drop another 40 to 50% to be affordable. In March Tokyo office rents declined for the first time since 1985.

Stocks and land are intertwined. The value of land holdings by major companies is a part of their stock valuation. Asako, et al. (1989) estimated that the stocks on the first section of the Tokyo stock exchange (TSE) from 1976 to 1987 were valued at only about 46% of the market value of the stocks and land they own. This relationship is explored in Ziemba and Schwartz (1991b).

Table 5.4
The Twenty-Six Declines of 10% or More on the NSA, 1949–92

Decline Number	Value at Peak	Value in Valley	Dates	% Decline	Duration (months)
1	177	85	9/1/49–7/6/50	-51.8	11
2	474	295	3/4–4/1/53	-37.8	2
3	367	322	5/6–6/3/53	-12.2	1
4	595	472	5/4–12/27/57	-20.8	8
5	1,830	1,258	7/18–12/19/61	-31.2	5
6	1,590	1,216	2/14–10/29/62	-23.5	9
7	1,634	1,201	4/5–12/18/63	-26.5	9
8	1,369	1,020	7/3/64–7/12/65	-25.5	13
9	1,589	1,364	4/1–12/15/66	-14.1	8
10	1,506	1,250	3/1–12/11/76	-17.0	9
11	2,534	1,930	4/6–5/27/70	-23.9	2
12	2,741	2,227	8/14–10/20/71	-18.7	3
13	5,360	3,355	1/24/73–10/9/74	-37.4	21
14	4,565	3,814	5/12–9/29/75	-16.4	5
15	5,288	4,597	9/5–11/24/77	-13.1	3
16	8,019	6,850	8/17/81–10/1/82	-14.6	14
17	11,190	9,703	5/4–7/23/84	-13.3	3
18	18,936	15,820	8/20–10/22/86	-16.5	2
19	25,929	22,703	6/17–7/22/87	-12.4	1
20	26,646	21,037	10/14–11/11/87	-21.1	1
21	38,916	28,002	12/29/89–4/2/90	-28.0	3
22	33,293	20,222	7/17–10/1/90	-39.3	2.5
23	26,980	22,176	4/17–6/8/91	-17.8	2.5
24	24,120	21,456	7/31–8/19/91	-11.0	0.5
25	25,222	21,503	10/31–12/11/91	-14.7	1.5
26	22,801	16,598	1/6–4/9/92	-30.3	3
Average				-22.7	5.5

Ueda (1990b), using a simple valuation model, argued that stock prices underestimated the value of the corporate assets during 1970–83 but overestimated the value of these assets since 1983. Figure 5.3 illustrates this. Stocks of companies with large land holdings trade at well below the market value of their assets. Typically such stocks trade at 10 to 15% of the value of their assets. The extreme increase in stock prices in the 1980s occurred during a period of declining required risk premiums in relation to rates of return. Hence, the sharp increase in prices of stocks prior to their steep decline in 1990 was at least partially based on expectation of future increases in asset prices of land and stock shares held. French and Poterba

(1991) and Ziemba and Schwartz (1991b) present similar analyses and conclusions.

Figure 5.3
Quarterly Tokyo Golf Course Membership Prices and the NSA, 1982–92 (Feb)

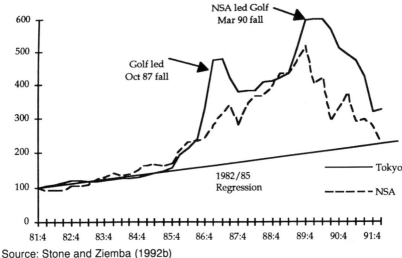

Source: Stone and Ziemba (1992b)

Speculative land is much more volatile than land used as an essential input for business operations or housing. Golf course membership indices for various cities compiled by the Nihon Keizai Shimbun, Inc., provide a measure of speculative land values. These indices, computed weekly since the end of 1981, are based on actual sales of memberships at the more than 400 golf courses in Japan.

The close relationship between the golf course membership index in Tokyo and the NSA is shown in Figure 5.3. The prices are generally in tandem, but there have been two gaps. In each case golf course membership prices rose far above the NSA, and the gap was eventually closed. The first gap presages and extends past the October 1987 stock market crash. Golf course membership prices started falling prior to the October 1987 crash. However, Stone and Ziemba (1990, 1992 a,b) found little basis for the argument that golf course prices generally lead the stock market. They did find evidence that golf courses lead land price returns and that stock price returns lead land price returns including golf course membership returns. The latter was the case in the 1990–91 decline. Stocks began to fall in reaction to higher interest rates (see Figure 5.4) in January 1990. Golf courses

Figure 5.4
Short Term Interest Rates in Japan, June 1984–March 1992

Source: Nikkei NEEDS

began to fall in March 1990 and all land in September 1990. The decline in golf course prices stopped in January 1992 with May 1992 prices slightly higher on the year.

Figure 5.5 shows the quarterly rates of return of Tokyo golf course memberships and the NSA since the beginning of 1982. Since March 1990 the golf course memberships fell every quarter until 1992. In the last quarter of 1991 the decline was nearly 25%. Figures 5.6 and 5.7 show the golf course membership prices in various cities and areas of Japan. The declines in Osaka and other cities outside Tokyo have been much more severe, just as their increases were much higher. In Wakayama prefecture the spectacular rise from 100 at the beginning of 1982 to over 4,300 in March 1990 has been followed by an equally spectacular decline to the 1,375 range at the end of 1991 and 1,411 at the end of February 1992. There is evidence that the decline in golf course membership prices was the bursting of a speculative bubble. Rachev and Ziemba (1992) have shown that these prices are non-normal and are well modeled by a stable distribution with extremely fat tails. There are very large rises and declines indicative of changes in investor perceptions of speculative returns or losses in the future.

Figure 5.5
Quarterly Rates of Return of Tokyo Golf Course Membership Prices and the NSA, 1982–92 (Feb)

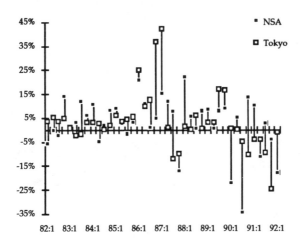

Source: Stone and Ziemba (1992b)

Figure 5.6
Quarterly Golf Course Membership Prices and the NSA in Various Japanese Cities, 1982–92 (Feb)

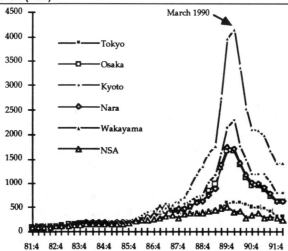

Source: Stone and Ziemba (1992b)

Figure 5.7
Quarterly Golf Course Membership Prices in the East, West and All Japan and the NSA, 1982–92 (Feb)

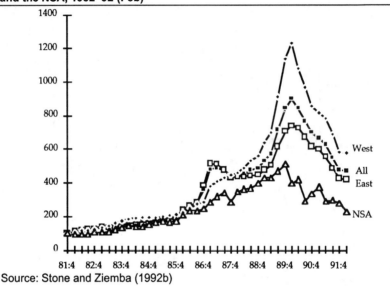

Source: Stone and Ziemba (1992b)

While speculative land including condos has fallen sharply (see Komahashi and Tsukada, 1991, and Shibata,1991), it is not clear how much essential use land might fall. Despite the dramatic declines in stock prices and speculative land, the fall in 1991–92 has been only about 15 to 20%. So land prices remain extremely high.

CONSUMER PRICE INDICES

Tables 5.5 and Figure 5.8 give CPI indices and their year-to-year change for Japan, as well as the U.S., Germany, France, and the U.K. for 1955–1988 (May). These indices are based on baskets of goods and *do not include housing*. The latter leads to many misconceptions because housing costs are a large fraction of a typical family's monthly budget.

CPI and fixed-basket indices of costs of living for families and business travelers provide insights into the cost of living in Japan. However, the consumption bundles and habits are very different in each country. The Japanese consume far less than U.S. or European counterparts and they save much more. It is not necessarily that their quality of life is lower,

Table 5.5
Inflation (1975–93), 1992, 1993 Estimated

	Japan	U.S.	Germany	France	U.K.
1976	8.3	5.8	4.3	9.7	16.5
1977	9.0	6.4	3.6	9.3	15.9
1978	-4.7	7.6	2.8	9.1	8.3
1979	12.8	11.3	4.0	10.8	13.4
1980	8.0	13.5	5.6	13.5	18.0
1981	4.9	10.3	5.9	13.4	11.9
1982	2.6	6.2	5.3	11.8	8.6
1983	1.9	3.2	3.6	9.6	4.6
1984	2.2	4.3	2.4	7.4	5.0
1985	2.1	3.5	2.2	5.8	6.1
1986	0.7	2.0	-0.2	2.7	3.4
1987	0.1	3.7	0.3	3.1	4.2
1988	0.8	4.1	1.2	2.8	4.9
1989	2.0	4.8	2.8	3.5	7.8
1990	3.3	5.4	2.7	3.4	9.4
1991	3.3	4.2	3.5	3.1	5.8
1992	2.0	3.0	3.9	2.5	3.3
1993	2.5	3.5	3.1	2.6	2.6

Source: Nikkei NEEDS

Figure 5.8
Consumer Price Indices in Major Countries (1975–93), 1975 = 100
1992, 1993 Estimated

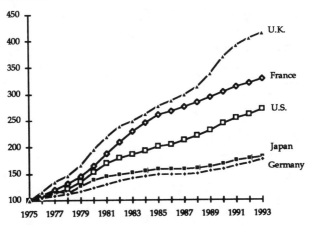

Source: Bank of Japan

despite how we might measure it on North American or European yardsticks. Their culture and living habits are very different. Many seeds of discontent exist, but there is a very strong contentedness that provides cohesion to the country and its citizens. Examples can be as misleading as they are instructive, but we provide one in the next section.

It is not our intent to suggest better consumer price index measures here, but the reader should be aware of the limitations of these measures. One must also adjust for currency changes. Table 5.6, based on casual observation, lists a number of items that locals, tourists and medium-term visitors might buy. Generally, most items cost about double the North American price, even for items that ought to have price parity, such as airline tickets and newsmagazines.

THE COSTS OF ENTERTAINMENT

Table 5.7 shows the extraordinary prices that must be paid for top entertainment. At ¥67,500 or about U.S.$500 in 1989 to attend a concert with Sammy Davis, Jr., Liza Minelli and Frank Sinatra, one sees just how high these prices can be.

The Hotel New Otani's 25-meter outdoor swimming pool is open for the summer season June 17 to September 10, hours are 10 a.m. to 5 p.m. the first month and then expand to 9 p.m. The weekday fee for adults is ¥7,500 and for children ¥5,000, rising to ¥10,000 and ¥7,000 on weekends. There are reduced evening rates of ¥3,000 and ¥2,000. A weekday package with dinner and drink is ¥9,000 and ¥6,000, while a gourmet package is ¥13,000 and ¥10,000.

A wine tasting dinner at the Tour d'Argent restaurant in March 1989 at the Hotel New Otani in Tokyo with nine courses with a regional French wine to accompany each course cost ¥40,000 per person. The ultimate is a restaurant in Tokyo where a special steak meal costs ¥100,000 about $700 per person![5]

---

[5]One loses a sense of proportion. We actually twice paid ¥5,300 for the three of us to swim in a lovely indoor pool in the Royal Hotel in Osaka.

Table 5.6
Prices in Yen and U.S. Dollar for Typical Items in Japan, December 1988
(Exchange Rate, 1 US$ = ¥ 125)

	Price in Yen	Price in US $	Comparable Price in California, U.S. $
Small apartment 1/2 hour commute from Central Tokyo	¥625 million	$500,000	$50,000–150,000
Rent for medium-sized apartment	¥750,000 per month	$6,000 per month	$600–700 per month
Furnished room rental in Tokyo at International Women's House	¥18,000–60,000 per week	$144–480 per week	$50–150
Subsidized 4-bedroom furnished apartment in suburbs for visiting scientist or professor	¥57,600 per month		
Subsidized room for young company employee of brokerage firm in main city or near factory	¥1,200 per month		
Rental for luxury apartment in central Tokyo district of Roppongi (242–269 sq.m., 4.5 bedrooms, study room, English TV, sauna, gym, swimming pool)	¥1,800,000 to 2,400,000 per month	$14,400 to 19,200 per month	$1,500–4,000 per month
Subsidized small apartment near factory for family of employee of manufacturing firm	¥12,000 per month		
Taxi ride in Tokyo	¥470 fixed fee for first 2 km plus ¥60 for each additional 390 km		
Top-quality large melon in Tokyo same melon in suburbs	¥8,000 to 10,000 ¥5,000	$64–80 $40	$2
Green Fees Good, but not best quality golf course, 18 holes	¥30,000	$240	$25–40
Private English-language instructor in suburbs	¥3,000–5,000 per hour	$24–40 per hour	$10–20
International Business Week At newsstand Yearly subscription	¥800 ¥16,400	$6.40 $131.50	$2.00 $95 in Australia, $18 in U.S.
Economist Magazine yearly subscription	¥24,500	$196	$69 in Korea, Taiwan, Thailand
Round trip flight Tokyo-LA-Tokyo LA-Tokyo-LA (at ¥296/$)	¥333,900	$2500	$1895

Oil prices in Japan are over $4 a gallon. This is even higher than Europe and over three times the U.S. price. Famous foreign brands cost 30% more in Japan than in Western countries.

The Cunard Line received a $50 million fee to moor the QE2 in Yokohama for 65 days. About 1,200 people per day paid ¥13,000 for a three-hour lunch and shopping tour. For ¥50,000 to ¥380,000, one could join the 700 a night who stayed over. Corporations bought tickets in blocks for employees and clients, and these accounted for 60% of the visits. Staff was increased from 21 to 112 for the 11 boutiques to stay open until midnight. High-priced items sold well, including ¥48,000 diamond and sapphire rings and silk scarves (a scarf that costs $125 in London sold for $190, below the $315 in Tokyo stores). Other services offered included Western-style weddings (there were 13 at a minimum charge of ¥53,000 per head). The Japanese consortium that chartered the QE2 may not have broken even, but members learned how to run cruise ships and top-class hotels. The QE2 plans another six-month charter in Japan, including three months in the port of Osaka.

In the last few years, the growth of the economy has been based on domestic consumption, reflecting a change in the attitudes of Japanese consumers. They are now less reluctant to use their savings for luxury goods. Many costly and once unusual items are now taken for granted. A ¥10,000 per person restaurant dinner is not considered a luxury nor is a stay at an overseas health care resort. The best tickets are now the first to sell out. The first-class green cars on the *shinkansen* fill up first during holiday periods. Table 5.7 gives the prices of a number of entertainment events.

Table 5.7
The Cost of Specific Entertainment Events in Japan, 1989

SIEGFRIED & ROY, Magic Show at Shiodome White Theater (Shinbashi)
Weekdays: (S) = ¥8,500   (a) = ¥5,000
Late show (Fri. & Sat. 9:30 p.m. only) (s) = ¥10,000 (a) ¥7,000
Sunday (all seats) - ¥5,000
SUPER CONCERT '89
Sammy Davis Jr., Liza Minelli, Frank Sinatra
(SS) = ¥67,500 (including the concert program)
Overnight accommodation plan available
Fee: ¥100,000 per guest, which will pay for cost of admission to the SS Arena of
the concert, and an overnight stay at hotels listed below, as well as breakfast on
Sunday morning. Tax and service charge included. Dinner at ¥20,000 per guest
can also be arranged.
Movie: Intolerance
Directed by D. W. Griffith in 1916
Music by New Japan Philharmonic Orchestra
February 27–March 1 at Nippon Budokan
(a) = ¥8,000   (b) = ¥5,000   (c) = ¥3,000

THE SKYROCKETING COST OF LIVING

The average Japanese earns more than his or her counterpart in some other
countries including the U.S. and West Germany. However, because of the
high cost of living, this income does not buy as much. During 1987, the
average Japanese, West Germany and American earned $23,022, $21,022
and $18,163, respectively. (Each of the 60.8 million actual workers in Japan
earned about $42,000.) In purchasing power parity, according to a study by
Balassa and Noland (1988), the Japanese, West German and U.S. incomes
were worth $7,302, $7,783 and $9,009, respectively. Figure 5.9 shows the
effect and in comparison with France, Italy and the United Kingdom.

Figure 5.9
Average Income and Purchasing Power Parity Per Capita, in 1987 in U.S. Dollars

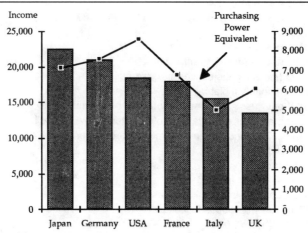

Source: Balassa and Noland (1988)

The price of a small apartment an hour and a half commute from central Tokyo, costs seven to ten times the annual earnings of its owner, some $500,000. For most European and U.S. cities, the cost is four and five times earnings and the living space is at least twice as large.

The Japanese also had to work longer hours for their wages. The average employee works 2,150 hours a year, compared with 1,924 hours in the United States, 1,938 hours in Britain, 1,655 hours in West Germany and 1,643 hours in France. In addition, Japanese workers spend more time commuting to work than their Western counterparts, with 13.7% of the workforce spending an hour or more going to and from jobs, compared with 6% in the United States, 3% in West Germany, and 2% in Belgium.

Riding the rail takes on a different meaning in Japan as they experiment with using the time productively. Ninety percent of the mobile phone market in Nagoya and Tokyo is on the rails. The East Japan Railway Co. offered 45-minute English classes on the commuter train between Odawara in Kanagawa prefecture to Shinjuku, Tokyo.

The retirement age for employees of the large firms is 55 to 58. It is typical then to buy a house with the lump-sum retirement payment and work at another, lower paying job, until the social security retirement is paid at 65. Often those working for the government or large firms live in subsidized housing while employed and lose that upon retirement.

This information, from the annual white paper issued by the Japan Labor Ministry in July 1988, also pointed out that Japan leads the world in average personal savings of $63,000 for each of the 60.8 million workers. The average wages of $42,000 U.S. represented a 2% increase in real wages for the second straight year, and savings per person increased by 11.8% in 1987 from the previous year, to $63,000. According to *The Economist* as of September 1989, the average Japanese household had ¥19 million or $135,000 in savings held in stocks, bonds, postal savings, insurance policies and similar financial instruments.

An average middle class Japanese male worker will spend half of his income on rent and utilities. Some 26% of the household income will be spent on food versus 15% in the U.S. Even if the worker could save enough for a down-payment on a house, his family would have to make do with 925 square feet, while the average American home covers 1,583 square feet. However, the average-sized home in many areas of Europe, including France and Italy, is not much larger than that in Japan. The average for Europe is 1,050 square feet.[6]

It is debatable whether more cars means a higher quality of life, but in Japan the average family has 0.88 cars, versus 1.3 in the European Economic Community, and a hefty 2.2 in the U.S.

For many Japanese, there seems little prospect of improvement. Plagued by extreme traffic congestion and a scarcity of greenery and other urban amenities, the Japanese capital seems trapped in an implosive cycle of overcrowding that is making it less comfortable for the middle class. After the 1986–88 boom in land prices (Tokyo up 24%, 76% and 44% in these three years), only Japanese who inherit land in Tokyo will be rich. Very few will grow rich by their own efforts.

The ministry report confirmed Japan's reputation as a nation of workaholics with little time for play. The report concluded that Japan— whose rapid post-war rise from a poor nation scarce in natural resources to an economic superpower has been dubbed a miracle—needs to help improve the living quality of its workers. It called for a reduction in working hours to "bring about a comfortable lifestyle." And it also recommended setting aside more land for housing in Tokyo, which has the world's highest real estate costs, and coaxing corporations to move to outlying areas while providing more low-cost rent accommodations.

---

[6]Japan, even in Tokyo, has an extremely high rate of home ownership. The Japanese do not consider that owning a condo is a replacement for a detached house. Those who work for a firm with housing benefits can live in company housing until retirement and then purchase a small house with their retirement money. Indeed, in the high interest rate period of 1989-91, condo prices fell sharply. Though prices for detached houses fell in late 1991, the decline has been modest. The rationale being that houses are paid for in cash and condos with speculative bonus money.

The population still totals about 12 million, though some 22,000 in 1988 moved to neighboring Chiba, Saitama, and other prefectures where land is cheaper. About 3.2% of the population of Tokyo is 65 and older. Companies normally pay ordinary transportation fees for their employees. With workers moving out of the city in search of affordable housing, many firms are now paying for higher priced *shinkansen* commutes. Shinetsu Chemical started paying ¥60,000 to ¥110,000 per month to 10 employees who live 50 to 150 kms outside Tokyo and spend 1.5 to 2 hours commuting. Another company pays 90% of the *shinkansen* costs.

Figure 5.10 describes a 1987 OECD study on purchasing power throughout Japan. It indicates that Japan is about par with West Germany and France, slightly ahead of Great Britain, but well behind the United States. Within Tokyo the purchasing power is even less. As shown in Table 5.8, based on a Union Bank of Switzerland study for 1987, Tokyo workers log more hours to have much less purchasing power than workers in New York, London, Paris and Frankfurt.

Figure 5.10
Purchasing Power of GDP in Real Terms in Five Countries in 1987, in Thousands, per Person

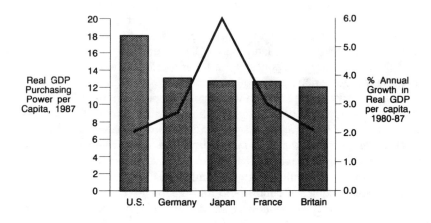

Source: OECD

Table 5.8
Standards of Working and Domestic Purchasing Power (Tokyo = 100) in 1987 in Five Countries

	Net hourly Earnings, $	Working Hours per Year	Vacation Days per Year, exc Public Holidays*	Net Domestic Purchasing Power	Average Rent 3-room Apartment, Monthly $
Tokyo	10.70	2,013	16.1	100	1.430
New York	9.00	1,867	13.0	200	1,150
London	8.00	1,754	24.1	154	860
Paris	6.60	1,730	28.2	135	750
Frankfurt	9.00	1,723	29.5	225	540

* Weighted average of 12 occupations excluding public holidays.

Source: OECD

This Union Bank of Switzerland study compared the costs of living (without rent, unfortunately) if one lives like a typical European family using a fixed basket of goods and services to reflect European consumption patterns. Not surprisingly, Tokyo heads the list and is way ahead of major European cities such as Stockholm, Geneva and London, all considered very pricey for North Americans (see Figure 5.11).

Figure 5.11
Cost of a Basket of European Goods and Services in a Variety of Cities, New York =100

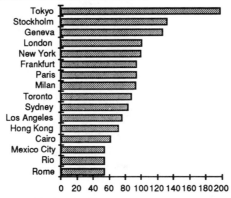

Source: Union Bank of Switzerland

What are the best places to live if one's income is in line with local norms? Los Angeles heads the list: its typical after-tax earnings have 33 to 55% more purchasing power than New York, Chicago, Houston, or Toronto and about 80% to 100% more than Paris, London, Milan, or Sydney. By contrast, net wages and salaries in Seoul, Hong Kong, and Tokyo buy only 26% to 38% of the goods and services that Los Angeles workers can afford.

For business travel, Tokyo and Osaka-Kobe have cost indices of over 200 compared with New York, the most expensive U.S. city, with the base of 100. This is detailed in Table 5.9 which was compiled from the Geneva-based Business International's twice yearly survey of living costs. The survey takes into account the cost of a shopping basket of food items, alcoholic drinks, household supplies, personal care items, tobacco, utilities, clothing, domestic help, recreation, entertainment, and transportation, but not housing.

Table 5.9
Living Costs for Business Travel in Various Cities, Fall, 1988

City	Index Rating (NY=100)	Annual Inflation %, 87–88	City	Index Rating (NY=100)	Annual Inflation %, 87–88
Tokyo	203	2.20	Paris	109	3.10
Osaka-Kobe	201	2.20	Brussels	104	2.60
Tehran	189	15.00	Frankfurt-am-Main	104	2.40
Libreville	162	5.60	Milan	104	7.00
Brazzaville	155	14.00	Algiers	103	25.00
Oslo	138	6.00	Dusseldorf	103	2.30
Taipei	133	3.50	Melbourne	103	11.00
Helsinki	128	5.40	Rome	103	7.20
Dakar	127	5.50	Seoul	102	9.20
Geneva	123	3.00	Toronto	102	6.50
Tel Aviv	123	22.00	Montreal	101	6.00
Zurich	123	3.10	Port Moresby	101	6.80
Copenhagen	120	7.00	Sydney	100	10.50
Vienna	118	3.70	Madrid	99	7.50
Stockholm	112	6.80	Singapore	95	N/A
Hamburg	111	2.80	Hong Kong	88	N/A
Munich	110	2.90	Manila	72	N/A
London	109	3.80			

Source: Business International, Geneva

CHAPTER 6
OPERATING AS A CREDITOR NATION:
WHERE IS JAPAN INVESTING ITS HUGE WEALTH?

Thank you, Japan. The world's biggest creditor has played a similar role in the 1980s to that of America in the 1920s. So far, it has done a better job.
        The Economist editorial headline, December 23, 1989

The Economist praised Japanese participation in the world financial markets. By providing the steady financing for the U.S. twin deficits and steadiness during the October stock crises in 1987 and 1989, the Japanese have helped save the financial system from collapse. This is not manipulation by the Ministry of Finance but an indication of the speed with which markets have been deregulated.

However, *The Economist* expressed other sobering thoughts. At the end of the 1920s the U.S. was in the same position as Japan, with the aftermath of WWI turning it into the major creditor. Then came the crash of 1929. *The Economist* points to the speculative run up in land and stock prices in Japan and called for a tightening of credit in Japan to head off the problems of the 1930s. This they believe would make Japan a better creditor.[1]

Japan has become the world's largest creditor nation. Many come to Japan seeking more investment. Its foreign reserves were about $70 billion U.S. in May 1992, but down from a peak of about $101 billion in 1989. In addition, the major companies have cash and other liquid assets. Meanwhile, the land and stock market booms have made thousands and thousands of people instant millionaires with huge assets. Since stock market profits by individuals in Japan were not subject to any capital gains taxes (and now only 20% or less) and banks have been willing to loan money at relatively low interest rates based on land collateral (of up to about 80% of appraised value and sometimes 95%) these gains have been readily transferable at low cost into cash that can be used to buy assets elsewhere. With the price of everything sky high in Japan and the yen

---

[1]Indeed, they were right on the mark and this has changed things dramatically. In Chapter 11 we discuss this and the future.

strong, it is little wonder that many Japanese institutions and individuals look to the U.S. and elsewhere to make investments. In general, the Japanese have been cautious, careful investors who like to invest where they are familiar and comfortable. But they are willing to pay high prices if the proposed deal looks good over the long horizon with the relatively low required rates of return that they normally employ.

Japanese management techniques are having an important effect on industry in the host countries. But the workers need much training. They lack, in the words of one Japanese manager, *ishin-denshin*, the ability to comprehend without verbal instructions. For example, a secretary does not have to be told to proofread a document before sending it out. American workers must be told what to do. They lack the concept of teamwork and consider that their job is limited to their own assignment, so they ignore problems that might arise in other areas. American workers resented the Toyota practice of making mistakes public in order to prevent a recurrence even though the company promised there would be no punishment.

GROWING WEALTH AND JAPAN'S FINANCIAL INSTITUTIONS

On the basis of high savings and exports, Japan became the world's largest creditor nation. In 1986, Japan became the largest net investor in the world with $180 billion (versus only $7 billion in 1976). Its net claims grew to $241 billion in 1987, $325 billion in 1988, and were $400 billion by the end of 1989. Its foreign reserves reached $100 billion U.S. before weak yen problems led to spending about a quarter of these reserves to support the yen.

Table 6.1 illustrates some of the Japanese wealth and its concentration as well as the concentration of economic power. The Japanese are not only richer externally because of the rise in the value of the yen but they are also richer internally. In April 1989, *The Economist* noted: "The *increase* in the value of Japan's financial assets in 1987 . . . was bigger than the country's GNP; the same was also true for the increase in the value of fixed assets including land [italics theirs]." This rate of increase occurred again in 1988. To compare with the U.S., in 1986–87, financial assets increased an average 30% of GNP, while in 1981 in Japan it was only 15%.

Table 6.1
Concentration of Japanese Wealth and Power in 1988–89

Japan has amassed the world's largest fortune, and that wealth is concentrated in a few institutions.

A Japanese regulator need only talk to a handful of individuals at 25 financial institutions to move markets; the same individuals can move world markets in a matter of hours.

The top 21 financial institutions in the world (by capitalization) are all Japanese. So are the top ten banks. By some accounts the world's two wealthiest individuals are Japanese as are six of the top ten. Some 41 of the world's top 226 billionaires are Japanese.

In 1988, the big four Japanese securities firms, Nomura, Daiwa, Nikko and Yamaichi, had more than 60% of all trading volume in Japan. Nomura alone had about 30%. While this dropped in 1990–92, they still have much of the volume.

	U.S.	Japan
Commercial banks	14,000	158
Life insurance companies	1,550	24
Property & casualty companies	1,775	23

Japanese and Japanese-owned banks now supply more than 20% of all credit to the state of California. They have about 25% of the banking assets in California.

Nomura Securities has enough capital to buy all the leading Wall Street companies.

The Japanese Postal Savings System, which is a huge government-owned bank, has assets larger than the top 12 U.S. banks combined as of 1988.

Because of a mistranslated press report, Japanese fund managers withdrew their funds, causing the failure of Continental Bank, the seventh largest U.S. bank, in 1984. This caused an over reaction that led the FDIC to insure all deposits, even those above the original stated limits.

Japanese also pulled massive funds out of the U.S. bond market causing a sharp rise in interest rates a few days before the October 1987 stock market crash.

Adapted from Murphy (1989)

As of the end of 1987, the 20 largest financial institutions in the world measured by capitalization, be they banks or brokerage firms, were all Japanese. No U.S. bank made it into the top 20 listed in Table 6.2. The Bank of America, the world's largest bank in 1982, was no longer in the top 100 financial institutions.

Table 6.2
The World's Largest Financial Institutions Measured by Market Capitalization at the end of 1986 and 1987

Rank 1987	1986		Market Value, $ Billion 1987	1986
1	1	Sumitomo Bank	58.85	35.16
2	5	Fuji Bank	55.60	27.04
3	4	Dai-Ichi Kangyo Bank	55.32	29.47
4	5	Mitsubishi Bank	48.62	26.90
5	3	Industrial Bank of Japan	46.38	32.06
6	7	Sanwa Bank	44.20	21.82
7	2	Nomura Securities	38.37	33.71
8	13	Mitsui Bank	28.45	13.26
9	12	Long-Term Credit Bank	27.46	13.58
10	18	Tokai Bank	27.34	12.24
11	8	Sumitomo Trust & Banking	21.07	16.78
12	9	Mitsubishi Trust & Banking Co.	20.70	16.65
13	21	Bank of Tokyo	15.79	13.07
14	14	Daiwa Securities	15.79	13.07
15	17	Mitsui Trust & Banking Co.	14.66	12.57
16	15	Nikko Securities	14.51	12.98
17	26	Tanyo Kobe Bank	14.22	7.22
18	22	Daiwa Bank	12.75	9.81
19	25	Nippon Credit Bank	12.39	7.89
20	23	Yasuda Trust & Banking Co.	11.14	9.07

As of July 1990, in the middle of the 1990 stock market declines, the top ten banks in the world by capitalization were still all Japanese. See Table 6.3. By assets, the top six and seven of the top ten were Japanese. However, by profitability, based on return on equity adjusted for one-time tax benefits, differing capital ratios, inflation and tax returns, there are no Japanese banks in the top ten. This reflects the high price earnings ratios and huge land holdings of Japanese companies compared to those in other countries. On this measure, five of the top ten banks are in the U.S.

Table 6.3
The Top 10 Banks by Stock Market Capitalization, Assets and Profitability Indices, June 1990

Rank by Capitalization, Billions of Dollars		Rank by Assets, Billions of Dollars		Rank by Profitability Index	
Industrial Bank of Japan	67.6	Dai-Ichi Kangyo Bank	370.5	Wells Fargo/U.S.	1.239
Sumitomo	55.8	Sumitomo	370.0	BankAmerica/U.S.	1.217
Fuji Bank	53.2	Fuji Bank	364.9	Banco Bilbao Viscava/Spain	1.214
Dai-Ichi Kangyo Bank	49.6	Mitsubishi Bank	362.2	Scadinaviska Ensikilds Banken/Sweden	1.192
Mitsubishi Bank	47.2	Sanwa Bank	355.9	NCNB/U.S.	1.175
Sanwa Bank	45.6	Industrial Bank of Japan	248.7	National Australia Bank/Australia	1.167
Long-Term Credit Bank of Japan	32.4	Credit Agricole/France	242.0	Security Pacific/U.S.	1.161
Mitsui Bank	25.7	Banque Nationale de Paris/France	231.4	First Chicago/U.S.	1.126
Tokai Bank	23.5	Citicorp/U.S.	230.6	Paribas/France	1.125
Nippon Credit Bank	19.2	Tokai Bank	229.2	Abbey National/Britain	1.125

Source: *Business Week*, July 2, 1990.

The Japanese big four brokerage firms are compared to the top 18 U.S. brokerage firms in Table 6.4. With four times the expenses, the U.S. brokers produced only slightly more than double the Japanese revenues. Hence, U.S. pre-tax margins were about one-sixth those of the Japanese and return on equity was one-fifth.[2] The subsidiaries of Japan's largest brokerage firms are already represented in the top 50 U.S. brokerage firms: Nomura Securities International, 20, Nikko Securities Co. International, 28, Daiwa Securities America, 32 and Yamaichi International (America), 34. These firms are not profitable yet, but if they develop better retail and other operations and buy subsidiaries they may well move to the top in size and financial strength. Some of the massive Japanese insurance companies such as Nippon Life have holdings and market values that place them above many of those institutions listed in Tables 6.3 and 6.4. The insurance companies have vast holdings of stock, which they seldom trade, and cash instruments, some of which are held to pay claims and the guaranteed

---

[2]*The Economist,* using new data, claims that the Japanese-owned U.S. firms are profitable and are sheltering income.

payments on the policies they sell. Typically, these policies guarantee the purchaser that part of the cost is paid back on maturity, and dividends of about 5% on this principal are paid as well. Such policies are extremely popular.

Table 6.4
Japan's Big Four versus the U.S. Top 18 Brokerage Firms, in Millions of Dollars, 1988

Category	Nomura	Daiwa	Nikko[1]	Yamaichi	Total	Largest 18 U.S. firms
Brokerage commissions	4,629	2,396	2,202	2,534	11,780	8,750
Underwriting & distribution	1,400	835	774	940	3,949	4,750
Net gain on trading	1,024	306	474	5	1,809	5,750
Interest and dividends	1,401	1,398	67	694	3,560	23,150
Other	62	183	180	211	636	5,250
Total revenues	*8,516*	*5,118*	*3,697*	*4,404*	*21,735*	*47,650*
Compensation & benefits	1,088	623	564	719	2,995	14,250
Interest expense	781	1,093	194	403	2,471	21,175
All other expenses	2,016	1,084	1,063	1,113	5,276	9,925
Total expenses	*3,885*	*2,800*	*1,821*	*2,236*	*10,742*	*45,350*
Income before taxes	4,631	2,318	1,876	2,168	10,993	2,300
Nonoperating income & other	0	(39)	31	15	8	na
Taxes	2,503	1,264	1,055	1,168	5,990	na
Net Income	*2,128*	*1,016*	*851*	*1,016*	*5,010*	*na*
Pre-tax margin[2]	60%	58%	54%	54%	56%	9%
Av shareholders' equity	6,950	3,413	3,287	3,197	16,845	19,000
Pre-tax ROE	67%	67%	58%	68%	65%	12%

[1]Excluded unconsolidated subsidiaries. [2]Includes net interest.

Source: Sanford C. Bernstein and Co. and Forbes, November 28, 1988

Since stock market profits by individuals in Japan have not been subject to any capital gains taxes and banks will loan money at low interest rates (about 6% until 1990) based on land collateral (of up to about 80% of appraised value and sometimes 95% or even 100%), these gains are readily transferred at low cost into cash that can be used to buy assets elsewhere. The 1989 tax reform added taxes on capital gains, but they are small. One can pay 1% of the sale value or add 20% of the profits to income. With the price of everything high, the need for funds low in Japan, and the yen so strong, many institutions and individuals look to the U.S., Europe, and elsewhere to invest their funds.

Figure 6.1
The Ten Largest Insurance Companies in the World, in Billions of U.S. Dollars in Assets at Dec 31, 1987, Values and Exchange Rages

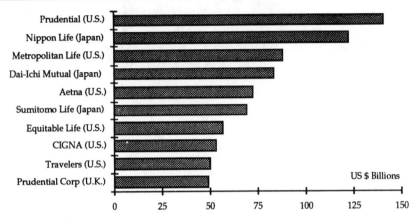

Source: Worldscope

Calculations in terms of capitalization (market value) show the size of Japanese institutions.[3] In terms of assets, U.S. firms still appear large. For example, of the ten largest insurance companies in the world ranked by assets as of the end of 1987, only three were Japanese and six were American(see Figure 6.1). Japanese life insurance companies had assets of $760 billion by the end of March 1989, a 22.5% increase from the previous year and three times bigger than in 1981. They have been buying American and other foreign stocks and bonds and overseas property.

Nippon Life receives ¥12 billion in premiums *daily*. Deregulation is permitting the life insurance companies to diversify. Since they are still restricted to generating income rather than capital gains, the Tokyo stock exchange is not as attractive to them, although the insurance companies collectively own about 15% of the TSE. They now have 20% of their money in property, and 30% in foreign-denominated assets. Nippon Life lost ¥3 trillion, mainly in higher yielding Treasury bonds, when the dollar fell in 1985–87, so it has had to reconsider its currency hedging policies.

---

[3]Indeed, this is precisely why the 1990-92 stock market decline has occurred—to bring these excess valuations back into line.

JAPANESE OVERSEAS INVESTMENT BOOMS

The first Japanese overseas investment boom was in U.S. investments from 1985–87. Banks, insurance companies and brokerage firms set up offices in North America. Some established real estate subsidiaries, improved their understanding of the U.S. market, and capitalized on higher U.S. property yields.

The second phase was the move into Europe. This began in the early 1980s and was in full bloom in anticipation of the 1992 European unification. The third phase, which is just beginning, is the move into Asian equities. The sums so far are less in Europe and Asia because the capital markets are smaller. But with the Asian markets just opening, this investment is increasing rapidly. Statements like that of Yasuhiko Ueyama, the president of Sumitomo Life, that his firm would like to increase the Asian share of its foreign securities portfolio from 3% to 33% over the next ten years echo the sentiments.

A Yamaichi Securities survey found that, since 1985, Japanese companies bought 1,017 foreign companies, while foreigners made 91 purchases in Japan. Another survey by *Nihon Keizai* found that 72% of Japanese executives are favorable to mergers and acquisitions. Nissan expects to cut its car exports to half the 1985 peak by the late 1990s on the basis of its foreign production. Other auto producers have similar goals.

As of April 1988, total Japanese direct investments abroad exceeded $180 billion. Of this, over $30 billion was invested in the U.S., some 3% of total U.S. assets. In fiscal 1988, these investments totaled $33.4 billion, up some 49.5% from 1987, according to Japan External Trade Organization (JETRO). The U.S. took 46% of the investments in 1988, but investment in Asia and Europe increased faster. They were up 100% and 90%, respectively, in 1987 and 1988 compared to the previous year. Securities houses and banks held 73% of overall direct investment overseas, followed by manufacturers, with 23.5%. The manufacturers' share represented a 200% gain over the previous year. Real estate investment went up 50.7% in the U.S. and 81.7% in Australia. The 1988 investment overseas was $22.8 billion in the first six months, and exceeded $40 billion for fiscal 1988.

In 1988, of 143 acquisitions whose prices were made public by Japanese corporations, 116 were overseas, amounting to $12.65 billion or 97% of the total of $13.07 billion. U.S. companies accounted for 67.8%, followed by Australian companies with 8.5%, French with 4.0%, British with 3.4% and Hong Kong with 2.8%. The total investment was higher because a record 229 companies were acquired in 1988.

Political turmoil caused more violent price swings, leading to a sell-off by foreign investors. Foreign investment in Japan is about 0.3% of the GNP and falling; Germany the next lowest, is at 10%. Foreign investors sold a net $1.95 billion in Japanese stocks in April 1989 ($288 million net purchase in March) for the first time since September 1988. They also sold a net $2.98 billion in Japanese public and corporate bonds ($1.1 billion net purchased in March). Japanese investors bought $1.67 billion of foreign stocks in April, especially British listed stocks. Japanese investors had been net sellers, $2.31 billion, of foreign bonds in March following net purchases of $11.18 billion in February 1989. Foreign investors have bought heavily in Japan during 1991 and 1992.

Japan's direct foreign investment[4] rose 35% to $30.82 billion in the six months to September 1989 compared with a year earlier (see Table 6.5). Finance and insurance represented 24%, real estate, 19.3%, and services, 12.9%. At the same time Japanese investment in Europe increased 90%. The share in Europe increased to 24.9% versus 17.7% with declines in the U.S. and Latin America. The share in the Asian Pacific rose as well, while that in Africa declined.

Although savvy and shrewd, the Japanese are not usually prone to hard bargaining. If the price is fair, they buy; if not they pass. More often than not they buy. Often they have overpaid from foreign points of view.

Figure 6.2 shows the net outflow of long-term capital from Japan (direct investment plus portfolio investment in shares and bonds) for the years 1980 to 1991. From 1987 to 1990 the outflow averaged $100 billion per year. However, the outflow changed to an inflow of $36.6 billion in 1991. This was the first net inflow of long-term capital since 1980. The steep decline in the stock market in 1990–92 left investors with less cash to invest abroad. There has been some selling of foreign assets to pay for losses in Japan. However, the largest flow change has been foreigners' demand for Japanese securities. Total foreign purchases of stocks and bonds in 1991 were $115.3 billion, versus $34.7 billion in 1990. While foreign investors sold about $10 billion of equities each year from 1987 to 1990, they bought $45.7 billion net in 1991. This caused the yen to rise during 1991 as discussed in Chapters 2 and 11.

---

[4]Direct investment is when foreign interests own or control 10% or more of a U.S. business.

Table 6.5
Japan's Direct Foreign Investment, April to September 1989

Country	Investment, Billions	Growth Rate, %
Holland	$2.81	325%
Britain	2.44	23
Germany	0.68	296
France	0.55	272
U.S.	13.13	15
Canada	0.65	93
Asia	3.91	47
Hong Kong	0.94	na
Singapore	0.81	na
South Korea	0.37	na
Indonesia	0.33	na
Pacific Region	2.36	90
Australia	2.27	100
Latin America	2.76	-3.7

Figure 6.2
Japan's Net Long-Term Capital Flows, 1980–91

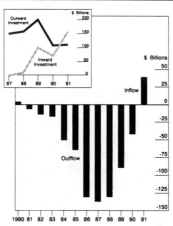

Source: Bank of Japan

SOME NOTABLE PURCHASES

Let's look at some of their purchases.

- The Hama Kikaku Tokyo real estate company bought the 4,900 square meter property of the St. Augustin Catholic Church at $45 million. The price per square meter was more than double the previous high in all of

Hawaii for the property on a main road facing Waikiki Beach. The church which began missionary activities in the 1830s is a local tourist attraction. Local residents called church officials to protest the land deal and bought protest advertisements in major newspapers. Church officials said they will build a new church on another site.

- Kirin Brewery purchased a 30% interest in Twyford International Inc., a Santa Paula, California, biotech firm, for $6.2 million. Kirin is now Twyford's largest shareholder and will send one director to the board of the firm which researches, produces and markets tissue culture plants. Tissue culture is a method of removing small fragments of tissue from plants and growing them in a culture medium. It is used to cultivate foliage and flowering plants.

- The Japanese, who like to ski, have purchased several major skiing resorts. The Victoria Company bought the Breckenridge resort in Colorado for $65 million in 1988. Breckenridge, which has about 100 acres, was priced at about 65 times 1988 earnings.

- Nomura International Ltd., a wholly owned subsidiary of Nomura Securities Co., the world's largest securities firm, acquired 3% of J. Francois Dufour-J.L. Kervern S.A., France's sixth largest securities firm for ¥100 million. Nomura increased its stake to 10% by 1990 to strengthen its business in Europe. It is the first such purchase of an equity stake in a French brokerage firm by a Japanese company and follows the lifting of a ban on foreign capital participation in French securities firms as part of its financial market reform program.

- Japanese investors bought several prime U.S. ranches, feedlots and packing houses. Zenchiku, a meat importer, bought the 80,000-acre Selkirk Ranch near Dillon, Montana, in October 1988 for $13 million. It plans to export 80% of the ranch's production to Japan. Japanese companies invested $50 to $100 million in the U.S. beef industry since 1987. Mt. Shasta Beef, a company formed by Masa Tanabe and three California cattle ranchers, spent $2.2 million for a 6,000-acre ranch in northern California. In August 1988, a Japanese import-export firm, Farmland Trading Co., bought a packer, Washington Beef Inc., of Yakima, for $200 million. It plans to export 45% of the output. Japanese bought a 1,490-hectare ranch in Nebraska and shares in Iowa Beef Processors Inc., a giant packer in Nebraska. These purchases have been encouraged by Japan's easing of imports of U.S. beef. The Japanese own only a small fraction of the industry because American producers have been getting into the market.[5] They are also buying cattle operations in Australia where the cattle are grass fed.

Now that Japan is opening its markets to more imported food, the Japanese are also acquiring U.S. food companies. A broad range of products is involved, including juice, soft drinks, processed meats and vegetables. Zennoh, the commercial group of Japan's National Federation of Agricultural Cooperative Associations, joined with C. Itoh to buy Consolidated Grain and Barge of St. Louis. Consolidated owns 33 grain elevators. Kagome Co., a maker of tomato products, has a processing plant in California, giving it access to tomatoes at one-fifth the cost in Japan. Glico Dairy Co. built a $5 million grapefruit processing plant in Florida. Naigai Chikusan, a livestock wholesaler, bought 50% of Colonial Beef Co. of Philadelphia. Hansen Foods has started bottling soft drinks under special labels for the Japanese market, sparking Japanese interest in acquiring the company. Kirin Brewery bought Coca-Cola Bottling Co. of northern New England, and it has signed a contract with Molson Breweries of Canada to bottle Japanese beer for sale in the U.S.

- Lucky Taxi Corp of Nagasaki acquired the 18-story 328-room Outrigger Malia Hotel in central Waikiki Beach for $30 million. The hotel, which had revenues of about $5 million in 1987, was formerly owned by Outrigger Hotels, Hawaii, which will operate the hotel for the next five years. Lucky Taxi is engaged in taxi, restaurant and real estate business in Fukuoka, Tokyo, and Nagasaki. Its travel agency division has sent 50,000 tourists to Hawaii since 1973.

- Akio Nishino, director of the art division of the fashionable Mitsukoshi Department store in the Nihonbashi section of Tokyo, bought Pablo Picasso's painting *Acrobat and Young Harlequin* for £20.9 million ($37.6 million U.S.) at Christies' auction house in London. Nishino is exhibiting the painting at the department store. The somber study of two circus figures dates to Picasso's Rose Period in the winter of 1905. *Acrobat and Young Harlequin* had been banned as decadent and was confiscated by the Nazis in occupied Europe in 1939. Just before the outbreak of World War II, the Picasso painting, with subtle blue and pink tones, passed into the hands of a Belgian collector and had been kept in private collections for the past four decades.

---

[5] In 1988, the U.S. exported 4,841 million head of beef to Japan. This was expected to grow by 30% for the next few years. Fully 42% of Japan's beef is from the U.S. up from 8% in 1976. U.S. exports to Korea are also growing. The Japanese taste is for fat beef.   Eight percent of U.S. beef went to Asia. The Japanese consume only 12 pounds of red meat per capita annually versus 75 pounds in the U.S.

This is not the highest price paid by a Japanese for a Picasso. The Japanese firm Nippon Autopolis bought *Les Noces de Piemetto*, a poignant group portrait from the painter's blue period, for 300 million French francs ($48.9 million) at the Droust-Montaigne auction house in Paris in November 1989. This is the current record for a Picasso surpassing the old record of $47.85 million for Picasso's *Yo Picasso* set in New York in April 1989. In November 1989, another Picasso, *Au Lapin Agile*, was bought for $40.7 million in New York.

Prices of the top paintings are so high that when Yasumichi Morishita, consultant and chairman of Aska International (a gallery with some of the world's best Impressionist art) in Tokyo and a major art collector bought *La Maternite* for £7.15 million ($11.2 million), well below its £10+ million estimate at a London auction in November 1989, he simply bought two more paintings with his excess cash. They were Monet's winter scene, *L'Eglise de Jeufosse*, for £3.85 million, and Renoir's *La Famille*, for £2.42 million. Morishita recently bought a 6.4% stake in Christie's. He owns 20 to 25 Monets. He plans to open a museum where he will display 30 paintings each season from his vast collection.

- Ryouhei Saito, 74, bought the world's two most expensive paintings at a Sotheby's auction in New York in 1991. Dutch artist Vincent van Gogh's *Portrait of Dr. Gachet* sold for $82.5 million, and Pierre-Auguste Renoir's *Au Moulin de la Galette* depiction of an outdoor Parisian dance hall went for $78.1 million. Saito's more that $160 million purchases were reportedly paid for with mortgage land money.[6] Apparently, by mid-1992, he has paid back about half his cost by charging high fees to see the paintings.

- Japanese steel makers want access to the U.S. market, and the U.S. steel makers want access to Japanese technology. This has led to numerous joint ventures with the Japanese supplying the capital, such as $350 million for a 40% stake in the Eastern Steel Division of Armco sold to Kawasaki Steel Corp. Some of the major Japanese-American joint ventures in steel are shown in Table 6.6.

- In 1989, Toray Industries acquired the 545-employee Samuel Courtland Division of Courtlands PLC of Nottingham, England, for ¥5.8 billion.

---

[6]The previous world record for a single work of art is for Dutch artist Vincent van Gogh's *Irises* sold at Sotheby's in London in 1987 for $53.9 million to Australian tycoon Alan Bond. To show the liquidity in the marketplace that leads to higher and higher prices for these top paintings, Bond borrowed half the money from Sotheby's and the other half from an Australian bank. None of the payment was cash. Bond subsequently got into a financial cash crunch and *Irises* was sold for an undisclosed sum to the Getty Museum in Malibu. The Japanese, however, usually pay cash, although Saito is an exception.

This division weaves and dyes heavyweight polyester filament. The purchase enables Toray to stay closer to trends in the European market as it develops textile products and applications for sale in Europe. The company was renamed Toray Textiles Europe Ltd. The Japanese parent provided executive personnel, including the chairman and managing directors. Courtlands PLC was the first fiber manufacturer to have commercialized chemical fibers. The new company makes, among other things, woven fabrics from heavyweight polyester filament for use in skirts, trousers, and dresses. Some 8 million yards were shipped in 1988.

- In 1986, Dainippon Ink and Chemicals (DIC) purchased the graphic art materials division of Sun Chemical, the world's largest ink maker, at a cost of ¥87 billion.

Table 6.6
Major U.S.-Japan Steel Ventures

Japanese*	U.S.	Date	details
Nippon Steel	Inland Steel	Jul 1987	auto cold-rolled sheet steel
		Sep 1989	auto surface treatment sheet steel
NKK	National Steel**	Aug 1984	capital participation
	⌠National Steel ⌡Dofasco	fall 1989	auto surface treatment sheet steel
Kawasaki Steel	Rio Dose (Brazil)	Jul 1984	acquired former Kaiser Steel Fontana works
	Armco	Mar 1989	Acquired Armco Middletown and Ashland works, carbon steel
Sumitomo Metal Industries	LTV	Jan 1985	auto surface treatment sheet steel, electrogalvanizing line
		May 1989	sheet steel
Kobe Steel	USX	Jul 1989	acquired USX Lorain steelworks
Nisshin Steel	Wheeling-Pittsburgh	Jul 1984	auto surface treatment sheet steel

*Other ventures include National Steel and Marubeni Corp for a slitting operation; Baker Hughes Inc. and Sumitomo Metal for steel-pipe; Armco Inc and C. Itoh, steel processing; and Steel Technologies and Mitsui for a service center.

**National Steel is the joint venture between National Intergroup Inc. and NKK Corp.

Source: *Tokyo Business Today*

- The Bank of Yokohama bought the British merchant bank Guiness Mahon Holdings PLC for £94.5 million. This is the first offer by a

Japanese company for a British investment bank and the largest public takeover bid by a Japanese company in Europe. It was a friendly takeover with the bank continuing to operate independently. The Japanese firm will have three seats on the expanded board of 12.

- In 1989, Canon, the camera and electronics giant, paid $100 million for a one-sixth interest in Steven Jobs' computer company NeXT. Canon is a major supplier of laser printers, copiers, and related office equipment. Jobs, whose personal $7 million investment is now worth $600 million, was a co-founder of Apple Computer, and his vision led to the development of the popular Macintosh computer. Jobs' NeXT machine utilizes advanced sound and visual features. NeXT did not need the Canon investment for production because it already had a factory that could produce $1 billion of product per year. The funds are earmarked for research and development into new components of future NeXT computers. This cements an important link via the printer technology. Both these are consistent with the Japanese long-term view of business.

- Roy Ormiston, one of Canada's most celebrated dairy cow breeders, auctioned off his herd of 75 cows and bulls in 1991 after 54 years in the business for more than $1 million. The average price was $14,000, but a seven-week-old bull calf sold for $140,000 to a Japanese buyer. Ormison is credited with substantially improving the Holstein breed and a statue of one of his bulls stands in Sapporo.

- Japanese have become large buyers of gold. In 1980, the retail price of gold reached a high of ¥6,495, or about $45, a gram. In February 1989, the price had fallen to a ten-year low of ¥1,500, or about $12, a gram. From the Depression in 1931 through World War II and in the post-war rebuilding, gold holdings were banned in Japan. Gold holdings were turned in during the war and, until 1968, the government banned private dealings in gold. Imports were not allowed until 1973, and exports were not permitted until 1978. Social attitudes and official rules limited sales to a trickle until 1978. The nation's prodigious savings was invested, and much of this was kept in savings accounts. The lifestyle reflected conservative habits; gold jewelry was rarely seen except among the rich and the aristocracy. Gold was a luxury and not for the common middle class. Extravagance was against society's norms.

Now, and especially after the shock of the October 1987 stock market crash, Japanese are buying gold by the ton. Some 240 tons were imported in the first ten months of 1988, with the year's sales expected to top 300 tons. Of this some 15.9 tons were gold coins, a 16-fold increase compared to 1980. Many customers are women who buy 500 gram bars for about $7,400. Privately held gold supplies, virtually non-existent in Japan at the end of World War II, now exceed 1,000 tons. France has the most in private hands at 6,000 tons collected over 200 years. With the tax changes eliminating the breaks from investment in low-yield bank and postal savings accounts, some of the estimated $4.72 trillion in private savings will find its way into gold. The government also has over one billion of its $70 billion foreign reserves in gold and major companies have vast holdings as well.

The infatuation for gold turned a bit to the bizarre. In some fancy Tokyo restaurants, there is gold leaf sushi, gold dappled omelets, gold leaf curry, golden curry, and gold ice cream, all made with thin sheets of gold leaf. In one restaurant near Tokyo, three or four dishes of the gold garnished sushi are sold each day at about $41 a piece.

Mitsubishi Metal Corp. is selling gold meishi (business cards) capitalizing on the importance of these cards in Japanese business. The cards contain one gram of pure gold coated with a thin film on which the bearer's name, position, etc., are printed. The cards sell for ¥6,000 with a guarantee by Mitsubishi to buy them back at the market price of gold, currently ¥1,686. It plans to add to the enjoyment of Japan's age of affluence with gold greeting cards and certificates.

One can also buy gold golf balls, that are 99% pure and weigh 810 grams, for ¥1.9 million from a firm on the Tokyo futures commodity exchange.

- Diamonds are also popular with the Japanese. Imports in 1988 were up 400% from 1987. And the buyers, mostly young wives of the super-rich, bought bigger and bigger stones. Unlike in the west where men buy jewelry as gifts for the women in their lives, Japanese women buy for themselves. But the men are catching on a bit; the average diamond engagement ring has risen in size from 0.3 to 1 carat.

- The Japanese have bought more top thoroughbred racehorses. A Japanese law taxes horses brought into the country by about $30,000. This tends to increase the quality of the blood stock because it does not pay to import cheap horses. Throughout the 1980s, the prices of the best thoroughbreds have been largely set by the friendly bidding of the four Maktoum brothers from the reigning family of Dubai, a Middle East oil kingdom, and the lottery magnate Robert Sangster. Now the Japanese have moved into the picture at the highest levels. At the July 1989 Keeneland sale, the highest priced yearling was a Northern Dancer colt that sold to Japanese horseman Zenya Yoshida for $2.8 million. Yoshida has also purchased a one-quarter interest in the 1989 Kentucky Derby winner, Sunday Silence, for $3 million. Later he bought the whole horse for a total price of $10 million. The horse now stands at his Hokkaido farm. In November 1989, the top sale again went to the Japanese, this time to Kazuo Nakamura who paid $4.6 million for Open Mind. At the January 1990 sale, 128 horses were sold for $7.9 million. The Japanese spent $3.4 million for 17 horses, including a sale topping $2.1 million for Goodbye Halo, who was purchased by golf course developer and manager Yoshio Asakawa. After winning the 1988 Japan Cup, Pay the Butter, a California horse, was sold to Koichiro Hayata, a veterinarian who operates Hayata Farms on Hokkaido. Hayata has been very active in purchasing other U.S. stallions and mares for himself and other Hokkaidan's. Tomonari Tsurumaki bought the sale topper, a $2.9 million yearling, at the July 1990 Keeneland sale. The colt, A.P. Indy by Seattle Slew, whose dam is a Secretariat brood mare, is a leading three-year-old in 1992.

- Kentucky issued a 10-year yen denominated bond (known as Samurai bond) to raise ¥10 billion.

- TDK bid $200 million for Silicon Systems, a California firm which produces semiconductors for machines related to personal computers.

- Japan imported a record 127 helicopters, with 80% coming from the U.S. and France.

- Japan oil firms are planning U.S. exploration: a joint venture by Nippon Oil and Chevron Corp. in the Gulf of Mexico that has so far drilled 50 wells; a Nippon Oil joint venture with Texaco in Alaska that is producing; acquisitions of partial drilling rights by Idemitsu Kosan Co. in the Gulf of Mexico from Frances' Societe Nationale Elf Aquitaine and offshore California from Atlantic Richfield Co.; and a 1988 venture between Japan Petroleum Exploration Co. and Tenneco in the Gulf of Mexico.

- NKK has contracted with Battel Memorial Institute of the U.S. to jointly develop vaccines for virus-related respiratory disease.

- Nissan invested $500 million to double its capacity in the U.S. to 440,000 units, bringing its total U.S. investment to more than $1.2 billion.

- Suncall Sanko Corp. the U.S. subsidiary of Sanko Senzai Kogyo Co. will form a joint venture with Peterson American Corp. to produce transmissions in Detroit. The parts will be sold to Toyota, Nissan, and Honda.

- Aisan Industry Co., an auto parts maker affiliated with Toyota Motor, has set up a wholly owned subsidiary in Franklin, Kentucky, called Franklin Precision Industry, to supply parts to Toyota and other Japanese auto makers in the U.S. It will build a plant to manufacture fuel injection parts.

- Japan Storage Battery Co. and Exide Electronics Groups of the U.S. have a joint venture to market backup power sources for computers in Japan. They aim to acquire 10% of the domestic market. Exide will make those for large computers, while JSB will make them for personal computers.

- Boeing is discussing a joint venture with three Japanese companies to develop and produce its next airplane, a wide body jet to carry 285 to 350 passengers.

  The total market for planes is expected to be 850 to 900 a year for the next ten years to be shared among Boeing, McDonnell Douglas and Airbus Industrie. Boeing has a backlog of 1,600 orders so it will subcontract. It is moving more and more into being a designer, assembler, and marketer rather than an integrated manufacturer. To succeed in this, it must find reliable suppliers that can do their own R&D.

  It has nothing in the niche created by Airbus (300 passengers and 4,000 miles). So it is attempting to redesign its 200-passenger 767. Boeing has worked well with Mitsubishi Heavy Industries, Kawasaki Heavy Industries, and Fuji Heavy Industries. Japan accounts for one-third of Boeing's orders.

- Taiyo Kogyo has acquired a 50% stake in O.C. Birdair which makes roof sheeting for domed stadiums in the U.S. It hopes to expand into Europe and the Middle East. It acquired the stake from Owens-Corning Fiberglas. The remaining 50% is held by Chemical Fabrics Corp. of New Hampshire.

- Kao bought 75% of the stock of Goldwell Germany's second largest maker of hairdressing and cosmetic products. It plans to acquire the remaining 25% in five years and will establish a marketing network in Europe.

- Sumitomo Metal Industries Ltd. has a plan for a joint plant with LTV Steel for producing electrogalvanized steel, corrosion resistant sheet steel, to be sold to U.S. and Japanese auto makers with plants in the U.S. in time for the 1992 model year (October 1991). It will be run by L-S II Electro-Galvanizing Co. Each firm is contributing $100 million and 100 employees and it will be sited in Columbus, Ohio. They also have been operating a facility in Cleveland since April 1986, which produces 360,000 to 400,000 tons per year.

- JDC, a general construction company, signed a cooperation contract with McDevitt and Street Co. a major U.S. construction firm. They will exchange technology, personnel and information on projects in the U.S. and Japan. M&S will open an office in Japan, and JDC will help. M&S is the fourth largest construction firm in the U.S and mainly builds hospitals and luxury hotels.

- Futaba Industrial Co., an auto muffler maker, has entered a technical venture with Walker Manufacturing Co., a U.S. auto parts maker, to supply mufflers to Japanese auto makers overseas. Futaba will provide expertise on development and quality control for Walker. Walker has factories in North America, Australia, and Europe. They are already cooperating for the Canadian and Australian-based Japanese auto makers.

- Toray Industries and Monsanto Chemical, which is affiliated with Mitsubishi, will form a 50-50 joint venture to be located in Detroit to produce nylon resin compounds for sale to Japanese customers operating in the U.S. Toray has been working with auto, electrical, and electronics industries to develop new types of nylon compounds.

THE FAST PACE OF JAPANESE INVESTMENTS IN THE UNITED STATES

The large number of U.S. acquisitions reflects a belief that the U.S. will be one good base for internationalization of Japanese businesses. In 1989, Japanese institutions helped finance 50% of new housing starts in California (*Business Week*, April 23, 1990). From 1983 to 1991, the 12 Japanese banks were the major source of U.S. commercial credit.

The largest number of buyers were in commerce, some 18.8% by major trading houses. The chemical industry was next with 10%. When Sony Corporation purchased Columbia Pictures, this was described as selling the world series or mom; yet this was soon followed by the purchase of the Rockefeller Center and the linkup with Michael Jackson. Even the trademark *Indy* for the Indianapolis Motor Speedway was sold to a Japanese real estate company. The company plans to build a high-speed oval race track near Tokyo to host an Indy-car race by about 1994.

The Sony purchase of Columbia Pictures at $4.2 billion set a record in 1989. Subsidiary deals associated with this purchase put the total size of this one acquisition at about $5 billion. Sony's stake in the U.S. reached $7 billion or 12 times the net income in FY 1989. Matsushita Electric Industrial's purchase of MCA, parent of Universal Studios in December 1990 was a larger deal of 97% of $6.27 billion. The total acquisition price was $6.46 billion and the deal closed in early 1991.

The value of publicly reported Japanese investment in the U.S. in 1988 was at least $8.4 billion for 45 corporations and $16.54 billion in real estate for a total of nearly $29 billion. Table 6.7 shows the largest purchases in 1988, which were all companies except for Seibu/Saison's $2.15 billion purchases of the Intercontinental Hotel complex. The latter was purchased at an extremely high 41 times earnings. Presumably with Japan's increasing tourism abroad and the Seibu/Saison large hold on travel with its 6 million credit card holders, this should be a good purchase. The chain has hotels on several continents, including such landmarks as the Mark Hopkins in San Francisco and the Willard in Washington, D.C.

The strong yen, high corporate profits in Japan, low price earnings ratios (PERs) in the U.S. and an increasingly aggressive attitude towards foreign acquisitions led to more of this activity in 1988 and 1989. Many Japanese companies are looking for production plants and distribution channels in the U.S. So far, essentially all of the acquisitions, mergers and takeovers are friendly. However, hostile takeovers may not be far away. The two largest purchases in 1988 beat the previous record of $2 billion paid by Sony for the CBS record business that produces the recordings of such stars as Michael Jackson and Bruce Springsteen. The scale of these activities has also increased. In 1988, the tenth largest acquisition was for $300 million U.S. compared with $45 million in 1987. Japanese commercial banks, particularly Sumitomo, are playing a larger role in this activity and were the lead advisor in six of the ten largest transactions. Also, Nomura, Nikko, and Yamaichi securities each bought stakes in U.S. merger boutiques in 1988 signaling their growing interest in this activity. But as the 1980s ended, the financial excesses of the debt decade began to take their toll and the takeover era and the very high yielding junk bonds used to finance these activities became a thing of the past.

By 1990, of the nine largest acquisitions in the U.S., only the largest, Matsushita Electric Industrial's purchase of MCA, was by a Japanese firm.

Table 6.7
The Ten Largest Japanese Acquisitions in the U.S. in 1988

Japanese Acquirer	U.S. Target (Parent)	Price $mils	Japanese Advisor (U.S. Advisor)
Bridgestone	Firestone	2600	Sumitomo Bank/Lazard Freres (Goldman Sachs/Blackstone Group)
Seibu/Saison	Intercontinental Hotels	2150	LTCB-Peers
Group	(Grand Metropolitan PLC)		(Morgan Stanley)
Nippon Mining	Gould	1100	IBJ-Schroder (First Boston)
Paloma Industries	Pace Industries/ Pheem Mfg	850	Sumitomo Bank (Shearson Lehman/Merrill Lynch)
Calif. First Bank (Bank of Tokyo)	Union Bank of Calif. (Standard Chartered)	750	None (Goldman Sachs)
Settsu	Uarco (Kohlberg Kravis Roberts)	550	Sumitomo Bank/First Union Bank (Merrill Lynch)
Shiseido	Zotos International (Conair)	345	Daiwa Securities (None)
Jusco	Talbots (General Mills)	325	Dai-Ichi Kangyo Bank/Paribas (Dillon Read)
Ryobi	Motor Products Division (Singer)	325	Bankers Trust (Shearson Lehman)
Kao	Andrew Jergens (American Brands)	300	None (Morgan Stanley)

Source: Ulmer Brothers Inc. reported in the *Asian Wall Street Journal*

The Japanese have a long way to go to replace the British, who have been investing in the U.S. since colonial days, as the leader in direct investment. But they did move up fast (see Table 6.8). As of early 1992, they were above the Dutch but still trailing the British in total investment. Total direct foreign investment in the U.S. increased 10.5% and a further 21% in 1988.

Japanese companies were number one in terms of sales, which increased 9.4%. Although employment increased 28.9% (284,000), they still ranked only fourth.

Table 6.8
Cumulative Direct Foreign Investment in the U.S., Billions of
Dollars, 1989–91

	1983	1987	1988
Britain	32.1	74.9	81.9
Japan	11.3	33.3	44.8
Netherlands	29.1	47.0	52.0

Much of the Japanese non real estate purchases in the U.S. are in direct investments in cognate companies to strengthen their U.S. presence and in new factories to produce products. These include the following:

- A $2.6 billion merger with Firestone Tire and Rubber by Bridgestone, Japan's largest tire maker,
- A $660 million Nissan plant to build light trucks in Smyrna, Tennessee,
- Toyota's $800 million Camry plant in Kentucky; a second plant is currently under construction to build an additional 200,000 cars per year,
- Sony's $20-million video disc plant, its seventh in the U.S,
- Hitachi's purchase of Systems Magnetic, its sixth plant, and
- Mineba was negotiating a seventh plant.

A study of Martin Starr (1987) gives the Japanese firms top results. The development of a newly merged U.S./Japanese style leads to a lower rate of defective goods (95% of the plants had 5% or fewer versus the U.S. average of 10%), and less absenteeism (95% had 5% or less versus 8%).

The Japanese became such a major player on the U.S. scene that when anything is placed on the block rumors quickly fly about potential Japanese purchasers. For example, it was reported and denied that Tokyu was interested in Bloomingdale's, part of the troubled Campeau Corporation.

INVESTMENTS FOR THE VERY LONG TERM

In typical Japanese fashion, investors are also thinking about the non-real assets and the long term. Japanese firms are endowing chairs and programs at U.S. universities. This is often perceived as a threat, but perhaps it should be considered a boon and a good example of corporate citizenship. As of July 1988, 16 chairs at about $1.5 million each have been endowed at MIT, as shown in Table 6.9. Chalmers Johnson estimates that 80% of the money for research about Japan comes from Japanese sources.

More than 50 Japanese companies pay up to $100,000 per year for access to pre-published papers at schools such as MIT and Stanford. For a

Table 6.9
Japanese Endowed Chairs at MIT

Dai-Ichi Kangyo Bank	Finance
Fujitsu	Electrical engineering
Fukutake Publishing	Media laboratory
Kokusai Denshin Denwa	Media laboratory
Kyocera	Material sciences
Matsushita	Electrical engineering
Mitsubishi Bank	Finance
Mitsui	International mgt, contemporary technology (2)
NEC	Computers/communications software
Nippon Steel	Civil engineering/policy
Nomura Securities	Finance
TDK	Materials
Toyota	Materials

Source: *Business Week*, July 11, 1988

donation of $500,000 the firm can send researchers to university labs; a favored one is the Media Laboratory at MIT. In turn, through the connections established, MIT is sending 20 students to Japanese labs. This program is sponsored by U.S. companies. Japanese companies donated $4 million to build a computer laboratory at the University of California, Berkeley.

Japanese companies are setting up research labs at U.S. colleges. The Japanese have long supported research projects and fellowships and endowed professorships but now they are also paying for the buildings. The Hitachi Chemical Ltd. Lab at University of California, Irvine, cost $15 million. Hitachi has a 40-year lease on the site, after which it will revert to the university. Some projects are listed in Table 6.10.

Silicon Valley is attracting more Japanese companies. They are willing to supply patient capital as well as access to Japanese manufacturing expertise and entrée into Japan's and Asia's growing markets. They are apparently less driven by capital gain and more driven by the creation of partnerships, technology transfer, and joint product development. Venture Economics estimates that, from January 1988 to the end of June 1989, $380 million was invested in 64 startups, including $100 million for Canon's 16%

Table 6.10

Japanese Research Laboratories in the U.S.

Company	University	Subject
Otsuka Pharmaceutical	Univ. of Washington Biomembrane Institute	Medicine
Kobe Steel	N. Carolina State Univ.	Diamond films
NEC	Princeton	Advanced computers
Hitachi Chemical	University of California, Irvine	Chemistry

purchase of NeXT. Nippon Steel, Kobe Steel and Kubota are very active. Kubota has spent over $120 million on six electronics startups. Technology from these has led to the assembly of mini-supercomputers in a Japanese factory.

CANADA

Japan, as of early 1992, was Canada's largest creditor in the bond market with over $35 billion. Direct investment in Canada has doubled in the two years 1988 to 1990, and $4.5 billion of British Columbia's $18 billion exports went to Japan.

Many firms have been announcing joint ventures and other forms of investment in Canada especially since the beginning of the free trade agreement with the U.S. The Japanese are now trading more actively than in the past and are looking at short-term bonds, bills, and notes. Their interest in Canadian stocks is still minimal.[7] Direct investment was $626 million in 1988, for a cumulative $3.2 billion. With only 2% of the total Japanese investment, compared with 46% for the U.S., the Canadian government perception is that Canada is not getting its share of Japanese investment. It is believed that Canada should be able to attract 4 to 5% of Japanese investment, and the government is lobbying to attract more. A delegation of 50 senior businesspeople from Japan, led by the president of Mitsubishi

---

[7]Poor long-term performance of Canadian equities may be part of the reason for this. But more plausible is the fact that the Japanese simply are more comfortable with banks.

Corp., Shinroku Mosobashi, made a ten-day investment tour of Canada. If limits are placed on foreign investment in the U.S., this should help Canada.

AUTOMOBILE MANUFACTURING INVESTMENT

The Toyota Motor manufacturing (TMMC) plant, a $400 million project in Cambridge, Ontario, was attracted to Canada by access to skilled labor force, low energy costs, and low medical and social security overhead (social security costs U.S.$3,000 per person in the U.S. and only C$400 in Canada). Toyota is striving for 50% North American content to meet the free trade rules. It has been judged the most efficient plant in North America.

TMMC recruited people with certification in various skills not necessarily auto production. Only 2% had prior auto assembly experience, though 15 to 20% of the managers had experience in the auto industry. Toyota began training employees in August 1988. Bill Easdale, vice president of administration, comments on the extensive training program: four months at TMMC, a one-week orientation, one month in Japan, two months at Conestoga College (the local college worked with Toyota to develop courses and even sent personnel to Japan), and back to TMMC for more training. The new employees work on a special training line and then move onto the middle of the regular shift for four hours under the supervision of Japanese trainers and their team and group leaders (teams of five to seven undergo training). This experience continues for two weeks. There are two rates of pay: the assembly workers begin at 85% and reach the full rate of $17.25 in 18 months; maintenance workers get 95% and reach the full rate of $19.92 at the end of six months.

Cambridge is noticing the development of an industrial psychology from the impact of Toyota. After Toyota announced the plans, other investment money began to flow to the town (they say within 48 hours). The unemployment rate fell from 22% to 4 to 7%.

Language courses were quickly made available: Japanese classes were offered so that the children could maintain their Japanese schooling. English classes were offered for families of the Japanese employees. The Japanese felt comfortable in the area. It was easy for them to buy Japanese food near the University of Waterloo and they appreciated the natural environment.

Toyota Canada began a second shift in October 1989 and produces about 50,000 cars per year from its $400 million plant. In one year, total employment increased from 500 to 900. The plant builds only Corolla four-door sedans.

Fifty percent of the steel for the body panels is purchased from Stelco and Dofasco; the punching of the steel blanks is done by A. G. Simpson at Oakville, and the stamping is completed in their Cambridge plant. Twenty Canadian and many U.S. suppliers are involved. The major imports from Japan included in the cars are specialty anti-corrosion steel, car transmissions, and engines. Planning is needed to ensure just-in-time delivery. Stelco has announced a possible joint venture with Mitsubishi in which Mitsubishi will become a half owner in Stelco's new $200 million manufacturing plant. As the car meets the 50% North American content rule, 60% of the production goes to the U.S. under the Free Trade Agreement (FTA).

The plant is the smallest built in Canada by Japanese and Korean auto makers. There is room for a further doubling of capacity at Cambridge. Hyundai is producing 100,000 cars in Bromont, Quebec; Honda 80,000 at Alliston, Ontario, and CAMI of Ingersoll (joint venture of GM and Suzuki) will produce 200,000.[8]

Six Japanese companies have set up an auto parts manufacturing and sales company one of which is Canada Mold Technology to manufacture metal molds of experimental plastic auto parts for Japanese auto and auto parts makers in Canada and the U.S. It is capitalized at $275 million, with 51% put up by Magase, Japan's top trader in chemical products, and 20% by Asahi Chemical Industry Co. The remaining 29% is held by four Japanese makers of auto metal molds, including Nihon Proto Corp. It is located in Woodstock, Ontario.

OTHER INDUSTRIAL INVESTMENT

Canada has also seen Japanese investment outside the auto industry. Sanyo has agreed to a joint venture with Mosaid of Canada to develop and produce 4-megabit dynamic RAM chips.

Sumitomo Heavy Industries acquired Lumonics Inc., a Canadian laser equipment maker. Lumonics had asked to join the Sumitomo group because diversifying its products requires technology and funds. Sumitomo bought 96% of its stock for about ¥10 billion. This is the first Japanese firm to make a takeover bid for shares of a Canadian company. The government initially objected on the grounds that Lumonics' laser

---

[8]In 1992, the U.S. ruled that the Honda Civics produced in Canada failed to meet the 50% North American content requirement for duty-free entry into the U.S.

oscillators are also used by the military, but it approved the deal under assurances that the present leadership will continue to run the company. Lumonics is the world's number two producer of integrated laser equipment. Sumitomo has been selling Lumonics' products in Southeast Asia and Japan. Possible development of machine tools and medical systems combining Lumonics' laser oscillation technology and Sumitomo's precision instruments technology is being considered.

Nagase and Co. and Asahi Chemical Industry Co. will set up Canada Mold Technology Inc., a plastic mold production company, in Toronto, to supply parts for Japanese auto makers in North America. It is capitalized at C\$2.5 million or ¥275 million, with Nagase investing 51%, Asahi 20%, and four other Japanese mold makers for the remaining 29%.

Minebea Co., the world's top miniature bearing manufacturer, will establish in Canada Manitoba Breeders Canada Co., a large-scale hog-raising subsidiary for ¥2 billion.

The Alberta government has leased forest land equivalent to the size of Britain to six pulp companies. After the fact, the government agreed to an environmental assessment for the Alberta-Pacific Forest Industries Ltd. mill, a \$1.3 billion bleached kraft mill about 100 kms northeast of Edmonton. Alberta-Pacific is controlled by Mitsubishi Corp and Honshu Paper Co. This project has received approval and is underway.

In October 1991, Daishowa Paper Mfg. Co. of Japan announced that it would sell its Canadian pulp and paper subsidiary in Alberta to a joint venture it owns with Marubeni Corp. This is part of a plan to reduce Daishowa's debt by \$3.78 billion. While the factory cost about \$1 billion to build, they are asking \$756 million. Also at issue are the claims of the Lubicon Cree Indians to the land that would be logged.

An investment with a long-term payback is the 1991 purchase by Mitsubishi of a 5% share of the Syncrude project.

Table 6.11
Japanese Investment in Canadian Bonds and Stocks in 1990

By type of debt			By type of institution	
Bonds				
Federal government		$22.3	Life insurance companies	$23.6
Fed. govt. enterprises		0.6	Trust banks	2.4
Provincial government		4.5	Government	7.2
Prov. govt. enterprises		3.6	Investment trusts and	1.7
Municipal government		0.4	management companies	
Private corporate		4.3	Non-life insurance	2.4
Treasury bills		0.1	Banks	6.0
	Bonds Total	36.7	Leasing companies	0.4
Stocks		0.4		
Loans		7.8		
	Overall Total	43.6	Total	43.6

Source: Canadian Embassy in Japan

Japanese institutional investors, particularly the life insurance companies, hold $43.6 billion in Canadian bonds, stocks, and direct loans to the Canadian government and public corporations according to a survey conducted by the Canadian Embassy in Tokyo for the 1990 fiscal year which ended in March 1991. Most of the money, some $36.7 billion, is in bonds with $7.8 billion in loans and only $400 million in stocks. Another $2.4 billion in investment is estimated to have not been captured by the survey. The survey received detailed responses from 92 financial houses, including insurance companies, government institutions, trust banks, long-term credit banks and commercial banks (see Table 6.11). The life insurance companies hold about $23.6 billion, almost 60% of the total, and the fire and marine insurers have some $2.4 billion more. Each insurance company has large stakes. The four largest insurers hold more than $2.5 billion; six more have over $1 billion, and five others have more than $750 million. Total investment in Canada increased slightly over 1989 largely because of the high bond and loan yields. Japanese investors hold 24% of all Canadian bonds held by non-residents and fully 41% of non-resident holdings of Government of Canada bonds. This investment is part of the reason for the strength of the Canadian dollar from 1989–92. Their investment, or lack of it, greatly affects the Canadian dollar. Concern with Quebec separatism, a reduction in the spread over U.S. interest rates, as well as the rejection of free trade status for Japanese Hondas made in Canada all led to some

Japanese selling Canadian dollars in early 1992. This contributed to a fall of 5¢ in the Canadian dollar. Overall in 1990, the Japanese were net sellers of U.S.$16 billion in U.S. securities, $2 billion in German securities and $1.1 billion in Australian securities. Other net purchases of securities include $860 million Canadian, $1.9 billion British, and $5.5 billion French securities.

AUSTRALIA

Japan was the largest direct investor in Australia with A$5.4 billion (a 69% increase) of the total approved investment of A$24.8 billion in 1988. Investment from Britain rose 124% to A$4.7 billion. Investment from New Zealand fell 20% to A$2.8 billion, and from the U.S. fell 53% to A$1.7 billion. Almost 60% of the Japanese investment went into tourist facilities and other real estate mainly in Queensland and New South Wales.

Daishowa Paper Manufacturing Co. is planning to build two pulp plants in Australia, one in New South Wales, and one in Tasmania for a total cost of ¥200 billion and a combined capacity of 800,000 tons.

Nippon Shinpan Co., jointly with Australia and New Zealand Banking Group Ltd., will handle overseas real estate backed loans.

The Japanese leisure giant EIE, the largest investor in Australian property, is considering a stake in Qantas Airways as well as Australia's domestic airline, Australian Airlines. EIE owns the Sanctuary Cove Resort in Queensland and acquired a stake in Air Pacific, Fiji's airline and Air Caledonia.

New Zealand has put 550,000 hectares of softwood plantations or about half its commercial forests up for sale.

EUROPE

Europe is also generating increased interest from Japan in preparation for the united market of 1992. The European Community (EC) represents about one-fourth of world gross national product.

The Japanese are buying property in France. Paris, at $740 per square meter per year, has the world's fourth highest office rentals behind Tokyo at $2,060, London at $1,650, and Hong Kong at $1,115. Japanese property developers have increased their holdings of French commercial property from FFr500 million to FFr7 billion. Golf courses are a bargain with the cost per hole only 1 to 18 in comparison with Tokyo. The Japanese are second behind the British with FFr10 billion. While the British increased their holdings 20% last year, the Japanese increased theirs 30%. Kowa accounts for 50% of Japanese investment in France. C. Itoh is also heavily invested. Japanese life insurance companies are also beginning to invest.

The EC's trade deficit with Japan in 1988 was ¥3 trillion.

Europe battled Japanese imports successfully but now finds that the Japanese are producing locally. One study indicated that there are only three major industries in which Europe is more competitive than Japan: pharmaceuticals, chemicals, and telecommunications equipment, and a few areas where Japan is dominant but where Europe still has a presence: autos, consumer electronics, and industrial equipment.

The pace of Japanese investment is accelerating: in the U.K., 50 plants opened between 1971 and 1986; and 50 more from 1987 to 1989. Japanese firms have made 365 manufacturing investments in the EC. Margaret Thatcher encouraged Japanese investment and by 1989 the U.K. had 35% of all Japanese investment in Europe. To counter this, France attempted to impose an 80% European content on Nissan's British Bluebird cars. Table 6.12 shows Japanese cumulative investment in Europe in four manufacturing sectors. In 1989, direct Japanese investment in EC countries is about $8.6 billion.

Table 6.12
Cumulative Japanese Investment in European Industries, US$ millions, March 31

	1988	1983
Electronics/electrical	704	226
General machinery	365	145
Cars, trucks, transport	797	115
Pharmaceuticals, chemicals	347	158

Source: *The Asian Wall Street Journal*

Incentives to lure Japanese manufacturing have been large. Fujitsu received £30 million for a £400 million microchip factory in northeastern England. Robert Bosch of West Germany also received assistance for a 320 million mark car generator plant. U.S. local governments have used this tactic. Ohio won the Honda plant, which promised 3,000 jobs by providing a $22 million package. Kentucky paid five times as much to get the Toyota plant in 1985.

Autos

British plants of Toyota, Nissan and Honda expect to be producing 500,000 cars per year in the mid-1990s.

Toyota is building a $1 billion plant in Britain without state aid to avoid delays in approval and criticism by European rivals. Toyota is being offered other concessions. The Derbyshire County Council offered to put £20 million of its pension fund's £450 million into Toyota shares, the biggest investment it has made, and it will convert a mansion, which is surrounded by a golf course 10 kms from Burnaston, into apartments for Toyota executives. Toyota wants to establish a strong presence and expects to produce 200,000 cars by 1992.

Nissan's U.K. plant has been producing Bluebirds since 1986. They expect to make 200,000 by 1992. Some of these will be exported to Japan. Honda produces 5,000 per year with the Rover Group at a plant in England and it expects to produce 40,000 cars by 1992.

A gentlemen's agreement limits Japan to 12% of the EC auto market. Japanese auto makers, Nissan with the Infiniti and Toyota with the Lexus, are now competing head on with the prestige European auto makers Daimler-Benz, BMW and Porsche first in the U.S. and soon in Germany itself.

Germany's share of the luxury auto market is still 80% in Europe, 78% in the U.S. and 85% in Japan. But this could be changing as the Japanese producers move upscale. Four out of ten U.S. buyers of the Lexus are trading in German cars.

ELECTRONICS

NEC and Fujitsu expect to invest in semiconductor plants, Matsushita plans a highly automated fax machine plant, its 15th factory in Europe.

Fujitsu plans to build an integrated chip plant in northeast England for £400 million. Many others have only assembly plants, but this step will give Fujitsu duty-free access in the EC. Toshiba, the largest maker of one-megabit dynamic random access memory chips will likely also build a plant either alone or as a joint venture with a European firm. NEC, the first, built in Scotland in 1987. The Japanese have 40% of the market in Denmark, Ireland, and Greece, countries with no domestic production; while they have only 3% in France, Italy, and Spain. To avoid charges of dumping, Japan chip makers set a floor price. Sony and Matsushita have been charged with dumping CD players.

Dai Nippon Printing will produce wide-screen projection TVs in Denmark, with no built in picture tube, through a 100% owned subsidiary.

Toshiba will provide Siemens A.G. of Germany with gate array design technology (semi-finished integrated chips for computers and electronic equipment that can be wired in various ways to enable manufacturers to speed up deliveries).

Sanyo Electric Co. plans a joint venture plant to produce facsimile machines with Olivetti. The plant will be capitalized at U.S.$8 million with Olivetti investing 51%, Sanyo 39%, and Mitsui 10%. Of the annual production of 200,000 units, half will be sold in Europe under the Olivetti name and half under Sanyo's.

OTHER INVESTMENTS

Japan's European investments are numerous and various as the following demonstrates:

- Italy will allow foreign banks to be lire bond lead-managers and is looking for reciprocity. Hitachi Construction is working in Italy on a joint venture with Geotech, the construction machinery arm of Fiat.

- Suntory, in a joint venture with Garantie Mutuelle des Fonctionnaires, a French insurance company, will manufacture and sell fine wines. Gagrands Millesimes de France capitalized at FFr674 million is 81% French owned and 19% Suntory. Suntory has proposed to increase its share to 40% if approved by the French government. The insurance company has two wineries in Bordeaux (including Chateau Beychevelle) and has been selling fine wine since 1984. Sales in 1988 totaled ¥1.5 billion Suntory has wine producing facilities in Germany and the U.S.

- Idemitsu Oil Development Co. and the state-owned Japan National Oil Corp. together bought about 4.7% of the North Sea Shore oil field from the Norwegian state oil corporation. The field has an exploitable oil reserve of $700 to $800 million barrels.

- The Japan Highways Public Corporation issued bonds for 150 million in European currency units in June 1989. Fees were high at 9.17%.

- Mitsubishi Trust and Banking Corp. was the first Japanese trust bank to be listed in London. As part of the expansion into Europe, Nomura Securities bought a $93 million stake in Banco Santander, Spain's fifth largest bank and owner of the largest investment bank there.

- Sumitomo Electric will establish a West German subsidiary to produce cemented carbide tools.

- Sekisui Jushi Co. and Hunter Douglas NV of the Netherlands set up a joint venture to produce blinds in Holland for assembly and sale in Japan.

- There is a plan for a fiber optic cable to Europe via the CIS which would be 17,000 kms long.

- Mitsubishi Corp. and Meiji Milk Products bought a combined 21.7% share in Bio Isolates PLC a British protein manufacturer, for $2.85 million.

- Nestle KK, a wholly owned subsidiary of Nestle S.A., formed a joint venture with Fujiya, a Japanese confectioner (called Nestle Mackintosh KK) to market chocolate and products of Rowntree Mackintosh Confectionery, a subsidiary of Rowntree PLC a British company, that Nestle purchased.

- The Japanese are buying luxury goods in France including cognac. Comité Colbert is an association mandated to promote the French *art of living* and to protect the luxury industry from cheap rivals.

- Swissair and JAL are working together to bring Europe and Japan closer. They introduced a non-stop trans-Siberian flight from Zurich to Tokyo. Swissair will provide DC-10s for the service, and JAL will be responsible for half the seats and will provide some flight attendants. The time to Tokyo is less than 12 hours while the return trip with a stopover in Moscow will take under 14 hours. The current flight takes 18 via the North Pole with a short stopover in Anchorage.

EASTERN EUROPE

Japan is poised to take advantage of the opening of Eastern Europe, especially the big trading houses. In 1991, Prime Minister Kaifu offered $2 billion in soft loans and technical aid to Poland and Hungary.

Japanese activity in the CIS has been slowed by the need to negotiate the status of four islands claimed by the Japanese that the USSR occupied following WWII. Once these are turned over to Japan, trade and investment opportunities will be very attractive to the Japanese and will benefit the development of the CIS.

Even by 1990 a number of projects were already under consideration:[9]

- A joint venture for petrochemical development in Western Siberia with Combustion Engineering Inc., of the U.S., Neste Oy of Finland, Mitsubishi, Mitsui and the Ministry of Chemical & Oil Refining Industry of Soviet Union. Total investment is $2.2 billion. Mitsubishi

---

[9]Japan in the 1990s, *Tokyo Business Today*, January 1990.

Corp. is the sole coordinator in another petrochemical project for western Siberia. Mitsui and Chiyoda Corp and Combustion Engineering will also participate.

- A joint venture lumber mill in Siberia with C. Itoh & Co.

- A natural gas development on Sakhalin.

- A fertilizer plant in the Amur River region with Marubeni and Mitsui considering.

Marubeni is considering meat and fruit juice processing and export in Hungary; an appliance repair plant in joint venture with a Japanese appliance manufacturer; a joint venture with Bulgarian state-run pharmaceutical company to establish a trade company in Japan; and consignment production of men's clothing in Romania.

Other smaller projects also being considered for Eastern Europe are: a joint venture by Toyo Menka Kaisha Ltd., seventh largest sogo sosha, to produce glass fiber in Hungary for export to the USSR; a joint venture by C. Itoh and Suzuki Motor to produce compact cars in Hungary; Mitsubishi plans a development-import for garden furniture; and a production plant for Daihatsu cars by Sumitomo and Mitsui in Poland.

Sumitomo is to purchase half of the silicate of soda produced in Poland. Mitsui is negotiating to introduce an account settlement method in Bulgaria so that a ¥10 billion plant will be paid off through products.

Before the breakup of the USSR, the Soviets had commissioned Japanese firms to build 103 ships including 200,000 ton tankers and a deluxe passenger ship. They were looking for credit and wanted delivery between 1991 and 1993.

ASIA

Japan is becoming the engine of growth and stability for many countries in Asia and an economic sphere is evolving. Table 6.13 gives the cumulative Japanese investment in Asia as of 1989. The Taiwanese are installing rooftop satellite dishes to receive Japanese television broadcasts, and Japanese designers and pop music are becoming popular. More magazines are available in Japanese than English. In Korea, it is still illegal to import Japanese music, but bootlegged copies are available. Singapore tour guides are learning Japanese. Hong Kong sends trade missions to Tokyo. Japanese consumers buy Taiwanese bicycles and Korean video cassette recorders. Japan's imports from Asia rose almost 70% from 1986 to 1988, compared with 32% from the U.S.

Table 6.13 Cumulative Japanese Investment in Asia, as of 1989

Country	Investment	Employment
China	2.3	28,775
Hong Kong	7.1	38,494
Indonesia	10.1	61,611
Malaysia	2.1	70,324
Philippines	1.2	36,183
Singapore	4.6	67,441
South Korea	3.6	179,269
Taiwan	1.9	171,851
Thailand	2.6	109,831

Source: Ministry of Finance

It is no longer the lure of cheap Asian labor that attracts Japanese investment. Workers are no longer cheap nor docile. Labor shortages are a problem in Taiwan, Hong Kong, and Singapore. Taiwan's manufacturing sector is short 200,000 workers in footwear, construction, knitwear and toys. Hong Kong also has 200,000 vacancies especially in construction, hotel, retail and garment industries. Singapore needs 80,000 workers. Japan's interest transcends cheap labor.

Japanese auto makers are aware of the potential growth of production, income and demand in Asia. Nomura Research Institute projects that by 2,000 only Indonesia and the Philippines will have less than $2,000 income per capita, the level that brings high car purchases. They are moving production offshore. Toyota has a joint venture in Taiwan, the Kuozui Motors Ltd., with local content of 70%. The production line includes robots which replace labor intensive methods. Nissan Motor Co. has a stake in Yue Loong Motor Co. of Taiwan. It has plans for large-scale renovation. It is considering exporting to Thailand and other countries in Northeast Asia from this plant. Honda produces its cars in Thailand in a factory previously owned by GM. It is planning and producing for the future; its current production is only a few thousand vehicles a year.

The Japanese are already developing regional production. They build large parts factories in different locations to satisfy local demands for investment and employment, but they are manufacturing at high enough volumes to attain production efficiencies. ASEAN accepted a Pacific area production plan proposed by Mitsubishi Motors. Under the plan, Malaysia, the Philippines, and Thailand agreed to cut tariffs on imports of Mitsubishi truck transmissions and stamped metal parts from each other's factories. Toyota plans to spend $215 million on a program to concentrate production of diesel engines in Thailand, gasoline engines in Indonesia, steering systems in Malaysia, and transmission equipment in the Philippines. Nissan will spend up to $400 million to produce engines, axles, and transmission systems in Asia. Though to North Americans the whole process seems like too much work, the Japanese, who care about each market, are patient.

Similar trends are under way in Asian retailing. The Japanese retail giants are dominating Asian markets with more than 60 department stores, supermarket chains, and offices across Asia. They hold as much as 80% of the retail market in Singapore and 60% in Hong Kong. Aiwa makes half its products in Singapore (CD players, radios, and cassette recorders). Minebea has invested $400 million in five plants in Thailand and plans an additional $240 million. Toshiba is investing $130 million in a number of projects in Thailand, making appliances for export. Shipping companies are also thriving on the trade, which is growing 30% a year within the region and is likely to surpass the $250 billion bilateral trade with the U.S. soon.

Japan is training software writers in Malaysia and Thailand. Canon and Matsushita Electric Industrial have set up research centers in Taiwan. The Japanese are beginning to seek out information and a presence in Hanoi and remote places in China. They are providing good after-sales service (quoting *Business Week* "the Japanese send an engineer where the Americans would send a telex").

According to Kobayashi (1988), the Japanese are the major investor in Thailand: there were 204 separate deals in 1987, a four-fold increase over 1986. Investment in China, which began in 1978, continues to expand. Some 150 deals have been made.

A wood processing company was set up as a joint venture between Tairikuboeki and Soviet interests at a site near Lake Baikal. This was the first joint venture between the Soviet Union and a Western country. More joint ventures in resort and hotel management are planned.

Major firms doing business in Asia include Hitachi (producing TV sets), Orient Lease, and Otsuka Pharmaceutical. Small businesses include Rikio Tabi's production of *jiki-tabi*, traditional Japanese rubber-soled, split toed shoes for workers.

Brother Industries a manufacturer of sewing machines and typewriters, has a wholly owned subsidiary in Malaysia to manufacture components of office automation equipment.

Fujisawa Pharmaceutical will set up a joint venture with Dong-A Pharmaceutical of Korea to produce and sell medicines.

Hitachi Maxell has set up a wholly owned subsidiary in the Malacca free trade zone in Malaysia to produce videotapes and videocassette cases. It was capitalized at ¥250 million, with an initial work force of 220.

Indonesia plans three new oil refineries, adding 500,000 barrels a day capacity, by the early 1990s to meet growing regional demand, especially from Japan. Existing capacity was 750,000. The largest refinery, 250,000 barrels a day, would use Saudi Arabian crude. This one is planned with Pertamina, Mitsubishi and the Arabian American Oil Co. Another is planned with Taiwan's Chinese Petroleum Corp to produce low sulfur fuel for Taiwan's power plants. The third is also for motor fuel and has a number of firms involved.

Japan's direct investment in Indonesia, Malaysia, Thailand, and the Philippines was about $400 million in 1986. In 1988, it was about $1.1 billion. Changes to encourage deregulation and the lifting of bans on foreign companies entering the distribution system, allowing retail operations and abolishment of restrictions on capital inflows, are taking place to encourage this investment.

HONG KONG

There is much Japanese investment in Hong Kong. A low 16.5% tax rate on corporate income is a major plus for this investment. China has been wooing Japan to continue investment and maintain confidence as others withdraw. Chiba Bank upgraded its office to a branch in April 1989 citing that 150 of its home clients have offices or factories in Hong Kong. Japan has a stake in a smooth transition in 1997. Dai-Ichi Mutual Life Insurance bought a 1% stake in Hong Kong and Shanghai Banking Corp. to gain assistance for Asiawide investment.

There are 22 regional banks and five prefectural government offices in Hong Kong. Juroku and Ogaki Kyoritsu banks have full licenses. And there is more interaction of south Japan (Kyushu) and Hong Kong. Nippon Life, Nomura, Nikko Securities and others have newly established offices in Hong Kong. Japan is also making a contribution of ¥25 million to repatriate Vietnamese refugees. Hong Kong received the second largest direct aid of $1.1 billion.

Japan is the second largest cumulative investor (27%) versus the U.S. at 36% but is the largest manufacturing investor year-by-year. There are 500 companies in the Japanese Chamber of Commerce and 11,000 Japanese residents in Hong Kong. Nissho Iwai, C. Itoh, and Kumagai Gumi have increased their property activity. Some estimate a doubling of Japanese money into the Hong Kong property market in 1989 as compared with the previous two years, or about HK$10 billion ($1.25 billion).

Japanese tourism to Hong Kong is also increasing.

Matsushita will produce VTRs in Beijing. Hitachi signed an early agreement for technology transfer. U.S. regulations had prohibited Hitachi from joint venturing in the USSR, but they obtained a rule relaxation for China. A plant will be built near a color TV cathode ray tube plant in Beijing, also a joint venture. During the problems in China in June 1989 leading to the Beijing massacre, there was strong trade in the Hong Kong dollar with support from the Bank of China along with its 13 sister banks. The Bank of China sold hundreds of millions of U.S. dollars. The stock markets fell about 25% and property shares were down about 35%. One suspects that the Hong Kong dollars they received were later put into the stock market to bolster it. The Hong Kong stock and property markets had recovered most of their losses in this crash by December 1989. In 1992 prices are much higher. Hong Kong is one of the few property markets that had an increase in 1991. The increase, which was 25% in 1991, continued in 1992.

But one must be alert to the impact of the massacre in China on the future value of investments in China and Hong Kong. China's debt may be a time bomb for Japan. It currently has $45 billion in foreign debt. Of the $23 billion commercial debt, The Japanese account for about 70%. Payments now are about $7 billion per year and are scheduled to rise to $10 billion.

CHINA

The Japanese are in a good position to use their base in Hong Kong for investment in China's Guangdong province. Their investment in the area has lagged behind others including Hong Kong, the U.S. and Europe. This region of China went from 90% agriculture to 87% industrial in ten years and promises to be a main center in Asia. Labor costs are 27 times lower than in Japan. Production facilities have been established by firms such as Hitachi, Ricoh, Epson, Canon, and Sanyo.

THE LURE OF LION CITY—SINGAPORE

The Japanese net investment in foreign securities in 1987 and 1988 is listed in Table 6.14.

Table 6.14
Net Investment in Foreign Securities in 1987 and 1988, in Millions of U.S.
Dollars

Country	1987	1988
U.S.	2,618	350
Britain	267	350
Singapore	16	229
France	81	163
W. Germany	139	109
Netherlands	145	85
Hong Kong	26	78
Australia	49	23
Others	420	883
Totals	3,761	2,275

Source: Japan Securities Dealers' Association in the *Far Eastern Economic Review*

In 1988, one sees a shift from U.S. investments in the post-crash era to a sharp increase in investment in Hong Kong and especially in Singapore. The investment in Lion City went from $16 million to $229 million, a 14-fold increase. This investment is still small in total but it exceeded investments in France, West Germany, the Netherlands, Australia and Canada. Only Britain and the U.S. received more.

Why Singapore? The main lure is the tax incentive available to any foreign institution wishing to manage funds from Singapore. The tax rate for non-resident investments made from Singapore is zero and it is only 10% on the management fees. The Japanese corporate income tax rate, in comparison, is 54%. Moreover, Singapore is politically and economically stable, is far less expensive than Tokyo to operate offices, and has no exchange controls so funds can be repatriated whenever desired. Japanese life and other insurers can utilize all profits from such subsidiaries as dividends that can be passed on to investors. Only a small part of the $229 million investment actually found its way into Singapore equities. Much of it is invested back in the Japanese stock market by rich Chinese. Most of the rest is Japanese institutional fund management money invested around the world.

A number of leading Japanese insurance companies such as Nippon, Sumitomo, Meiji, and Yasuda have offices in Singapore. Sumitomo Marine and Fire Insurance Co. will open a wholly owned subsidiary in Singapore. Major securities houses such as Nikko and companies such as Mitsui have moved in as well. According to the *Far Eastern Economic Review*, this activity in Singapore and Hong Kong is the third phase of the Japanese overseas investment boom.

SOUTH AFRICA

Japan is South Africa's second largest trading partner at 12% second only to Germany at 17%, and bought more than 10% of its exports second only to the U.S. at 13%.

Japanese firms have not invested in South Africa according to the Investor Responsibility Research Center. The IRRC, a group that reports on South African ownership and advises pensions not to avoid those firms with South African holdings, has determined that the Japanese are clean, that is they get a rating of zero involvement in South Africa. Table 6.15 presents the IRRC's ratings of countries with regard to South African holdings.

Table 6.15
Adjustments in Worldwide Portfolios for Ethical Funds to Account for South African Investments

	% in world index	% removed for South African involvement
Holland	1	76
Germany	3	74
Switzerland	1	67
Britain	10	49
All Europe	21	46
USA	33	21
Japan	41	0

Source: *The Economist*

JAPANESE FOREIGN AID

The foreign aid budget of Japan for fiscal 1989 was ¥137 trillion or $11.1 billion (evaluated at ¥123/$) which is higher than the $9.1 billion of the U.S. This figure, like that of the U.S., includes grants as well as loans, including ¥804 billion of the latter to developing countries. There are many reasons for such aid: humanitarian, natural disaster relief, good will, investment, repayment of favors, military purposes, and the like. Traditionally, Japan has used its aid to promote exports and to help secure vital natural resources. Seventy percent of this aid has been given for industrial projects. But because of U.S. pressure Japan is no longer targeting its aid so narrowly and has promised to spend more outside of Asia. This will remove some of the U.S. aid burden. But internally there is much debate as to how this aid should be spent. Many would like Japan to go its own way and to strengthen itself for possible future trade wars. Others support the U.S. requests. Examples of this aid are:

- ¥2.95 billion to Bolivia to help build facilities to supply underground water in the city of El Alto and to develop a network of roads in Cochabamba state.

- ¥284 million in fiscal 1989 to the UN, a drop of 10.3% from 1988.

- ¥88 billion loan to the Philippines for infrastructure projects, public corporate-sector reform programs, forestry projects and import financing.

- ¥150 million grant to the West African country of Guinea-Bissau to help it increase grain production using agricultural chemicals and farm machinery.

- ¥1.23 billion in emergency aid to Soviet Armenia after it was devastated by one of the century's worst earthquakes. The aid was ¥1 billion cash plus ¥700 million of blankets, tents and other materials plus transportation cost.

THE DEVELOPING COUNTRIES

Japanese loans to and investment in developing countries rose to over ¥1.1 trillion in FY 1988, up 49.2% from the previous year, making this the largest aid program in the world. Direct loans to governments totaled over ¥1.09 trillion, up 51.8%, and loans or investments to companies were ¥8.6 billion down 52.6%. It has been suggested that Japan is long on yen but short on development experts because the number of personnel has not increased. Aid spending was $1.56 million per staff in 1977 and in 1988 was $5.34 million. The Japanese do not employ development experts but use personnel from consulting and trading companies. Britain's GE Company signed a $64.8 million deal to supply the Thai railroad with new signaling equipment; the project will be funded by Japan.

Turkey is attempting to get Japanese investors. Everyone is studying Japanese—urchins, carpet merchants, and tycoons! Since 1985 exports to Japan increased five-fold to $200 million per year, while imports have tripled to about $600 million. Four joint ventures and 20 representative offices have been established. Japanese are studying hotels, golf courses, car, gas lighters, and zipper plants. Political stability is an important concern along with the 64% inflation rate and red tape. Bridgestone, making its biggest investment in 1988, paid $60 million for a joint venture in the Turkish tire company Brissa, which plans to produce for the Middle East and Africa. Toyota is considering producing cars in Turkey via a joint venture with a Turkish financial group. It will invest $250 million. The investment is backed by export credits and government soft loans. Much investment is geared to trading.

An aid grant totaling ¥600 million has been given to India to help increase agricultural productivity. The grant will be used to purchase farm equipment and pesticides. Japan has been the largest supplier of development aid to India since 1987 and India is the fifth largest recipient of Japanese aid.

Guinea was the recipient of ¥290 million to help develop its fishing industry; the money will be used to purchase fishing equipment.

Japanese corporations are becoming more formally involved in aid programs. One hundred Japanese companies have founded the Japan International Development Organization to help provide aid to developing countries. This organization, chaired by Soichi Sawam former chairman of Toshiba, is jointly funded by private companies (¥4 billion) and by the government (¥2 billion).

The Japanese government plans to untie aid to Malaysia, Thailand, the Philippines, Korea, and Papua New Guinea by 1990 (Mansfield, 1989).

BRAZIL

Links between Japan and Brazil are strong. Brazil's ethnic Japanese population of approximately 1.2 million is the largest outside Japan. The colony began in 1908 when 781 Japanese arrived in Santos to work on coffee plantations. While the U.S. is focusing on Mexico, Japan appears to be focusing on Brazil. At least $1.5 billion in new loans was announced, though the U.S. investment in Brazil has a higher profile, at 3.5 times that of Japan. Brazil is number three in terms of Japanese direct foreign investment behind the U.S. and Indonesia. Kirin Brewery and Companhia Industrial E. Agricola Ometto of Brazil invested $6.6 million to build a plant in Sao Paulo state to produce products made from yeast. Some $2 million was invested by Kirin which will also share technology.

Japanese investors in Brazil are concerned with the 934% inflation rate, possible debt moratorium, criticism of foreign investment and protectionism. Dai-Ichi Kangyo Bank via a debt-equity swap made a $100 million investment in Unibanco S.A. on the top five private banks. Japan has been criticized worldwide for supporting projects, including road building in the jungle, that are environmentally damaging to the Amazon.

The Japanese government agreed to reschedule ¥280 billion of Brazil's debt. Bishimetal, a subsidiary of Mitsubishi Metal, offered to buy Brazil's entire $115 billion foreign debt in exchange for mining rights over gold deposits in the Amazon estimated to be worth $260 billion.

The Japanese-Brazil Paper & Pulp Resources Development, financed by 20 Japanese organizations, will have a joint venture in Brazil to build a pulp plant in southeastern Brazil.

INVESTMENT IN FOREIGN SECURITIES

The International Monetary Fund (IMF) is working toward increasing Japan's role in coordination with a doubling of funding to $240 billion (Saudi Arabia, Britain and the U.S. have not yet signed).

The hold on the market of Japan's big four brokerage firms is weakening dramatically. In October 1989, Nomura's share of the turnover on the TSE fell below 10% for the first time in 20 years and the combined share of the four was 34%, down six points since March. In 1991 and 1992, the foreigners' share of trading exceeded 50%, and often it was about two-thirds of total volume; much of this is derivative securities trading. Three of the top earners in FY 1991, were U.S. brokers (see shown in Figure 6.3). Saloman's $176 million profit was only exceeded by Nomura.

The Japanese are keen on country funds including Spain, Germany, and Southeast Asia. According to *Forbes*, Japanese brokerage houses own up to 80% of the Germany and Spain fund and likely own most of the Thai, Malaysia, and Taiwan funds. As the brokerage houses hold the funds shares, none are available for arbitrage.

Figure 6.3
Reported Profits for FY 1991 (U.S.$Millions)

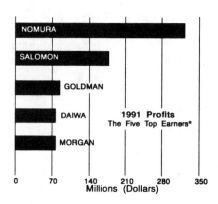

Source: *Asahi Shimbun*

Japanese investors escalated their purchases of stocks and bonds outside Japan rather dramatically as shown in Figure 6.4 and Tables 6.16-6.21. Net purchases in 1987 were more than tenfold those of 1985 but dropped dramatically in 1988. The growth in bonds which are bought on a much larger scale than stock has advanced at a steady pace and peaked in 1986. The sharp declines in the bond market in the U.S. and other parts of the world in early 1987 may have led to this decline. Still, net purchases of foreign bonds in 1987 were over ¥10 trillion, as they were in 1982.

Net Japanese investment in foreign securities was $85 billion in 1988, a staggering sum but still below 1986's record of nearly $100 billion. Nearly 70% of the foreign debt purchased in 1988 was in dollars. Hence, the Japanese purchased about 40% of the 1988 U.S. balance of payments deficit of some $140 billion. Much of the latter is purchased through U.S. T-bonds and T-bond futures traded at the board of trade in Chicago. The demand is so high that these futures are also, as of December 1989, traded in Tokyo.

In 1989, they bought $103 billion, but by 1990 total purchases worldwide were down to $42.3 billion.

Table 6.16
Japanese Investment in Foreign Securities (¥Billions)

	Stocks			Bonds		
Year	Purchases	Sales	Net Balance	Purchases	Sales	Net Balance
1979	36	44	-8	2,948	-1,493	309
1980	59	71	-12	5,237	-2,375	216
1981	201	149	52	2,002	767	1,236
1982	261	226	35	3,923	2,526	1,397
1983	520	364	156	5,651	2,575	3,076
1984	367	355	12	13,157	6,899	6,258
1985	1,364	1,118	246	72,938	59,6001	3,338
1986	4,169	2,760	1,409	277,707	258,562	19,145
1987	10,945	8,316	2,629	198,106	186,712	11,394
1988	10,393	10,025	369	185,702	174,123	11,580

Source: Ministry of Finance (after 1980), Japan Securities Dealers Assn. (1980 and before)

Table 6.17
Japanese Investments in Foreign Currency Bonds, Years Ending June 30, 1983–88, ($ Millions)

Foreign Currency Bonds	1983	1984	1985	1986	1987	1988
Purchases	26,510	77,587	291,376	1,473,248	1,228,026	806,307
Sales	12,822	47,108	237,860	1,374,283	1,165,173	753,386
Net 13,688	30,479	53,516	98,965	62,853	53,021	

Source: Bank of Japan

Table 6.18
Japanese Investment in Foreign Stock, ($ Millions)

Foreign Equities	1983	1984	1985	1986	1987	1988
Purchases	2,080	2,318	5,484	32,049	75,911	47,013
Sales	276	2,185	4,489	21,293	64,140	42,915
Net 804	133	995	10,756	11,771	4,098	

Source: Bank of Japan

As of the end of 1987, the U.S. net debt to foreigners was some $368.2 billion of which $80.7 billion was owed to Japan. Most of the Japanese investments were in Treasury bonds to recycle the trade surplus. This can be seen from the other side: in order to help fund the U.S. deficit without inflation, the trade surplus filled the goods gap! Net Japanese assets abroad at the end of 1987 totaled $240.7 billion with the private sector owning $146.5 billion and the government $94.3 (see Table 6.21).

Table 6.19
Net U.S. and Japanese Purchases of Debt and Equity

	Purchases of Japanese Securities by U.S. Investors			Purchases of U.S. Securities by Japanese Investors		
	Stock ($1989M)	Stock (% TSE)	Bonds ($1989M)	Stock ($1989M)	Stock (% NYSE)	Bonds ($1989M)
1970	–	–	–	31.9	0.001	6.4
1971	–	–	–	147.0	0.007	5108.0
1972	0.511	0.143	–	471.5	0.019	8824.8
1973	-0.700	-0.152	–	1382.4	0.064	2097.4
1974	-1.589	-0.476	–	-113.2	-0.008	-3314.5
1975	-0.093	-0.029	–	50.7	0.004	-631.3
1976	-0.335	-0.091	–	146.0	0.009	-1568.8
1977	-1.233	-0.298	–	67.5	0.004	8875.2
1978	-0.966	-0.174	–	138.8	0.010	9103.3
1979	-0.045	-0.008	–	217.0	0.015	-466.4
1980	1.447	0.287	–	-233.2	-0.015	-2437.6
1981	0.752	0.139	–	160.9	0.010	1781.1
1982	0.937	0.185	–	0.0	0.000	1034.4
1983	1.587	0.260	–	339.9	0.020	3153.5
1984	-0.367	-0.049	0.898	-156.4	-0.009	8958.3
1985	-0.454	-0.052	0.278	343.5	0.018	27989.3
1986	-9.300	-0.566	-0.818	3727.6	0.163	15754.5
1987	-11.811	-0.490	-1.851	12402.7	0.521	2691.2
1988	1.562	0.046	-1.622	2014.6	0.084	30856.4
1989	5.105	0.126	-2.605	3348.0	0.122	8724.0

Source: French and Poterba (1990)

Table 6.20
Cross-Border Ownership of Japanese and U.S. Equities, 1985 and 1989

	Percentage of U.S. Market Owned by Japanese	Percentage of Japanese Market Owned by Americans
1985	0.15	1.11
1989	1.04	0.22

Source: French and Poterba (1990)

Table 6.21
Japanese Assets and Liabilities Abroad in U.S. Millions, End of 1987

Assets		Liabilities	
Long-term assets	646,81	Long-term liabilities	236,181
Private sector	565,100	Private sector	178,810
securities	339,677		
Government	81,081	Government	57,321
Short-term assets	425,450	Short-term liabilities	594,706
Private sector	343,261	Private sector	583,057
Government	82,189	Government	11,649
Total assets	1,071,631	Total liabilities	830,887
Net assets	240,744		
Private sector	146,494		
Government	94,250		

Figure 6.4
Japanese Net Investment in U.S. Securities, 1984–90, Billions of Dollars

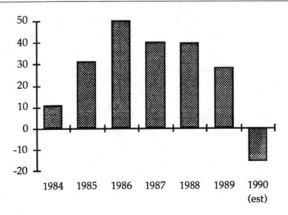

Source: TSE

FINANCIAL INSTITUTIONS AND THEIR INVESTMENTS

Japan's financial institutions have overseas activities worth more than twice those of its carmakers and consumer electronics firms together. They went abroad for a variety of reasons:

- To follow their manufacturing clients.

- To seek higher returns there was a net outflow of capital with elimination of foreign exchange controls in 1980, along with less borrowing by government and corporations

- To learn business, they were not yet allowed to engage in at home.

Japanese banks are entering the international aircraft leasing and financing business. They are using innovative financing techniques, including leveraged leasing. A leasing company sets up a limited partnership with nine investors. The partnership finances 20% and the banks finance 80%. From December 1988 to July 1989, one hundred aircraft were leased this way.

Aircraft are considered less risky than Third World loans because one has the planes as security. It is projected that 12,500 commercial aircraft will be needed to meet the growing travel demand by the year 2000; there are about 8,500 in 1992. The total replacement demand of about 2,400 plus additions to the fleet, means financing will be needed for about 7,000 new planes with an average price of $50 million for a total cost of $350 billion.

Airlines lease about 12% of their fleets. This is expected to rise to 25%. The largest leasing company is the GPA Group based in Ireland. Mitsubishi Trust and Banking and the Long-Term Credit Bank of Japan have shares along with Air Canada, which is the largest shareholder at 22%. Five Japanese banks (Mitsubishi Trust, Industrial Bank of Japan, Bank of Tokyo, Tokai Bank, and Daiwa Bank) are lead managers in a $1.25 billion financing deal under GPA. This venture, totaling $10 billion, was the ninth major deal with Japanese bank participation in the last three years. Mitsubishi Trust and the Long-Term Credit Bank are the most active and are involved with all the deals. Mitsubishi Trust was the lead lender for United Airlines $1 billion loan in December 1988 and for British Airways PLC $2 billion loan in June 1988. Not only are the loans secured but the banks also receive 1 to 2% of the value in commission and interest.

To further their understanding of the business, Sumitomo acquired a 5% stake in International Lease Finance Corp of Beverly Hills, the number two aircraft leasing company, and Industrial Bank of Japan bought a 20%

stake in D'Accord Inc. (a U.S. company). Through its leasing unit IBJ Leasing Co., Mitsubishi Trust and Banking Corp. has agreed to form a London-based aircraft finance and leasing company along with Rolls-Royce Motors Holding Ltd., National Westminister Bank PLC and Chrysler Corp.

Nomura, the largest brokerage firm in Japan and the world, had 12,000 employees in 38 offices in 21 countries and earned $2 billion in 1987, nearly five times as much as Merrill Lynch. It beat out Toyota as the most profitable firm in Japan. It is number one in the Eurobond market after only six years in London (13.2% versus 7.7% for Credit Suisse First Boston). It is supported by sophisticated research and technology. Nomura has $270 million in mainframe computers and 45,000 terminals worldwide. A Nomura broker anywhere in the world can quickly retrieve information. When opening offices abroad, it goes local, only 300 of its 2,000 overseas employees are Japanese, though Japanese executives dominate top management in the branches. Nomura was one of the few companies able to keep its name after the war (mostly by procrastination, it never got around to complying, and the rules changed).

Many of these deals cannot be put together without the Japanese. The power of the Japanese banks was felt when the UAL deal collapsed and sent the DJIA into a 190-point tailspin in the last hour of trading on Friday October 13, 1989. Unhappy with the terms offered by the main bankers, Citibank and Chase Manhattan, the Japanese gave only a third of the $3 billion they were expected to provide. Japanese banks have lent as much as $20 billion to U.S. leveraged buyouts and are committed to an additional $15 billion. They provided $5.8 billion for the Kohlberg Kravis Roberts & Co. buy out of RJR Nabisco, and lent to Al Checchi to complete his takeover of NWA Inc. Table 6.21 summarizes the loans outstanding and total commitments by nationality of bank participating in leveraged buyouts.

The Bank of Japan urged caution and the Japanese banks were concerned about the collapsing junk bond market and the slowing U.S. economy in 1991. They were critical of the Time-Warner deal.

Table 6.22
Participation in Leveraged Buyouts by Major Country, in Billions of Dollars

	Outstanding Loans	Total Loan Commitment
U.S.	$45.0	$72.0
Japan	20.0	35.0
France	8.5	10.2
Britain	7.5	9.0
Canada	7.0	8.4

Source: *Business Week*, Oct 30, 1989

Japanese banking institutions in California have experienced dramatic growth. In 1987 they accounted for 21.7% of the California market, with assets of $76.1 billion. They have one-quarter of the market for commercial lending. They accounted for four of the top ten banks, numbers six, seven, eight, and ten as follows: California First Bank with $6.3 billion, Sanwa Bank California, $5.9 billion, Bank of California, $4.9 billion (Mitsubishi), and Sumitomo Bank of California, $3.5 billion. In 1989 they had five of the top eleven. The Bank of Tokyo owns 76.7% of Union Bank and claims to do business with 80% of the Japanese companies operating in California. After buying Union, it merged it with its California First Bank of San Francisco. The New York Fed estimated the Japanese control 14% of U.S. banking assets.

Financing of real estate is increasing. The Japanese appear to be more comfortable dealing with currency risk and may be lowering their risks as they have yen cash flow, so are likely targets of yen financing. Olympia & York took a mortgage of $800 million for an office building in Manhattan's World Financial Center (the largest for a single building). Nomura Securities Co. and its real estate affiliate Eastdil Realty Inc. arranged this ten-year loan. This is a risk splitting arrangement with the borrowers borrowing at about two percentage points below the going dollar rate, and the lenders receiving 2.5 percentage points more than the 5% yen rate. The interest and principal are payable in dollars, but the amount of principal at maturity is linked to the yen dollar exchange rate. If the dollar falls, Olympia & York will pay more, and if the dollar rises the Japanese lenders receive less than the $800 million. The break-even point is in the 120 to 125 yen to dollar range though the rate was 132 when the deal was made. The May 1992 exchange rate was about 130.

First Boston brokered one of the first yen-financed acquisitions of U.S. real estate when Katoh Kagaku Co. (a Japanese corn syrup manufacturer) purchased the Hyatt Regency in Chicago for $255 million with a yen mortgage from Orient Leasing Co. This loan is reasonable because Katoh has large yen receipts.

In another deal, a $72 million retail development expansion arranged by Sonnenblick-Goldman, the yen financing cost was only 6% compared with an expected 10.25% if dollar financed. Again, the deal made sense because the tenants would pay in yen.

Los Angeles County issued $100 million of ten-year yen denominated bonds, making it the first municipality to do so. The debt was placed privately with Nippon Life Insurance Co. and the Long-Term Credit Bank of Japan and is taxable. First Boston is advising on the deal. They will buy high-yield securities of which at least half will consist of dollar-denominated foreign securities. They engaged in currency swaps to lock in interest rates and avoid currency risks. They are playing with money for employee pensions.

In 1988, 85% of new international banking claims involved funds flowing to or from Japan. Much of the activity reflects Japanese lending in Asia and the Pacific Rim and is due in part to the low rates of interest in Japan as well as the U.S. banks' caution due to the Third World debt crisis.

Some acquisitions in September 1989 included the following: the Fuji Bank Ltd. took over Kleinwort Benson's Chicago-based primary dealership of U.S. government securities; Dai-Ichi Kangyo Bank (DKB) bought a 60% interest in the business lending unit of Manufacturers Hanover Corp for $1.4 billion (it was then the largest investment by a Japanese bank in an American financial company). The Sony deal for Columbia Pictures Entertainment also occurred that month. Kyocera Corp and AVX Corp undertook a $531 million stock-swap merger, the first ever between publicly held companies in Japan and the U.S.

Table 6.23

Mergers and Acquisitions

a.

Industry	Number Acquired 1985–87
Chemical and allied products	70
Nonelectrical machinery	69
Electrical and electronic machinery	62
Business services	53
Printing and publishing	53
Photo, medical and optical instruments	45
Distribution and wholesale trade	36
Food and allied products	32

b.

Country	1986	1987	1988	1989 (first half)
U.S.	126	120	167	84
Europe	28	35	52	40
Asia/Oceania	36	61	79	34
Other	14	12	17	12

c.

Industry	US 1987	US 1988	J 1988
Chemicals	18	11	64
Electrical equip	18	15	63
Foods	20	15	56
Paper & forest	16	12	65
Textile products	16	14	79

Source: *Business Tokyo*, November 1989

In 1984, there were only 44 mergers or acquisitions (M&As) of foreign companies by Japanese companies; by 1988 there were 315 and the total value rose from $1 billion to $11 billion (not counting real estate). The total U.S. M&A market was $230 billion in 1988. For information on merger and acquisition activity in Japan, see Kester (1991).

Three of the big four brokers are affiliated with foreign M&A specialists: Nomura with Wasserstein, Perella; Nikko with the Blackstone Group, and Yamaichi[10] with the Lodestar Group.

Sumitomo has a stake in Goldman Sachs sometimes giving it the advantage of belonging in Japan and also networked in the U.S.

---

[10] Yamaichi had the first dedicated M&A group in 1973 headed by Masaki Yoshida who now has his own firm, the RECOF Group.

JAPANESE LIFE INSURANCE COMPANIES

Japan's 25 life insurance companies (seiho) have grown too big, too quickly. They have developed the financial muscle of a Goliath, while retaining the investment sophistication of a David.

Tony Shale

As of mid-1989, Japan's life insurance companies had combined assets of over ¥95 trillion some $720 billion (see Shale, 1989). This is over twice the combined GNP of Taiwan, Korea, Singapore, and Thailand. Nippon Life, by far the world's largest life insurance company, had assets over $170 billion, some 50% larger than Prudential. Now that postal savings are no longer tax-exempt, reducing their effective yields from about 7.6% to 3.7%, about 25% of the ¥30 trillion ($231 billion) expected to flow out of these accounts is destined for the life insurers. The insurers have policies that return most of the investments in the form of guaranteed payments over time plus bonuses in addition to the principal at expiry of the policy. The *seiho* already own about 15% of the TSE. Moreover, domestic bonds returned coupons of 4 to 5%—until the rise in interest rates in 1990 to the 7 to 8% range and their decline to the 5 to 6% range in early 1992. Hence, there is a serious problem about where to put the current and new money (about $26 billion per year for Nippon Life) to return enough—around 10%—to cover commitments and make a profit. Their commitments include the 5 to 6% they must pay individuals and policy holders. Unrealized gains cannot be used for this purpose, neither can realized profits on stock sold in Japan. Bond, money market and stock income as well as income and capital gains from foreign subsidiaries and *tokkin* (private, pooled equity trust) accounts do count. Table 6.24 shows the asset allocation of the 25 *seiho* for 1980 to 1988.

Tables 6.24 and 6.25b show the principal assets and their allocation for the life insurance companies by month from November 1988 to April 1989. Table 6.25a,c have the asset allocations for the much smaller non-life insurance and mutual insurance federations of agricultural cooperatives for the same period. One sees substantial increases in equities and foreign securities and decreases in loans.

The mutual insurance federations of agricultural cooperatives mainly invest in cash instruments, bank debentures, corporate bonds and loans for business and industry The life insurance companies have their assets mainly in domestic stocks and foreign securities with substantial assets in domestic bonds. The non-life insurance companies have their assets largely in stocks, bonds and loans with some assets in foreign securities.

Table 6.24
Asset Allocation of Japanese Life Insurance Companies 1980–88, ¥100 Million

	Securities							
	Cash Deposit	Subtotal	Bonds	Equities	Foreign Securities	Loans	Real Estate	Total
1980	6,601	79,760	27,859	45,201	6,689	156,850	16,477	262,570
1981	7,169	96,909	31,931	58,842	14,126	175,045	18,417	300,980
1982	11,051	113,278	35,270	55,847	21,693	196,692	20,863	346,130
1983	17,788	136,530	43,250	62,118	30,639	211,575	24,066	395,260
1984	31,589	160,504	50,136	69,216	40,286	230,639	27,405	457,400
1985	63,951	189,813	60,783	81,138	46,681	243,522	31,962	538,700
1986	77,006	267,918	78,373	111,005	75,252	256,366	37,770	653,170
1987	96,285	349,336	89,453	155,888	98,029	285,632	44,861	792,580
1988	108,592	421,279	98,210	184,644	120,857	324,324	52,944	924,550

	Cash Deposit %	Subtotal %	Bonds %	Equities %	Foreign Securities %	Loans %	Real Estate %	Total
1980	2.5	30.4	10.6	17.2	2.5	59.7	6.3	100.0
1981	2.4	32.2	10.6	19.6	4.7	58.2	6.1	100.0
1982	3.2	32.7	10.2	16.1	6.3	56.8	6.0	100.0
1983	4.5	34.5	10.9	15.7	7.8	53.5	6.1	100.0
1984	6.9	35.1	11.0	15.1	8.8	50.4	6.0	100.0
1985	11.9	35.2	11.3	15.1	8.7	45.2	5.9	100.0
1986	11.8	41.0	12.0	17.0	11.5	39.2	5.8	100.0
1987	12.1	44.1	11.3	19.7	12.4	36.0	5.7	100.0
1988	11.7	45.6	10.6	20.0	13.1	35.1	5.7	100.0

Source: Daiwa Europe Limited

Figure 6.5
EPFA Trust Bank Performance Yield and Total Return for Year Ended
March 1987

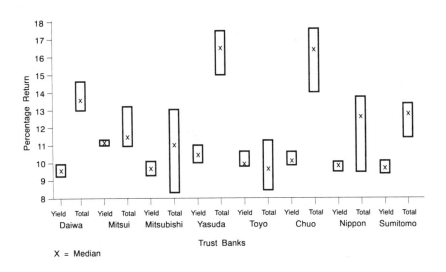

X = Median

Source: Myers and Ujiie (1988)

For regulatory purposes in Japan, insurance portfolios can only count dividends received and not the total return as usually defined. Dividends include cash received from stock dividends, bond coupons, interest and profits from realized capital gains. This usually amounts to 6 to 8%. In 1988, the highest such return was 7.8%. Most *seiho* earned less, about 6 to 7%. It is difficult to obtain information on total returns that is income plus realized gains. The reported returns do not include unrealized gains from securities, land, and other assets held. Since the NSA and TOPIX indices were up about 40% in 1988 and the *seiho* own 15% of the first section, their total return was well above that reported. According to *The Economist* in 1988, 54% of their inflows of ¥6 trillion was invested in securities. The inflows totaled about ¥6.3 trillion in the first ten months of 1988. Some 39% was invested in stocks and a further 46% in corporate loans. Figures 6.5 and 6.6 from Myers and Ujiie (1988) give some insight into the actual rates of return earned. One sees that for trust banks, the total return is in most cases is 4 to 5% higher than the reported return for FY 1986. Still as shown in Figure 6.5 their total return was well below the TOPIX index for the two years ending in March 1987. The trust banks generally have returns that exceed those of the *seiho* because of their emphasis on separate accounts which have high performance in relation to the *seiho's* pooled accounts.

One way to improve this performance is to move into more risky but higher yielding equities, companies, and properties. To improve their know-how they have purchased small stakes in leading foreign brokerage firms to learn from them. An example is Nippon Life's 13% stake in Shearson Lehman Hutton in 1986 for $580 million which, according to Haruaki Deguchi, a senior manager of the financial and investment planning department, "was purely to allow us to educate our personnel in all areas of international finance."

Figure 6.6
EPFA Trust Bank Performance Two year Return ended December 1987

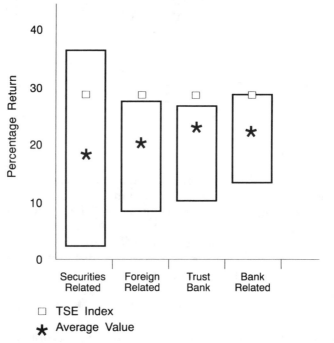

Source: Myers and Ujiie (1988)

Since then the pattern has continued with the acquisitions in Table 6.26. Many other joint ventures, largely to learn investment technology, are in the works.

Foreign investments are limited to 30% of the total and have been in the 20% range. The *seiho* had massive losses in U.S. bonds because of the dollar's fall from 1985 to 1987. These losses were about ¥500 billion in the FY 1988. In 1986–87 the losses were even larger. In 1986 they were $17.8 billion. They also had massive losses in U.S. equities during the October 1987 crash. The emphasis thus shifted to investments in Australia, Canada, and Europe. For example, Nippon Life's bond portfolio, which constitutes 70% of it overseas investments, is 52% in the U.S., 16% in Canada, 12%

Table 6.25
Asset Allocation of Japanese Nonlife and Mutual Insurance Companies End of 1988, ¥100 Million

a: Principal Assets of Mutual Insurance Federations of Agricultural Cooperatives

	Oct-88	Dec-88	Mar-89
Cash deposits with others	33,125	34,467	33,060
Deposits with affiliates	18,287	18,504	19,278
Total Securities	78,047	80,206	84,428
Govt. bonds	6,496	7,168	8,203
Local Govt. Bonds	6,090	6,339	6,833
Bank debentures	16,212	16,373	17,546
Govt. guaranteed bonds	9,032	9,264	9,861
Public corp. bonds	8,226	8,360	8,461
Corporate bonds	10,921	11,242	11,334
Stocks & shares	7,034	7,166	7,570
Total Loans	34,861	34,546	37,997
Loans for business & industry	23,747	23,591	25,225
Loans for housing construction	462	457	445
Loans on policies	817	778	709
Loans on restorations	517	452	434
Loans to other financial institutions	3,159	3,174	4,864
Real estate	595	600	559
Total operating funds	146,630	149,821	156,045
Total assets including other assets	147,978	151,253	162,963

Source: The National Mutual Insurance Federations of Agricultural Cooperatives

Table 6.25 (continued)

b: Principal Assets of Life Insurance Companies

	Nov-88	Jan-89	Mar-89
Cash deposits with others	99,896	105,144	109070
Call loans	3,559	4,354	2180
Total Securities	413,470	431,526	447491
Govt. bonds	51,203	55,010	58358
Corporate bonds	8,810	8,953	9256
Stocks & shares	36,963	38,240	39594
Foreign securities	180,667	188,390	196941
Total	128,184	133,198	135956
	321,141	326,229	334828
Loans based on insurance provision	24,704	24,748	25091
Ordinary loans	296,437	301,481	309736
Fixed asset construction program			
Total	51,357	53,940	55557
Land	23,212	24,574	28471
Building	19,405	19,885	21297
Constuction in progress	8,739	9,480	5788
Total operating funds	889,425	922,195	919287
Total assets including other assets	907,845	939,733	970827
New contracts	207,659	85,325	168922
Contracts outstanding	11,906,598	12,064,474	12321343

Source: The Life Insurance Association

c: Principal Assets of Non-Life Insurance Companies

	Oct-88	Dec-88	Mar-89
Deposits with others	20,089	22,566	25,766
Money in trust	8,666	8,884	8,762
Call loans	567	3,791	3,254
Total Securities	91,205	91,629	95,067
Govt. bonds	11,091	10,810	11,331
Local Govt. Bonds	3,925	3,923	3,938
Corporate bonds	16,646	16,089	16,747
Stocks & shares	30,301	30,831	32,799
Foreign securities	19,737	20,453	21,100
Total Loans	41,115	42,246	46,595
Loans based on insurance provision	1,775	1,784	1,842
Ordinary loans	39,340	40,461	42,753
Fixed assets	8,544	8,714	9,220
Total operating funds	174,679	177,832	187,522
Total assets including other assets	190,760	196,356	206,693

Source: The Marine and Fire Insurance Association of Japan

Table 6.26
Acquisitions by Japanese Life Insurance Companies.

Company	Purchase	Cost
Yasuda Life	18% of Paine Webber	$300.0 million
Dai-Ichi Life	1% of Hong Kong and Shanghai	$48.1 million
Sumitomo Life	15% of Edinburgh-based Ivory & Sime	£7.5 million
	also small investments in Kleinwort Benson, Banque Paribas, Berliner Handelsund Frankfurter Bank (BHF) and Credit Agricole	
Asahi Life	5% of Group AG, Belgium's largest insurance group	$81.3 million
Meiji Life	5% of Equitable Life Insurance, the U.S. third largest	

in England, 11% in Australia, 5% in West Germany, and 3% in Euroyen, ECU and New Zealand dollar bonds. Nippon's current goal is to achieve a total dividend return of at least 8.5%, hence low return bonds such as those in Germany are being phased out. With Nippon's reluctance to buy bonds with ratings less than AA, this may be difficult. Investments in funds run by others, such as Salomon Brothers' high yield fund set up for Japanese investors which yielded 10.48% in 1988 are increasing. It is clear that making their 6 to 8% *dividend* return with the low risk they desire will be difficult.

The vast size of these insurance companies makes investing difficult. For example, the total size of the open Asian markets other than Australia is only ¥60 trillion ($46 billion), which is about 12% of the TSE's ¥550 trillion and less than a third of the *seiho* total assets of $170 billion. Real estate and equity markets are underweighted and may well have their exposures increased in subsequent years.

Changes in regulations have had a dramatic effect on the insurance companies, opening the market and their choices. Only recently they had to keep their assets in government bonds and domestic equity of certain types. The fall in the yen in 1989 and 1990 has associated with it huge Japanese investment around the world, including major investment in Eastern and Western Europe and the U.S.

ACTIVITIES OF JAPANESE BANKS

Japanese banks, already the biggest in the world based on capitalization, are growing larger through mergers. Mitsui and Taiyo Kobe Banks (numbers 7 and 8 in terms of assets) have merged, forming the world's second biggest bank. The lineup now is Dai-Ichi Kangyo, Sumitomo, Fuji, Mitsubishi, Sanwa all with assets of over ¥35 trillion or $250 million. This was the first big banking merger in Japan in 16 years. The new bank is named Mitsui Taiyo Kobe Bank. The merger was prompted by Mitsui's need for more branches as its shifts from reliance on corporate customers. It also follows on deregulation of deposit rates and growing competition among retail banks.   With the growing liquidity in the financial system in Japan, corporations are relying less on banks and more on the capital markets (as well as internal savings) for funds. As well as the competition for personal savings is growing with securities firms, insurance companies and the Post Office are all competing for customers. Regional banks, such as the Bank of Yokohama, Chiba Bank, and Hokuriku Bank, are also growing and have a more secure place in their localities.

Other niches are also giving the banks trouble:

- Many were caught in the foreign exchange business with the dollar's increase against the yen.

- Bond profits are down in part because the government is issuing fewer bonds and foreign banks and securities dealers have been given more share (Mitsui profits of ¥21.7 billion in 1987 went to a loss of ¥5.7 billion in 1988).

The city banks reported a record after tax profit of ¥1.2 trillion up 35%, but a third of this is non-continuing, arising from the sales of hidden assets.

Mitsui is the oldest commercial bank in Japan and was the center of the Mitsui shipbuilding and trading empire that was broken up after WWII. It has been living off its past. Though its revenues rose 20%, its operating profit fell 38%. In a real sense, it is the smaller Taiyo Kobe that is taking over Mitsui, TK's president Yasuo Matsushita will be the chairman and the new headquarters will be in TK's main Tokyo branch. Its Japanese name recognizes this new twist of power. TK has the most branches, so its profit per branch is low, and it could be helped by the merger to use its plant more efficiently.

Apparently, there was insider trading in June and July 1989 as TK head offices told branches to tip off customers. A new insider trading laws went into effect in April 1990.

The Bank of Tokyo is burdened with Third World debt.

Sumitomo considers profit more than assets, it is number one in profit in Japan, fourth in the world. While Dai-Ichi Kangyo is number one in assets, Sumitomo is number two. (Citicorp is the highest in profit in the world.)

The Bank for International Settlements (BIS) risk-asset ratio is forcing Japanese banks to pay more attention to profits. Many have issued stock and convertible bonds and sold off stockholdings in other Japanese companies.

In 1987, Sumitomo bought Heiwa Sogo Bank, a failing Japanese-style S&L. It immediately wrote down the losses. But Sumitomo still gained, without the merger it would have been unable to grow in Tokyo because there restrictions on branches and the supply of office space is tight. Sumitomo is now working on the retail market because it is has been easy for firms to raise equity on the TSE. They are targeting smaller businesses and consumers and are also working in leveraged buyouts. The bank was the advisor to Yamanouchi in the $395 million takeover of Shaklee, arranged Japanese financing for Campeau's buyout of Federated Department Stores and earned a $2.5 million loan commitment fee from Paramount in its failed bid for Time. Its president, Tatsumi said "we don't want to miss any chance to earn commissions overseas." The bank is active in Europe through a London investment banking subsidiary and Banca del Gottardo, a Swiss bank it acquired in 1984. In 1986, it paid $500 million for a 12.5% share of Goldman, Sachs' profits but the FED restricts extensive business development.

Dai-Ichi Mutual Life of Japan acquired a 1% stake (the maximum allowed any investor) in the Hong Kong & Shanghai Banking Co.

The Ministry of Industry and International Trade (MITI) will expand its insurance on overseas investment in an attempt to encourage Japanese investment in countries with high investment risks such as wars, civil unrest as well as foreign exchange fluctuations. This will be provided at a risk premium of 0.3 to 1.3% from the current 0.55 to 0.65% and the period of coverage will also be expanded to 3 to 15 years. Insurance will also be available on debt-equity swaps and portfolio investment in developing countries.

Japanese banks may appear to be very conservative but that's because their speculative operations are kept in secret accounts called *tokkin* and *kingaishin* (T&K funds) held anonymously by friendly investment firms or trust banks. There is reportedly ¥3 trillion in *tokkin* accounts (investment pools) the banks set up in 1980 and they are a major force on the TSE. While sales of stock managed in house portfolios are treated as capital gains, *tokkin* profits are treated as ordinary income, thus they can be used to mask the results of their ordinary business and inflate net operating profit.

Mitsubishi Bank, which favors reform, receives less than 1% of their operating profit this way compared with 10% for Sumitomo Bank and the Industrial Bank of Japan, and up to 28% for the Long-Term Credit Bank of Japan. New rules will make the accounts more transparent by accounting for a variety of classes of income: revenue from funds management, revenue from service transactions, revenue from non-core businesses, and other current revenues. Income from foreign-exchange trading, bond trading, and bond redemptions will come under non-core businesses, while revenue from stock transactions will be entered under other current revenues. The *tokkin* come under the *other* category. Banks had been disguising bond trading losses by transferring bonds with losses out of trading accounts to portfolio accounts; while revenue from *tokkin* trusts was used to window-dress banks' accounts, making it hard to determine real value from published data.

This will have two effects on the market. One will be to value more strongly those banks that are profitable on the basis of their real banking business. The other effect is the fear that the *tokkin* funds will dry up and cause a decline in the market.

Japan's banks can count 45% of the unrealized gains in their portfolios toward their capital for the accounting by the BIS standards that will come into effect in March 1993. Each time the NSA falls or the yen falls against the dollar (40% of the banks' assets are denominated in foreign currencies), concern for capital adequacy is revived (see Figure 6.7).

Table 6.7
The Relationship between the Banks' Capital Ratios, the NSA and the Yen

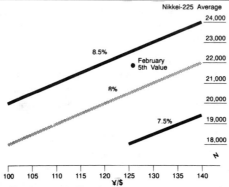

Source: Salomon Brothers and *The Economist*, February 8, 1991

In 1992, there is much trouble in the banking industry because of non-performing real estate and stock market loans. The banks have not been calling in the real estate loans. This has caused more trouble for the already weak stock market, which has fallen from its December 1989 high of 38,916 to as low as 16,500 in April 1992. Banks have been selling stock to cover their non-performing loans and to raise their capital ratios to comply with the BIS standards.

Japanese banks may count 45% of their unrealized gains on their stock portfolios towards their capital. By March 1993 banks must have capital equal to 8% of their risk-weighted assets to meet the BIS standard. At least half of these assets must be *tier-one* equity, which is shareholders' assets and retained earnings. The rest of their capital, called *tier-two* includes subordinated debt, a portion of loan loss reserves and unrealized stock share gains. As pointed out in the *Economist*, banks can expand tier-two resources in various ways such as by lending money to offshore subsidiaries to help them buy the same bank's subordinated debt.

The essence of the bank's problem is a lack of tier-one capital, which in February 1992 was only slightly more than 4% of assets for all the banks. This constrains bank lending and may have prolonged the 1991–92 slump in Japan.

There are several ways, according to David Atkinson, a Salomon Brothers banking analyst in Tokyo, that banks can increase their tier-one capital:

- They may issue new equity, but with the weak stock market and the MOF informal ban on new equity imposed in April 1990, this is not currently a very good option.

- They can increase their return on assets to enlarge their retained assets, for example, by selling stock with a dividend yield of 0.7% and replacing it with assets with higher yields. Since there has been some cross-holding selling by various financial institutions, the banks have not been large stock sellers.

Selling pressure by various institutions peaked in early April 1992 and then subsided somewhat. Should there be a rally in the stock market from the very depressed 18,000 level on the NSA in May 1992, the banks' positions would be greatly improved. This current situation and future prospects are discussed in Chapter 11.

RESENTMENT AND PRAISE FOR JAPANESE INVESTMENT ABROAD

The Bridgestone case is interesting. Bridgestone bought a truck tire plant from Firestone Tire and Rubber in LaVergne, Tennessee, in 1983. The plant had labor problems and very poor productivity. Within six years Bridgestone turned it around and went on to buy the rest of Firestone in May 1988 for $2.6 billion. Firestone, focusing on maximizing return to shareholders, had been cutting back on its manufacturing and concentrating on auto service centers. Firestone had halved its labor force, shut down ten of its 17 North American plants, and sold some of its businesses. It created a mess of problems with inefficient plants, poor labor and dealer relations, as well as poor supplier relations. Productivity at Firestone plants was about half that at Bridgestone.

Bridgestone is still 40% held by the founding family. The company began as a manufacturer of tabi, traditional footwear. It has half the replacement tire market in Japan and 35% of the new car tire market. It purchased Firestone in an attempt to follow its customers into North America. But immediately on acquisition, GM, purchasing 20% of its output, dropped Firestone as a supplier. Though it won a contract with Honda, this does not compensate.

Atlanta has openly asked Japanese investors to buy its trophy buildings. Kentucky recently took a ¥10 billion loan in yen specifically to give concessions to Japanese corporations relocating there. The Toyota Camry factory in central Kentucky has been a very successful venture for Kentucky as well as for Toyota. On the other hand, communities in the Gold Coast of Australia, in Hawaii, in Anchorage, Alaska, and elsewhere are up in arms about being priced out of the market and for their land falling into foreign hands.

The Japanese globalization will not come without its costs, particularly with the not untypical plan to completely take over and to vertically integrate. Some Australians complain that the Japanese never spend any Australian money on a vacation there. Everything is paid to Japanese corporations in yen.

The Japanese are increasingly aware of this resentment, which is natural for virtually any outsider. A growing number of deals have been canceled, and although this is most publicly discussed in the real estate and mergers and acquisitions area, it happens elsewhere as well. Some Japanese companies have also faced strikes and other frictions with trade unions when they absorbed foreign subsidiaries as well as disputes with local residents and foreign governments. Their presence in South Africa has not helped. It will be a real challenge for the Japanese expansionists to use the vision necessary to bring out the positive aspects of these acquisitions for the benefit of all.

Japanese companies are usually not vertically integrated; they depend on suppliers. For example the just-in-time inventory of Toyota and other firms saves a lot of money and gains them much flexibility. Much of the costs borne by suppliers might burden a large, vertically integrated firm. On the other hand, leisure firms tend to be more integrated, with pre-sold packages including travel, tours, accommodations, and meals paid for in yen and spent in Japanese-owned facilities. The profit is yen-based. And it is the profit that provides for regeneration.

The Japanese are attempting to be good neighbors as they follow their investments. In Norman, Oklahoma, the Japanese employees of Hitachi drive U.S. cars and spread themselves around different neighborhoods. Hitachi has set up the Hitachi Foundation in Washington, headed by former cabinet member, Elliot Richardson, with an endowment of $25 million. Hitachi is buying $350 million annually of capital goods for their Japanese plants.

Mazda's Flat Rock, Michigan, plant received tax concessions for 12 years with a total incentive package of about $120 million; in turn, it is giving $100,000 a year to the town and an additional $1 million for a sewage project, as well as $70,000 to the United Way.

The Japanese government is considering tax deductions for Japanese companies if they give money to hospitals, schools, and other charities in the U.S. This would put them on par with U.S. domestic firms and overcome the difference in tax codes in Japan and the U.S.

AND THE OTHER SIDE—SUPPORT

Walter Yetnikoff, president of CBS Records, interviewed in *Forbes*, December 11, 1989, said he believes Sony has been a good parent. Sony purchased CBS Records in January 1988. First it freed CBS Records from the bureaucracy, enabling creative people to begin a turnaround of the company. Over the years, the company had come to depend upon superstars and had neglected developing new artists. It did not have enough talent coming up to provide income in cycles when the stars were not producing. Sony got some negative press and, in the year following its purchase, income fell dramatically, but this can be attributed to the problem of the lack of new talent that occurred in the years before the sale. Their whole strategy of development has been revamped. Previously, CBS Records would put out two songs giving a new artist or group two tries at competing with the superstars to get on the Top 40. If they failed, that was that. Now new artists start with MTV videos, concert tours, college radio, and other promotions. CBS Records is also beginning to spawn new labels, which will enable it to promote more artists.

WHY DID THE JAPANESE INVEST SO MUCH ABROAD?

There are many explanations[11] for the acceleration of Japanese investment abroad from 1985–90, including the following:

- The yen was very strong. At ¥125 to ¥160 per dollar, assets in the U.S. are cheap.
- Japanese investors were willing to consider and purchase investments with relatively low rates of return because their cost of capital has been extremely low from 1989 to early 1991. They have long investment horizons.
- With so much money available, the Japanese simply had to spend it somewhere. Domestic savings far outpace domestic investment needs. Japanese net external assets at the end of 1987 were more than $1 trillion U.S., up 47.3% from 1986. Private savings are accumulating at the rate of about $1.8 billion a day, and this is only a part of the growth in wealth.
- The increase of trade protectionism in the U.S. and other countries as trading blocks are formed makes it advantageous to buy or build plants and produce in the home market for sale there or elsewhere or even for export to Japan.
- Japanese firms wish to establish overseas operations for long-run technological development.
- Many foreign districts, such as U.S. states, are eager for the Japanese to build plants and create jobs for their people and to have the resulting highly efficient and productive activities and the positive educational, economic, and other benefits. Rather than band together, individual regions compete against each other and further the process of Japanese investment under advantageous terms for the Japanese.
- The foreign operations allow the Japanese firms to expand and capture new markets abroad without fear of quotas, with lower worker costs, and with a positive reaction by the locals and the host government.
- The global strategy is to expand and strengthen overseas production for the long term.
- The Japanese wish to secure long-run supplies of natural resources and raw materials. This includes large recent purchases of agricultural land for cattle and citrus orchards.

---

[11]Thanks to Kobayashi (1988) for some of these.

- The developing subsidiaries can pass on valuable information to the headquarters in R&D, technology, marketing, finance, global trends and the like.
- Corporate tax rates in certain foreign financial centers, such as Singapore and Hong Kong, are much lower than in Japan.
- Profits from subsidiaries in foreign countries can be used to pay dividends to insurance company investors.
- There is a rapid influx of imports from the newly industrialized economies (NIEs) particularly those in Asia, and it is profitable to simply produce there in Japanese-owned facilities for export to Japan.

For example, imports of office equipment from Southeast Asia in fiscal 1987 increased 91% over 1986, while imports of audio-visual equipment including TVs and videocassette recorders grew 85%. A survey by the *Oriental Economist* of 54% of the manufacturing companies and 48% of the publicly traded companies found that Japanese corporations have 15,000 subsidiaries and affiliates in 120 countries. They have 1,540,000 local employees on their payrolls and about 32,000 Japanese employees on overseas assignments.

An Economic Planning Agency survey in April 1988 found that two-thirds of the responding firms either have overseas operations or were planning them. However, overseas production is still extremely limited—2.6% versus 17.3% for the U.S. in 1986. This is expected to reach to 6.2% in 1992 with some of this moving to EEC countries. Mergers and acquisitions are preferred to development by 32% of the firms.

Though overall Japanese exports are only about 10% of production, for a number of corporations, exports are a high or sharply rising percentage of production; for example, they are 99.7% for Uniden, 80.4% for Minolta, 75.5% for Canon, 66.6% for Casio, and 62.9% for Honda. Disposing of this production domestically would be extremely difficult. Meanwhile, overseas production as a percentage of total sales is 30.8% at Nissan and Yakult, 38.2% at Sanyo Electric, and 25.7% at Kumagai Gumi.

A new big player in Japan is also entering the scene: the massive Japanese pension funds. Until 1989, they were allowed to invest only 3% of their fund assets abroad. Now they are permitted by the Ministry of Finance to invest up to 20%.

CHAPTER 7
JAPANESE INVESTMENT IN U.S. AND OTHER FOREIGN REAL ESTATE

Toshi Sato owns a 135-square-meter apartment in downtown Tokyo. He bought it for a half-million dollars five years ago. Now its official market value is $8 million. Half of that apparent appreciation is real: the other half comes from the devaluation of the dollar.

Earlier this year, Sato talked with a bank in Tokyo and decided to borrow money with his apartment as collateral. The bank offered to loan him $6 million— the usual 80% of current value minus his housing loan—at the prevailing interest rate of 6%.

(H)e looked at Southern California where $1 million, or a small fraction of his lending limit, can buy a nice five-bedroom house on the waterfront. With several direct flights a day from Tokyo, it doesn't take much longer to reach Los Angeles than his Karuizawa country home (only 150 km from his Tokyo apartment) in holiday traffic. Sato and his family now visit his Newport Beach house in California more often than his villa outside Tokyo.

Kenichi Ohmae, *Japan Times*, December 12, 1988

A CASE STUDY OF REAL ESTATE PURCHASES IN THE U.S: GENERAL KAWAMOTO

I absolutely will not sell. I'm talking about holding for 20 years or more.
Genshiro Kawamoto, Japanese Real Estate Magnate

Genshiro Kawamoto is said to cruise around Honolulu in the *Kawamotomobile* picking out properties and has his aides negotiate their purchase. According to *BusinessWeek*, he has at least 178 rental properties in Hawaii for which he paid $173 million, including the $46 million Kaiser estate. He bought so much that public backlash led to a legislative proposal to ban home ownership by non-residents. So he moved on, at least temporarily, to other areas such as Santa Rosa, near the Napa Valley, and Sacramento.

There he plans to invest some $500 million to build some 245 single-family homes in Santa Rosa and 350 near Sacramento. He also plans to buy 1,000 homes from builders in Sacramento, nearly 100% of the area's annual production, then watch the reaction before buying more. Kawamoto considers Sacramento cheap, and because of its fast-growing electronics industry and still-reasonable home prices, he thinks it's the best market in the U.S. Sacramento Mayor Anne Rudin asks, "We want foreign capital. Why is this different from a New York company investing here?" Kawamoto started in the 1950s by building a home for resale while he was running the family kimono business. This grew into his realty firm, Marugen Corp., which owns 3,000 apartments and numerous office buildings in Japan, worth over $1 billion.

In the 1980s, there was a dramatic increase in the wealth of Japanese corporations and individuals who own land and stocks. No tax is owed on these gains until the land is sold and the gains realized. Even then, capital gains are taxed at a much lower rate than income. Hence, there was a great attraction to borrow on the value of the land at Japan's low interest rates to buy additional investments. Property is priced very high because of the scarcity of land, the unwillingness to sell because of the tax implications, the fear of losing out on still more gains, and the need to live somewhere. Add to this a near doubling of the value of the yen, from about 260 in the fall of 1985 to the April 1990 value or about 155 to 160, against the U.S. dollar and you have enormous buying power.

Another factor contributing to high land prices is that the Japanese corporations and individuals have a lot of money (recall household savings increase by $1.8 billion a day), and there is a strong desire to invest at home first.[1] This affects many other relationships in the economy, such as vacations and consumption.

Japan's land has been thought to be a safe but expensive investment. In comparison, real estate in the U.S. looks very attractive to the Japanese. Not only is the price low, but the interest rate on the loans, denominated in yen has also been fairly low. There is, of course, exchange rate risk. Although much of the money used to buy foreign real estate is composed of funds already in U.S. currency, Treasury bills, bonds, and the like, some holdings have already incurred large currency losses. Procedures such as those we discussed in Chapter 6 of Ziemba and Schwartz (1991) can be used to minimize risk for direct yen investments in U.S. dollars or other currencies.

---

[1]This is often called a cultural bias and somehow interpreted as a negative; but, it is a strength. It means that factories are built and people employed. Also, alternatives are only recently becoming available, as foreign investment was strictly limited until recent openings of financial markets, and Japan for decades was involved in economic rebuilding and needed all its funds for investment at home. Other developing countries should take note and prevent capital flight.

In this chapter, we review these purchases and the dramatic rise in Japanese ownership of U.S. real estate in the period 1985 to early 1992. Since the stock market decline in Japan in 1990–92 and the decline in real estate prices in the U.S. in the 1991–92 recession, some of these purchases have lost considerable value. According to Daniel Neidich, head of the real estate department of Goldman Sachs and Co., "the Japanese supported the U.S. market long after other players had withdrawn." Some of these losses are reviewed as well.

AMERICA IS SELLING ITSELF CHEAP

This year when they turn on the lights of that Christmas tree in Rockefeller Center, we Americans are going to have to come to grips with the reality that this great national celebration is actually occurring on Japanese property.

Connecticut Senator Joseph Lieberman

In the late 1980s, Japanese individuals and corporations bought choice parcels of U.S. real estate. The trend accelerated until, in 1990, the Ministry of Finance asked buyers to ease off and lenders to stop lending. The U.S., preoccupied with its trade deficit, has even encouraged the financial markets to devalue the dollar which has encouraged the purchase of land and other assets as we saw in Chapter 6. Instead of emphasizing the manufacture and sale of high-quality products in the U.S. and abroad, the emphasis has been to let the dollar slide, so U.S. goods will become so cheap abroad someone will buy them, and the superior Japanese and German goods will become so expensive that U.S. consumers will stop buying them. This is the conclusion of some econometric models, but it does not seem wise.[2] Where goods are cheap, incomes are low, and the people are poor. Where products cost a lot, incomes are high, and people are wealthy. An exchange rate policy that cheapens U.S. products also impoverishes Americans. Before the accounts are balanced, vast amounts of choice U.S. real estate and other valuable assets will be in Japanese hands, and Americans will be poorer.[3]

---

[2] Analyses such as Sato (1988) and our discussions elsewhere in this book suggest the U.S. is still on the wrong part of the J-curve. An excellent analysis along these lines is Marris (1985, 1987). If one simply lets the economics speak, then the arguments lead to a lower dollar, and Marris' predictions of the yen/dollar exchange rate were remarkably close to the actual rate in 1985–87.

[3] This is also a problem for other countries whose currencies are loosely tied to the U.S. dollar, such as Australia and Canada.

Proponents of this fire sale argue that Japanese direct investment in the U.S. is still low compared to many other countries. From 1965 to 1989, foreigners had acquired about 19% of the prime office space of 335 million square feet in New York. The leading nationality of the purchasers is Canadian (7.3%), Japanese (5.4%), British (2.7%) and Dutch (1.4%). Olympia & York of Toronto is the largest single foreign owner. They began acquiring property in the depressed mid-1970s. More than half the office buildings in Los Angeles are foreign owned; in Atlanta, 12%.

Since 1986, Japanese investors have acquired such commercial real estate as the Exxon, Citicorp, Mobil, ABC, and Paine Webber buildings and hotels such as the Algonquin, the Stanhope, the Intercontinental, and the Essex House. As of June 30, 1988, Japanese investment in U.S. manufacturing was only the eighth highest, well behind Britain, the Netherlands, Switzerland, West Germany, and France. But when real estate is included, Japan trailed only Britain and the Netherlands in total U.S. investment at the end of 1987. The Japanese have subsequently passed the Netherlands. Japanese companies invested $15.08 billion in U.S. land and manufacturing in 1988. Total cumulative investment was $40 billion, versus $90 billion for Britain.

The Japanese emphasis on real estate is very high and escalated in the 1980s. During 1987, three-quarters of all the foreign investment in U.S. real estate, some $12.77 billion out of about $16.50 billion, was Japanese. The Japanese invested $16.54 billion in U.S. real estate in 1988, an increase of nearly 30% over 1987. Cumulative investments in U.S. real estate at the end of 1988 were about $42.88 billion, according to the Los Angeles accounting firm Kenneth Leventhal & Co. By 1991, these investments were at least $76 billion in commercial projects alone. California ranked first among the states with $5.62 billion in Japanese real estate investments in 1988, followed by New York at $2.8 billion, and Illinois at $1.87 billion. Los Angeles topped all cities with $3.05 billion, with New York City in second at $2.8 billion. Figure 7.1 shows the growth from 1985 to 1991, and the distribution of purchases across states in 1988. Table 7.1 shows the distribution of the investments in 1987 and 1988. Although still small, the largest increase in investments is in golf courses; look for much more of that in the future. In 1988, there was less emphasis on Hawaiian purchases and more on those in Chicago with continuing interest in New York and Los Angeles. In 1990, a survey of U.S. based Japanese corporate executives found that California remains the favored state for Japanese real estate investment, New York was second, followed by Hawaii (with 75, 42, and 32 votes, respectively).

Figure 7.1
Japanese Investment in U.S. Real Estate (1985–91) and Where the Japanese Invested, in 1988, Billions of Dollars

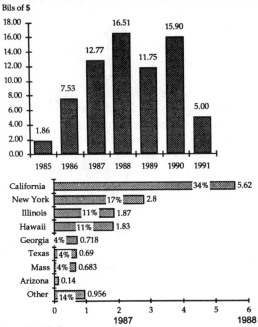

Source: Kenneth Leventhal & Co.

Table 7.1
Types of Japanese Investment in the U.S.

Type of Property	1987		1988	
	$ millions	% total	$ millions	% total
Office	5,190	41	8,310	50
Hotel/resort	4,570	36	3,577	22
Mixed use	740	6	2,415	15
Residential	1,300	10	702	4
Retail	560	4	644	4
Industrial	30	0	310	2
Land	470	4	302	2
Golf courses	10	0	202	1
Other	0	0	81	0

Source: Kenneth Leventhal & Co.

Figure 7.2 shows the direct foreign investment in U.S. real estate in 1989 and 1990. Some $35 billion was invested in 1990 with the Japanese buying $15.9 billion. In 1990, investors from the Netherlands outpaced investors from the U.K. and Canada for a total of $5.2 billion, versus $4.20 and $4.00 billion, respectively. Those from the U.K. and Canada were net sellers of U.S. properties. The Canadian portfolio was reduced 22%. Even Japanese and Dutch investment was much lower. A number of conditions had led up to this: oversupply of U.S. properties, overvaluation of those properties reflected in the gap between sellers' and buyers' expectations concerning value and, for foreigners, the decline in the U.S. dollar, resulting in fear of currency exposure, problems at home, for example, and, for the Japanese, the decline in the NSA and rising interest rates.

Table 7.2 shows the investment by metropolitan area and Table 7.3 shows the type of acquisition made. The Japanese prefer to buy an existing property outright or as a joint venture, or to construct a new property as a joint venture. Table 7.4 shows the property acquisition method by investor type in 1988.

Figure 7.2
Direct Foreign Investment in U.S. Real Estate in 1989 and 1990 in Billions of U.S. Dollars

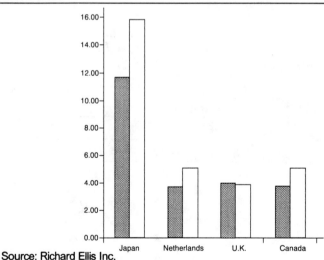

Source: Richard Ellis Inc.

Table 7.2
Japanese Investment in U.S. Real Estate by Metropolitan Area through 1988

Area	Through 1987 Total $ millions	%	1988 Total $ millions	%
Anaheim	360	1	506	3
Atlanta	130	–	718	4
Boston	162	1	683	4
Chicago	1,060	4	1,871	11
Dallas	950	4	505	3
Honolulu	4,420	17	1,325	8
Los Angeles	4,570	17	3,049	18
New York	5,831	22	2,802	17
Phoenix	1,590	6	140	1
San Diego	400	2	421	3
San Francisco-Oakland	1,172	4	740	5
Seattle	731	3	341	2
Washington, D.C.	431	2	638	4
Others	4,493	17	2,805	17
Total	26,340		16,544	

Source: Kenneth Leventhal & Co.

Table 7.3
Japanese Investment in U.S. Real Estate by Property Acquisition Method in 1988

Property acquisition method	1988 $ millions	1988 %
Existing property, full ownership	5,384	33
New construction, full ownership	909	5
Existing property, joint venture	4,276	26
New construction, joint venture	5,975	36

Source: Kenneth Leventhal & Co.

The rise in U.S. investment by the Japanese seems accounted for by the strong yen, the relaxation of Ministry of Finance restrictions on foreign assets, and the perceived security of U.S. land investments. According to the Real Estate Research Corporation, Los Angeles is the best market for real estate in the U.S. despite its traffic congestion, smog, ridiculously high housing prices, and regulatory barriers. Its research suggests that Houston, Denver, and Dallas are places to avoid. The positive aspects of Los Angeles and the whole Southern California region, namely economic diversity, job growth, climate, quality of life, and access to the Pacific Rim, outweigh the negative aspects. Growth restriction is actually a plus for Southern California because one does not have as high housing prices relative to incomes as New York, Washington, and Boston. The RERC's research indicates that fewer and fewer people can afford to live in or near these latter centers, and that will limit economic expansion. Indeed, their real estate prices have been flat or even declining since 1987.

Table 7.4
Japanese Investment in U.S. Real Estate Property Acquisition Method by Investor Type, 1988 in Millions of U.S. Dollars

| | Full Ownership | | Joint Venture | | |
InvestorType	Existing Property	New Construction	Existing Property	New Construction	Total
Construction	362	111	0	2,916	3,389
Development	513	315	456	1,483	2,767
Life insurance	560	0	1,707	343	2,610
Misc. public & private≠	723	193	142	525	1,583
Individual investor / investment co.	1,054	77	432	0	1,563
Retail	660	0	228	0	888
Trading	125	0	191	412	728
Securities	0	0	420	0	420
Finance and leasing	245	24	0	0	269
Financial institution	0	0	225	0	225
Total *	4,242	720	3,801	5,679	14,442

≠Represents all public and private companies for which a category was not previously identified.

*The amounts are based on the transactions for which the necessary investor and deal information could be ascertained or about 87% of the total transactions.

Source: Kenneth Leventhal & Co.

Because of an increasing familiarity with U.S. real estate, Japanese investors are adding to their low risk trophy properties, greater risk office buildings, and new construction projects via joint ventures. Japanese investors are also buying in locations other than California, New York, and Hawaii. Investments in Illinois and Georgia are increasing. During the first eight months of 1988, more than half of the Japanese investment was from land development and life insurance companies, but investment and leasing companies, securities firms and trading houses are starting to enter the market, according to Kenneth Leventhal Co. Of new Japanese investment, nearly 60% is in office properties. The Japanese are also linking up with U.S. real estate firms. For example, Sumitomo, with about 100 offices in Japan, has affiliated with Fred Sands. Together they sold over $25 million of residential real estate in California in 1988, not a large amount but a start to a much greater activity in the future.

Nomura Securities offered individuals as well as institutional investors in Japan and Europe a unique way to bet on the future value of a vacant skyscraper in Manhattan, the old J.C. Penney building. Ten-year bonds were offered with a 3% premium. The investors receive back their principal plus half of the building's independently appraised value over $600 million on expiry of the bond. When the building is rented, the 3% will be topped up to 5% with the net rentals, and further net rental income, once 5% is reached, will be split 50–50 with the bondholders and the partnership. Should the building be sold before the bonds expire, the bondholders receive their principal and coupon payments plus half the amount of the sale over $600 million.

The partnership bought the building for $352 million in May 1988 and spent about $100 million in renovations. The supposition is that the building will be worth about $1 billion on expiry, providing good cash flow and capital gains to the largely Japanese bondholders and a fine profit for the organizers, Tishman Speyer Properties of New York, Trammell Crow Co. of Dallas, and Nomura, which are selling the $600 million paper. Half is backed by the building with these bonds and the other half is owed by the partnership at 1 to 1.5% above the T-bond rate of 8.3% when this deal was set in June 1989. To show the complexity of modern deals of this sort, the financing involves two Netherlands Antilles shell companies, a private trust registered there, and five law firms. U.S. investors cannot buy such bonds in their initial offering, but they can in the secondary market. The deal allows medium-sized players to own part of trophy buildings, most of which are bought by huge Japanese insurance companies and banks.

Daiwa Securities and Goldman Sachs negotiated a joint venture for the sale of U.S. real estate securities to Japanese investors. These include mortgage bonds and shares in real estate investment trusts. Daiwa would find the Japanese investors, and Goldman Sachs would handle the investments.

The Japanese follow through on their investments and are attempting to fit into the community. Soon after buying the 52-story Arco Plaza in Los Angeles, Shigeru Kobayashi, head of the Shuwa Investment Corp., paid a visit to Mayor Tom Bradley. In the Japanese tradition of bringing gifts, he presented a check for $100,000 for a monument Bradley wants to erect to welcome immigrants. Bradley has received $200,000 in donations from more than a dozen Japanese firms during the last four years.

TROPHY BUILDINGS AND SPECIAL PROPERTIES

Georgia invites Japanese investors to buy Atlanta's trophy building

John A. Bolt

Japanese investors like to invest where they are comfortable and where they believe their money is safe. In fact, in many cases, it is not their money at all. It is not hard for them to obtain substantial loans at relatively low interest rates for so-called trophy buildings (world class buildings in premium locations) and choice resort rental property. Assuming the rental return becomes larger than the 6% (or so) interest rate on the loan, the purchaser will eventually get the building more or less free. For example, if the net initial return is 7% and grows by 5% per year, and the cost of the loan is 6%, the entire building will be paid off in less than 20 years, even if the investor gets a loan in yen for the whole amount. Yen/dollar fluctuations and other factors make the transaction more complicated than this, but the point is that even with slightly rising rents or losses in the early years, there are considerable profits in the long haul by buying these choice properties with their well-established and secure tenants. Since much of the value of the property is the building, its depreciation provides a substantial paper tax loss in Japan as well. Buildings in so-called second-tier cities such as Atlanta are available at much cheaper prices than those in first-tier cities such as New York, Los Angeles, Chicago, Boston and Washington.

There are a number of advantages for the U.S. in selling these buildings, plus some disadvantages in selling off the country cheap. Jobs are the main reason for Atlanta's interest in selling its trophy buildings, such as the IBM Tower, which the Sumitomo Life Insurance Company is buying for $300 million. The headquarters tower of Georgia-Pacific Corporation and the CNN Center, where Ted Turner's broadcasting empire is centered, are also reportedly for sale. Japanese investors already have a large presence in

Table 7.5
Japanese Trophy Building/Property Purchases in the U.S.

Bldg/prop	Location	Price	Buyer	Date
Pebble Peach Complex	Monterey	$841 M	Minoru Isatani	1990
Hotel Bel Air	Los Angeles	$110 M	Sekitei Kaihatsu Co.	1989
IBM Tower	Atlanta	$350 M	Sumitomo Life Ins.	1989
Intercontinental Hotels	chain	$2.15 B	Seibu/Saison Group	1988
Kaiser Estate	Hawaii	$46 M	Genshiro Kawamoto	1988
Wells Fargo Building	Los Angeles	$147 M	na	1988
Marriot Hotel	Century City	$85 M	na	1988
Hyatt Regency	Chicago	$260 M	na	1988
3 First National Plaza	Chicago	$254 M	na	1988
Madison Plaza	Chicago	$235 M	na	1988
Westin Hotels	chain	$1.4 B	Aoki Corp. (with RM Bass Group)	1987
Building at 666 Fifth Ave	New York	$500 M	Sumitomo Realty	1987
Meridien Hotel	San Francisco	$100 M	All Nippon Air	1987
Dunes Hotel and Casino	Las Vegas	$155 M	Masao Nangaku	1987
Arco Plaza	Los Angeles	$620 M	Shuwa Investment Corp.	1986
Exxon Building	New York	$610 M	Mitsui Fudosan (N Y)	1986
Tower 49	New York	$303.5 M	Kata Kagaku	1986
Hyatt Regency	Waikiki	$270 M	Azabu	1986
Capital Cities/ ABC Inc. Headquarters	New York	$174.2 M	Shuwa Investment Corp.	1986
Paine Webber Building	Boston	$100 M	Shuwa Investment Corp.	1986
Tiffany Building	New York	$94 M	Dai-Ichi Real Estate	1986
US News & World	Wash., D.C.	$80 M	Shuwa Investment Corp.	1986
Aladdin Hotel and Casino	Las Vegas	$54 M	Ginjo Yasuda	1986
Headquarters of Wang Laboratories	Near Boston	na	Sumitomo Life Realty	1985

Source: various, including Viner (1988)

Georgia with 236 Japanese-owned entities employing 12,100 people, with an investment of some $810 million as of July 1988, according to the Consulate General of Japan.

Besides paying high prices (often outbidding others and setting new records in the process) and not defaulting, Japanese investors have been good and stable landlords. According to a 1987 study by MIT Professor Lawrence Bacow, the Japanese are interested in all types of rental property except single-family housing. Because the investors are largely institutional, they have a strong interest in maintaining their properties for a long period rather than engaging in speculative purchases. Table 7.5 lists some of these trophy buildings purchased by the Japanese.

Perhaps the most eye opening purchase in 1989 was Mitsubishi Estates' acquisition of 51% of the 19-building complex known as Rockefeller Center for $849 million. The deal was a good one for the Rockefeller family because they were too heavily concentrated in properties. This cash allowed the Rockefellers to diversify. The deal was also perceived to be a good one for Mitsubishi Estates, which owns at least 24 major buildings in downtown Tokyo. With prices in downtown Tokyo more than $500 million for a single building, half of Rockefeller Center for $849 million is not that expensive. A real estate investment trust, Rockefeller Center Properties, bought a $1.3 billion mortgage in 1985 on most of the buildings and has the option of converting to 71.5% ownership in 2000. Famous tenants of the Rockefeller Center include Time Warner, Celanase, General Electric, and Simon & Schuster. Concerned about backlash, the Japanese government is discouraging the purchase of landmark sites and Japanese interests did back away from the Sears Tower in Chicago. Days after the Rockefeller Center sale, a consortium led by Mori Building Development paid $300 million for 85% of Houston's Four Oaks Place office center.

Minoru Isatani bought the fabled complex of four golf courses at Pebble Beach near Monterey, California, for $841 million in 1990. The complex, which is about 5,300 acres, includes the Pebble Beach Lodge and the Inn at Spanish Bay as well as three of the top one hundred courses in the U.S. Pebble Beach itself rivals St. Andrews as the world's most famous golf course. Isatani owns nine courses in Japan, two in France and one in Austria. In addition to Pebble Beach, he is building a $200 million golf course and hotel on a 1,881-acre tract near Las Vegas and is co-developing a $357 million golf and hotel complex on a 1,100-acre site along the Kona coast in Hawaii. The vendors were a group led by financier Marvin Davis, who made a profit of some $500 million since their purchase of the property in 1983.

Isatani's plans for Pebble Beach include selling memberships to Japanese for $750,000 each. Months of negotiations and ill-will led to the local authorities blocking the plan. The locals did not like privatizing America's top course. This, plus the general decline in U.S. commercial and resort real estate prices, led to intense financial pressure. The sharp decline in golf course prices in Japan during 1990–92 (see Figures 5.4–5.7) put additional pressure on Isatani's position. He offered the Pebble Beach property for sale in the $500 million range in early 1992. That translated into a loss of $341 million plus a year and a half of effort and interest. The purchaser was Masatsuga Takabayashi, chairman and president of the Lone Cypress Co.

Dai-Ichi Mutual Life Insurance bought the New York Citicorp Center in 1987. Other new high technology buildings such as Kumagai Gumi's Worldwide Plaza are strong competitors for tenants.

Japanese investors own at least 25 of the major buildings in Los Angeles, including 30% of the rental office space in downtown Los Angeles, and a 49% interest in the Riviera Country Club. In 1989, Sekitei Kaihatsu Company paid a record $1.2 million for each of the 92 rooms (a total of $110 million) for the legendary Hotel Bel Air sitting on a 4.5-hectare plot in Los Angeles, Sekitei is a closely held 95-year-old company operating luxury hotels, restaurants, and resorts in Japan. Other bidders, all willing to pay more than $1 million per room included Tobishima Associates, a construction company, and Seibu Saison, which owns Intercontinental Hotels. The price for this luxury hotel, sold by oil heiress Caroline Hunt, surpassed the previous record room price of $757,000 the Sultan of Brunei paid to acquire the Beverly Hills Hotel in 1987, and it more than doubled the $496,000 per room Donald Trump paid in 1988 for the Plaza Hotel in New York. As with many other luxury hotels purchased by the Japanese, the present management, in this case Dallas-based Rosewood Property Co., owned by Moss Hunt, will continue to operate the hotel for at least ten more years.

Large property investments in the U.S. may be peaking for the simple reason that not many more trophy buildings are available for sale. The Japanese paid top dollar for these choice properties. Many believed at the time that they overpaid.[4] They set the market, and other properties came up to their price. Since they did not plan to sell, they reasoned that a slightly higher price paid would not matter much many years down the road. While the Japanese are the top foreign buyers of prime U.S. real estate, there is increasing competition from Holland, South Korea, Sweden, and Taiwan. The Japanese money bound for the U.S. competes with opportunities primarily in Europe, Australia, and Hong Kong.

The strategy of Mitsui Fudosan in New York, a wholly owned subsidiary of the 323-year-old Mitsui Development Corporation, sums up the Japanese approach:[5]

- When acquiring existing buildings, Mitsui seeks natural stone such as granite, limestone, or marble, eschewing glass curtain wall, concrete, or brick. They also seek corner locations.

- When building, *Mitsui builds to hold forever.* The same philosophy applies to acquisitions; thus it seeks trophy buildings that will remain so for the next 100 to 200 years. Because Mitsui's philosophy is to hold

---

[4]In general, such analysts have proven right in 1991–92 during the U.S. real estate recession. A very good analysis of why the U.S. real estate market was likely to decline based on demographic changes was made in Mankiw and Weil (1988).

[5]Adapted from William Howell, director acquisitions, in an interview with Holly Sraeel.

forever, it is difficult for it to do joint ventures with U.S. investors who typically have short horizons, unless there is a buy/sell agreement for 100% ownership.

- In order to hold forever, Mitsui does much preliminary work before investing. Before the Japanese came to New York, they studied the city for five years.

- Mitsui looks at transportation, accessibility, quality of life, and always considers how it is likely to be assessed in 50 years.

- Any deal must pass on the four criteria of location, quality, need, and personality.

- The Japanese are both patient and thorough. "If it's a deal we're trying to close, by the time we get close to the final contract, I know ten times more about the property than you, even if you're the owner."

LAS VEGAS

The Japanese are heavily invested in Los Angeles, owning about 40% of the downtown plus many other significant holdings in the area. Further purchases are proceeding, but the prices have become very high. They see Las Vegas as a low-cost alternative and adjunct to Los Angeles and had already invested about $800 million there. The resort city still has low real estate prices and taxes, a low cost of living, a strong real estate market, a receptive municipal government, a warm climate and an attractive lifestyle. It is also reasonably close to the large markets of Southern California (and not much further by plane as a vacation spot from Japan).

About 400,000 Japanese visit Las Vegas each year. More than half of the Japanese tourists who come to Los Angeles also visit Las Vegas. Nevada has a trade office in Tokyo. It is the sixth fastest growing metropolitan area in the U.S. One aim is to make the city even closer to Los Angeles via a high speed train that travels up to 300 miles an hour which, by as early as 1995, could be shuttling passengers back and forth in 70 minutes instead of the current five hours. C. Itoh and Co., the big Japanese trading firm, has committed to 40% of the cost of the $3 billion project which includes fast local trains as well. (The justly famous Japanese *shinkansen*, or bullet train, makes this an interesting venture.)

True to form, the Japanese buy top properties with good revenue potential. Japanese businessman Ginji Yasuda became the first non-U.S.-resident to own a major Las Vegas casino when he bought the Aladdin for $54 million in 1986. In 1987, billionaire Masao Nangaku bought the Dunes

Hotel and Casino for $155 million. He also built a $120 million, 35-story non-gaming hotel, which was completed in 1991. Ginji Yasuda bought the Aladdin Hotel and Casino and has invested over $120 million in it. Another Japanese group, led by Katsuki Manabe, who is affiliated with one of the city's largest suppliers of gambling devices, Sigma Game Inc., has its sights on the 400-room Holiday International, which it has leased, renamed the Park Hotel. They have an option to buy it. Universal Distributing of Nevada, another Japanese group dominant in the market for slot machines in Las Vegas, recently bought eight hectares near Las Vegas.

Sukeaki Izumi, who owns five major hotels in Japan and Guam, purchased the 324-room Treasury Hotel and renamed it the San Remo. He invested $30 million for the hotel's purchase and renovation and made another $30 million 340-room addition in 1990 followed by further expansion of the hotel and casino. Izumi, who first came to Las Vegas in 1957, has moved there to personally supervise the project.

The electronics giant Cosmo World is planning a huge golf resort project just outside Las Vegas at a cost of some $200 million. Completion is scheduled for 1993. The resort will include 45 holes of golf, 2,700 condominiums, apartments, and luxury homes, a tennis stadium, and a 700-room hotel. Besides its investments in Japan, Cosmo World also has investments in Europe, Hawaii, Los Angeles, San Francisco, and Tucson.

Business in Las Vegas is good and especially so for hotels and casinos. Circus Circus, for example, typically has an occupancy rate above 98%. Some 16 million tourists including 1.7 million conventioneers went to Las Vegas in 1987 filling its 61,150 hotel rooms 83.3% of the time. They spent $8.6 billion, of which $2.7 billion was in the casinos. The current construction boom has 10,000 hotel rooms on the drawing board. The largest are a $565 million 3,600-room Golden Nugget on the Strip and a 4,000 room addition to Circus Circus. The Japanese are not dominant in Las Vegas, but they have a growing piece of the action.

HAWAII

We interrupt this program with a special bulletin . . . the Japanese have just bought Pearl Harbor . . . I repeat the Japanese have just bought Pearl Harbor.

The Japanese love Hawaii. It has a warm climate. It is close to Japan. Twenty-five percent of the population are of Japanese descent, and many more have roots in China, Korea and other Asian countries. Nearly 2 million Japanese tourists go there each year, out of the nearly 10 million foreign visits. The average Japanese tourist spends $400 a day, which is four times as much as the average U.S. mainlander.

The Japanese have bought numerous hotels and other valuable properties. About two-thirds of the new luxury hotels purchased or built are in Japanese hands. Table 7.5 lists two of the notable purchases, the Kaiser Estate and the Hyatt Regency in Waikiki. Another was the $600 million Hyatt Wailea Hotel on Maui.

AUSTRALIA

Air travel between Australia and Japan is convenient, with many direct flights, and the Japanese feel comfortable going there for vacations. The costs of traveling and staying there are relatively low, and the reversed seasons is a plus. Of particular interest to the Japanese is the Gold Coast. Huge vacation villa complexes have been built there and more are planned.

An example, as reported in the *Japan Times*, is the 50-50 joint venture between Orient Finance and Mitsui to build a large-scale leisure complex in the fashionable Surfers' Paradise area, for about ¥7 billion. The complex will include luxury condominiums, including one 43-story, 187-unit complex with an average unit price of ¥70 million. The condos will be marketed in Japan and Australia. The complex, to be built by the Australian construction firm, the Hulbert Group, will occupy a 17,000 square-meter plot and include such leisure facilities as swimming pools, tennis courts, gymnasiums, a yacht marina, and six detached houses when it is completed in 1992. Orient Finance intends to make the joint venture the first of a chain of resorts in the Pacific, with complexes in the South Pacific and on the west coast of the U.S. It decided to develop the overseas resorts "in the hopes of cashing in on the spreading trend of long vacations among Japanese workers and the overseas travel boom."

The ultimate in Gold Coast luxury living is provided by the $3.65 million Australian penthouse apartments in Grand Marnier at Paradise Waters on an island served by a causeway a few minutes from Central Surfers. This complex is a $150 million project of Kuji Property Ltd., a joint venture of the Australian subsidiaries of Orient Finance and Mitsui Construction, both major Japanese firms. Prices in the 43-story complex range from $340,000 to $3.65 million for one of the two penthouses. The design is like the Empire State Building, with five tiers narrowing up the structure and gardens laid out on the tiers. The complex has spas, barbecues, entertainment halls, lounges, tennis courts, plus a marina for 34 boats along the 120-meter waterfront.

It is now common for large companies or conglomerates, such as Daiwa and Nikko Securities, to build their own rest and health resorts for their employees to use for short vacations. The overhead savings and ability to provide perks for employees provide part of the motivation to build.

Nikko spent some ¥1.5 billion for 116-square meters on the Gold Coast to build such a resort. Daiwa has a 400-square meter facility at Nar-Darak near Melbourne. It planned to build a more massive resort in Fremantle, a port town near Perth on the Indian Ocean, at one of the most beautiful locations in the world. Daiwa originally negotiated to buy 33,000-square meters of publicly held property there, but massive property investments by Japanese corporations have stirred anti-Japanese feelings, causing the parliament of the State of Western Australia to refuse permission to Daiwa to purchase the property alone. Queensland now has set up a register to check foreign ownership of land in that Australian state. Some 75% of the Gold Coast is owned by Japanese.

Daiwa had planned to build housing units for its employees and retirees, who planned to spend one to six months in Fremantle. After negotiations, it was allowed to buy a two-thirds interest, some 6,600 square meters, in a 9,900-square-meter plot for about $1 million Australian. Daiwa bought the land and will re-evaluate what it will do with it since it is much smaller than that required for the original plan.

Other purchases (in Australian dollars) and planned projects by Japanese on the Gold Coast are:

- $341 million for the Sanctuary Cove development at Hope Island which was sold in 1988 by Ariadne Australia to EIE Developments.

- Daikyo's $200 million Palm Meadows Golf Resort at Merrimac.

- Matsushita Investment and Development Company's $260 million Pine Lakes resort on 243 hectares at Ashmore Waters.

- Shinko Ltd.'s $300 million Hope Island Resort on 369 hectares.

In total, $2.5 billion worth of resort projects on over 2,000 hectares are planned, the lion's share by Japanese or with their involvement.

Orient Finance and Daikyo Inc., a builder of condos and resorts, joined to purchase the Cairns Parkroyal Hotel in Australia for A$130 million. This after a Japanese project to build a resort in Cairns was stopped by critical press and opposition of the state government. Toko Haus Co. withdrew its application for permission to buy land to build a resort. Though the Australian government welcomes foreign investment, it has expressed the desire to broaden the investments to include more manufacturing.

In fiscal 1987, total direct investment in Australia by the Japanese was A\$5.4 billion, up 68.8% from the A\$3.2 billion in 1986, which was up 68.4% from A\$1.9 the previous year. The Japanese investment is about one quarter of total direct investment in Australia, some A\$24.8 billion up 34.1% from A\$18.5 billion in fiscal 1986. Britain, New Zealand and the U.S. followed Japan with A\$4.7 billion, A\$2.8 billion, and A\$1.7 respectively. The U.S. and New Zealand investment is dropping. Fully 60% of the Japanese investment in Australia is for buying and developing tourist facilities and other real estate.

HONG KONG

The Japanese occupied Hong Kong from 1942 to August 1945. Forty years later they are buying property there. At a time when many Hong Kong citizens are wary of their future and are using their cash to buy Canadian real estate, particularly in Vancouver and Toronto, the Japanese have been confident about Hong Kong being a good investment. Hong Kong is one of the few markets in the world with sharply rising land prices in 1991 and projections for further rises in 1992. A high inflation rate, low cash equivalent yields and a shortage of other investments except for property and stocks (many of which are property firms or hold much real estate) is fueling the increase. In 1987, the Japanese bought $650 million worth of real estate, triple their 1986 investment, becoming Hong Kong's largest overseas real estate investor. The Japanese began buying Hong Kong property heavily in 1985 when the yen started its rise against the U.S. dollar. Because the Hong Kong dollar is pegged to the U.S. currency, the prices in yen were dropping. High rent yields, 5-10%, compared to 3% or less in Japan, booming prices, and no capital gains taxes add to the appeal. Hong Kong is also only five hours from Tokyo by air, and this proximity to Japan is viewed as a big plus.

Hong Kong is seen as a good market, particularly for speculators who buy commercial, residential, and hotel properties. Most of the buying is by so-called third-tier Japanese companies and entrepreneurs willing to take risks because of the strong yen. Many Japanese believe that China will be the fastest growing place in the world in the coming century (often called the China century). So they wish to set up their front line bases in Hong Kong, which enjoys both the advantages of proximity to China, and a modern, sophisticated business infrastructure.

While most projects are $13 to $30 million, there are some larger ones. One notable purchase, by Paul Sun, a Japanese born Chinese, was $113.5

million for land in the tourist and hotel district of Tsimshatsui. Sun's recently completed Sun Plaza is valued at $384.6 million.

The negatives of Hong Kong are, of course, the return to Chinese sovereignty in 1997 with the considerable uncertainty once this transfer takes place and the reputation of the territory as a place with quick deals while the Japanese have tended to invest for the long-term. The June 1989 Tiananmen Square massacres in Beijing have added substantially to the risk of Hong Kong. The stock market quickly fell 20-25% and property values fell 30-35% in the aftermath of this fear. By the end of September the market had recovered about half of these losses (see Figure 7.3). The return to pre-June 1989 and higher valuations is largely dependent upon a peaceful period in China. Since property stocks trade at low PERs and at a considerable discount, i.e., low Q value from net asset value, much of the risk is already factored in. By worldwide standards, the valuations are very cheap, even if the properties are worth much less after 1997. Indeed these valuations have led to sharply higher prices in 1991 and early 1992. The price earnings ratios are in the 10-11 range, which is well below those in Japan or the U.S.

Figure 7.3
Hong Kong's Heng Seng Stock Market Index, April to September 1989

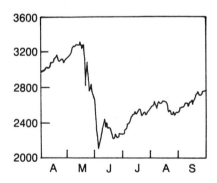

Source: *Asian Wall Street Journal*

Figure 7.4
Investments in Hong Kong in 1988, Transactions of $6.4 Million or More

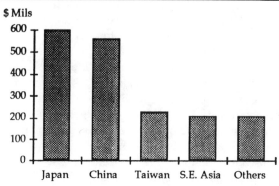

Source: Richard Ellis, Ltd.

Hong Kong has been grown strongly. The Chinese have been buying almost as much as the Japanese, which seems to bode well for a strong future. Figure 7.4 shows the 1988 purchases of properties above U.S.$6.4 million. All land is now leased to the British Colony, with the leases transferring to China in 1997 for another 50 years. After that, nobody knows. But for now the pre-1997 period is enough to be concerned with.

CANADA
EVEN NANCY GREENE HAS SOLD TO THE JAPANESE

So far the Japanese have not invested very heavily in Canada. In 1987, Japanese investment there amounted to only about 2% of the total overseas investment. One reason is because the Japanese have been more interested and comfortable with U.S. investments. The small Japanese population base in Canada and the lingering World War II internment stigma (which was largely lifted by the Mulroney conservative government's compensation payments to those interned) kept Japanese investment low. This seems to be changing: the government agreed to compensation payments to those interned; Canadian government officials are encouraging investment; ease of obtaining Canadian citizenship; and the Free Trade Agreement have all made Canada more attractive and inexpensive compared to Japan, Hong Kong, and Taiwan.

Current legislation encourages foreign investment in all parts of the country including Banff, a Japanese favorite in the Canadian Rockies. The government leases park land to businesses and residents. No investment proposal has yet been refused by Robert de Cotret, Minister of Regional Industrial Expansion. Only properties with a value of $5 million or more come under this jurisdiction. An example is the Banff Park Lodge which Fuji Projects bought in 1988 for some Cdn$26 million. The ten-year-old, 210-room lodge behind the historic Banff Springs Hotel is the park's second largest hotel. This was the first major national park property acquired by foreign interests. It has raised local fears of a foreign takeover. About a third of all businesses in Banff are Japanese-owned, and in the summer one sees about the same share of Japanese among the tourists in the area.

Choice rental properties and golf courses have been the major targets. Cheap farmland to produce food is also a likely area for considerable future investment. Pork is very popular in Japan, and the Minebea Corporation of Japan, the world's major bearing manufacturer, is diversifying by investing ¥2 billion to establish a large hog raising subsidiary in Manitoba, named the Northern Manitoba Breeders' Company.

Japanese investors have become interested in hotel property in Canada. One Japanese company, Jasmac Canada (a subsidiary of a Tokyo-based hotel, restaurant and development company) bought Toronto's Windsor Arms Hotel for $30 million, a premium price as the previous owners, Upper Canada Land Corporation, earned $1 million per month for its eight-month ownership. Jasmac has also been buying land in Yorkville, which is considered to be among the best commercial real estate in Canada. Upper Canada Land Corporation has also sold three other properties to Jasmac. Two other major hotels (Inn on the Park Four Seasons and Harbour Castle Westin) are actively seeking Japanese buyers.

Another Japanese firm set a record in October 1989 with the purchase of a Vancouver hotel. Japan Palios Developments Canada Ltd. bought O'Doul's Hotel, a 130-room Robson Street hotel, for $23 million or $175,000 per room. The price requires a room rental of $175 per night to recoup their investment at the normal industry standard of 0.1%/night. (The average in 1992 is $125 per night.) Le Meridien, an elegant hotel built for Expo86, fetched only $118,000 per room for a $47 million total, while the Hotel Georgia sold for $127,000 per room (a $40 million total). Most of the city's downtown hotels have been sold in 1989–90, primarily to offshore investors.

The Whistler-Blackcomb complex, some seventy miles north of Vancouver along the coast, is Canada's top skiing resort. It hosts many top international events and is considered of Olympic quality. The vertical drop at 4,200 feet is North America's longest run and the season is very long, typically running from early December to the end of May. Helicopter skiing on the high mountains makes it so one can practically ski all year. The two mountains branch off from the European-style Whistler village. It's an attractive location, complete with many fashionable shops, restaurants, condominiums, and hotels. It's also a short hop from Tokyo on direct flights to Vancouver (the shortest air distance to North America except for Alaska).

With excellent facilities, partly due to the friendly rivalry between two mountains, it's a prime spot for Japanese tourism. The largest hotel there is the 400-room Canadian Pacific hotel, the Chateau Whistler. This upscale resort has rooms renting in the $150 to $500 range. But one of the most famous hotels is the Nancy Greene Olympic Lodge that Nancy Greene, the 1968 gold medal winner of two events in the Grenoble Olympics owned with her husband, Al Raine, her former coach until IPEC, Inc., a Japanese firm, paid $8.5 million for it and $7.5 million for the nearby Crystal Lodge in 1989. The two hotels are being amalgamated into the Nancy Greene Lodge.

The Japanese own at least two other major hotels in Whistler. In 1988, Listel Canada, Ltd., a Japanese firm, bought the International Hotel (renamed the International Listel Hotel) for $7.2 million. Listel also owns three hotels in Japan. In 1989, the Mitsui Corporation bought the Fairways Hotel for $12 million. Other hotels in Whistler, such as the Delta Hotel, are owned by Hong Kong Chinese. The major developments have moved the resort upscale with much higher prices, so it seems likely that the new investors will reap handsome profits on their investments. There is also much use of the facilities by Japanese tourists. In the 1989/90 season, just one tourist agency booked 14,000 Japanese skiers to visit Whistler-Blackcomb on four night trips, costing ¥130,000. With the economies of scale, the whole trip, with ground travel to the resort, lodging, lift tickets and many meals and frills, costs much less than the airfare to Vancouver.

Kenchiku Shiryo Ken Kyusha Co., Ltd. of Tokyo will build the first North American resort with year-round skiing on three glaciers in the rugged Purcell Mountains in southeastern British Columbia. It would provide helicopter-style powder skiing for ordinary lift ticket customers. Plateau Rosa in the Alps is the only operating resort of this type in the world.

Tod Mountain was sold to Nippon Cable Company of Tokyo in 1992. The company will spend $50 million developing the mountain resort over the next 10 years. The purchase price was about $5 million, slightly above the $4.75 million asking price.

Other resort purchases include Harrison Hot Springs, bought by Itoman & Co., and Radium Hot Springs, acquired by a subsidiary of the Chotokan Group of Hamamatsu for $20 million. The Chotokan group spent an additional $5 million expanding and upgrading the facility. They plan to bring Japanese tourists to the resort in the winter normally a slow season for the resort. Employees of the resort are trained at Chotokan facilities in Japan.

EUROPE

Real estate investment by the Japanese in Europe is expanding rapidly. The Japanese life insurance companies were off to a slow start because of regulations, then they were shut out of the U.S. property market due to adverse reactions to the purchase of Rockefeller Center and the subsequent request from the MOF to *lay off* purchases of U.S. trophy properties. So, they moved to Europe. They are especially interested in bargain properties in Paris.

Restrictions are tighter for foreign investment than in the U.S., Canada, Australia and other places. As in the U.S, the Japanese like choice properties. In an eye-catching deal, Nippon Life purchased nearly a third of the Halles shopping center, a thriving new complex that is considered as much a part of Paris as Rockefeller Center is of New York. It is a large multi-story complex near the Louvre on the site of the old central fruit and vegetable market. It sits atop the Halles Metro Station and commuter rail service and it's topped by walkways and parks, and surrounded by cafes and boutiques. It is Paris's busiest shopping center. The price was FF420 million or about $70 million (purchased in partnership with Credit Lyonnais). Although this is Nippon Life's first real estate purchase in France, the company already owns part of the French travel firm Club Mediterranee and the construction group Bouygnes.

Sumitomo Life purchased a stake (about $8.7 million, large by Paris standards but small compared with the $50 million a day in premiums) in Europolis, a multinational property development company based in Paris. Meiji Life purchased the French department store Au Trois Quartiers in partnership with Postel, the British post office pension fund. Still, the life insurance firms would prefer to avoid currency risks and invest in Japan. Nippon Life owns more commercial property in Tokyo than does Mitsubishi Estate.

THE INFLATION MOTIVE IN U.S. REAL ESTATE[6]

It is said that stocks are a hedge against inflation. Inflation has gone up and so have stocks, bonds and, real estate. Figure 7.5 provides some data for the 65 years from 1926 to 1990. By moving U.S. funds from stocks and/or bonds

---

[6]See Sharpe and Alexander (1989).

into U.S. real estate, the Japanese may really be protecting themselves against inflation. If the U.S. government pursues policies to inflate itself out of its deficit problem, there may be a hefty bout of inflation ahead. Whether or not this happens, the advantage of paying off this debt in cheaper dollars and receiving more taxes by inflating people into higher brackets is a very real one.[7] Let's see how the inflation hedge in U.S. real estate works.

Consider the following model for the return R_i from security i:

$$R_i = a_i + b_i I + c_i J + e_i$$

where

   a_i is a constant,

   b_i is the security's sensitivity to expected inflation, I,

   I is the expected rate of inflation,

   c_i is the security's sensitivity to unexpected inflation, J,

   J is the unexpected inflation, the difference between the actual rate of inflation, and

   e_i is the uncertain part of the return of the security that is not related to inflation.

An estimate of the short-term expected rate of inflation is the short-term Treasury rate, the T-bill rate as it is more commonly called (see Ibbotson and Associates, 1992, for up-to-date data and calculations). The T-bill rate adjusted for inflation is very close to zero over long periods. It is often used as a measure of the risk-free rate of return in asset pricing models. The unexpected inflation can then be estimated as the difference between the actual rate of inflation in, say, a six-month period, and the T-bill rate at the beginning of this period. One can then use the model above to estimate the effects of inflation on various assets. Using data over six-month periods from July 1959 to July 1971, Fama and Schwert (1977) used multiple regression techniques to estimate the b's and c's for government bonds of various durations from one to five years, common stocks as measured by the NYFE index (a value-weighted average of all stocks on the NYSE) and private residential real estate. Table 7.6 summarizes some of their results.

---

[7] The latter point has been eliminated in large part by the reduction in the number of brackets and the new limits on the top tax rate; also, the government has been forced to index brackets to avoid bracket creep.

Figure 7.5
Wealth Indices of Investments in the U.S. Capital Markets, 1926–90, Year End, 1925 = 1.00

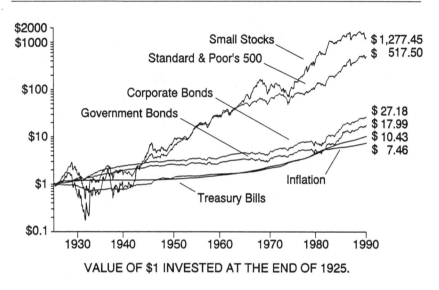

VALUE OF $1 INVESTED AT THE END OF 1925.

Source: Ibbotson and Associates (1991)

Table 7.6
Sensitivities of Government Bonds, Residential Real Estate and Unexpected Inflation over Six-Month Holding Periods, July 1959 to July 1971.

Asset	b_i	c_i
6 month U.S. Treasury bills	1.0	0
1 –2 year U.S. government bonds	1.08	-1.15
2–3 year U.S. government bonds	1.03	-1.75
3–4 year U.S. government bonds	.88	-2.37
4–5 year U.S. government bonds	.79	-2.75
Private residential real estate	1.27	1.14
Common stocks	-4.26	-2.09

Source: Fama and Schwert (1977)

By construction, the T-bills move one-to-one with expected inflation and are not affected by unanticipated inflation, so b=1 and c=0. The government bonds become less sensitive to short-term expected inflation the longer their maturities. For the four- to five-year bonds, the sensitivity to short-term expected inflation is less than 80%. However, all the bonds react very negatively to unexpected inflation and more so the longer the term of the bond. This is not surprising because if you had a bond fairly priced at today's inflation rate of 6% and inflation suddenly goes to 10% you would expect the price of the bond to fall and the more so the longer the maturity.

Stocks turn out not to be inflation hedges at all. They fall more than four times as fast as expected inflation rises, and they fall more than twice as fast as unexpected inflation rises. Stocks, at least from 1959 to 1971, certainly did not react positively to inflation. They do the best in periods of falling, not rising, inflation.

Real estate, on the other hand, reacts very positively to both increased expected and unexpected inflation. This makes their returns a good diversifying part of a large investment portfolio if increasing inflation is a major fear. Many factors must be considered in one's investment mix to develop the preferred risk-return balance in the currency(s) of choice. But this effect is one that must be considered in the minds of Japanese executives contemplating U.S. investments, particularly for funds already in U.S. currency that may have a previous exchange rate loss.

CONCLUSION

The Japanese came on the world property market quickly and decisively. Then the lending bubble was burst and with it the worldwide property market. If they can hold on in the tough times they will have a strong international base to work from in the future.

CHAPTER 8
ORGANIZING THE GOVERNMENT AND LARGE CORPORATIONS FOR MAXIMUM ECONOMIC GROWTH

Marco Polo and a blind, wise Japanese potter are discussing the Mongol's hopes to conquer Japan in the third quarter of the 13th century.

- I want to ask you about your country, the Kingdom of Islands.

- Why? There is fear in your voice, a threat.

- No, you hear a desire to learn, a desire to tell the true from the false.

- It seems, my friend, that you are as blind as I am. At this moment I must rely on memory. My people are divided by many things—religious quarrels, possession of land. Rich lords jealous of what they have and always ready to fight each other for more. Then there is the pride of the great families of the men of war we call samurai. They are both generous and cruel. Born to fight, they never lay down their swords, one against the other, family against family.

- How could a country so divided drive back a Mongol invasion?

- These fingers are different from each other, are they not my friend? But watch. Now they have become a fist, united and strong. When my country comes under attack all disputes and quarrels end at once. Everyone obeys the emperor's wish and that of the Shekon, his regent, and that of the Shogun, his great general. It is as though Japan had only one heart. No foreigner will ever dominate our country. The only domination we will ever accept is from our own lord. To protect our land, each man is ready to sacrifice everything. Even the sight of the glorious sun.

Some call the salaryman the modern samurai.

What hurts Japan's image the most is that it is a market economy that has retained its social connections as valued and has used this to its benefit.

Though the Japanese may be behind on financial options and other derivative financial instruments, they have their own type of options called loyalty which allows firms a free hand in developing their strategies.

HOW EFFECTIVE IS THE JAPANESE GOVERNMENT?

Japan has a different focus for its economic decisions. It is design oriented and based upon a crafts approach to production. Does this different economic focus lead as well to a different conception of the role of governmental institutions in the economic?

Yes and no.

During the aborted NYSE crash of October 1989, commentators noted that the TSE did not fall and trading volume was thin and suggested that there had been rumors the government had asked institutions not to sell. The universal comment was that the government has more control in Japan. This carried a negative judgment concerning the openness of the country's markets. Yet, they are in awe at the power of their government to be in control.

Forgotten in the ensuing rally on the U.S. markets was the very large part played by the weekend announcement that the Federal Reserve Board was prepared to make funds available to all those who needed it. This was not seen to be government intervention but *wisdom* on the part of government.

It is just as wise to *ask* people not to sell as it is to provide low-cost money to *induce* people not to sell.

We live in an age where all economies are mixtures of private enterprise and government intervention. All modern economies expect government to set the rules of the game and these rules vary from country to country. We are so used to our own rules and procedures and expectations that we forget that the hand of government has been involved.

It is incumbent upon potential players in the Japanese market to understand the Japanese rules and not complain that they are not the rules they are used to.

The discussion of issues in comparative economic systems and the role of government in both Japan and the U.S. is confounded by the desire of people to believe two different things at once:

- They like to believe that government is ineffective so they can argue that government has no place in the marketplace.

- They like to believe government in Japan has been behind Japan's economic success so they can be excused from their failures.

They cannot have it both ways: if government is ineffective, then how can Japan's success be explained?

Both statements are probably untrue. Japan's government was effective in allocating very scarce investment funds at low interest in the early years of reconstruction. But they were lucky too as war time demand (first Korean then Vietnamese) and proximity brought them a good customer in the U.S. government.

Funds are no longer scarce: the problem for Japan is a surplus of funds, too much savings, trade surplus, and profits. Now government is less powerful, and it has little or no direct control in the allocation of investment funds, though it has the indirect tool of moral suasion. This is how it should be as an economy evolves.

We have explored many of these issues in previous chapters. Japanese firms are remarkably flexible, as we discussed Chapter 3. An example is the booming floral business as rice farmers switch to flowers. Okinawa has increased flower production to 10% of its total agriculture. Meanwhile, per capita flower consumption is still less than one-third that of Europe, and there is room for both domestic production and imports.

Now the U.S. wants government to protect competition for U.S. firms and the U.S. government, especially Congress, is becoming more involved in defining rules. The Japanese government is good at defining rules. Let's look at some of the areas in which the institutions differ and some of the rules and debate linking the two countries, using them as a metaphor for the world economic system at its transition into the new age of information and services.

WHO RUNS JAPAN ?

Karel van Wolferen's book *The Enigma of Japanese Power* (1989) has received extensive coverage in Japan. He claims Japan has no leader. What runs Japan is neither the prime minister, the ruling party, the bureaucracy, nor big business, farms. What runs Japan is the *system*: LDP, ministries, business and agricultural groups, the police and organized crime, everything and everybody together. Other writers including David Howell and James Fallow support this view of Japan. They pose the question for Japan but one wonders how they would answer it for the U.S. and other countries. In any event some of the aspects of *the system*, as it is perceived by outsiders, are presented in Table 8.1.

Table 8.1
Some Attributes of the Japanese System:

- No checking accounts, hard to spend money
- Government policy to encourage cooperation
- Works in tandem, brokerage firms in lock step to carve up the market
- Picks losers as well as winners
- Business groups cooperate on fundamental research and on phasing out dying industries
- Makes it easy to export
- Makes it hard to import (perpetuation of myths like foreign skis are no good in Japan as the snow is different)
- Subsidies (rice farmers can keep prices high)
- Hard to sell land—up to 80% tax
- Perks as inducement to work hard, all tax deductible
- Peer pressure: look around at 5:30, one person gone; 5:45, two persons; 6:00 and the rest can then go home
- Look busy
- Domestic distribution not efficient, but as effective as unemployment insurance
- Retail prices kept high domestically on things that do not face import competition, for example electricians, rice
- Wholesale prices kept low
- Strong nationalistic pride and feeling of specialness

Writing in the *Japan Times,* Howell related a story told by former Prime Minister Takeshita: He said that when he resigned, the British press assumed that Japan had been hit by a major political earthquake while China, on the other hand, appeared disinterested in his resignation. The British assumption is that prime ministers and ministers are real leaders, so they matter. China accepts that Japan is a key player in Asia with or without a leader and that China and Japan are entering a period of rapprochement. They see major forces in history transcending individuals.

An article in *Business Week*[1] following on those by Fallows and van Wolferen shows that the U.S. is disappointed to see that Japan operates by different rules. The U.S. cannot see the benefits of diversity and defines all things from its own point of view.

---

[1]Rethinking Japan, *Business Week,* Aug 7, 1989.

One example of loyalty within groups is easy access to lending and purchasing. In a Mitsubishi Estate-owned building, one sees a Mitsubishi Electric Co. elevator; Sumitomo Bank executives choose to eat at restaurants serving Asahi beer (well, they might say, if not us then who!) These decisions are not at arm's length.

The prime minister's activities are well known and published daily in the newspapers as shown in Table 8.2.

Table 8.2
The Prime Minister's Schedule for October 20, 1988

8:52	Leaves private residence for Diet
9:25	Meets Jacques de Larosiere, governor of the Banque de France
10:00	Attends Lower House ad hoc committee on tax reform
12:21	Is briefed by Deputy Chief Cabinet Secretary Ichiro Ozawa
1:06	Attends Lower House plenary session
2:22	Attends Lower House ad hoc committee on tax reform
5:20	Returns to Kantei
5:21	Has talks with Masayoshi Ito, chairman of LDP Executive Council
5:45	Meets editors of Japanese-language dailies abroad who are here to attend the annual meeting of the Japan Newspaper Publishers and Editors Association
5:55	Has talks with Masaharu Gotoda, head of LDP Election System Research Council

Van Wolferen explores two related myths: that Japan is a parliamentary democracy and that Japan is a modern capitalistic, free-market economy. It is important to remember that today all economies are mixed and that Japan's mix is different from the U.S. mix.

Take for example the auto inspection fee of U.S.$1,500 that the Japanese pay for the world's highest quality cars. Japanese cars must be inspected every other year until they are six years old and annually thereafter. We had to practically give away an excellent eight-year-old Toyota Cressida because there is little market for any used car let alone one that is old enough to need an annual inspection. Selling a car is a complex process that requires about four inspectors who check all the minor dents even more carefully than the engine. They calculate the price from a book that includes minor repairs a North American would never consider making. When one sells a used car, one is liable for any faults. The car dealership must exercise care and make full repairs because it takes on the liability from the previous owner.

This extra care may strike us as unnecessary, but it, along with other social costs, may be less than the costs of the 602,000 private security guards regularly employed in the U.S. and the costs of drug enforcement, crime, and lawyers. Certainly, if even the costs are the same, they contribute more toward stability and ease of living.

Van Wolferen criticizes Japan for not meeting European ideals of state, power, and control. For example, Europe assumes that irrationality in politics leads to tyranny, and van Wolferen suggests that irrationality in Japan politics has led to totalitarianism.

THE MINISTRIES HAVE A HAND

The bureaucracy has much power in Japan, providing stability. Seven out of eight bills considered in the Diet are initiated by bureaucrats rather than the government. We also need to understand the often conflicting roles of the different government ministries. The Construction Ministry will give approval to placing optical fiber cables in sewage pipes, though we in the West might assume the Ministry of Posts and Telecommunications (MPT) would have the important roles.

Yet despite the apparent primitive political gaming, sewer systems are sophisticated and do not use valves. Robots have been developed to lay the fiber cables in sewer pipes 20 to 30 centimeters in diameter and the costs should be less than ¥10,000 per meter.

The roles of MITI and MPT have also conflicted in terms of collection of savings and allocation of those funds.

MITI and MOF might have different views on the best interest rate and exchange rate.

The transformations in the Japanese economy could result in some interesting bureaucratic fights between MITI and MPT and also in determining the role of the privatized Nippon Telephone and Telegraph (NTT). These three organizations along with the Ministry of Finance, the Ministry of Agriculture, and the Ministry of Education all have their own constituencies and have been important at different times and different ways in shaping the Japanese economy. By some accounts, the major influences were:

1920–45	Ministry of Home Affairs
1955–80	MITI
1980–90	Ministry of Finance
1990–2000	Ministry of Health and Welfare

The Ministry of Health and Welfare has important regulatory power and will take on more importance with the greying population. The various ministries are also involved with the continuing liberalization of the Japanese economy.

As with much in Japan decisions are generally arrived by a long process of arriving at consensus. Ministries encouraging change and educating people to new policy initiatives begin the debate years ahead of time and keep a focus on the future. First, provocative statements are made. Then there is debate in the press. Small changes are made and all of a sudden true change is under way. The degree of preparation ensures an easier transition. Back in 1988, the first steps toward a shortened work week were tentatively taken. Saturday trading days were reduced first to three Saturdays in a month, then to two, and finally to none.

With the Consumption Tax, the government felt under more pressure and rammed the change through before consensus was reached on the design and before the population was in agreement. The tax was hated.

Kang (1989) illumines the role of the group in Japan. Comparing Korea and Japan, he notes if one were to pit individual against individual, then the Koreans would win, but if you put together teams of five on each side, then the Japanese would win. In Japanese factories, workers and engineers are knowledgeable about their own jobs and the manufacturing process in general. In Korean factories, workers know only what they are told to do. That the Japanese factory can better adapt is no surprise.

Japanese use the term *peace of mind* ten times more than Koreans, reflecting the role this plays in leading to harmony and few surprises through long-range business relationships, reliable products, etc. However, Kang notes the strains of change that are arising with a generation gap in which young Japanese stress less work, more free time.

Many criticize the Japanese for a lack of transcending values. Yet this may be part of the secret of their success. The ancient Shinto[2] value in the cycles of nature may have helped them to understand the continuity of change.

MITI: THE MINISTRY OF INTERNATIONAL TRADE AND INDUSTRY

MITI was an important player in the early post-war development of Japan. In a country with limited foreign exchange and a huge appetite for investment, the Ministry controlled the allocation of investment funds and the access to foreign currency. In the new Japan, with excess savings and a huge stockpile of foreign reserves, the role of MITI is changing.

---

[2]Japan has trouble separating religion and state because under the Meiji Restoration the state used the body of folk beliefs under the name Shinto for state purposes. Shinto has no theology.

In times of transition, MITI sometimes oversees orderly cutbacks. For example, government-facilitated gentlemen's agreements allocated plant closures which helped revive the shipbuilding industry. By 1988, about 50% of Japanese shipyards had been shut. Shipping lines did the same thing and allocated tonnage to be scrapped. South Korean competition had reduced Japan's share of the world market from 57% in 1984 to 38% in 1988.

The Japanese government even shared information on plant closures with the South Korean government. Actually the Japanese are willing to let the Koreans get the small contracts, while they defend their share in the supertanker market, where they command a 54% share. This market is poised for expansion because half the fleet is about 15 years old. Meanwhile, in Korea, there have been strikes and higher wages to depress the industry.

MITI has begun to help foreign firms overcome non-tariff barriers. It offers advice on the distribution system and has set up a network to link overseas manufacturers with Japanese domestic retailers. In attempting to make industrial standards more transparent. MITI has even invited John Stern, the vice president of the American Electronics Association, to sit on the committee for optoelectronics. Former MITI employees are now allowed to work for foreign firms; for example, Makoto Kuroda, who recently retired as vice minister of MITI, is now an advisor to Salomon Brothers.

To encourage imports by example, MITI has added two imported cars to its fleet. Importers of manufactured products will be offered ¥30 billion in tax incentives and low rate import loans. MITI met with major trading house officials to encourage them to aim for 30% growth in finished product imports, versus plans for 15% growth. The aim is to increase the ratio of finished goods to raw material imports from about 45% to about 75%. To help encourage consumers to try foreign products, MITI earmarked ¥4.5 billion for a variety of advertising projects. The textile and leather industries are under pressure from increased imports, especially from Italy. Independent importers are now bringing in many items including watches, jewelry, handbags, compact discs, automobiles, and whiskey.

Interestingly, the Post Office has gone into the direct import business. The Japanese can order American products—from beef and oranges to toys—at the Post Office and pay the postal carrier upon delivery.

On the other hand, MITI continues to set up research consortiums pooling R&D funds for greater effectiveness. These help to reduce uncertainty and risk. Such consortiums include computer programs for language translation, and a marine biotechnology project to breed organisms to eat pollution. These projects with very high social rewards are considered unfair intervention by U.S. firms, even though there is no way in which the unaided market can address them. However, there is a lessening of government-sponsored consortia in Japan as electronics companies are now reluctant to work closely for fear of loss of information to competitors.

In 1988, MITI announced an expanded program for research into superconductive materials, including plans to hire 100 specialists from academic and corporate research centers. The institute was set up under the International Superconductivity Technology Center which has 102 members (97 Japanese, two U.S., two U.S. affiliates in Japan, and one British firm). Forty-five of the firms take part in the activities by paying an annual fee of ¥12 million and an initial donation of ¥100 million. MITI plans to double its initial contribution, which was ¥680 million.

In the past most research in this area has been independent work at the various corporate research labs. In this area, they are taking a lead in research and applications. Some data is presented in Table 8.3.

Table 8.3
Comparative Statistics on R&D and Scientists, Japan and the U.S.

	Japan	U.S.
Total R&D spending	$258 million	$256 million
Industrial R&D	$146	$97
Scientists and engineers	1,066	625

Source: *Business Week*, 1988

Some of the innovations from Japanese company research are:

- Matsushita Electric Industrial developed a method of depositing up to four layers of thin superconducting films.

- Sumitomo Electric Industries developed a thin ceramic film that conducted a record current.

- Mitsubishi Metal Corp. and Kumamoto University have developed a superconducting wire coil that carries a current load five times as strong as any previous wire.

- Hitachi Ltd. developed a thallium-based ceramic superconductor.

- Sumitomo Electric has applied for 600 to 1,000 patents related to warm superconductors.

U.S. scientists have called for cooperation and an opening of R&D labs to foreigners, but 70% of the 54 companies do not plan any international cooperation let alone cooperation among themselves, because the work is now in the stage of commercial development rather than basic research. The commercial development is still 15 years away, but to the Japanese this is imminent!

One factor slowing the U.S. is that 70% of U.S. R&D is defense-related and so is without commercial considerations. In 1988, U.S. companies formed two new consortiums: Superchip Corp. to develop microchips and electronic applications, and Superconductivity Applications, Inc. to concentrate on wires and electrical products.

Foreign participation is welcomed at Japan's International Super-conductivity Technology Center, but as yet no U.S. company is willing to pay the $890,000 full membership fee. Only DuPont and Rockwell International Corp. have paid the $15,000 for associate status which allows limited access to research.

The U.S. is trying to use the MITI model of private/government cooperation. One example is Sematech (semiconductor manufacturing technology), which has 14 corporate members and has been studying production equipment for computer chips.

SCIENCE CITIES

The establishment of Science Cities is a way of formalizing the cooperative nature of research among firms and between firms and government and academia.

The trend in Japan to establish synergetic R&D centers is reflected in Tsukuba, where there is a university, 50 public sector and 70 private sector labs. The establishment of Tsukuba shows again the care and patient planning of the Japanese. Tsukuba celebrated its 25th anniversary in 1988, but 1963 was merely the date of the legislation to sponsor government research there. The first labs did not open for almost 15 years. The Japan Auto Research Lab, among the oldest there, recently celebrated its tenth anniversary. The government began to shift 7,000 researchers in 1980, spending ¥1.3 trillion. About two thirds of all public sector research is conducted in Tsukuba. At the time, the land was cheap, about 90% less than in Kawasaki, though it has recently risen sharply. The rise was partially predicated on the future availability of a fast train to Tokyo—in 2005!

Kansai Science City is planned in the hills near Kyoto, Osaka, and Nara. Already located there is Advanced Telecommunications Research Institute (ATR) and branch campuses of Koshisha and Doshisha Women's Universities. ATR's projects include one to develop the technology for telephone systems to analyze sounds and voices to lead to instant translations of two-way phone conversations in two languages. They anticipate having 200 scientists including some from North America and Europe.

Unlike Tsukuba, Kansai will cover the entire range of cultural and scientific studies and not be limited to the natural sciences. Also, Kansai is led by business rather than the national government. The International Institute for Advanced Studies (IIAS), which does for interdisciplinary work on the frontier of science, will have a scholar village to accommodate visitors to Kansai.

Another government research program, ERATO was set up to help creative young scientists bypass the power of elder scientists and professors. The program is also attempting to cross ministry boundaries, including the funding of research in universities under the domain of the Ministry of Education.

The Japan Key Technology Center funds high-tech ventures and consortia. It accepts applications each September. Since 1985, it has granted ¥32 billion in capital to research groups. Both MITI and MPT oversee the center. Before the center, government planners identified key sectors which were dominated by large firms and took few risks. Now small start up companies can identify areas of interest. According to Mr. Eda of MITI , they will attempt to use the private sector to advance technology that Japan has in the past been accused of neglecting. This has also been an avenue for foreign subsidiaries to join in funded research, for example DEC and Hoffman-La Roche.

GOVERNMENTS ARE INVOLVED IN THE TRADE DISPUTES

The Japanese are making the FSX fighter plane with the U.S. They are making the electronics and we are making the hamburgers for the pilot.

Jay Leno

Many of the current trade problems between Japan and the U.S. reflect judgments concerning proper socio-economic rules and regulations. Each country has a list of objections concerning the other. The debate is formally called the SII or the structural impediments initiatives.

The U.S. criticizes Japan for:
- Japan's consumer price mechanism (gap between foreign and domestic prices)
- Inefficiencies of the distribution system
- Over savings and shortfalls in domestic investment

- High land prices
- Restrictive trading practices by Japan's large corporate groups (*keiretsu*)
- Discriminatory practices that restrict foreign firms

Japan criticizes the U.S. for:
- Under-savings and excessive consumption
- Declines in investment and productive vitality of U.S. firms
- Poor corporate performance
- Antimarket governmental regulations
- Imbalance of R&D (military at expense of commercial)
- Failure to promote exports
- Need to improve education and training
- Overemphasis on the short- term and mergers and acquisitions

Some suggest that 80% of the U.S. problem is internal, including budget

Table 8.4
The Micro and Macro Economic Causes of the Trade Gap

	Micro		Macro	
Causes	Nontariff barriers	$6 bil	Delayed effect of $ drop	$25 bil
	Lagging technology	$20 bil	Government deficit	$25 bil
	Poor product quality	$6 bil	Slow growth of developing countries	$12 bil
			Slow growth of industrial countries	$ 9 bil
Cures	Delayed impact of $ drop	$11 bil	Further cut in $ value (20%)	$36 bil
	Planned budget cuts	$28 bil	Added cuts in budget deficit	$25 bil
	Increased private savings	$12 bil	Growth in industrial countries	$10 bil
	Improved U.S. technology	$5 bil	Debt relief to developing countries	$13 bil

Source: Hufbauer (1988)

deficits, a flawed education system, and inattention to quality, but like the Sufi story of the drunk who searches for his keys under the light rather then where they were lost in the dark, they are going after the 20% or so that can control unfair trade. For example, Hufbauer (1988) estimated the micro and macro economic causes of the trade gap and made policy recommendations for eliminating it as illustrated in Table 8.4.

This adds up, but a simple listing will not create a cure or take away the pain of cutting back on spending. It is not clear that all of these so-called policies are beneficial. For example, why should the industrial countries grow more, pollute more, and use resources faster? A further cut in the value of the dollar is unlikely, and the costs of the benefits will be great. It didn't work the first time, so why continue? What is clear from the table is that the role of nontariff barriers being pursued under Super 301 is small compared to lagging technology, poor quality, and the impact of the deficit. Under Super 301, the U.S. Congress can declare countries unfair traders and has done so to Japan and other countries.

Japan is not the only country rejecting or faulting U.S. goods. The Europeans are concerned about design problems with Boeing 747-400 jets and have asked for modifications on the floor beams supporting the upper decks and separation of electrical circuits.

The U.S. government has few, if any, levers available to improve domestic product quality, so it is focusing upon trade regulations. Super 301 is an example. It is interesting that supercomputers and satellites were chosen: these products are not made in competitive markets, and in all countries, governments play a significant role in their development and use.

Europe is now objecting to the U.S. labeling other countries unfair and the EC, in self protection, has listed 40 U.S. trade barriers. It lists all the usual things that the U.S. holds against others, including the directive to buy American, rules on intellectual property, testing standards, counter-vailing and antidumping duties, export controls on technology transfers, ship repair services, tax barriers, and financial institutions. Also included is the tax on imported oil (which probably should be on all oil) and for cleanup of toxic waste. Unfortunately, the U.S. believes it is the only arbiter of fairness.

The U.S. is not concerned about level playing fields and fairness when it comes to higher taxes. For example, in Japan, oil and gas cost three to four times the price in the U.S., almost all of it taxes.

The FSX controversy provides a view of how it all hangs together in Japan as well as an example of Japan-U.S. bargaining. Various issues are raised. The U.S. worries that Japan will use the skills and technology gained in the production of this military plane for commercial planes. This is probably true, and we hope the U.S. firms are doing this and not keeping the two separate as individual profit centers.

Japan has no incentive to buy the plane off the shelf from the U.S. Japan brings financing as well as some technology to the venture. For example, it has developed carbon fibers for the wings, and a superior radar system.

Mitsubishi Heavy Industries Inc. and General Dynamics would jointly develop the FSX. GD would receive 35 to 40% of the funding allocated by the Japanese government for planning and design. They plan to spend more than $1 billion to improve the F-16 and then produce 130 jets. The F-

16 is a single-engine tactical fighter plane, the most maneuverable in the U.S. arsenal and the top export fighter. Seventeen air forces have ordered the jet.

It has been suggested that joint weapon development is the wave of the future. Many believe that other nations, now customers of U.S. products like Europe, Korea, and Singapore, will demand a similar deal. France already produces its own planes, and a British, Italian, and German joint venture is building the Tornado jet fighter.

Japanese companies are making inroads in the U.S. military and space markets. The Pentagon placed two contracts worth $6 million with two groups that include nine Japanese companies to jointly develop specific defense systems for the Strategic Defense Initiative. The system is aimed at countering medium- and short-range missiles in the western Pacific. One group is headed by Mitsubishi Heavy Industries and includes NEC, Hitachi, and Fujitsu, and the other group is headed by LTV of the U.S. which included Kawasaki Heavy Industries and Westinghouse. Other contracts have also been concluded with German companies for $47 million, British for $43 million, Israeli for $12 million, Italian for $48 million, and French for $6 million.

FOREIGNERS IN JAPAN—DO THEY NEED GOVERNMENT HELP?

Successful foreign companies in Japan are very quiet; they have no desire to attract attention.

Kenichi Ohmae
President, McKinsey Japan

Market share of Western products in Japan (by volume unless noted):

Schick:	70% of the safety razor blade market
McDonald's:	30% of the fast food hamburger market (sales)
Coca-Cola:	30% of the market for carbonated soft drinks
Pampers:	20-22% of disposable diaper market
German cars:	2.6% of auto market
U.S. cars:	0.4% of auto market
Braun:	40% of electric shaver market
Kodak:	12-15% of amateur color film market
Cigarettes:	11.5% of the market, mostly U.S. made

Source: *Asian Wall Street Journal*, March 1989.

There is little incentive for those who are making it in Japanese business (IBM, Xerox, McDonald's) to call attention to themselves. However, U.S. companies are finding the Japanese are interested in franchising their services and products.[3] There are seven Nautilus Clubs in Tokyo and 100 Jazzercise instructors. Domino's Pizza is represented by 54 licensees. Unfortunately, many of the U.S. entrants sold out for short-term gains and ignored the longer term—Nautilus and 7-Eleven, though very successful, have no U.S. ownership. Nautilus exported equipment worth $14 million. Seibu has a license to open Ralph Lauren stores in Japan. Tiffany's earned $26.5 million from outlets in Japan. Toys-R-Us is working with McDonald's to open 100 stores, including one in Niigata.[4] MTS, the owner of Tower Records, has grown to nine stores with sales of $36 million, and the Tokyo store sells more per square foot than any of its U.S. outlets.

The U.S. and Japan agreed in 1986 that U.S. firms would capture 20% of the Japanese chip market by 1991. The progress is better than expected. In 1986, imports were $248 million or 8.6% and by end of 1988 had increased 2.2 times to $540 million, but this represented only 10.6%. In 1990 they were up to about 18%. In 1987, the U.S. government charged that Japan was not living up to its agreement and put 100% tariffs on US$165 million of Japanese exports.

NEC bought 20.8% of its chips from foreign firms but finds it hard to maintain that level unless the U.S. and other makers produce more of the chips it needs. Toshiba bought 16% from foreign sources (up from 12% in FY 1986) but states it needs chips for consumer electronics and foreign makers supply few of them. Hitachi echoes the concern. It now buys 15% of its chips from foreign sources. NEC claims it will be difficult to maintain its high level unless U.S. firms produce more of the chips it needs, for example, memory chips. Mitsubishi Electric bought more than 20%, and Fujitsu bought 15% while Oki Electric Industry Co. bought 22%.

The U.S. chip producers are learning to market to smaller users and to provide what the customer wants. In May 1989, Matsushita (buying from Signetics), Sanyo (buying from Motorola), and Sony all announced they would increase imports of U.S. chips. Japanese users are also reaching out to U.S. semiconductor firms. Sony and Sharp held exhibits for them to

---

[3]Again note the hidden importance of service trade and the need to consider the combined current account.

[4]They want to open a 5,000-square-meter discount toy store in Niigata. Japanese regulations require that all stores over 500 m^2 must gain approval of the local small stores. The 63 stores in Niigata that sell toys have annual sales of ¥4.4 billion and Toys-R-Us anticipates sales of ¥5 billion. They fear that their numbers are threatened and cite the example in Britain where the number of toy stores declined from 6,000 to 1,500 in 10 years due to Toys-R-Us expansion.

display their wares. Sony also sent a team of buyers to the U.S. West Coast to advise U.S. chip designers on types of chips needed in Japan.

The U.S. merchant producers of computer memory chips are making inroads in Japan by trying to provide what the Japanese factories need. Intel's sales increased 72% to ¥41.7 billion and profit rose 41%, Motorola's sales grew 60%, and Texas Instruments (TI) grew 47% to $591 million. Yet TI is concerned because its market share in Japan is 3%, compared to 6% worldwide.

Some Japanese firms are beginning to work with the U.S. companies. Matsushita Electric Industrial is working to design chips for videotape recorders, air conditioners, and other consumer items; Intel is beginning to sell chips to Nissan that would control the engines in a new auto.[5] Toyota Motor Corp in June 1989 agreed to use Motorola's cellular telephones in luxury cars marketed in the U.S. Japanese auto parts manufacturers have agreed to increase their purchases of foreign chips.

Total chip imports increased 35.8% in 1988 to ¥32.9 billion, and imports accounted for 3.3% versus 2.7% in the previous year. Their successes puts them in an awkward position of still supporting efforts for further opening while they are doing well. Motorola, TI, and Intel, all have a presence in Japan—Motorola and TI have plants and Intel has design facilities. The three control 5.8% of Japan's $20 billion chip market.

An interesting case is that of Motorola. Sony was very reluctant to buy Motorola's chip in 1985. The chip was hard to adapt to consumer products, Motorola offered only an English manual, and deliveries were slow. Then Motorola changed. It translated the manual, hand delivered the chips and shared future design secrets with Sony. Motorola tried to please the customer, then Sony was willing to design the chip into future products. On the basis of the success of the five chips in Sony's new camera, Motorola has also earned other Japanese customers. Unfortunately, Motorola's spokesperson still says: "The market is definitely not open enough for foreign suppliers. But it's probably more open than most U.S. people would think."

TI is beginning to customize chips for Japanese companies rather than attempting to sell off-the-shelf ones. It has opened chip design centers in Osaka.

---

[5] Is this a false victory? Are the U.S. consumer electronics and auto companies also working with these firms? Again the domestic market may be more important than making in roads into Japan and the trade deficit is misdirecting. The U.S. chip consumers may still be left out in the cold, and the final consumers may still buy foreign high value added products.

U.S. investment in Japan has increased. Total U.S. capital outlays in Japan reached $2.3 billion in 1988. Motorola joined a venture with Toshiba for a new $270 million semiconductor plant.

Firms are opening R&D labs to tap into Japanese talent as well as to better design for the Japanese market. Japan is becoming an important R&D site for firms interested in the global economy especially for high-tech materials and high added value products. Upjohn opened a $113 million facility to work on developing drugs for vascular and central nervous system disorders. DuPont established a central research lab in Yokohama in 1987 and an agricultural research center at Tsukuba in 1988. Nihon DEC is opening an R&D lab in Tokyo and has several inspection and assembly plants near Tokyo, though its focus is on soft ware development and systems engineering. Annual hiring is 500 to 600, so it competes for engineering graduates in Japan. Other companies, including Hoechst Japan and Bayer Japan, also have R&D labs in Japan.

One misunderstood result of this successful investment is that when a Japanese firm buys from a U.S. firm with a subsidiary in Japan, the sale is not counted as a U.S. export and has no effect on the trade balance.

Foreign firms are finding that specialty boutiques in department stores provide a foothold into the Japanese market. Mitsukoshi opened five in-store leather goods shops in an exclusive agreement with New York's Coach Leatherware Co. Coach is also developing new products to meet Japanese demands, including a leather train-pass holder (there are 8 million commuters in Tokyo alone) and a wider business card holder. Other in-store boutiques include Tiffany's and Etro, an Italian accessory shop. Takashimaya set up in store shops with Dalmeiyer to sell German sausage and Peck to sell Italian pasta. Tokyu has a joint venture with Williams-Sonoma for an in-store kitchenware and line shop. Jusco has set up Laura Ashley clothing outlets and recently bought Talbot's, which specializes in women's business clothes.

Foreign investment in Japan tripled in the period 1985–88. Estimates of the total range from $2.58 to $3.24 billion by 1988.

U.S. Ambassador Armacost, by going to the freight terminal at Hanada Airport, saw first hand that the notion of Japan as a closed economy is outdated (Table 8.5 presents a list of the fastest growing foreign firms in Japan as of November 1989).

A MITI study found that 47% of the 2,700 foreign firms were U.S. Foreign firms together accounted for 1.9% of capital, 2.2% of sales and 0.8% of employees in Japan. They are responsible for 3.3% of exports and 13.9% of the imports (1986 data). They produced a *net trade surplus* of ¥1.7 trillion (about $12 billion). Meanwhile a MITI survey of problems faced by foreign executives yielded this as the most frequent response: no particular problem. Those who had problems cited competition from domestic firms, sales channels, local customs, and high corporate taxes.

Table 8.4
Fastest Growing Foreign Firms in Japan

Company	Parent	87 Pretax Income, ¥ bil	83–87 Growth CAGR *%
Amway (Japan)	Amway	25.48	142.1
Miles-Kyawa	Bayer	1.97	130.3
DuPont-Mitsui Polychemicals	E.I. DuPont	3.45	90.9
Dow Corning	Dow Corning	.99	87.6
Dow Kahoh	Dow Chemical	1.40	77.8
Nippon Boehringer Ingelheim	Boehringer Ingelheim	5.08	58.3
Japan Upjohn	Upjohn	4.98	58.0
ICI Japan	ICI	3.63	55.6
Yokogawa Medical Systems	General Electric	4.80	52.4
Zimmer Japan	Bristol-Myers	3.25	47.9
Nihon Digital Equip	Digital Equipment	9.82	44.1
Searle Yakuhin	Monsanto	1.46	44.0
Bayer Yakuhin	Bayer	10.02	41.4
Sumitomo Eaton Hydraulics	Eaton	.94	40.7
Medtronic Japan	Medtronic	1.32	40.4
Kasei Hoechst	Hoechst	1.10	33.4
Nippon Brunswick	Brunswick	1.49	32.7
AM Japan	AM International	0.15	30.9
Ortha Diagnostic Systems	Johnson & Johnson	0.88	29.8
Levi Strauss Japan	Levi Strauss	2.28	29.1

*CAGR= compounded annual growth rate

Source: *Business Tokyo* (November 1989)

PROGRAMS TO INCREASE FOREIGN DIRECT INVESTMENT IN JAPAN

A number of new programs have been designed to increase foreign direct investment in Japan. MITI is relaxing restrictions on new technologies, targeting computers, electronic components for fifth generation computers, equipment for laser processing optical communications, new materials and off-shore oil production, to facilitate entry of foreign companies with advanced technology.

A MITI report in 1989 indicated that at least 156 research facilities are planned. The report projects that most of these will be in the provinces, and MITI has a variety of incentive packages to encourage this. MITI has a plan to create a world business zone to facilitate the entry of firms by providing short-term rental space and tax incentives. The Japan Regional Development Corp. under the supervision of MITI and the National Land Agency, plans to create 58 industrial parks. MITI has an International Industrial Forum Project aimed at site development to promote internationalization and to facilitate exchange of information on R&D, and market development between foreign and Japanese firms. MITI also has a Cosmopolis Model Project to create international industrial cities around Japan.

Myths tested and found to be just myths:

- Foreign products must be high priced to succeed.

- Foreign products must be changed to sell in Japan (manufacturer must take account of obvious differences).

- Japan is a homogeneous market.

Well-designed, quality products will sell in Japan.

CHAPTER 9
SCANDALS AND REFORM
THE ROLE OF THE STOCK MARKET IN POLITICAL CHANGE

In the early 1980s it was reckoned that each vote was worth a refrigerator.
                                                                    The Economist

People with high ideals don't necessarily make good politicians. If clean politics is so important, we should leave the job to scientists and the clergy.
                            former Japanese ruling-party Michio Watanabe
                                                     Newsweek, June 12, 1989

In Japan, we say we are a nation that turns disaster into good fortune. We tend to think the Recruit scandal will be looked back at as a blessing in disguise.
                            Masaya Miyoshi, president of Keidanren

This chapter discusses the role of gift giving in Japan and the financial pressure that this puts on politicians. This created an environment for the Recruit scandal that involved many top Japanese politicians. This scandal has shaped the future of Japanese politics and changed society's view of insider trading. This discussion will follow the sequence of events and the aftermath that has led to the resignation of two prime ministers and many other major politicians and business leaders. The stock market scandals of 1991 as well as two new scandals uncovered in early 1992 are also discussed. These scandals have had a profound effect on investor sentiment which has been a factor in the 1990–92 stock market decline.

THE RECRUIT SCANDAL

The outrage expressed when it was learned that leading political figures (and even minor ones) bought low cost preflotation shares in the Recruit company and subsequently sold them at high post-listing prices. In total 760,000 shares were offered to political, bureaucratic and business leaders, including aides to former Prime Minister Yasuhiro Nakasone and then Prime Minister Noboru Takeshita, cabinet members, and party leaders. Also Recruit gave hundreds of millions of yen as donations and to buy tickets to political fundraising parties. This scandal is a reminder of the vulnerability of the closely networked Japanese political and corporate systems.

THE HISTORY OF MONEY POLITICS

The Recruit scandal is rooted in two Japanese rituals: the need of government officials to give gifts at weddings, funerals, and other occasions and the definition of the name stamp as the legal signature.

The average parliamentarian must collect ¥100 to ¥130 million (around U.S.$1 million) just to survive in office each year. This is for gifts at weddings, typically ¥10,000 to ¥30,000, and other such gifts. Faction leaders and other major politicians need more. The 1989 election cost the Liberal Democratic Party (LDP) about ¥210 billion for two weeks campaigning, or about $1.5 billion, compared with $400 million spent by all candidates for the year-long election campaign for president in the U.S. in 1988. This is about ¥650 million each for the 323 LDP candidates seeking election. Incumbents need little money, while those in marginal seats may spend $10 million. The Japanese Socialist Party (JDSP) spent about ¥2 billion, the Democratic Socialist Party (DSP) about ¥1 billion and Komeito ¥400 million. Many Diet members are in favor of placing limits on donations.

Holding a name stamp grants complete power of attorney to act in one's name. As a result, the high-level ministers could claim ignorance because their secretaries dealt with the Recruit shares for them.

Politicians have a number of heavy financial obligations:

- staff and office expenses—the government pays only for two assistants so additional staff as well as supplies, telephones, and other office expenses must be paid

- campaign expenses

- constituents including cash gifts of anywhere from $35 to $400 for weddings and funerals. A survey of 89 Diet members for *Asahi Shimbun* found that they averaged $4,200 *per month* (about 7 weddings and 27 funerals).

- junior politicians—contributions are made to younger faction members

  Typically the money is raised as in other countries by:

- direct contributions to the politician

- political support groups

- fundraising events

The major trade groups and corporations that contributed political funds in 1990 are listed in Table 9.1.

Table 9.1

Major Contributors of Political Funds as of 1990

Rank 1990	Trade Group	Total	LDP	JDSP	Rank 1989
1	Petroleum Assn. of Japan	690	628	62	1
2	Japan Iron & Steel Fed.	676	621	55	4
3	Japan Automobile Manuf Assn. Inc.	656	587	69	2
4	Assn. of Tokyo Stock Exchange Regular Members	631	419	21	3
5	Real Estate Companies Assn. in Japan	573	537	36	5
6	Japan Petrochemical Industry Assn.	555	521	34	7
7	Second Assn. of Regional Banks	552	482	69	6
8	Japan Department Stores Assn.	424	414	10	17
9	Osaka Securities Exchange Regular Members Assn.	414	345	69	10
9	Japan Chemical Fibers Assn.	414	345	69	8
	Corporations				
1	Mitsubishi Bank	654	605	48	9
2	Fuji Bank	633	585	48	1
2	Dai-Ichi Kangyo Bank	633	585	48	1
4	Sumitomo Bank	632	584	48	3
4	Sanwa Bank	632	584	48	3
6	Mitsui Taiyo Kobe Bank	632	584	48	–
7	Industrial Bank of Japan	632	583	48	5
7	Long-Term Credit Bank of Japan	631	582	48	5
9	Bank of Tokyo	629	580	48	7
10	Tokai Bank	627	579	48	8
11	Nippon Credit Bank	615	568	47	10
12	Daiwa Bank	607	561	46	12
13	Kyowa Bank	585	540	44	16
14	Saitama Bank	561	519	41	17
15	Nippon Steel	569	517	41	15
16	Hokkaido Takushoku Bank	538	496	41	20
17	Taisei Corp	517	455	51	52
18	Mitsubishi Corp	486	472	14	18
19	Mitsubishi Trust & Banking	485	470	15	25
20	Kumagai Gumi	473	450	23	47
21	Toyota Motor	469	425	44	34
22	Kawasaki Steel	457	416	41	35
23	NKK Corp	455	414	41	36
23	Sumitomo Metal Industries	455	414	41	36
23	Kobe Steel	455	414	41	36

The Recruit Cosmos company was innovative in its attempts to gain favor. It sold stock to politicians or their families, aides and supporters before public offering after which it could be sold at a profit. Ezoe and Recruit offered stock at $20 a share to individuals in the Diet and the bureaucracy over a period of two years before going public. After listing the price rose ¥2,200 per share. In total 760,000 shares were offered to political, bureaucratic and business leaders. The shares were unavailable to the general public. The Takeshita and Nakasone groups are known to have purchased 12,000 and 29,000 shares, respectively. As well Recruit donated $259,000 to Takeshita's organization in 1986–87 and they bought more than $570,000 in tickets to two fundraisers in 1987.

Because of the gift giving rituals, even the voters themselves, the recipients of the largess, were involved in the scandal. The whole scheme was so massive that it is indeed hard to find who did not gain. It was a massive redistribution like a potlatch.

Well, perhaps Recruit Cosmos was not really innovative, according to Viner (1988):

> *Although not clearly documented, it is well-known in Japan that politicians procure campaign funds from stock market investments. That many securities firms ramp stocks in order to fill political campaign coffers is also well-known. Indeed, many individual Japanese investors will buy any stock rumored to be on the current buy list of a politician. Although fund raising through stock market manipulation is illegal in Japan, authorities are not motivated to conduct investigations or prosecutions.*

This statement was of course confirmed by the events of the Recruit scandal as Viner continues:

> *The Securities and Exchange Law of Japan does prohibit insider trading, including the manipulation of information in order to cause investors to buy or sell a stock (company directors are specifically excluded from these regulatory restrictions and are freely permitted to deal in their own company shares.) Nonetheless, only a handful of insider trading cases have ever gone to court.*

In a case against a former Nomura Securities executive it has been charged that Nomura has a special account for politicians to launder their funds where the money can yield 100% of the principal.

Other cases involving listed companies include Shokusan Jutaku and the *Toshi Journal*. The lack of a capital gains tax makes it easy to launder covert donations in stock manipulations.

Table 9.2 lists the major post-war bribery scandals prior to Recruit.

Table 9.2
Postwar History of Bribery Scandals

	Scandal	Defendant	Position	Charge	Judgment
1948	Shoden	Hitoshi Ashida	ex-prime minister	accepting bribe, etc	acquitted
		Takeo Kunusu	economic stability chief	accepting bribe, etc	8 months prison, 1 yr stay
		Suehiro Nishio	JDSP Diet member	accepting bribe	acquitted
		Banboku Ono	ex-Sec Gen, Liberal party	accepting bribe	acquitted
1948	Tankan	Kakuei Tanaka	parliamentary vice minister for justice	accepting bribe	acquitted
		Tamaichiro Fukatsu	Democratic Liberal Party (Minjito)DM	accepting bribe	2 yrs prison, 4 yr stay
1954	Zosen	Jiro Arita	Liberal Party DM	giving and accepting bribe	2 yrs, 3 yr stay
		Katsutoshi Sekiya	Liberal Party DM	accepting bribe	1 yr, 2 yr stay
		Goro Okada	Liberal Party DM	accepting bribe, etc	10 months, 2 yr stay
		Kisaku Sato	Sec Gen Liberal Party	violating political fund control law	acquitted in amnesty
1957	Prostitution	Shinpachi Sudo	LDP DM	accepting bribe	acquitted
		Takashi Shina	LDP DM	accepting bribe	10 months, 3 yr stay
		Giju Manabe	LDP DM	accepting bribe	10 months, 3 yr stay
1961	Bushu RR	Watanu Narahashi		accepting bribe	2 yrs, 4 yr stay
1967	Kyowa Seito	Shigeaki Aizawa		accepting bribe	withdrawn
1967	Taxi	Katsutoshi Sekiya	LDP DM	accepting bribe	withdrawn
		Shoichi Suhara	LDP DM	accepting bribe	withdrawn
1968	Nittsu	Masanosuke Ikeda	LDP DM	accepting bribe	1 yr, 6 month stay
		Seiichi Okura		accepting bribe	withdrawn
1976	Lockheed	Kakuei Tanaka		accepting bribe	on trial
		Tonasaburo Hashimoto		accepting bribe	on trial
		Takayuki Sato		accepting bribe	2 yrs, 3 yr stay
1986	Nenshi	Fumio Yokote		accepting bribe	on trial
	Koren	Sakonshiro Inamura	LDP DM	accepting bribe	on trial
1988	Jarisen	Fujio Tashiro		accepting bribe	

Source: *Japan Times*

THE RECRUIT COMPANY

The Recruit Group consists of 28 companies with interests in job-placement, information, telecommunications and real estate. Its accumulated bank debt is large—¥1.86 trillion or 30% more than Nippon Steel's ¥1.1 trillion—creating considerable uncertainty in financial markets. Recruit's core business is the fastest growing in Japan: information services.

Table 9.3
Recruit's Top Lenders, December 1988, ¥ Billion

Sanwa Bank	109	Sumitomo Trust	90
Mitsui Bank	108	Ind Bank of Japan	87
Toyo Trust	94	Mitsubishi Trust	83
Nippon Credit	93	Fuji Bank	81
Dai-Ichi Kangyo Bank	91	Mitsui Trust	80

Source: *The Economist*

Recruit Cosmos, the real estate arm, had meteoric growth in 1985 going from ninth to second among condominium developers. Its growth depended in large part on very heavy borrowings. It developed land under its own name and bought, for resale, buildings developed by smaller real estate companies. With this large need for funding, Recruit Cosmos began to rely on its own financial company, First Finance which raised money from the city banks and then relent the funds at higher interest rates to smaller developers. Paying interest rates that were about 1.5 points higher than major manufacturing companies like Toyota, First Finance had very thin margins. They were forced to abandon plans to issue shares on the Tokyo OTC market when the Recruit scandal hit in June 1988.

Condo prices in Tokyo fell 20 to 30% from the peak in late 1987 to the spring of 1989. Recruit acquired much of its land at the peak, so it had as much a ¥2 trillion of land to be devalued. Recruit owed money to 30 banks, for a total debt of ¥1.7 trillion. Mitsui, Sanwa, the Industrial Bank of Japan, Nippon Credit Bank as well as others all have lent heavily to Recruit Cosmos. The top lenders are listed in Table 9.3.

Other Recruit businesses include two employment magazines (*Bing* and *From A*), employment film and videos, and in-house communication networks that resell high-speed digital circuits leased from NTT.[1] Some of the group enterprises experienced financial problems in the wake of the scandal. Advertising revenue was off. One of its biggest advertisers, the Housing and Urban Development Corporation, was affiliated with the government, and many of the education authorities ceased advertising with Recruit.

The three main companies, Recruit, Recruit Cosmos, and First Finance Company, increased their earnings in 1988 with a total income of ¥74.11 billion, up 65% over 1987. Their combined profits exceeded those of Kirin Brewery, which ranked 52nd in corporate earnings for 1988. Notable were

---

[1]Some of the problems related to NTT share prices are a result of its role in the scandal.

the brisk sales of placement magazines published by the groups. Income by Recruit Co., the parent, grew 23.7% to ¥37.77 billion ranking it 109th. The declared income by Recruit Cosmos increased 52.7% to ¥1.28 billion, putting it in 217th place from 286th the previous year. First Finance Co. had returns of ¥17.06 billion, a 9.5-fold increase.

THE HISTORY OF THE RECRUIT SCANDAL

The full ramifications of Recruit are still not completely known. Scandals of this proportion in conjunction with the other socioeconomic changes underway take a long time to work their full metamorphosis on a nation. Indeed, the scandal was so long in evolving that the *Economist* had a numbered series of news articles. Until there is real political reform or some other crisis intervenes, the situation will not be resolved. Table 9.3 presents a chronology of the Recruit scandal from 1986 to 1989.

THE SCANDAL UNFOLDS

Arrests included Takao Fujinami, former chief Cabinet secretary and Katsuya Ikeda, former Komeito deputy secretary-general were both accused of accepting bribes.

Kunio Takaishi, vice minister of education, received 10,000 shares in exchange for eliminating regulations that would have hurt Recruit's employment magazines. Among the regulations are time deadlines: in the gentlemen's recruiting game, the beginning of the recruiting year for new graduates is strictly specified.

Recruit is also said to have special contacts with thousands of high school guidance counselors. They established a network of information about students seeking enrollment in universities, colleges and vocational schools. They had on file the names of 30,111 teachers who gave career advice to second-year students and 29,783 who gave advice to third-year students. We like the precision of this that was reported in the *Japan Times*. There are 5,500 public and private senior high schools in Japan; these lists covered 70% of them. Recruit distributed questionnaires to students every fall. They also sent out free literature that was paid for by the private vocational schools and colleges and universities. It was suspected that the network was facilitated by the Education Ministry as it is a huge undertaking.

Table 9.3
The Recruit Scandal, Major Events, 1986–89

1986	Recruit Co. sells unlisted shares in Recruit Cosmos Co. a subsidiary, at low prices to 160 politicians, businessmen and officials. Shares are listed on October 30 and many profit.
1988	
Jun 18	Newspaper reports that a city official got low-priced shares in exchange for favors in a building project
Jun–July	Involvement of other officials revealed including aides to PM Takeshita and former PM Nakasone
Jul 6	Hiromasa Ezoe resigns as Recruit chairman, Recruit stock transactions by former secretary of Takeshita revealed
Sep 5	Opposition DM Yanosuki Narazaki says he was offered a bribe by Hiroshi Matsubara of Recruit to go easy on investigation of Recruit
Oct 20	First arrest, Mr Matsubara on bribery charges
Dec 9	Finance Minister Kiichi Miyazawa resigns under pressure from aide's stock purchases
Dec 15	Hisashi Shinto, chairman of NTT, resigns after acknowledging Recruit profits in his bank account
Dec 30	Justice Minister Takashi Hasegawa, acknowledging Recruit donations, resigns just 60 hours after being appointed in a cabinet reshuffle
1989	
Jan 24	Ken Harada, head of Economic Planning Agency, who earlier headed a Diet committee, investigating the scandal, resigns because of Recruit links
Feb 13	Hiromasa Ezoe arrested for giving a bribe
	Hiroshi Kobayashi, president First Finance, arrested for giving a bribe
	Toshihiko Hasegawa, ex-NTT director and president Recruit International VAN Co., arrested for accepting a bribe
	Shikiba, ex-NTT director, arrested for accepting a bribe
Feb 15	Shunjiro Mamiya, Recruit director, arrested on violation of Securities Exchange Law
	Seiichi Tateoka, Recruit director, arrested on violation of Securities Exchange Law
Feb 17	Shigeru Kano, Labor Ministry, member of employment security bureau, arrested for accepting a bribe
Feb 18	Toshiro Ono, private secretary to Recruit president, arrested on violation of Securities Exchange Law
Mar 6	Hisashi Shinto, ex-NTT chairman, arrested for accepting a bribe
	Kozo Murata, ex-secretary to former NTT chairmen Shinto, arrested for accepting a bribe
Mar 8	Takashi Kato, ex-vice labor minister, arrested for accepting a bribe, he received 3,000 shares.
Mar 28	Kunio Takaishi, ex-vice education minister, arrested for accepting a bribe, 4,000 shares.
Apr 11,12	Takeshita tells Diet of ¥130 million ($990,000) donation from Recruit, acknowledges that donations exceeded legal limit
Apr 22	Reports that Recruit loaned Takeshita ¥50 million
Apr 25	Takeshita announces resignation
Apr 26	Mr. Aoki, the secretary and financial advisor to Takeshita, cuts his wrists and hangs himself

Source: Adapted from the *Japan Times*

In an unrelated incident, Junya Yano, Komeito chairman (ironically Komeito is the clean government party!), resigned after being accused of accepting ¥200 million in stock from a Meidenko Co. affiliate. He is the third political chief who has resigned. Democratic Socialist Party chairman Saburo Tsukamoto, in February, 1989, and Prime Minister Noboru Takeshita were the others. Yano denied that claim but was accused by Isao Nakaseko, a former top adviser to Meidenko, who was given a jail term for tax evasion.

Nakasone is believed to have helped NTT purchase four Cray supercomputers for Recruit and approved the appointment of Ezoe to government commissions that had direct bearing on Recruit.[2] Apparently Ezoe was not only buying favors but also was trying to establish a political career. Also implicated are NTT shares pre-privatization that were sold to large investors: originally there were to be 300,000, of which 100,000 ended up with the Ministry of Finance (parked so to say), and 200,000 were put up for auction. Some 33,000 that were originally in the auction were not picked up. Some suggest that 20,000 of these prefloation shares went to Ezoe, and their sale netted ¥6 billion ($50 million) in profit. Also uncovered are off-the-books slush funds, involving Japan's 97 hospitals.

Former Prime Minister Nakasone finally testified but it was a non-event. He said that he had done nothing questionable though he apologized to the nation for events that had occurred during his tenure. He also said he could not resign, as it was his duty to facilitate reform. Two secretaries and a female assistant of Nakasone had together bought a total of 29,000 shares in 1986 and quickly made ¥64 million in capital gains or about ¥2,200 per share. The two secretaries bought the shares with loans from First Finance. He claimed that they used the funds for their own jobs. It was rumored that Nakasone's assistant received 200 shares of NTT from Ezoe in November 1986. Nakasone refused a request to make public donations to the Sanno Economic Research Institute, a political fund raising organization.

It appears that it is hard to prove that bribery actually happened, as it must be proven that the recipient had the ability to affect the laws and deliver goodies.

The Recruit scandal is changing the political face of Japan. By late 1989 Takeshita had already been welcomed back into the LDP. Until there is some political reform, the situation will not be resolved.

---

[2] This raises the concern that there is some U.S. involvement because the U.S. government has pushed the purchase of supercomputers in Japan.

THE LDP PARTY—FACTIONS AND POWER

The LDP is a party of factions and power, not ideology. The LDP was formed as a coalition between the Liberal and the Democratic parties. The two parties were originally formed in 1953, when Shigeru Yoshida and Hatoyama split. Neither party won, so in 1956 the two parties merged opposition to the JDSP, so the LDP never really had a coherent program. In the beginning there were eight divisions. There has been some fluidity among these factions as divisions, and mergers, and leaders came and went. The coalition was supported by a business community that wanted stability.

From the beginning, factions disagreed on policies except holding office, and compromise has been important as a way of winning. It has historically had legislation approved by dealing with its factions and the opposition and rarely by having contested laws debated in the Diet. Some suggest that the cost of gluing together the party has been the equivalent of about ¥3 million a year transferred from the cities to each farming household. Then Kakuei Tanaka, in office in the 1960s, helped fuel a building boom and gained both personally via his own companies and politically by creating a network of loyal building and material firms and small contractors. He built the largest faction, once controlling 143 votes in the Diet. The major part of his faction is now headed by Takeshita. Though out of favor after the Lockheed bribe surfaced, no one could be prime minister without his approval, and in 1982 he and Kishi together crowned Nakasone as a stopgap prime minister.

Nakasone attempted to reform the party: he wanted to take power away from the traditional groups and garner more power himself. He set up advisory councils composed of businessmen and academics. One businessman who rose with Nakasone was Hiromasa Ezoe. His Recruit Co. concept for information business required access to the Ministry of Education and to cheap telecommunications (NTT). An added political device for raising money was selling tickets to fundraisers. The sums raised in rival parties in the summer of 1985 were staggering: Abe raised the equivalent of U.S.$10 million, Miyazawa $8 million and Takeshita $17 million. These figures are for one fundraising party each! Another round of parties was held in October 1987, and this time Recruit bestowed huge sums on each faction: Takeshita, Abe and Miyazawa each received about $1.6 million.

When it became apparent that Nakasone was losing power, Recruit looked to see who would be next. Because of the faction system, there were many candidates to choose from (see Table 9.4). Recruit drew up a list of 78 politicians, officials and journalists to be bought off with stock shares. Because so very many were tainted, it will be hard to enforce the faction system in the future.

Even in February, 1992, no real ideological platforms appear to distinguish the factions. Factions stay together in order to share power. As the factions become stronger, it becomes harder to determine who should be the head of the LDP and thereby the prime minister; see Table 9.5. As a way around the impasse, a more or less informal agreement was made to limit the prime minister to two or three years and to rotate power among the factions.

The vast sums collected and spent hide a trend away from the factions in the LDP and toward the central headquarters, giving more power to the party.

Table 9.4
The Factions and Their Pre Recruit Support in the Lower and Upper Houses in 1988

Faction Leader	LH	UH	Total
Takeshita	71	49	120
Nakasone	64	24	88
Abe	58	29	87
Miyazawa	60	27	87
Komoto	23	7	30
Independent	9	5	14
Tanaka	11	3	14
Old Tanaka	2	3	5

Elections are held every three years for the lower house, and half of the upper house is elected at that time. In the midst of the Recruit scandal, the LDP lost the upper house election to the JDSP headed by Takako Doi. However, the LDP, headed by Prime Minister Toshiki Kaifu, was able to maintain a majority in the February 18, 1990, lower house elections. To counter the loss of the women's vote due to the sex scandal of Sousuke Uno and the popularity of Doi, Kaifu was quick to appoint Mayumi Moriyama as chief cabinet secretary.[3] Doi resigned as the head of the JDSP in the summer of 1991.

---

[3]There were no women elected in the LDP so the two women ministers were absent from the new cabinet he appointed in February 1990. Overall, however, the number of female members has increased, with the JDSP in the lead with seven.

Table 9.5
Prime Ministers and The Factions in Office

	1955	1956	1972	1980	1987	1991 (Sept)
		Hayato Ikeda	**Masayoshi Ohira**	**Zenko Suzuki**	Kiichi Miyazawa	**Kiichi Miyazawa (21%)**
	Shigeru Yoshida					
		Eisaku Sato	**Kakuei Tanaka**	Tanaka	**Noboru Takeshita**	**Noboru Takeshita (27%)**
Former Liberal Party					& Shin Kanemaru Susumu Nikaido	
	Taketora Ogata Banboku Ohno	Mitsujiro Ishi Ohno				
		Ichiro Kono	**Yasuhiro Nakasone**	**Nakasone**	**Nakasone**	Michio Watanabe (17%)
	Ichiro Hatoyama				& Sousuke Uno	
		Tanzan Ishibashi	Sunao Sonoda Elsusaburo Shiina			
Former Democratic Party						
	Nobusuke Kishi	Kishi	**Takeo Fukuda**	**Fukuda**	Shintaro Abe	Hiroshi Mitsuzuki (23%)
				Ichiro Nakagawa		
	Takeo Miki	**Takeo Miki**	**Miki**	Toshio Komoto	Komoto	Toshio Komoto (8%)
	& Kenzo Matsumura				& Toshiki Kaifu	

Those in **bold** have served as prime minister.

Source: *Tokyo Business Today*, October 1991

Under the agreement, Shintaro Abe was to become prime minister after Takeshita, but, because he was tainted by the scandal, he was prohibited from running at the time and he died in 1991 before having his chance at the office. Toshiki Kaifu, considered clean because he took only ¥14 million in handouts from Recruit, became the third prime minister in less than a year. He was only 58 at the time and lacked a power base within the LDP, though he was a supporter of Takeo Miki, the reformer prime minister of the 1970s.

Table 9.6
The Factions and their Leadership Contenders

Takeshita	Ryutaro Hashimoto, 51	9 times elected from Okayama, transport, health and welfare, finance minister
	Ichiro Ozawa, 46	7 times elected from Iwate, building industry
	Tsutomu Hata, 53	7 times elected from Nagano, agriculture, he made the infamous statement that Japanese cannot eat foreign beef as their intestines are shorter than western ones
Nakasone	Takeo Fujinami, 55	8 times elected from Mie, education, very tainted by Recruit
Abe	Hiroshi Mitsuzuka, 61	6 times elected from Miyagi, transport, trade and industry
	Yoshiro Mori, 51	former education minister, chairman of party's national organization committee
Miyazawa	Koichi Kato, 49	defense and deputy cabinet secretary, confessed early to Recruit involvement
	Yohei Kono, 51	8 times elected from Kanagawa, education
Komoto	Toshiki Kaifu, 57	10 times elected from Aichi, mentored by Miki[4]

Source: *The Economist*

Masayoshi Ito, 75, was the first candidate for the leadership. Though not in good health (or perhaps because of it as he would be seen to be a caretaker only), he had the image of a clean politician. In fact, he was too clean for the job. He threatened the party with *real* reform including passing the mantle of power to the younger generation. There were still a number of faction heads that had not yet been prime minister and they did not want to be passed over. Also Ito's suggested reforms would have struck at the heart of the faction system. Ito had been prime minister after Masayoshi Ohira died in office and he belonged to the faction headed by Kiichi Miyazawa who resigned over Recruit but still had aspirations to be leader.

The old guard faction leaders were Noboru Takeshita, Yasuhiro Nakasone, Shintaro Abe, Kiichi Miyazawa, and Toshio Komoto. Each wanted to have a chance to be prime minister before someone from the next generation was selected and they were all put out to pasture (Miyazawa succeeded). The next generation contenders are presented below. There is a sixth old guard, Michio Watanabe of the Nakasone faction, who is apparently transitional, neither a faction head nor of the young group. He, too, would like to serve.

---

[4]*The Economist* said that given the small size of the faction, lightning would have to strike for him to become leader, and it did.

The opposition parties agreed on how many candidates to enter so they would not hurt each other and thereby help the LDP. Table 9.7 shows the distribution of seats held before dissolution, the candidates run and the results of the February 1990 election.

Table 9.7
Distribution of Seats in the Diet

	Seats Held	Candidates	Results
LDP	295	325	275
JDSP	83	148	136
Komeito	54	58	45
JCP	26	131	16
DSP	25	44	14
Others & independents	12	77	26

The LDP won despite the continuing party weakness in light of the Recruit and sex scandals and the unpopular 3% consumption tax. The election itself was both a vote for change and confirmation of the LDP. Voter turnout was high at 73%. The LDP won 275 seats (257 are needed for a majority). The JDSP won 136 seats, up from 51. Yet all but two of the 16 candidates involved in the Recruit scandal were returned. With the upper house in the control of the combined opposition, the LDP will have to find support there in order to govern.

Since the LDP has been in power for over 35 years, they have appeared to provide continuity and a pro-business stance. However, there is still considerable infighting within the LDP. Kaifu was a compromise candidate and intended to be a caretaker until a more established and older party insider could take over. Foreign Minister Shintaro Abe was originally in line after Takeshita but was tainted by his Recruit ties. Kaifu has been popular with the Japanese people and business leaders and has done a creditable job. Since his appointment in the fall of 1989, the LDP has crept back from the brink of disaster. Until the LDP settles its internal squabbles, there will be political uncertainty, which translates into downward pressure on the yen and the stock market.

Kaifu successfully fought the LDP party brokers and kept tainted politicians off his cabinet. Two important continuing ministers were Finance Minister Ryutaro Hashimoto and Foreign Minister Taro Nakayama.

UNO, THE FIRST CARETAKER

The LDP had trouble finding anyone who was untainted by Recruit to replace Takeshita. Finally Sousuke Uno was chosen. He was clean regarding the money (he's very wealthy) but not regarding sex, having been involved in a scandal with a geisha. Prior to 1988, neither money nor sex scandals had been important in Japanese politics. Interestingly he was not on the *Economist's* list of contenders. He had been foreign minister since November 1987.

Under Uno's leadership, the LDP lost its upper house majority in July. This raised hopes for a true reformation of the LDP process. He then resigned after having been in office only about two months.

The traditional power base of the LDP has been a very broad coalition of farmers, small business and the bureaucracy. In the modern period, it is inevitable that the diverse interests of these groups would be very difficult to hold together. The farmers interests for protection and subsidies conflicted with both the interests of the industrialists for export market and the interests of households for more accessible land. However, the LDP managed to alienate all sides of the coalition by being held responsible for the whole range of transitions that Japan is currently facing: food imports, export backlash, high land prices, and the consumption tax. The policies of the party apparently were made with little consultation and consideration for the grass roots. Uno's affair with the geisha just added another element of general disdain, losing him the women's vote which had already been alienated by the consumption tax.

In December 1988, before the scandal was full blown, only 25% of the Japanese believed that the government policies reflected the popular opinion, while 64% indicated that they clearly did not.

KAIFU—THE SECOND CARETAKER

Toshiki Kaifu became the second new prime minister in less than four months. He was a former education minister and quite young at 58. He was *Mister Clean* as he took only ¥14 million in handouts from Recruit, though he had little political base inside the LDP. Kaifu was a supporter of Takeo Miki the prime minister who tried to reform Japanese politics after the scandals of the early 1970s.

In October 1989, he won election as party president for two years, thus stabilizing his role as prime minister.

Kaifu went after the woman's vote. He appointed Mayumi Moriyama chief cabinet secretary after her predecessor was felled by the sex scandal. She, in contrast to Doi, is a family woman.

In October, the LDP candidate in an upper house by-election won in Ibaraki. This calmed things for Kaifu and bought him more time to make his mark on the party.

Support for the LDP rose to 42% (up from 28%) under Uno's short reign in June. The LDP had a number of popular proposals: more spending on housing, review of the consumption tax, freeze of rice prices, and tax breaks for part-time workers (mostly women who were drawn to Doi). Kaifu's performance was good. There were few troubles and he was elected president of the party and was thought to be the likely candidate in the next election. Indeed his performance was good enough to drive small stocks up by more than 10% in early October 1989. This was driven by money left over from June bonuses that had not been invested by individual investors because of the Recruit trouble and China massacre.

Kaifu, considered by his party as a lame duck, staked his reputation on political and electoral reforms. He expected the Diet would sit in extra session for two months in the summer of 1991.

Kaifu's Package of Reforms:

- Lower house reduced to 471 seats from 512 with 300 from single seat constituencies and 171 from proportional representation.

  This is crucial to reform and cuts to the heart of the scandal ridden party system in Japan. At present 130 constituencies are represented by two to six members ensuring multi-party representation but also creating the LDP faction system pitting one LDP candidate against another. In three seat districts, for example, each voter gets one vote and the top three candidates win.

  In single-seat constituencies, it is more likely that policy rather than services will be debated. The LDP would be forced to become a party of policy rather than convenience.

  Single-seat districts would also cost less. The party would be in a better position to support the candidate as there would be only one.

  For the 171 seats in the national constituency, each voter cast a vote for the party of choice. Seats would then be allocated according to share of votes for all parties that get at least 2% of the vote.

- After five years, corporation and unions would be banned from making donations to candidates.

- Each politician could have at most two registered support organizations for soliciting donations.

- ¥30 billion in subsidies to parties will be based on number of Diet members and votes.

The Diet rejected the reform bill on September 30, 1991, with all parties opposed. Kaifu should have immediately called an election but waited for his fate to be sealed by the LDP. The dominant faction withdrew support. There was perhaps no way that the package would be passed as it would have been an endorsement of Kaifu. Probably under the next government a similar package will be passed and Japan will finally move forward.

Also being discussed at the extraordinary session were revision of Japan's security and exchange law and provision to permit the Security Defense Forces (SDF) to participate in UN peacekeeping operations. The securities bill was passed on October 4, and the SDF question will carryover to the next session.

DOI WAITED IN THE WINGS UNTIL THE APRIL 1991 ELECTION DEFEAT

Please vote Socialist, Japan.

The Economist editorial, July 9, 1989

Takako Doi, a 60-year-old, former university lecturer in constitutional law, was the leader of the Japan Socialist Party. She experienced great personal popularity, though her party has been unpopular. She took over the leadership of the JDSP in September 1986 and almost immediately the party's popularity rose 9 points to 24%. She learned to use the media. She even appeared on a popular TV quiz show (and even answered most questions correctly) and was at home playing Pachinko or singing songs at karaoke bars with news reporters. She instituted Operation Madonna in which 187 housewives ran for local office and 177 won.

Doi's popularity reflects the growing public role of women in Japan.[5] The July election for the upper house saw a record 22 women win seats (only 7 of the 497 in the lower house are women).

Doi attempted to modernize the party's platform to gain votes. The party is saddled with old, worn-out policies that she could not seem to shake free of, including a very unpopular pro-North Korea stand. There was a mini scandal in the fall of 1989 regarding Pachinko owners, who are

---

[5]Called *onna no jidai*, the era of women.

mostly Koreans, giving money to North Korea which then got funneled back to the JDSP. But the scandal died when it became known that the LDP also received money from the same source.

Doi resigned and took responsibility for the party's defeat in a local election in April, 1991. She had been more popular than the party and her resignation probably presages further decline of the JDSP. Doi herself did not use the opportunity to make the party more practical sometimes siding with the idealistic faction that included opposition to using the SDF in peacekeeping. Doi's replacement was Makoto Tanabe.

THE OCTOBER 1991 ELECTIONS

Though Kaifu was popular, he never formed a power base within the LDP as there were still too many older politicians vying for office. Abe did not have mass appeal but was known for his integrity and moderation. It had been expected that he would be given the nomination and then decline and pass it back to Takeshita. However, after Abe's death on May 15, 1991, the party was thrown into disarray. Many predicted that his death would give more power to the young generation.

The Abe faction was splintered into four groups. One group of about 40 members included Hiroshi Mitsuzuka (former MITI head) and Education Minister Yoshiro Mori. Mutsuki Kato headed a group of about 20 followers and former Education Minister Masajuro Shiokawa headed another group that included former PM Takeo Fukuda. Transport Minister Shintaro Ishihara had ten followers. Ishihara wrote the controversial book, *The Japan that Can Say No*, which sold over a million copies in Japan. An unauthorized English translation made the rounds of the U.S. Congress and caused its co-author, Sony chairman Morita to distance himself from the book. Though popular in Japan, Ishihara was tainted, having received ¥30 million in 1990 in political donations from Ken Mizuno, when the limit was ¥15 million/year. These groups were pulling in different directions. The Mitsuzuka-Mori group favored Takeshita while Kanamuru and Ozawa favored Kato. Mitsuzuka himself was a contender and Michio Watanabe, leaders of the third and fourth factions were also expected to run. Other contenders of young generation included Hashimoto (that's why he had to resign as minister of finance) and former LDP Secretary General Ichiro Ozawa.

Former Deputy PM Shin Kanemaru, 76, was a key power broker. He served as chairman of Takeshita's faction. Takeshita's faction was still the largest with 106 members. They were thought to favor Finance Minister Ryutaro Hashimoto who unfortunately had many enemies in the LDP and within the faction, but, like Kaifu, was popular. Other candidates included Secretary General Keizo Obuchi and former Agriculture Minister Tsutomu Hata.

Kanemaru favored reforms, and was a main backer of Kaifu but he preferred the reforms to come after the next election. On May 19, 1991, he declared that the faction would have a candidate for leader. He suggested that the new leader should be about 60 and that anyone over 70 should not be allowed. He has called for a grand coalition party uniting the LDP and the Social Democratic Party of Japan (SDPJ) which would reorganize Japanese politics. Perhaps the practical minded of the SDPJ will unite with the reform minded of the LDP and form a new party. To confuse things further, former PM Yasuhiro Nakasone was also readmitted to the party after a two-year exile.

Kanemaru first offered the support of his faction to Ozawa, a younger politician in the Takeshita faction. He turned it down, citing a recent heart attack, but he seemed to be concerned about the defeat of the LDP's candidate for governor of Tokyo. Ozawa had been important in the government of Kaifu. For example, he was crucial in getting approval for Japan's $9 billion (U.S.) contribution to the Persian Gulf war. In exchange for the cooperation of the Komei Party, he had to find a new candidate for governor of Tokyo. The Komei (supporters are largely from a neo-Buddhist sect, Soka Gakkai) had disapproved of the incumbent Shunichi Suzuki, 80, who spent lavishly on the new Tokyo city hall and development on landfill in Tokyo Bay. The candidate picked by Ozawa, Hisanori Isomura, was defeated. The Tokyo chapter resisted and Shumichi Suzuki got 50% of the vote though there were 16 candidates. Ozawa took responsibility for the chaotic candidate selection process.

In the end, Kanemaru supported Miyazawa, as did the Komoto faction of which Kaifu is a member. With the votes of his own faction he had 219 votes committed and he needs 249 for simple majority.

Kiichi Miyazawa, 72, is fluent in English, is strong in international economic and financial affairs and is known as an intellectual. He began his career as a bureaucrat in the finance ministry. He gets along with foreign statesmen and is internationally respected, perhaps in the mold of Yasuhiro Nakasone. His ease in dealing with foreigners has made him unpopular with politicians and he has an especially poor relationship with Kanemaru. He took a hands-on approach in the various ministries he headed including finance, foreign affairs, international trade and industry and economic planning agency.

It is thought that Miyazawa favors easing monetary policy and wants more investment. Miyazawa's win appears to white wash those with ties to the Recruit scandal.

Certainly the strategy of the leaders is to think long-term. The way they considered their choice in October 1991 was like a chess game. They thought about the next round as well. The next election may be in July 1992.

THE 1991/92 STOCK MARKET SCANDALS

Scandal is an inherent characteristic of the Japanese financial system.
                                          Robert Zielinski, Jardine Fleming Securities

In 1991 and early 1992, there have been continuing revelations concerning the stock-loss payback under which large clients were paid off for losses incurred on the TSE. This is a special form of portfolio insurance.[6] If you were a big investor and lost, then you were compensated for your losses, but small investors were not compensated. So many lost confidence in the stock market, especially in the wake of the steep stock market decline in 1990 and the market's failure to recover in 1991 and early 1992.

The market has been so weak that it could not even rally in January 1992. As discussed in Ziemba and Schwartz (1991b), January is the strongest month seasonally for the Japanese stock market so failure to rally in January is a signal for trouble ahead. The trouble is largely selling by Japanese firms, especially banks who need to liquidate stock to meet their BIS standards in light of falling real estate and stock prices and an unwillingness to call in non-performing loans.

The brokerages revealed stock-loss paybacks of nearly ¥44 billion to 380 corporations and six individuals during a two-year period up to March 1990. The big four securities firms Nomura, Daiwa, Yamaichi and Nikko had paid ¥128.3 billion to 228 corporations and three individuals beginning October 1987 for two and a half years. All together this amounts to about ¥173 billion. Later they admitted to continued compensations in the FY 1991 for an additional ¥43.5 billion. The ¥173 billion payback is small compared with the more than ¥200 trillion *loss* from the stock market decline from the end of December 1989 to early 1992.

From January 1991 to March 1992, a total of 235 companies have filed lawsuits against the practice of *tobashi* by securities firms. *Tobashi* is a system in which brokerages transfer securities with unrealized losses from

---

[6]Formally one pays a premium for a *guarantee* of a limited downside risk. For example, for about 3% one can insure a portfolio to not fall below its current level for one year. One then receives the full gain less the 3% but the worst case is no gain. An excellent discussion of the ideas of such modifications of return structures is in Hakansson (1990).

one client to another under repurchase deals to avoid reporting losses at year end. Fully 83 suits for a total of $154.2 billion are against the Big Four. Another 152 for $83.3 million were filed against the other brokerages. There may be as many as 350 *tobashi* lawsuits pending.

In March 1992, Daiwa Securities announced it would settle lawsuits by Tokyu Department Store and four others for ¥73.5 billion or about 8% of its shareholders' funds. The sum of the suits will place Daiwa in a net loss of $325.8 million for the year. The case is similar to that of Cosmo Securities which settled out of court for ¥36 billion with Skylark.

The reimbursements were not illegal but angered smaller holders. In late December 1989, the Finance Ministry issued a directive banning the practice. However, the firms continued the compensation program. For example, Nikko admitted that some ¥23.2 billion was paid after the directive. The list of firms is long with some appearing on more than one list; the actual number was around 200.

One of the recipients was Soka Gakkai, which received ¥457 million but claims the money was deposited without its knowledge. Nippon Kayaku Co., a pharmaceutical company chaired by Tsunekazu Sakano, former head of the Securities Bureau of the Finance Ministry, received ¥5 million from Taiheiyo Securities.

Matsushita Electric Industrial was reimbursed as much as ¥4.61 billion by eight securities companies, including three of the big four. Nippon Steel Corp., Toshiba Corp., Canon Inc., Mitsubishi Corp., Nippon Yusen KK, and Ishihara Promotion also received reimbursements, along with Dai-Ichi Mutual Life Insurance, Kyowa Bank, and Mitsui Bank. Toyota Motor received ¥2.2 billion and Nissan Motor ¥1.6 billion. Shinko Lease was at the top, with ¥1.36 billion, followed by Marubeni Corp. with ¥ 1.13 and Kokusai Management with ¥1.07 billion.

Investments in securities and bonds by companies on the TSE totaled ¥25.4 trillion ($186 billion) in 1989, a 76% increase since 1985. Table 9.8 indicates the top ten in terms of securities holdings.

With 230 brokerage houses, many are inefficient. Fixed commissions have been set high enough to ensure survival of the inefficient resulting in high profits for the larger, more efficient companies. Naoki Tanaka in *The Japan Times* suggested that the Finance Ministry had encouraged cross-holding and other measures by larger companies to bolster smaller companies.

Growing competition from foreign brokerage houses, including innovations such as index futures, has made it difficult to continue these special relationships among the members. The market plunge beginning January 1990 was triggered by high valuations relative to current interest rates and by index futures trading by foreign brokerages. When prices fell

Table 9.8

The Top Ten Securities Holders, 1989–90

Company	89 Securities assets, billions	90 Net sales, billions	Industry
Matsushita Electric	8.36	31.2	consumer electronics
Toyota Motor	6.50	58.8	automobiles
Nissan Motor	4.61	29.5	automobiles
C. Itoh & Co.	3.80	151.0	trading house
Mitsui & Co.	3.32	149.0	trading house
Mitsubishi Co.	2.88	123.0	trading house
Tokyo Electric Power Co.	2.72	30.1	electric utility
Marubeni Co.	2.61	134.0	trading house
Bridgestone Co.	2.59	5.3	tires and rubber
Fujitsu Ltd.	2.56	15.6	computers

Source: *Japan Times*

below prices sold to hedge foreign Nikkei put warrants, they were bought back, and cash shares were sold to complete the index arbitrage. And the market fell.

How did the securities firms actually pay off their clients? They had them buy convertible bonds or warrant bonds that yielded capital gains. Nomura did it by buying bonds from clients at above market prices among other means. The Finance Ministry had known of the payout practice since 1983.

The *eigyo tokkin* (investment trust) funds had an interesting role in the payoffs. These gave securities firms the right to be both broker and fund manager, and they gave investors unofficial return guarantees. These were phased out beginning in late 1989, creating a potential for trouble. The choice was to absorb the loss or let corporate clients take the loss (which meant that the taxpayer pays).

Future problems with unexercised convertible bonds and out-of-the-money equity warrants, which were originally a sweetener, were attached to warrant bonds so that the bonds could be marketed at very low interest rates. They started coming due in the fall of 1991. About 75% of these coming due in 1992 are out of the money, which amounts to about ¥14 trillion. Brokers sold these in an attempt to compensate clients for their losses. The banks alone have convertible bonds with puts of $5.6 billion that were issued when the NSA was at 30,000. Companies need to get alternative financing. Securities companies already began to buy some of these nearing expiry (including Sumitomo Realty, Sumitomo Metals, Shimadzu, and Nomura Securities).

Reform is sorely needed, and awaits the new government. Hashimoto and Kaifu disagreed on securities regulations. Kaifu wanted an SEC type body while Hashimoto claimed that it did not fit in well with the Japanese market and proposed instead to review its regulatory enforcement. Hashimoto was more concerned with preserving the power of the Finance Ministry, even though he resigned to take blame for the stock payback scandal. He announced a five-year plan to improve its securities and banking inspections. This would include major computerization.

Kaifu's suggestions included:

- A Securities and Financial Examination Committee affiliated with the Finance Ministry with semi-judicial authority to investigate alleged abuses and lay allegations but the right to impose discipline would be left to the Finance Ministry.

- Phasing out fixed commissions which were partially responsible for the kick back scandals.

- Licensing for brokers.

Hashimoto resigned in an attempt to preserve his future aspiration for the office of prime minister. His last act as finance minister was to attend the meeting of the G-7 in Thailand in October, 1991.

Some of the effects of the scandal were:

- The California Public Employee's Retirement System suspended all trading with Nomura Securities, though it will continue to deal with Nomura Capital Management Inc. the U.S. subsidiary. It has more than ¥1 billion invested in Japanese firms of which ¥385 million is managed by Nomura Capital.

- The Big Four security firms were suspended from the primary market for government bonds for one month. They were also suspended from trading on their own accounts for up to six weeks. The profits of the Big Four declined sharply, from 54% to 71% in the FY 1990 and even lower profits are expected for FY 1991.

In the early summer of 1991, the Finance Ministry pressured the Big Four to refrain from soliciting business from corporate clients for four days and asked Nomura and Nikko to close some head office operations for those days. This was considered too lenient, so the new penalties were imposed.

Suspension from the primary bond market might be costly to the government in terms of higher rates on new debt. The Big Four typically underwrite about 85% of all Japanese corporate and government issues.

By October 1991, there were a number of resignations. The presidents of Nomura Securities and of Nikko Securities both resigned. While other firms paid customers back for losses, these two firms had additional charges including allegedly ramping the stock of Tokyu Corporation.

Other scandals involve the banks. Sumitomo Bank is implicated with an Itoman scandal in which three men, Yoshihiko Kawamura, Suemitsu Ito, and Ho Yong Chung, were arrested. Kawamura, a former president of Itoman and once an executive at Sumitomo, allegedly illegally purchased Itoman shares to protect his position. At the time, Sumitomo, Itoman's main banker, was putting pressure on Kawamura to cut back on real estate and other purchases. Ito and Ho allegedly caused financial problems at Itoman by pursuing deals in art and real estate. Itoman group has total debts of ¥767 billion.

Toyo Shinkin Bank lent to Nui Onoue on the basis of forged deposit certificates as collateral without inquiring on the purpose of the loan.

These loose lending practices point to the problems attendant on having too much liquidity following the huge trade surpluses. There simply were not enough quality borrowers with quality ideas around to mop up all the money.

THE 1992 SCANDALS

Fumio Abe, a close associate of Prime Minister Miyazawa, was arrested and accused of accepting $830,000 in bribes from Kyowa, a manufacturer of steel frames. Zenko Suuki, former prime minister and member of the faction of Miyazawa, allegedly accepted a $92,500 honorarium; Jun Shiozaki of the same faction received $185,000 for convincing Marubeni Corp. to cover up a fraudulent deal involving Kyowa. Kyowa went bankrupt soon after the incidents. It is likely that money was used to fund Miyazawa's campaign. After Abe's arrest, Miyazawa convinced Shin Kanemaru to become party vice president.

Tokyo Sagawa Kyubin, a local moving company, was involved in a real estate speculation scandal that occurred during the bubble late 1980s involving *yakuza* and about 200 politicians and about $9.2 billion. This scandal was even more complex than Recruit. Tokyo Sagawa Kyubin gave $1 billion to Inagawa-kai, the number two crime syndicate. Sagawa Kyubin grew rapidly from a small delivery service in Kyoto to a nationwide company with $.4 billion in revenue and 76 affiliates. The founder, Kiyoshi Sagawa, has charged two executives, former president Hiroyasu Watanabe and former managing director Jun Saotome, with losing $116 million through bad loans. However, Sagawa himself is also involved.

POPULAR LEADERS AND THE FUTURE OF JAPANESE POLITICS

The legacy of both Doi and Kaifu will be the growing importance of popularity versus party discipline in the future of Japanese politics. In particular the legacy of Doi will be the growth in the importance of women and their vote in the Japanese system.

Unfortunately, both the LDP and the JDSP failed to take advantage of popular leaders to facilitate reform and restructuring.

BUREAUCRATIC POWER STRUGGLES AND OTHER RAMIFICATIONS

The political structure will not be alone in feeling the impact of the recruit scandal. The securities market will likely also change. The Recruit scandal directly affects two companies—Recruit Cosmos and NTT—and indirectly it affects the banks and other financial institutions that lent money to the heavily indebted Recruit group. The stock payoff scandal affects much of the investment community. There is already a new law banning paybacks for losses incurred with severe penalties, even jail terms.

Until now, the securities market has sold mostly to institutional investors, ignoring the small investor. Everyone gained something as stocks as a whole rose, but some gained a lot. Now voters and investors appear to want a more ordinary auction market, as in the U.S. This may also presage a shift to more reliance on shareholders and less on the company managers. There is also a major push to clean up the rules on insider trading, which have been very lax. One suspects that blatant violation of insider trading roles will no longer be generally tolerated, and this will be policed by the industry itself.

CHAPTER 10
TAKEOVERS JAPANESE STYLE
AND THE BOONE PICKENS-KOITO AFFAIR

What except for political gain would Boone Pickens want with an investment of $1 billion plus in a minor Japanese company that he cannot take over, whose profits have been relatively constant, its prospects fair, when its stock has already gone up 800% in the preceding two years?

This chapter discusses mergers and acquisitions and investigates the role of corporate loyalty.

BOONE VERSUS KOITO

T. Boone Pickens, a world famous greenmailer[1] bought a substantial interest in Koito Manufacturing and attempted to exercise shareholders rights as defined in the U.S. on the basis of his ownership. However, the other owners resisted, claiming that they could not trust him to have the long-term interest of the firm in mind but only the short-term gain of independent shareholders. The Pickens-Koito case illuminates the differences between the Japanese and American corporation, as discussed in Chapter 3.

Some compared the arrival of Pickens to that of Perry in 1853. Pickens, through his Boone Co., initially bought 32 million shares or 20.2% of the stock, for some $770 million in March 1989. Later he purchased an additional 6.2% for a total stake of 26.4%. The stock was purchased from Kitaro Watanabe a dealer in used luxury cars and a leading corporate raider in Japan. Toyota had paid off a greenmailer in 1988 but refused to pay Watanabe. He shopped around for a buyer for his shares, but there were no interested parties in Japan. He then tried the U.S. and made a deal with Pickens. Toyota, in turn, balked at buying out Pickens. Koito itself was prohibited from buying the shares.

---

[1]See Pickens (1987) and for example "Boone Pickens, Samurai Warrior," *Business Week*, May 8, 1989, pp 90-94.

Pickens' shares of Koito came from Azabu Tatemono Co., a member of the Azabu auto dealer group and formerly a major shareholder of Koito. They kept an additional 0.5%. Koito initially refused to register the shares under Pickens' name and asked the Ministry of Finance to investigate the Azabu-Boone Co. transaction. Azabu was in violation of the Securities and Exchange Law. They had failed to report when they had acquired a 10% stake. Then they turned the stock over quickly and made a profit of ¥1.17 billion from trading in Koito. Article 189 of the Securities and Exchange Law requires any holder of 10% or more of a company's stock to return any quick profit earned within six months of purchase if demanded by the company. The Ministry of Finance ordered Azabu to pay back the profits it earned by block trading the Koito stock. On May 17, 1989, Koito received the ¥1.17 billion in stock trade profits.

The law bans corporations making deals with *sokaiya*,[2] corporate meeting specialists who shake down company management, which is also why Koito could not pay greenmail to Pickens. A Sony meeting became a target in 1984 with nit-picking questions concerning the Beta format for their VCR making the meeting last 13 hours. This scared other companies into resuming payments. In May 1984 an employee of Istan Co., a department store, was arrested for paying off sokaiya. The distribution industry is most vulnerable as the sokaiya pose as consumer advocates. To defend themselves, a majority of companies hold their shareholders meetings on the same day (June 29).

KOITO

Koito's market value in 1989 was about $6 billion and its primary business is automobile lighting which constitutes about 91% of its sales. Koito also makes military-related aircraft parts. Aircraft parts manufacture accounts for a further 3%, and the rest of its business is in miscellaneous activities such as producing traffic signals, sanitary equipment and circuit boards. Its major customers include Toyota, Nissan, Mazda, and other leading Japanese auto makers. Toyota buys about 45% of its product as well as owning 19% of its shares and has three of the 20 board members. Only 3% of sales are to foreigners.

Koito was debt-free and has a good record of products. It had a 4% margin versus only 2% for Nissan suppliers. The stock rose eight-fold in 1987 and fell 25% since Pickens entered the scene. Figure 10.1 shows the price of the stock since 1985. The price was flat in the ¥500 to ¥600 range for

---

[2]The number of *sokaiya* have been declining since 1982 when there were 6,000. The estimates now vary widely from about 1,000 to as few as 200.

most of 1985 to 1987. It then rose sharply without much change in profits at the time of the Watanabe purchase. It peaked at ¥5,470 in March 1989. Pickens' initial purchase was at a price of about ¥3,800 at a time when the stock was selling for about ¥4,400.

Figure 10.1
The Price of Koito Stock, 1985–92

	High	Low	Yearly G/L, %
1985	655 (85)	10 (50)	
1986	722 (Jul)	505 (Oct)	-9.0
1987	1,650 (Dec)	510 (Apr)	182.6
1988	3,720 (Aug)	1,520 (Jan)	123.7
1989	5,470 (Mar)	3,300 (Aug)	3.2
1990	3,890 (Jul)	2,800 (Mar)	-6.8
1991	3,050 (Jan)	2,210 (Dec)	-17.5.
1992	2,500 (Jan)	1,210 (Mar)	-51.6

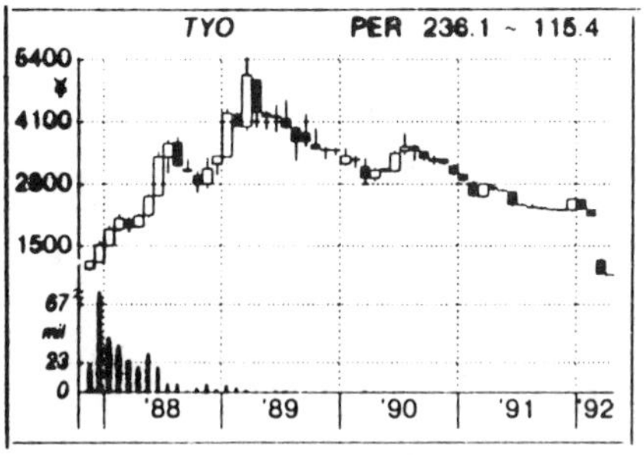

Source: *Japan Company Handbook*, Winter 1992

Toyota and others who have non-trading shares, including cross-held stock together hold 62%. Japanese law requires a two-thirds majority to determine major policy decisions. Some estimate that 10% of the companies listed on the eight Japanese stock markets have been bought into by greenmailers with firms too embarrassed to admit it. In October 1988, the rules on disclosure were tightened. Greenmailers seem to be attacking firms with land holdings threatening to force sale of prime sites for firms such as department stores like Matsuzakaya and small retailers like Chuijitsu-ya and Nagasaki-ya. These firms typically sell for 10 to 25% of the value of their stock, land and other assets.

Koito, like most Japanese companies, has substantial undervalued assets. For example, in 1989–90, its book value of land was ¥3.79 billion, but the estimated market value was at least ¥40 billion. Dividends are only ¥8/share or ¥260 million per year for Pickens' stake and the remuneration for three board members would not exceed ¥50 million per year. These returns cannot explain Pickens' interest in Koito.

Table 10.1 shows the profits earned by Koito since 1987. Although there is a slight growth of profits over this time, it hardly justified an eight-fold increase in the share price. With profits in the ¥20 range, Koito could afford to increase its dividend from its current ¥8 per year, but it is traditional in Japan to have low dividends. Watanabe or Azabu owned about 0.5% of the shares of Koito after their second sale to increase Pickens' stake to 26.4%.

Table 10.2 provides a summary of Koito's prospects as an investment. The October 1991 price of ¥2,804 is more reflective of the hidden assets. As of July 1991, Toyota owned 19%, Nissan 5.9%, Matsushita Electrical Industrial 5.3%, Nippon Life, 3.9%, Dai-Ichi Life, 3.1%, Matsushita Real Estate, 2.4% and Mitsubishi Bank, 1.5%.

Table 10.1
Financial Statistics on Koito Manufacturing, 1987–92 (in March), Consolidated Earnings, 1988–92 (in March)

Income		Profit					
¥ mil	Sales	Operating	Current	Net	EPS	Div PS	EquityPS
Mar 87	96,891	3,607	5,567	2,296	¥15.9	¥8	¥284.3
Mar 88	106,010	5,226	7,341	3,415	21.3	8	329.5
Mar 89	111,442	4,346	6,803	2,871	17.9	8	339.4
Mar 90	123,543	3,906	6,354	3,677	22.9	8	353.9
Mar 91	143,613	5,131	7,417	3,383	21.1	8	364.5
Mar 92*	160,000	3,500	5,500	2,700	16.8	8	
Mar 93*	175,000	3,900	5,900	3,000	18.7	8	
	Consolidated						
Mar 88	147,617	8,203	10,034	4,244	26.5		348.1
Mar 89	162,433	8,504	10,638	3,656	22.8		362.5
Mar 90	179,284	8,146	10,687	4,636	28.9		382.6
Mar 91	208,887	9,525	11,746	4,408	27.5		399.9
Mar 92*	225,000	8,300	9,500	3,600	22.4		

Source: Japan Company Handbook, Winter 1992

Table 10.2
Summary of Koito Prospects (Summer 1991)

Code	Price¥	CAP	Beta	Vol	PER	ROR	Div	Recommendation
7276	2804	4552	0.04	1081	23.6-209.1	44.84	8	Watch the action from the sidelines

The block of Koito stock owned by Pickens was originally held by a *shite*/speculator/rigger group called the Koshin Group. In early 1987, Koshin sold its block of 18 million shares to Azabu, which is another *shite* group formed by Kitaro Watanabe, president of Azabu Motors, who began a secret purchase of Koito shares, driving the price per share of ¥550 in early 1987 to as high as ¥3,820 in August 1988 (see Figure 10.1). Large blocks of shares are hard to come by in Japan.

Table 10.3
Ownership of Koito Manufacturing Co., Ltd. in 1990

Shareholders	Holdings (1,000s)	Share Ratio (%)
T. Boone Co.	41,934	26.40
Toyota Motor Co.	30,506	19.06
Nissan Motor Co.	9,543	5.96
Matsushita Electric Inc	8,558	4.94
Nippon Security Finance	7,905	4.94
Nippon Life Insurance	7,221	4.51
Dai-Ichi Life Insurance	5,310	3.32
Yamatane Securities	4,543	2.83
Daiwa Securities	4,143	2.83
Matsushita Real Estate	3,954	2.47
Mitsubishi Bank	2,442	1.53
Sumitomo Bank	2,442	1.53
Dai-Ichi Kangyo Bank	2,442	1.53

WHAT MOTIVATED PICKENS?

It does not seem to be a quick profit. Pickens claimed that he wanted Koito to become more profitable. This would include having it rethink its relationship with Toyota where he thought they were not earning enough, perhaps raising the price of its products, and raising its dividend from the current (and standard for Japan) level of ¥8 per share per year. His first specific request was that they raise the interim semi-annual dividend from ¥4 to ¥7.

Pickens was interested in four seats on the board of directors, roughly equivalent to Toyota (there are 20 seats). He complained that Matsushita Electric Industrial Co. was granted a seat on the Koito board though it holds only 5.3% of the stock. Pickens had an unprecedented number of interviews, storming out of meetings with Koito saying that he was discriminated against. He wanted to participate in management and improve shareholder rights and argued that Koito should have a better deal with Toyota. He wanted a dividend increase and treatment appropriate for a major shareholder. His Japan bashing in 1989–91 in an attempt to gain politically was a foreshadowing of the 1992 anti-Japan mood in the U.S. Congress.

BusinessWeek questioned whether Koito needed any help in its performance.

Much of this was a disagreement of shareholder rights, U.S. versus Japanese rules. The company in Japan is a social organization and not property. The main concerns of the company are customer, suppliers, workers, and management, and there is little concern for short-term financial gains. The board seats are for respected major shareholders and such seats are a privilege not a right. Japanese law does give holders of 10% or more of the stock the right to view all company records.

Pickens acted as though the Japanese were naive with his insistence that he meant to be a long-term holder of Koito stock. He did not understand that his reputation was worldwide. Indeed the business community in North America has developed sophisticated defenses against Pickens. For example, Unocol fought off a takeover by Mesa in 1985, beginning a string of unsuccessful raids.

Watanabe attempted to sell the shares to stable holders but could not make a deal in part because he refused to disclose the price he had paid for the stock. Watanabe then resumed buying shares and had 40 million in total or 25% of ownership by March 1989. The price per share was then ¥5,470 with a PER of more than 300. On March 31, 1989, Boone Co. bought 32.4 million shares at a cost of ¥109.35 or $770 million and a per share price of ¥3,375. Watanabe retained ownership of less than 10 million though he sold another 6%. (The price rose from ¥3,900 on March 1st to ¥5,470 on March 31st.)

After the announcement of Pickens' purchase, Koito stock fell from ¥5,470 to ¥3,980, which was still above the per share price paid by Pickens.

On April 19, 1989, Koito agreed to recognize Pickens' ownership and Koito president Takao Matsumura and the board met with Pickens. At this meeting, Pickens demanded three seats on the board. At later press conferences held in the U.S., it was suggested that Koito's profit level was too low due to low-cost sales to Toyota. He appeared to be appealing directly to protectionists in Washington by calling for freer financial markets in Japan and suggesting that the $55 billion trade deficit would not disappear until Americans could invest as freely in Japan as they do in the U.S.[3] Indeed U.S. trade representative Carla Hills was to put share ownership and control on the agenda of items to discuss with Tokyo.

In the end, in 1991, Pickens gave up. His efforts led to more and more hostility and resentment. The Japanese system won out. Minor profits, if

---

[3]Not aware that the net balances at all—though in truth, economists may not fully understand the role of the new financial institutional arrangements and the ability of borrowers and lenders to create money in whatever currency suits them at the time!

any, were swamped by the costs involved. Despite his considerable resources, the effects were minor. Any attempt he had to gain political points in the U.S. yielded meager results also. All Pickens was able to accomplish, after two years of hard and costly work, was a slight increase in the dividend which has since been rescinded. To end the affair, in early 1991, exercising the option he had when he purchased the shares, he sold his stock back to Watanabe through Azabu Tatemoto, who then owned 26.9%. Watanabe had 53 million shares again. Half of these shares were sold to the Sabia Carlson investment arm at the end of 1991.

The stock price then plummeted to ¥1,200 as of early March 1992. The price earnings ratio is 77.6, the market value ¥191.145 billion, and the net worth ¥365 per share. By May 1992, the price was ¥722 down fully 71.1% in 1992. This drop occurred with no essential changes in earnings; FY 1991 was ¥27.46 and 1990 ¥28.91. So the decline was based on other factors (as was the rise). In the ¥700 range, the stock price is now representative of the compnay's assets and earnings potential.

KEIRETSU

The Toyota-Koito relationship is an example of Japan's *keiretsu* or special relationship within a group of companies often rooted in the origin of the subsidiary company. The existence of Keiretsu both limits the local impact of Japanese foreign investment and makes it more difficult for direct investment in Japan to succeed. When Japanese auto makers entered the U.S. market with their own factories, they brought their Keiretsu parts makers and other service arms with them. In some cases the Japanese even brought their own service firms like catering, travel agencies, and even life insurance companies along.

In some regions, the Japanese firms are attempting to train U.S. suppliers to their exacting standards and interaction. This was discussed in Chapter 3 for the case of the automobile industry. When the Japanese transplants interact with local suppliers, there are spillovers of quality improvement on the domestic industry. Another indirect gain is that U.S. industry is also learning to work with local suppliers to obtain better quality products.

The Keiretsu system was under fire from the U.S. government as a market barrier and was one of three priority items in the Structural Impediments Initiative talks in 1992. Japan's Fair Trade Commission defended them, saying they are slowly reducing their reliance on each other. Each company within these groups held an average 1.42% of the total shares of another company in the same group in March 1990, compared with 1.52% three years earlier. Other members of the same group held an average 21.64% of the shares of a Keiretsu member company, down from 22.65% in 1987.

Professor Hiroshi Okumura, of Ryukoku University, pointed out that the decline has been caused by the issuance of large amounts of new stocks in the late 1980s rather than through conscious design.

According to the commission, the six company groups represent 0.008% of all Japanese companies but account for 13.54% of Japan's total business assets, 17.24% of total capital, and 16.23% of business sales. In the groups, the largest sales contributors, apart from banks, are general trading firms, which account for 60.7% of sales. Keiretsu members account for only 0.12% of each groups' trading companies' sales and for 0.38% of procurement.

Sales generated by intra-group business, excluding financial institutions, totaled 7.28% of the aggregate sales of member companies, down from 10.8% nine years earlier not counting indirect sales and transactions with subsidiaries. (*Nikkei Weekly News*, March 1992).

MOCHIAI, INTER—COMPANY SHAREHOLDING VERSUS MERGERS

Inter-company shareholding helps protect against hostile, outside takeovers and also helps to reinforce the long-term orientation of Japanese firms. These *mochiai* holdings are held for the purpose of maintaining good business relations and are rarely if ever sold. For some time after WWII, nearly 70% of shares had been held by individual investors. However, since the late 1960s, the share of individual investors has continually declined to about 20% in early 1992. Financial institutions own about 44%, business corporations about 20% and trust banks a further 8%; most of these holdings are mochiai and are never traded. The average mochiai holdings for 1978 listed companies in Japan in 1990 was 71%. Figure 10.2 shows the change of ownership patterns on the TSE between 1949 and 1987. Table 10.4 shows the mochiai percentages for the largest companies in each of the 28 sectors of the TSE in 1988. These holdings are extremely high and vary from 73 to 95%. Tables 10.5 and 10.6 show the lowest and highest cross-held companies as of late 1985.

Figure 10.2
Shareholders by Category

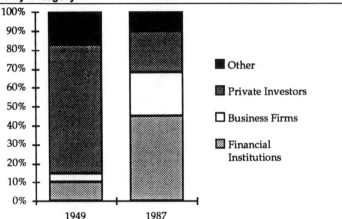

Cross-holding leads to a considerable overstatement of the value of companies in Japan. The total capitalization of $3.85 trillion at the end of 1988 was really about $2.93 trillion with some $924 trillion being double-counted mochiai holdings.[4] The size of Japan's market capitalization is such that the cross-holding bias was about the same as that in the six largest markets in continental Europe (Germany, France, Switzerland, Italy, Sweden, and Spain).

Recent legal changes have moved toward limiting the independence of shareholders. A 1982 law prohibited a subsidiary from buying shares in its parent (a firm holding more than 50% of the outstanding shares of the subsidiary). In the case of cross-holdings, if a company owns more than 25% of another then that second company cannot exercise its voting rights on the first (thus the subsidiary cannot vote on the policies of the parent). This reduces the incentive to be affiliated but not wholly owned (Pettway, Sicherman and Yamada, 1989). This, then, increased the incentive for subsidiaries to seek actively to be bought up and might lead to increased merger activity.

---

[4]McDonald(1989) has studied this effect. He used a sample of 75 major companies on the first section of the TSE that had about 53% of the section's capitalization. For these large capitalized companies, he counted the cross-holdings when they amounted to 0.05% or more. The analysis suggested for these companies that the real market capitalization in 1987-88 was about 76% of that reputed, namely the sum of the capitalizations of the individual firms. Since small and unreported holdings were not counted and lower capitalized firms may have higher mochiai holdings, the total effect is probably somewhat higher than the sample's 24%.

Table 10.4
Proportion of Floating Shares for the Largest Companies in the TSE Sectors, 1988

TSE Sector	Largest ¥ Companies	Price end Apr. 28/4/88	% Sector Mkt Cap Floating 1988	% Shares
Fishery, agriculture	Nippon Suisan	675	30	20
Mining	Arabian Oil	5,760	34	17
Construction	Kajima	1,590	9	15
Food	Ajinomoto	3,610	16	15
Textiles	Asahi Chemical	1,150	20	25
Pulp & Paper	Oji Paper	1,450	25	21
Chems & pharmaceutical	Takeda Chemical	3,050	8	17
Oil & coal products	Nippon Oil	1,190	39	27
Rubber Products	Bridgestone	1,460	49	12
Glass & ceramic	Asahi Glass	2,100	34	14
Iron & steel	Nippon Steel	465	27	20
Non-ferrous metals	Sumitomo Electric	1,660	19	24
Metal products	Toyo Seikan	3,210	41	10
Machinery	Kubota	700	10	12
Electrical machinery	MEI	2,790	12	17
Transportation equipment	Toyota Motor	2,440	33	8
Precision instruments	Ricoh	1,360	20	17
Other products	Dai Nippon	2,750	30	10
Commerce	Mitsubishi Corp.	1,330	8	12
Banking & insurance	Sumitomo Bank	3,800	7	5
Real estate	Mitsubishi Estate	2,410	45	16
Land transportation	Seibu Railway	4,550	16	8
Marine transport	Nippon Yusen	646	33	20
Air transportation	All Nippon Air	1,880	51	24
Warehouse & transportation	Mitsubishi Ware.	1570	24	17
Communications	NTT	2,490,000	73	5
Electricity & gas	Tokyo Electric	6,170	37	22
Services	Secom	7,110	15	23

Table 10.5
The 25 Companies with the Lowest Ratio of Stable Shareholders,
September 5, 1985.

Rank	Company	Ratio (%)
1	Heiwa Real Estate Co., Ltd.	7.13
2	Nankai Electric Railway Co., Ltd.	15.58
3	Teikoku Oil Co., Ltd.	15.68
4	Mitsui Mining and Smelting Co., Ltd.	17.85
5	Hankyu Corp.	18.08
6	Kirin Brewery Co., Ltd.	18.97
7	Seika Sangyo Co., Ltd.	19.48
8	Fujiko Co., Ltd.	19.53
9	Kitakawa Iron Works Co., Ltd.	19.62
10	Toyo Terminal Mfg Co., Ltd.	19.75
11	Noda Industrial Co., Ltd.	19.86
12	Nissan Chemical Industries, Ltd.	20.06
13	Nippon Steel Corp.	20.10
14	Nikkatsu Corp.	21.01
15	Kawasaki Steel Corp.	21.04
16	Sony Corp.	21.42
17	Miyairi Valve Mfg Co., Ltd.	21.51
18	Unichika, Ltd.	21.59
19	Shinki Bus	21.60
20	Nippon Dream Kanko Co., Ltd.	21.78
21	Ebara Corp.	21.80
22	Yamato Transport Co., Ltd.	22.03
23	Nippon Oil Co., Ltd.	22.40
24	Otori Senni Kogyo	22.48
25	Hitchi, Ltd.	22.62

Source: *Nikkei Sangyo Shimbun* and Kanji Ishizumi (1988)

Table 10.6
The 10 Companies with the Highest Ratio of Stable Shareholders,
September 5, 1985.

Rank	Company	Ratio (%)
1	Sanko Paper Mfg, Co., Ltd.	86.86
2	Ohtsu Tire Co., Ltd.	86.61
3	Toyo Bosuifu Mfg, Co., Ltd.	85.28
4	Shin Nippon Drop Foreign Co., Ltd.	81.40
5	Tokyo Toyota Motor Corp.	81.05
6	Zenistu Ryoko Concrete Co., Ltd.	80.68
7	Fuji Steamship Co., Ltd.	79.86
8	Hosui	79.82
9	P.S. Concrete Co., Ltd.	79.73
10	Yuraku Tochi Co., Ltd.	79.71

Source: *Nikkei Sangyo Shimbun* and Kanji Ishizumi (1988)

FOREIGN OWNERSHIP

For a foreign company to merge with a Japanese company it must first establish a subsidiary in Japan. In Japan, a foreign-owned firm is defined as one in which at least 50% of the equity is directly or indirectly owned by non-Japanese. As of March 1987, the total accumulated foreign investment was $7 billion representing 2,094 firms (Ishizumi, 1988).

In 1984, foreign capital investment represented 3.6% of the capital expenditures in Japan.

It is becoming easier for foreigners to acquire companies in Japan. Daiwa Securities reports that foreigners made 13 acquisitions for a total of $1.4 billion in 1991. Now 10% of the firms seeking mergers would be willing to accept a foreign offer, this is up from zero only two years ago.

Table 10.7
Distribution of Ownership of Foreign Firms in Japan, March 1987, from Sample of 894 firms

Country	% of firms
U.S.	48.5
German	7.7
British	7.4
Swiss	5.9
French	4.7
Asian	11.1

Source: Kanji Ishizumi (1988)

MERGERS AND ACQUISITIONS, JAPANESE STYLE[5]

Kanji Ishizumi sets out the procedures for acquisitions in Japan. He emphasizes the importance of doing things the Japanese way and of attempting to gain good will and cooperation before making any move. For example, it is useful to gain agreement from the target firm's bank, to offer a

---

[5]Thanks are due to   Ziemba's University of Tsukuba students Numako Masato, Adisak Taveerojkunsri, and Zoltan Zamori for helpful discussions and material in this section. Good discussions of this topic appear in the books by Ishizumi (1988) and Kester (1991).

mutually profitable business venture, to retain existing management, and to obtain cooperation from labor and other participants. One popular way to acquire a large stake in a company is to purchase stock from one of the major shareholders directly. Another way is to buy newly issued stock directly from the target company by private placement. In Japan, there are no laws protecting shareholders from dilution of their holdings by such private placement of new issues. These new issues have been offered at more than 50% discount from market. For example, when Sony acquired Aiwa at ¥70 the market closing price was ¥145.

By purchasing foreign convertible bonds, a would-be acquirer can maintain secrecy, as these are issued in bearer form. Some potential candidates are shown in Table 10.7. A related method is the purchase of newly issued convertible bonds from the company by private issue. Issuance of convertible bonds has also served to thwart takeover attempts.

The sale of shares by the major holder can create a large tax liability. The same is true when a Japanese company sells all or part of its business. For example, the difference between the book value and the selling price is subject to capital gains tax. So in consideration of the number of companies that carry land and other assets at original price, the unrealized capital gains liabilities are likely large. If a foreign company purchases assets at less than fair market value, this difference is considered a capital gain and is taxable.

Target acquisitions usually fall into one of the following categories:

Type 1   A company in serious financial difficulty that has expressed willingness to be acquired.

Type 2   A company that is in a good financial position and does not want to be acquired but might be willing to have a mutually advantageous business tie-up.

Type 3   A company that may be willing to be acquired but has not publicly expressed this.

The best targets are those in financial distress who need new money, those which have no successor for ownership or management, or those with long standing business partners. Acquisitions are easier if they have a low percentage of nonfloating shareholders and/or a large amount of convertible bonds issued. The most successful acquisitions are through some type of cooperation or joint venture followed by a merger or the gradual increase in friendly shareholding, which may end in the acquisition. Figure 10.3 shows the usual methods of acquiring Japanese companies.

For Type 1 companies the most important thing is to set the economic terms of the merger. Mochiai holdings usually block takeovers of Type 2 companies and there are virtually no hostile takeovers in Japan. For Type 3 companies, Japanese patience and nurturing is required for success. Secrecy is important and a public announcement is usually made only just prior to the completion of a deal. Successful mergers do not mention the term *acquisitions*, ask for too many board seats, let anyone lose face, remake the present management, or offend the labor union.

Figure 10.3
Methods for Acquiring Japanese Companies

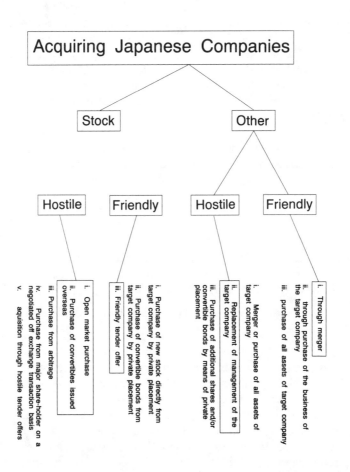

Source: Ishizumi (1988)

Strategies[6] to attempt an acquisition include one or more of the following aspects:

- Buying stock on the open market. This requires 6 to 18 months and secrecy is hard to maintain although professional *stock collectors* may be employed.

- Buying convertible bonds and/or warrant bonds issued in foreign markets. These can be acquired secretly. Among other advantages many of these derivatives are issued in bearer form and traded on OTC markets so the purchaser and/or price can be kept confidential.

- Friendly takeover tenders. The start is through additional share purchase which may eventually lead to the merger.

- Proxy solicitation as leverage to oust or select new directors.

Through shareholder resolution, control may be made with a two-thirds majority of some board seats to remove a director or simple majority to appoint a new director. Large shareholders, in good standing, can usually obtain seats in this way.

- Acquisitions through mergers. Mergers in Japan must be by share-for-share or stock exchange methods. Hence a prime concern is the exchange ratio for stocks. For a foreign company to acquire an existing Japanese company through merger, it must have a subsidiary in Japan which is the vehicle for the merger. Both boards must approve the merger and then the shareholders and creditors must approve. Shareholders who disagree have the right to demand that their shares be purchased at fair market value.

Mergers usually involve an informal preliminary contact with government agencies since their approval, though not required, is very beneficial. Notice must be given through the Bank of Japan before a 10% stake may be acquired. This contact, called *nemawashi,* is to inform all parties to attempt to secure a favorable opinion.

A merger must almost always have approval of the firm's largest commercial bank. Usually the bank is:

- The largest lender to the company.

- One with a long-standing business relationship with the company and any subsidiaries and affiliated companies in the lending business, deposits, foreign exchange, custodian and trustee service business.

---

[6]Adapted from Ishizumi (1988).

- One of the major shareholders of the company.

- Such that one or more bank employees are on the board of directors or the board of statutory auditors of the company.

- Fully committed to the company's funding operations.

- A close business liaison with the company so that it will usually be the lead manager of additional loans to the company.

The merger must be a mutually profitable business relationship to succeed. New technology or marketing channels may be crucial aspects of the merger.

Table 10.7
Companies with M&A Potential Based on Foreign Convertible Bonds.

Company	PCSE Ratio (%)	Potential Shares (1,000)	Nonconverted, Unexercised Amount (¥ mil)
Osaka Oxygen Kogyo	48.04	40,331	11,220
Minebea Co., Ltd.	42.93	93,821	65,718
Chujitsuya Co., Ltd.	39.38	22,935	15,521
Kenwood Corp.	34.73	18,256	13,431
Gun San	33.86	11,698	4,288
Renown Inc.	23.96	37,565	27,568
Daishinpan Co., Ltd.	22.85	8,845	6,609
Daido Sanso K.K.	22.48	10,070	2,537
Nakayama Steel Works, Ltd.	21.91	17,183	7,744
Asics Corp.	21.32	28,058	12,438
Nippon Shinpan Co., Ltd.	21.15	52,930	33,619
Ryobi Ltd.	20.51	24,974	10,123
Sanyo Electric Co., Ltd.	20.25	6,922	8,908
Maruzen Co., Ltd.	20.15	15,295	7,075
Durban Inc.	19.58	9,493	4,908
Gun Ei Chemical	19.40	10,494	9,668
Asahi Ka Forging	19.12	6,999	2,421
Tsubakimoto Precision Product Co., Ltd.	18.76	6,642	9,922
Takasago Thermal Engineering Co., Ltd.	18.58	8,551	4,899
Tuji Tech	18.50	11,948	8,942
Zeto	18.10	3,638	2,263
Tokyu Department Store Co., Ltd.	17.96	28,862	13,889
Showa Line, Ltd.	17.72	27,763	5,691
Pasco Corp.	17.46	6,350	8,934
Daiichi Katei Denki Co., Ltd.	17.26	11,879	7,828
Toshiba Plant	17.21	8,259	6,557
Osumi Howa	17.05	7,133	3,859
Han Wa Ko	16.93	29,101	20,567
Sonoike Took Mfg. Co., Ltd.	16.59	9,771	10,668
Sankyho Seiki Mfg. Co., Ltd.	16.56	11,649	15,111
Kayaba Industry Co., Ltd.	16.55	23,770	7,241
Tokyu Store Co., Ltd.	16.51	6,219	5,458
Silver Seiko Ltd.	16.49	7,999	4,615
Yamamura Glass Co., Ltd.	16.37	12,209	6,242
Yoeki & Co., Ltd.	16.06	26,049	10,075

Note: Potential share ratio is calculated based on the ratio of the potential share (non-converted convertible debenture and unexercised warrant) by issuring foreign bond to the issued share (as of the end of July 1985)

Source: *Nihon Keizai Shimbun*, Sept 21, 1985 as reprinted in Kanji Ishizumi (1988)

CHAPTER 11
WHERE DOES THE FUTURE LIE?

On Wall Street today, news of lower interest rates sent the stock market up, but then the expectation that these rates would be inflationary sent the market down, until the realization that lower rates might stimulate the sluggish economy pushed the market up, before it ultimately went down on fears that an overheated economy would lead to a reimposition of higher interest rates

The New Yorker Magazine (1981)

Japan changes rapidly and dramatically in response to economic forces. That doesn't mean it becomes more like us, or changes in ways that we like, but it does change.

Bill Emmott

In this chapter, we investigate both the financial and managerial future for Japan and its role in the world economy. Economic relations are always in flux as new conditions work their way through the global economy. A number of trends came together to contribute to Japan's dramatic rise to creditor status. The fall in real oil prices and thus imports contributed to the dramatic rise in Japan's current account surplus. Then when the surplus began its rise in September 1988, petroleum prices were 20% *lower* than the previous year, depressing oil imports 30% in value terms. As the yen increased in value, two things pushed exports unexpectedly higher: Japanese manufacturers switched to higher value added products, and increased foreign investment gave a boost to parts and equipment exports for the offshore plants. Exports actually increased about 15%.

Imports of finished goods did rise 39% in 1988 and accounted for 49% of all imports (up from 23% in 1980 and 31% from 1985). But imports from the U.S. rose at a below average 33%, those from Europe rose 37% and from Southeast Asia, 47%. Many of the imports are now firmly rooted in the Japanese production and distribution system. Trade relations are in transition.

One strength that Japan has had is an awareness that temporary gains are not permanent. The Japanese are aware of the need to be alert and responsive to future relative changes.

319

JAPAN'S ATTITUDE TOWARD THE WORLD

Japan has been a closed society and has created for itself the image of a pure society with a different, unique ethnic character. The cohesiveness, group camaraderie, and loyalty to one's company and the country is extraordinarily high. The work ethic and skill of the labor force are at the highest level. Outsiders, the *gaijun*, particularly those who are talented, are treated with great respect and courtesy. Their skills and knowledge are eagerly sought and the useful ideas pooled into the Japanese knowledge bank. They, like their fellow Japanese workers, must know their place, but with the communication and cultural differences this can be difficult. Few foreigners achieve any real position of authority. Though not impossible, it is very difficult to make business deals with Japanese firms except for the exchange of products and lease or sale of black box type products such as operating software.

Other Asians are discriminated against even if they were born there or have lived in Japan for a long time. Only recently has it been possible for non-Japanese to become citizens. There is only one permanent foreign professor at a national university, and he, a Korean, taught in Japan for twenty years before gaining this appointment. Yet the agricultural work force is increasingly composed of migrants from the Philippines and other countries. There is increasing confidence in their economic success and some arrogance towards the world and especially towards its number one benchmark, the United States. Japan has great pride in its economic success: the high yen, low interest, inflation, crime and drug rates, the low incidence of poverty and homelessness, the high educational level, and effective economy with saving surpluses.

James Taylor, an American expatriate born of missionaries in Japan, has lived there for twenty years. In his book *Shadows of the Rising Sun* (1985), he discusses Japan's national character, which he says has historically alternated between intense periods of servility and arrogance. He predicts Japan will show more of the world a superior attitude, that until now has been reserved for its Asian neighbors. This was the case in the late 1980s; however, the extreme financial problems in the stock, land and financial markets is tempering this. If troubles deepen, the Japanese may become more inward focused.

Although some of Japan's motivations to improve its wealth and status are admirable, there is now the feeling that the country has to run at full steam just to stay even.

Japan's national insecurity dates at least from the sixth century when they sent emissaries to China to learn about its more sophisticated culture. The Tokugawa shogunate closing of Japan more than a thousand years later revealed a confidence that there was little more worthwhile to be learned from the outside.

To understand Japan and the rest of modern Asia, one must understand the role of the Western powers in the 19th century. Much of the modern state of Japan was put into place under the Meiji Restoration and is a reflection of the paradox of insecurity at the forced opening of Japan and the strong desire to avoid the weakening and destruction that had happened in China. U.S. demands that Japan open up in 1854 changed things. This led to a frantic imitation of the communications, weaponry, and cultural aspects of the west. Japan felt the treaty to be very one-sided. The Japanese had no choice, having been overpowered, and they needed to learn to re-empower themselves. Military victories over China and Russia at the turn of the century restored Japan's sense of worth.

Paradoxically, the much admired Japanese education system was established both to westernize Japan and to secure for Japan a national identity. This led to the supremacy of education as a responsibility of the individual to the state. When Japan annexed Korea in 1910, it imposed this on the Koreans. Japanese was taught in Korean schools and there were efforts to stamp out the Korean culture and put in its place that of Japan.

Japan's defeat in World War II plunged Japan to extreme depths of inferiority. Now after forty years of hard work and with the economy in so much better shape than that of the U.S., they see themselves, in Taylor's view, as the older rather than the younger brother. There is some arrogance among those who grew up in the post-war era. Their impatience with the Western image of Japan as a brilliant imitator led to the increased emphasis on creativity and innovation in the mid-1980s. Still, the perception of Japanese arrogance may be largely grounded in a mixture of fear and admiration. Japanese people are still complacent about their relatively low standard of living relative to their income and the high prices they must pay for cameras, air travel and the like. The Japanese are used to accepting their condition. This is a great weakness and advantage at the same time, one of the vast number of contradictions of Japan.

To succeed as a global financial power in the long run, the Japanese will need to develop a social attitude reflective of a participant in the global community. Although there has been some progress, there is a definite feeling that Japan would like to take things more slowly on the world scene. The Japanese feel a larger worldwide political and economic presence could bring vulnerability to their domestic economic and cultural habits.

OPENING TO THE GLOBAL MARKET
IN THE SECURITIES MARKETS

The TSE began to accredit more foreign securities firms just as the securities market began its down turn in 1990.

The cost of joining the TSE was about $9.4 million, of which the equivalent of ¥500 million was membership with the remainder covering various exchange costs and financial guarantees. At current exchange rates the seats would cost 20 times the $470,000 of the NYSE. Despite the high costs, the TSE rejected the idea of creating a special limited membership.

The TSE previously admitted only firms that were trading on the NYSE or the American Stock Exchange but it has now agreed to allow firms on the OTC to also trade in Tokyo with a few additional requirements. These include a minimum net worth of about $70 million and pretax earnings of about $14 million in each of the last three years. Only about 69 of the 200 eligible have gone to the expense (more than $100,000) and time (about six months) of getting on the TSE. The volume of trading is low (as it is for most shares on the TSE). Individual investors cannot hedge the currency risk and institutional investors can buy in New York and avoid the high TSE commissions. Alcan Aluminum Ltd. of Canada was listed on the foreign stock section of the TSE.

Japanese companies are changing their names, simplifying them for the global economy, replacing Chinese characters with *katakana* and roman initials. About 20% of the 2,000 major companies on the stock exchanges use katakana and roman letters because the Kanji are considered out of date. Twelve new companies are in transition which will cost them from ¥10 million to ¥2 billion. Some examples are:

Teikoku Kako Co. Ltd.	Tayca Corp.
Kakuei Construction Co. Ltd.	L. Kakuei Corp.
Orient Finance Co. Ltd.	Orient Corp.
Daichi Construction Works Co. Ltd.	Ichiken Co. Ltd.
The Pilot Pen Co. Ltd.	Pilot Corp.
NTN Toyo Bering Co. Ltd.	NTN Corp.
Toa Electric Co. Ltd.	TOA Corp.
Omron Tateishi Electronics Co. Ltd.	Omron Corp.
Kubota Ltd.	Kubota Corp.
Kinki Electrical Construction Co. Ltd.	Kinden Corp.

NEW BANKING AND DERIVATIVE FINANCIAL INSTRUMENTS

The late 1980s saw a dramatic increase in the number of new financial instruments, especially *derivative securities* whose values depend upon the prices of underlying assets. Futures and futures options based on index values are examples. These changes in the financial sector became widespread and began to turn ordinary savers into speculators. One example introduced in 1989 by the Dai-Ichi Kangyo Bank and other city banks was an instrument linking time deposits to stock index performance. Depositors bet that the index will either go up (bull) or down (bear). If they are right, they receive a specified function of the full stock move. If they are wrong, they still receive a guaranteed minimum return of about 1%. Ordinary time deposits in contrast pay a fixed return of 4 to 5%.[1] The minimum denomination was initially ¥10 million with five maturities ranging from three months to two years. Later, the minimum deposit was phased down to ¥3 million.

Index arbitrage began in Japan in September 1988 with the Nikkei 225 on the Osaka Securities Exchange and TOPIX on the Tokyo. Their combined daily turnover by March 1989 was more than that of the S&P500. With the first expiry in December, 1988, arbitragers were short the underlying equity and last minute purchases dramatically moved the market. In March, they were apparently long on equities and expecting a sell off. Foreign brokerage firms were asked to place any large orders before the opening of the market March 7th, the expiry date, and to place any orders on their own account before the last 30 minutes. Domestic securities firms were asked not to engage in index arbitrage in Japan. However, they are active in index arbitrage in the U.S. and other markets. Also, some firms have invested in small boutique brokerages that were involved in similar arbitrages inside and outside Japan. In 1989-92, there was more programmed trading. Some trades have affected the market's returns and volatility because of hedge ratio adjustments of the Nikkei puts traded in the U.S., Canada and Europe.[2] We are also seeing new rules of disclosure on this activity. The Nikkei stock average futures contract has become the most successful contract in the world with trading in Singapore, Osaka and Chicago.

Major securities firms are looking for ways to increase the efficiency of trading. Yamaichi Securities began to use a Hitachi supercomputer in June 1989. Though only 10% of its capability will be used at first, these machines increase the processing of information on transactions and analysis of

---

[1] The pricing of this contract is formally a version of portfolio insurance as discussed in Ziemba and Schwartz (1992).

[2] On index arbitrage in Japan see Brenner et al. (1989, 1990 a, b) and Ziemba and Schwartz (1992). Shaw, Thorp and Ziemba (1992) have studied the Nikkei put warrant market.

investments more than 24 times over general purpose computers. These will speed up the development of financial products including derivative instruments such as those are being created on the New York, Toronto, and other stock exchanges.

The arrival of more sophisticated financial instruments will likely change Japan from a simple country with a high savings rate to one with a much more loose investment style.[3] Although on paper in continuous markets such instruments are fully safe, they require assumptions to execute them (see Grossman, 1988). In a crash, who knows? Japan is following the U.S. in this high-tech finance area. It may work well for Japan but it is not where Japan got its strength and assets. So far, the major profits from derivative trading have been made by foreign brokerage firms such as the Salomon Brothers, Goldman Sachs, Morgan Stanley and Baring Securities. They have made enormous profits. At the same time Japanese firms have had a very difficult time with the weak stockmarket. Profits are down sharply and there are cutbacks and some negative earnings.

NEW LISTINGS

Regulations passed in 1985 were designed to make listing on Japan's stock markets easier. From a base of about 2,140 listed companies in 1985, there were expected to be another 2,800 listed by 2001. These would be drawn for the large number of firms that earn the minimum profit level of ¥40 million required for listing. A number of factors are involved in the trend:

- Privatization of government companies.

- Modernization of traditional industries.

- Independent subcontractors.

- Independence of subsidiaries. The top 30 firms in terms of number of subsidiaries, have 6,600 subsidiaries and of the firms on the first section of the exchange, the total number of subsidiaries is 20,000.

---

[3]This is not really investment in the usual economist's definition of resources used for plant and equipment that contributes to higher output and productivity later. Non-consumption would be a better word. Perhaps the combination of high savings and the inability to afford housing will encourage gambling by many, which this is, rather than an investment which is no longer needed at a high rate.

Privatization of Japan Railways might be three times as large as NTT ($62 billion). The railroad shares would be more popular than NTT because of their property assets. The government is likely to sell all the shares in each individual company at once. The process began in 1991. Two proposals are being considered:

- List one company per year beginning with the three strongest regional companies that have 90% of the capital.

- Combine the stock of Japan Railways East and Japan Railways Tokai and sell it in two branches, followed by Japan Railways West and later the other, smaller companies.

The ministry also began land sales in 1991. The stock offering and land sales should raise as much as $187 billion over the three years. The stock sales alone will raise $102 billion or about two-thirds of the value of all new issues listed in 1990 in all Japanese markets. The railroad privatization is expected to spark takeovers once management decisions are freed.

The Japan National Railway (JNR) had been a company at the mercy of governing politicians some of whom gained by building bullet trains direct to their own ridings, however remote (Niigata). Also it fed subcontractors inflated prices. There are even stories of supervisors burying nuts, bolts and spare parts so they would have them when needed. Since the breakup the individual companies have improved profits and image in anticipation of privatization. Group profits in FY 1989 were a pretax equivalent of $1.8 billion, up 40% over the previous year.

The Economist predicted a restructuring to unwind the many diversifications undertaken with *endaka*. Added to this is the court ruling that forbids selling shares at low prices to white knights. Another possibility is the unbundling of subsidiaries by selling shares on the stock market. Asahi Breweries recently did this with Nikka Whiskey. The advantages of unbundling include the following: money can pay off now more costly bank loans, internal loans to the subsidiary can be recalled, and a market value can then be put on any retained holdings in the subsidiary. *The Economist* suggests that likely candidates include Fuji, Xerox, NTT Data Communications from NTT, Sumitomo Pharmaceutical (from Sumitomo Chemical). Nippon Light Metal will float ten subsidiaries over the next 10 years.

Foreigners may have an advantage in future mergers and acquisitions in Japan because they can cut across *keiretsu* lines.

THE FUTURE OF THE STOCK MARKET

Stock prices are determined by the market not by the Finance Ministry
                                           Finance Minister Tsutomu Hata

In the period from January 1990 to early April 1992, the stock market as measured by the Nikkei Stock Average fell from its historic high at 38,916 to as low as the 16,500 range. This is a decline of well over 50%. The dramatic increases in stock and land prices in the 1980s (see the Figures 5.1 and 5.4-5.7.1) led to immense paper profits and enormous leveraging. While Japan has the world's highest savings rate among major industrial nations, it is also the most leveraged. Loans were readily available for speculative land and stock purchases in the late 1980s, and many individuals and institutions were highly leveraged. The dramatic increase in interest rates during 1989-90 (see Figure 5.3) was intended to destroy or at least dampen the speculative *bubble* economy. The rise from 2.5% to 6.0% in the discount rate accomplished this very effectively with speculative investments such as condos, golf courses, and many stocks falling sharply.

The decline in stock prices has caused countless bankruptcies, margin calls and pressure on the banking system. The stigma to bankruptcy is high with job loss likely for a salaried worker who declares bankruptcy. Savings remain high but these funds are not going into stocks because investors fear they would lose their funds. While speculative land has fallen 50% or so, regular use land has fallen far less. But the decline is still a very substantial 15 to 20% in the official land price indices. Osaka land prices, which rose sharply in the late 1980s, have fallen back to previous levels, which are 30 to 40% below their peak. Tokyo prices have fallen about 20%. Figures 5.1 and 5.4 show that the decline in the last quarter of 1991 has put stock and land prices back in balance. Stocks have fallen more in 1992, while land prices have stabilized in the first quarter of 1992.

Attempts by the government to revive the stock market in 1992 have been feeble and have met with little success. For example, at the beginning of April 1992, the discount rate was cut 0.75% to 3.75% and the market had a sharp selloff. The problem in 1992 is such that there is a large backlog of sales that must be made by accounts that must sell or accounts of the banks which must sell stock to raise their capital ratios if they do not wish to call in non-performing speculative land loans. Selling in the first quarter of 1992 was feeding on itself. Price declines led to more margin calls and still lower prices particularly in the case of low trading volume for many stocks. A proposed change would be to allow firms to buy their own stock. This would bid up prices and also reduce the oversupply of shares. Another is to have a new entity formed to buy stock, as was done in the 1985 crisis.

Investor sentiment is at a very low level and any excuse to sell leads to swift declines. Even minor pieces of bad news leads to sharp selloffs in thin volume. For example in mid-May the NSA fell 470 points, nearly 2.5% when the MOF announced it was calling a news conference to disclose a new violation. The market perceived that this was a new case of insider trading or a scandal. Instead, it was a tempest in a teapot arising from the rice cracker company Nitto Arare Company's false statements in its 1988 and 1990 financial reports to the MOF. Stock have a difficult time advancing in such a market. Foreigners who rely on economic valuation models are major buyers arguing that the market is cheap and simply oversold. This is probably a good investment strategy.

Regulations prohibit Japanese firms from buying their own shares. The big four securities companies have created an investment fund that circumvents the regulations. Nikko Securities, in March 1992, was the first to sell ¥200 billion of a 10-year trust fund invested in mainly by listed companies. The new investment trust fund will buy, for example, ¥10 billion of stocks from a certain company if the company invests ¥10 billion yen in the fund. In addition to helping companies maintain their stock prices, the fund will stimulate the flow of cash into the stock market in the short term. The Ministry of Finance expected that this new instrument would raise approximately ¥2 trillion yen.

Stock prices are far less important than land prices in Japan, and despite the huge fall in stock prices the damage to the economy has not been very dramatic. That is not to say that there are not severe problems, but the Japanese economic miracle built on production is not in severe danger. Indeed, an unnamed spokesperson for the Bank of Japan said "the BOJ has no intention of moving toward lower interest rates . . . the BOJ will not take bond or stock prices into consideration when discussing monetary policy in the future."

There is considerable tension and misinformation from various governmental groups, but it is clear that stock price levels are deemed to be much less important than the economy and land price levels. Small declines in the later are tolerated and are indeed encouraged but a full scale collapse would be avoided if possible. Meanwhile, the decline in interest rates has made stock prices cheap using traditional measures such as adjusted price earnings in relation to required rates of return (see Chapter 5 of Ziemba and Schwartz, 1991). While earnings have dropped 15 to 25%, interest rates have declined about 40% (for example in April 1991 the short term prime was 8.25%; in April 1992 after seven cuts it is 5.25%) to make the stock market much cheaper than in 1989. Still, the sentiment in the marketplace by Japanese investors with massive losses and the pent up demand to sell is a severe damper on the market.

Equity warrants in 1992 are trading at very low prices, and many issues are at or close to zero volatility pricing. Should the market recover as it always has in the past, there will be large gains on the upside. Eventually, the market should return to make higher levels once the lower interest rates work their way through the economy and into higher earnings. Despite the recession in 1991–92, real GNP is still increasing at about a 2 to 3% rate. Stock investors with long run horizons are likely to be rewarded for their patience. Many British pension plans have increased their allocation of assets to Japanese stocks to 30% from 20%, returning to the level they had in 1988. Net foreign buying on the Japanese markets was $2 billion in February and March of 1992.

Most of the warrants trade in London in U.S., German and Swiss currencies on individual Japanese stocks. A few trade in yen in Tokyo. They have expiry dates from 1992 to 1998 and represent a slight dilution of the underlying equity. Initially, the warrants were attached to bonds to be sold with lower coupon rates. For example, an equity warrant bond might yield 4% in U.S. dollars versus 8% for a regular bond. By converting the bonds receipts into yen and hedging the effective interest rate for the loan was -2 to +2%. This was one of the major sources of funds in the low interest rate bubble economy of the 1980s. The cheap money is predicated on having a market for the equity and Japanese interest rates below those in the issuing currency. Both of these factors ceased to exist in the 1990s; hence, there are few new issues of such warrants. An additional problem will occur if the equity warrants expire worthless. If that happens, the firm does not obtain this financing and in addition must refinance or pay off the bonds. Since this market is in the billions, this is a serious problem for the financial markets.

Whether and when such activities as warrant bonds providing nearly zero percent financing and related instruments will return to the market is not clear. Many observers expect a period of one or two years of trouble in the equity markets to sort out the decline of the *bubble* economy.

THE LAND BUBBLE: WILL IT BURST OR HAVE SOME AIR LET OUT?

There is something grossly wrong with a system that allows such insane (land) prices.

Nashiro Amaya

By the late 1980s, analysts began to worry that high land prices would threaten economic growth in Japan. Tokyo land prices had risen 10.4% in 1987, 57.5% in 1987, and 22.6% in 1988, more than doubling in three years (almost doubling in two). The price of a house in Tokyo came to exceed 15 times income. Total asset value was ¥5.338 quadrillion (or about $43.48 trillion) at the end of 1987, for 20 times GNP. Land values are 66.2% of net national wealth (excluding financial assets), compared with 24.2% in the U.S. At first this housing boom fed the economic boom. The proceeds from land sales canceled profit declines and made landowners feel richer and spend more. But a pyramid is always vulnerable.

The Bank of Japan and the Ministry of Finance, fearing a negative effect on growth, began to limit real estate lending for speculative purposes. However, their initial attempts to restrain land value increases in Tokyo only spread the increases to other areas: residential land prices in Tokyo rose 3% in the year to September 1989 after a 24% increase the preceding year, but they rose 95% in Chiba, 37% in Osaka, and 28% in Kyoto. These areas continued to have high price rises into 1990. Though the banks had been restrained, the life insurance companies put about ¥2.9 trillion into property between April and September 1989. New rules will enable the MOF to oversee all loans over ¥1 billion. Meanwhile expectations are that prices will continue to increase, as evidenced by the increase in share prices of property developers.

Foreign embassies have even sold land in Tokyo. The Australian Embassy had a fine garden, until it sold some land for about $1.5 billion to pay down some of its budget deficit. Land prices are also considered a barrier to foreign investment and the U.S. has asked Japan to lower real estate prices. High land prices also make the improvement of public infrastructure costly. The Japanese government is considering a variety of changes including abolition of tax incentives for farmer ownership in urban areas and relaxation of construction codes.[4]

The land prices in Tokyo reached levels that may be termed a speculative bubble. Will it go the way of many other bubbles in the past,

---

[4]The Canadians had their new Embassy built in exchange for 20 years free rent to the construction company in a part of the building.

such as those in South Sea land, tulips and silver, and completely collapse? The high prices are the result of too much money chasing too few available desirable properties. Fundamentally, there is too much saving and the desirable outlets for that savings in Japanese property are limited. Though land is hard to make, the Japanese *are* making some, which we discuss below. With only 2% of Tokyo's land changing hands each year, there is not much for sale. In this thin market, a few sales determine the price for large amounts of property that are not for sale.

There was a leveling of the prices in 1989 in Tokyo while the suburbs and other cities caught up. Rumors floated of large sales in Tokyo with prices a little off the peak. But buyers were ready to pick up choice properties, particularly if they could purchase them at a discount to what they feel is the market price. Additional steps were taken to cool off the market.

It is hard to say what the future will bring, but it seems most likely that steps will be taken to ensure that the basic market remains stable. A small 20 to 30% decline might be tolerated, but a crash of over 50% would be devastating to the country's financial well-being, and its image as a major financial center would be seriously damaged.

Historically, the land index has had only one correction in any six-month period since 1949 before the 1990–92 decline. That fall was a modest 5 to 8% (depending on the index used) due to the first oil crisis in the late 1970s. The danger and challenge is how to have a minor correction without a blowout, because the leveraging on land is extraordinarily high and the pyramid effect could be widespread.

The consequences of a crash in land prices with its certain fallout of a similar decline in stock prices is simply too devastating to Japan to be tolerated. By a crash, we mean a fall of 50 to 90%. With an acre of choice land in Tokyo at $800,000,000, a 90% fall still leaves it at $80 million. History tells us that it may not be possible to avoid a crash. But with the strong government and business ties and so much of the wealth highly concentrated in the control of the corporation, the loose collusion of cooperation through gentle government prodding that led to the rise in the first place will likely prevent it from collapsing. We say this with less confidence in May 1992 than in 1989. As we have seen in the stock market corrections of 1990–92, the deregulation of financial markets has led to less and less cooperation and more and more foreign influence.

Finally, to deal with the fundamental land shortage, more accessible land through expansion into Tokyo Bay and other areas is planned, along with better transportation into Tokyo to lighten the commuting burden. Japan has already added about 400 square miles to its land area with artificial islands and other coastal extensions and there are plans for much more of this activity. The entire land mass for Tokyo Disneyland is reclaimed land. The largest artificial island complex in the world is Port Island, which is in Osaka Bay, near Kobe. According to Dwight Holing, writing in *OMNI* magazine, this nine-square-mile island took some 15 years to build at a cost of over $2 billion. Some 20,000 people live there in modern apartments surrounding four parks with nearby office buildings, restaurants, a hospital, and a convention center with hotels and conference halls. Transportation to and from Port Island and the mainland proceeds via an electric powered rail system.

For the future, many other projects are on the drawing boards. The most ambitious is Japanese architect Kisho Kurokawa's $1 trillion proposal for a giant island complex in Tokyo Bay to be completed around 2016. His vision is for a self-contained modern city with 5 to 7 million residents. The construction would be complex. Just the landfill would be about 13 billion cubic yards, but the dream may well become a reality. Despite the huge price tag, the cost to live there would be much less than currently in Tokyo in constant yen. Moreover, there would be more livable space and a better physical and geographical environment, convenient commuting into Tokyo if needed, and less risk in a large earthquake. It sounds like science fiction. Other islands, at much lower cost, are also planned. They would have the great advantage of real estate and rental costs of about one-tenth in constant yen of those currently in central Tokyo. Obviously, these additions are only part of the steps needed to take air out of the bubble, but they may well be a significant part of this activity.

Another proposal is Aeropolis, the city in the sky. This gigantic 2,000-meter apartment/office mini-city has been proposed to solve land problems in Tokyo. The idea is simply an extension of the vast network of underground malls found throughout Japan. Indeed some of the underground transfer stations are a kilometer long. Aeropolis would be a living city with 35,000 homes and space for 135,000 jobs and all the amenities for high-quality living. The cost would be about $336 billion. In comparison with other major buildings in the world, Aeropolis would be very tall indeed, comparisions are given in Table 11.1.

It is hard to imagine a building so tall, almost four times the height of the CN Tower currently the world's tallest structure, stretching a mile and a quarter into the sky. To get some perspective, new buildings in Vancouver are limited to less than 100 meters, and Aeropolis would be 20 times that. Geting to the top would require a *fifteen minute* commute. Aeropolis would have 500 floors. Ohbayashi Corp. designed the structure which would be home and workplace for 300,000 people. It would take 25 years to build on an artificial island in Tokyo Bay and would cost Cdn$381 billion. Robots supervised by computers would do the construction. It would be designed

Table 11.1
Aeropolis Compared with the Tallest Buildings in the World

Building	City	Height in meters
Harbour Center	Vancouver	147
Eiffel Tower	Paris	300
Empire State	NY	381
Sears Tower[5]	Chicago	443
CN Tower	Toronto	555
Aeropolis	Tokyo	2,000

to withstand earthquakes with a foundation sunk into bedrock at 200 meters square; it would sway like a pendulum. The top floors would contain water that would be pumped around to counter wind. Engineers and architects claim the structure is technologically feasible, though the construction technology is not yet available nor have the psychological problems of living vertically been considered. It has been estimated that the building would employ 370 full-time janitors and require advances in heating and electricity.

Aeropolis would have a base of 11 square kilometers. It would have its own train station and subway link to downtown Tokyo and Narita Airport. It would contain hotels, hospitals, parks and convention centers. It would be an entire medium-sized city on an island. Aeropolis would be a mountain unto itself, almost double the height of Grouse Mountain and only a bit shorter than Whistler. Feasible or not, the concept shows that the Japanese are brainstorming images of the new Tokyo, and they are very much aware of the constraints imposed by being an island nation.

WHERE WILL THE YEN/DOLLAR EXCHANGE RATE GO?

A stronger yen would not help one jot: they will pay more for the same Japanese products and we will buy up America even more cheaply
                                                                    Akio Morita, Chairman of Sony

The outlook for the yen in early 1992 seems to indicate a strengthening because of worldwide demand for yen while interest rates are relatively

---

[5]This is the tallest office tower. Chicago has approved the construction of a 595-meter office tower that would be the tallest office tower and the world's tallest building.

high. At the end of 1988, the U.S. dollar traded at about 125 yen. After its dramatic fall from the 260 range in 1985, it bottomed at about 121 in January 1988, and has stayed in a trading range of 120 to 160 since. Figure 2.3 shows the exchange rate over time.

Table 11.2, largely based on a survey of the literature by Balassa and Noland (1988), summarizes the conclusions of a number of exchange rate studies. Price parity suggests a yen of 140 to 180, while sustainability and lowering or eliminating of the deficit suggests an exchange rate in the 80 to 130 range. This implies that despite its strength in 1990, there will be likely more downward pressure on the dollar until the trade deficit problem is solved or put aside; then there will be upward pressure on the dollar to return to a value more consistent with its true purchasing power. Yamaichi Research Institute's estimates, based on Japan's export price index computed by the Bank of Japan and U.S. industrial good wholesale price index computed by the U.S. Commerce Department manufactured goods as shown in Figure 11.1, show a steady drop in the price parity down to a level of about 110¥/$. This is a painful reminder for residents of Japan who must live with the high prices of an extraordinary number of markups before an item gets to the retail level, but it is a burden that many have been willing to accept for social cohesion.[6]

---

[6]Actually, the goods are not the same in Japan and the U.S. The Japanese goods come with low crime, low unemployment, and income equality, while the U.S. goods come along with high crime, etc. We think we can easily unbundle the goods from the distribution, but the cost may indeed be great in non-market incommensurables.

Table 11.2
Yen-Dollar Exchange Rate Purchasing Power Parity and Future Value
Estimates

Study	Year	Purpose of Research	Exchange Rate Estimate (¥/$)
McKinnon & Ohno (1987)	1st Quarter 1986	Purchasing Power Parity: to equate differential rates of inflation using a given price level index, exchange rate estimates varies with index used.	180-200
Krugman (1986)	1st Quarter 1986	Marston (1986) demonstrated that productivity increases in the Japanese traded goods sector have increased those in the non-traded goods sector. Assuming these growth rates remain constant gives the lower exchange rate that Krugman found.	140
Bergsten and Cline (1987)	1987	Exchange rate estimated to induce a current account balance consistent with capital flows determined by savings-investment balance (i.e., a sustainable equilibrium). It is the exchange rate that given the current fiscal and monetary policies equal commodity flows.	140-145
Marris (1987)	1987	Econometric analysis similar to Bergsten and Cline (1987) but assuming deficit reduction is not on schedule. Bergsten, in the September 17, 1987, *Washington Post,* revised the B-C (1987) estimates to this value.	115
Krugman (1985,88)	1990–91	Based on debt/GNP ratios	>140
Krause (1986)	early 1990s	To balance the U.S. current account	100
Dornbusch (1988)		To achieve a desirable U.S. current account may require a drop in the rate of up to another 40%.	70 -80
Yamaichi Research Inst (1989)	early 1990s	Based on wholesale prices of manufactured goods in Japan and the U.S.	118

Source: Partially based on summary in Balassa and Noland (1988).

Figure 11.1
Yen/Dollar Exchange Rate and Purchasing Power Parity, 1973–1992 (February)

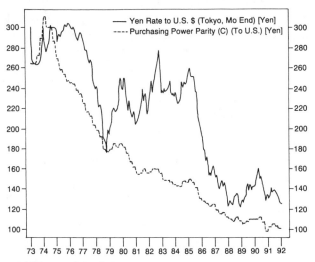

Source: Yamaichi Research Institute

Marris (1985, 1987) analyzed the U.S. deficits and their probable impact on the yen/dollar exchange rate. His predictions using econometric models were remarkably accurate. At the time he predicted a further strengthening of the yen. Others such as Martin Feldstein, the Harvard economics professor and head of the National Bureau of Economic Research in Cambridge, Massachusetts, and Fred Bergsten, head of the Institute for International Economics in Washington, D.C., have similar views. Under the yen/dollar rate must overshoot to cure the U.S. trade deficit problem.[7] Econometric models predict that U.S. exports will increase because they are cheap for their foreign purchasers, while simultaneously imports of foreign goods will fall at their much higher prices.[8]

---

[7]Unfortunately, the fall in the dollar will not cure the basic problem: the fundamental imbalance is the U.S. economy's a very low savings rates with a high propensity to spend. The trade deficit is secondary not primary. Solving it alone is like solving high blood pressure that results from some other imbalance such as diabetes but ignoring the diabetes. The symptom is cured but the disease remains.

[8]The predictions of these models were wrong in 1989 and 1990 when the dollar firmed to the 160 level. But the dollar weakened substantially in early 1992 with an exchange rate as low as the 125 range with a value in the 130 range in May 1992.

In volume terms, this effect has occurred: the net physical trade balance has shrunk as the dollar has fallen. But because the imports are valued more expensively and exports are valued inexpensively, the net effect, called the J effect, does not significantly decrease the trade balance in dollars. It is for this very reason that analysts such as Marris argue there likely will be a hard landing and the dollar will overshoot on the downside. We have argued, as have others, that econometric analyses cannot capture some important aspects of the trade balance problem, such as the weakness of the U.S. export market. U.S. products do not sell overseas because of perceived inferior quality, the same reason they do not sell domestically unless protected by a low dollar exchange value, and because of barriers to entry of U.S. products due to cultural differences.

The recession in the U.S. and the substantial Japanese bashing and the trouble in the Japanese stock market point to less investment in the U.S. and other foreign regions and more repatriation of funds back to Japan, which indicates increased demand for yen and hence a higher price.

An interesting effect will be the flow of U.S. trade from Japanese firms in the U.S. In the initial phase, these ventures contribute to increased imports of machinery and demand for yen. As they begin production they should have a positive influence of the U.S. balance of trade and create a demand for dollars. Canon Virginia is expecting to export production to France. Japanese manufacturers accounted for about 10% of U.S. exports in 1987 including: eight factories sent color TVs to Canada, Latin America, Japan and the rest of Asia; two plants exported personal computers to Canada; two produced diskettes for Japan, Europe, Canada and Latin America and automakers exported cars to Europe and Japan.

Obviously, decisions made in Washington and Tokyo and in the financial markets around the world will affect this path. Although central banks will try to prop up the dollar from time to time, the real power at any moment is the market sentiment of approximately 25 major foreign currency traders who trade about $1 trillion each day in the cash and futures currency markets. The supply and demand of those they represent will determine the current market price. It is quite plausible that the dollar will hit new lows below 120 in the next few years, and then as the budget deficit situation is dealt with the dollar will rise well above 150. With the huge budget deficit and corresponding trade deficit, savings and loan crisis and Third World debt problems it is difficult to imagine the dollar not coming under selling pressure again until the U.S. fiscal house is in order.

THE JAPANESE ECONOMY: SHORT- AND MID-TERM PROSPECTS

Some analysts project in the next decade, the Japanese economy will grow another 40 to 45% in yen and its foreign investment will reach U.S.$1 trillion. The 1990s recession is a mild one by worldwide standards with essentially full employment, a 2 to 3% real GNP growth, low inflation at about 1.8% and the government has a surplus of over 2% of GNP.

The Japanese bubble peaked in 1989. By then, the global economy had entered its seventh year of expansion. The U.S. trade deficit was still large though in 1988, it had experienced its first year-by-year reduction in real terms since 1981. After the initial contraction; it rose again in 1992. Currency adjustment will not be enough and it is easy to argue that this approach is not really a sound one for the U.S.

The Asian economies, with Japan in the lead, are in a very strong growth position. In 1989, Nomura expected that Japan would continue its strong economic progress and enter a new phase of prosperity based upon its status as a lender nation. Feeding into this is the concern for generating profits rather than the focus on market share, as in the past. The profit ratio on sales in manufacturing rose to 5% for the first time in 15 years in 1989. This is accompanied by a low rate of inflation, so real profits were high. Also, there is a greater focus on domestic market sales. Unprofitable exports have been dropped and manufacturing overseas has increased. Both reflect that foreign exchange is no longer a constraint on the economy. Investment also reflects a restructuring with more going to information processing equipment, and research and development.

Meanwhile, expansions in overseas manufacturing, mergers, and acquisitions provided avenues to funnel the excess savings and return future profits.[9] The sum of these effects provided for a strong stock market until the end of 1989. In 1990, we saw a temporary new era with a weak yen, high interest rates, inflation and a weak stock market. How long it will take for Japan to turn this around is not clear. One thing is clear, though. They will need to basically do it alone. The request to the U.S. to lower interest rates in March 1990 fell on deaf ears even though Japan maintained lower interest rates to help the U.S. dollar in 1986–89.

This is the challenge facing Japan. No previous country entering this phase has been able to turn the status of lender into earned income and continued growth. Generally, when this phase has been reached, the home

---

[9]Though Nomura does not make the distinction, it is important to sort out the difference between those financial dealings that reflect a call on domestic resources and generate domestic income and those that have their primary production and income generating effects outside the domestic economy or that only reflect wealth transfers.

economy becomes stagnant and is no longer fed by new import replacing ideas (see Jacobs, 1984).

Supporting transition is a shift to investment in Japan by foreign investors. During the 1984–87 bull market, and the resultant huge gains (nearly tripling in the Tokyo market in yen and nearly sixfolding in U.S. dollars) foreign investors were actually net sellers of Japanese stocks.[10] For the U.S. this was the time of the shift from net creditor to net debtor status. The foreign share of trading has dropped from 10% to 2% of the volume on the TSE. Finally in 1988, with a floundering New York market and many nervous markets elsewhere, foreign investors became net buyers of Japanese stocks. This trend continued. A typical example was the decision in the spring of 1989 by Pictet and Co. of Geneva, the largest private Swiss bank, to downgrade the U.S. while upgrading Japan. This was the first time in Pictet's 200-year history that it recommended investing more money in Japanese rather than U.S. stocks. According to Iain Little, general manager of international investment at Pictet (Japan) Ltd., the Tokyo subsidiary:

The reasons for preferring Japan to the U.S. are simple. In the U.S. there is a poor outlook for interest rates. These may remain high because of the U.S. familiar problems. Economic growth in Japan, however, is steady and well balanced. In addition, the corporate sector is full of companies capable of adapting to change, such as dramatic currency appreciation. Japan seems a safer place to put clients' money at the moment: opportunities seem greater and risks less.

The PERs based on trailing earnings were still high in 1989, about 59 at the beginning of 1988, but they were higher in 1987. With earnings expected to increase about 25% in the year ended March 1989 and projected to rise a further 17% for the year ended in March 1990, there was room for a substantial increase from the record end of 1988 valuations. According to *The Economist's* sources, as of January 14, 1989, private economists saw GNP rising 5% in 1989, just below 1988's 5.5%, and wage increases averaging 6%. The low interest rates, low inflation and strong yen were good for the market in 1989. The main danger in the near term was possible interest rate hikes if there was a worldwide inflation binge. That was the case in 1990.

Profits of Japanese firms slowed rapidly in 1990 due to higher raw material costs, weaker yen, higher competition from imports and slower export growth. Profits increased 27% in 1989. Profit increases slowed in 1990 and 1991 and 1992 showed declines. This is leading to lower bonuses and lower domestic consumption. Also, expect lower investment (23% of

---

[10]Co-incidently they have been net buyers in the 1990–92 decline.

GNP in 1989, the highest since 1955) which has been financed mostly by retained earnings and lower TSE prices. Most recent investments have gone to robotics, R&D labs and diversification abroad, all very long term.

There is a major division between the MOF and Bank of Japan (BOJ) on the appropriate level of interest rates and relative threat of inflation. (The MOF wanted low rates and the BOJ wanted higher rates placing a greater weight on inflation.)

Future economic growth seems weaker. In recent years, there have been a few quarters of negative growth, though not yet (until 1992) two quarters in succession to qualify for a recession. For example, the GNP declined by 0.8% in the second quarter of 1989 and declined as well in the final quarter of 1991. Much of the inflation in the late 1980s was from lower valued yen, as 94% of Japanese imports are U.S. dollar denominated. With each 10% increase in the U.S. dollar, the Japanese wholesale price index increases by 1.17 percentage points.

R&D INVESTING FOR THE FUTURE

U.S. firms neglect academic research, while the number of agreements among U.S. universities and foreign corporations are growing. In 1989, Hoechst AG, a German chemical corporation, signed a $70 million ten-year research agreement with Massachusetts General Hospital, which is affiliated with the Harvard Medical School. DIFIA Pharmaceutical, an Italian company, agreed to fund a $62 million 20-year study on the working of the brain at Georgetown University. U.S. companies avoid such long-term commitments. Total research in 1982 at universities was $7.26 billion; only 5% was funded by industry. The approaches to R&D differ:

> Technological innovation no longer fits the simplistic straight-line view to which America clings: of basic research leading to applied research, leading to technological development, leading to new products. Today's successful innovation is a complex blending of skills, best described as technological fusion. Japan's microchip industry gained pre-eminence only after fusing the know-how of camera makers (who developed new ways of printing microcircuits) with that of crystallographers (who perfected the purest of silicon wafers) with that of builders (who had learned how to make rooms dust free). The line of innovation has curled into many circles. No longer does control of access to one bit of technology necessarily check the progress of others (*The Economist*, April 1, 1989).

One area of controversy is differing patent systems. The U.S. debates fine points of law, while Japan's system works more effectively. Japan's reply to the U.S. accusation that its patent system is a barrier to trade was that its system resembles that of Europe. The U.S., Canada and the Philippines share a system based on the first-to-invent principle; most other nations, including Japan, have systems based on first-to-file. Many international disagreements revolve around this difference. Under the Euro-Japanese system, patent information is secret until the patent is filed, and patent information is public 18 months after filing. Scientists prefer to publish before seeking a patent. They prefer the U.S. system. Lawyers also like the first-to-invent principle as legal disputes are more likely to arise under this rule. First-to-invent encourages sitting on patents and slows innovation and change.

The differences are fundamental. Japan takes a social view of intellectual property rights, believing ideas belong to everyone; while in the U.S. property rights are primarily the right to exclude.

The U.S. claim that it takes 5 to 7 years to gain a patent in Japan was countered with the Japanese claim that on average it's three years, one month. Japan's patent office receives more applications than any other in the world.

In Japan, the social ideal is the hard-working, low-keyed craftsperson. Japan is challenging the U.S. reputation for creativity and innovation. In 1987, the top three recipients of American patents were Canon, Hitachi, and Toshiba. GE, which had been number one for 25 years, was in fourth place. Foreigners obtained 47% of all U.S. patents in 1987, up from 34% in 1977. Japanese patents grew 25% to 17,288, followed by Germany led by Siemens, with 8,030 (up 15%), and France with 2,990 (up 19%). Canon had 887 new patents, up from 158 a decade ago. (GE fell to 784 from 822.)

Another standard, citations by other inventors, also finds Japan in the lead, at 26% more than Americans. Japanese patents cover a wide range of industries: a computerized auto carburetor by Nissan was cited about 50 times; Canon's patent for the optical disc was mentioned 56 times; an antibotic by Takeda Chemical Industries was cited more than 100 times. Hitachi patented higher resolution TV (HDTV); floppy computer disks, and the Walkman. Now researchers are denying the importance of patents, claiming they are important only in slow moving technologies. Of course patents do not tell the whole story but are an interesting measure in light of previous chastisement of Japan.

In Japan, 79% of funds for R&D come from firms. In 1986, the U.S. outspent Japan $119 billion to $72 billion, but 50% of U.S. research funds came from the government (mostly the Pentagon). The Japanese are increasing their spending on R&D. Only half the consumer electronics firms are spending less than 4% of sales on R&D. Aiwa, Fujitsu General, JVC, Pioneer, and Sanyo spend about 5%, Sharp about 7%, Matsushita, 9%, and Sony, 12%. With R&D so high in Japan now, 30% of new investment is being directed at new product and service development, and 30% goes to the creation of new methods of development, design, production, and distribution. Only 40% goes into capacity expansion, half of which is for new products. So the bottom line is that *only 20% of the investment is directed at the past economy.*

The look in Japanese labs is loosening up with jeans, t-shirts and other symbols of freedom of expression.

Although the VCR was invented by the U.S. firm Ampex and further developed at RCA, Sony and JVC bought the rights and, *10,000 patents* later, made it a commercial success.

Inventors are relying more upon basic research with a shortening of time between basic research and commercial success. A reflection of this is that universities are playing a larger role in new product ideas. The citations in patent applications support this.

Esther Dyson in *Forbes* suggests that most of the new software requires craftsmanship, attention to detail, and integration, not creativity and daring. Modifications and upgrades must fill needs of multiple users and systems.

Crafty innovations noted by *Business Week* that appear first in Japan before being marketed abroad include:

- Electrically heated carpets in Persian designs for $7,000.

- Hand held scanner shaped like a thick six-inch ruler that instantly translates words scanned in Japanese; it's by Seiko Epson and sells for $220.

- Alarm clock that fills the air with eucalyptus a half minute before sounding the alarm. (It flopped.)

- Rock'n Flowers.

- Phones that dial on voice command and a waterproof phone for steamrooms and baths.

- Lamps, fans, alarms, etc., activated by heat generated by humans.

- Ski jacket developed by Mizuno and Toray Industries that darkens as the temperature drops to absorb more sunlight.

- Adjustible cross-country skis: pour boiling water on tips and curve them for deeper snow.

- $200 battery-powered ski goggles with a push-botton tint control and defroster.

ENERGY

Nuclear power output declined 5.8% due to accidents and problems at nuclear power plants in Japan in 1988. Meanwhile demand for electricity increased.

Three utility companies, Tokyo Gas, Osaka Gas, and Tobo Gas, and Fuji Electric Co. will develop a system for generating electricity and heat without pollution in a process that catalyzes natural gas or liquid petroleum gas employing phosphoric acid in cells. They plan to have two units producing 50 and 100 kilowatts for sale in 1993. The power will cost about ¥7 per kilowatt, which is less than the average of ¥25 charged by electric power companies.[11] They plan to sell 500 units per year mainly to hotels, restaurants, hospitals, and sports facilities.

Other countries are learning to use more energy efficient methods of steel production cutting into the edge enjoyed by Japan as shown in Table 11.3. This would begin to close the cost advantages of steel production in Japan.

Table 11.3
Energy Efficiency in Steel Production, Japan=100

	1987	1980
U.S	141	147
Britain	120	133
France	117	122
Japan	100	100

FOREIGN GOODS AND JAPAN'S DISTRIBUTION SYSTEM

The U.S. has attacked Japan's distribution system, labeling it a barrier to trade because of the high markups that accumulate at each level. Yet an effective campaign to reduce Japan's distribution system means asking for an elimination of small shopkeepers. There are 1.62 million mom-and-pop shops and small distributors employing 6 million people; shops with one or two employees account for 57% of all retail outlets. The wholesale and retail trade account for 14% of GNP and about 20% of employment, more than in most industrialized countries, providing for a huge middle class. The large-scale retail law regulates business hours and holidays, giving neighborhood shopkeepers a veto over new stores larger than 500 square meters. The network of small shops actually grew during the 1970s and early 1980s

---

[11]This is interesting—utility companies getting into the business of selling capital equipment to their customers and in the process losing customers.

under the protective legislation. Like the protection of small farmers, this is a social measure to help ameliorate the impact of unemployment. Already the mom-and-pop stores are being squeezed. One shopkeeper reported in the *Japan Times* claimed the shop was now forced to sell only lower-priced lines, and cut markups.

Through their regulations and willingness to keep mom-and-pop stores and urban rice farmers people are paying for:[12]

Quality: Daisies cost $4 per stem but are beautiful; apples cost $2 each but there are no rotten ones.

Service: Service people are well paid and do not expect a tip.

Humanity: The remnants of rice fields and mom-and-pop stores, the crooked streets, and lack of skyscrapers all inefficient uses of land in a crowded expensive city actually help to make the city both more humane and safer. The mixed uses mean people are always around. The elderly shopkeepers who also tend grandchildren and avoid living off social security would be put out of business by the rational distribution system favored by the U.S.

Drucker has pointed out that Japan is the largest buyer of *U.S. brand* products. However, most of these are made in Japan by wholly owned U.S. subsidiaries rather than imported. Japan is the largest buyer of U.S. farm products, and the Japanese pay the full price and in cash. This trade needs to be preserved against loss to the EC or other countries. Drucker sees that the U.S. is wasting bargaining power on relatively minor products such as beef, rice, pineapples, and citrus fruit (he suggests that the high rice price encourages the Japanese consumer to buy wheat products and other substitutes). A major area that is worth bargaining for, according to Drucker, is services, including banking.

THE GREENING OF JAPAN

Japan is in a paradoxial position regarding environmental concerns. Nearly 25% of the Japanese population lives in the Tokyo region much of which is on reclaimed land and would be inundated if the sea level were to rise with a global warming. This should make Japan a leader in research on greening. However, as an importer of raw materials, Japan has always been sensitive to threats of long-term access to raw material supplies.

The World Wildlife Fund charges Japan is a villain in the destruction of Southeast Asia's rain forests, which are most affected by logging. In 1986, SE Asia sold $2.9 billion of logs and products to Japan and the EC, more

---

[12]Fred Hiatt of the *Washington Post* in the *Japan Times*.

than twice the value from Africa and Latin America combined.[13] Each took about one-third the volume of exports which means that per capita Japan took three times as much. However, exporters earned 20% more from the EC because they purchase more processed products. Japan concentrates on buying the cheapest and least processed, especially logs clearcut without replanting. Unfortunately, the logs are often used as moulds for concrete and not directly in houses—even including mahogany. In the mid-1980s, the Philipines and Indonesia banned the export of raw logs and, in 1989, Thailand banned logging.

Some other issues include:

- MITI recently joined the ban on ivory imports. The Japanese are working on substitutes, including mammoth tusks from Siberia (it is estimated that 10 million mammoths have been preserved under the Siberian permafrost) and cow bones. Japan was the biggest ivory consumer using 40% of the world total and employing 30,000. One of the main uses of ivory is for *hanko*, the stamps that replace signatures.

- Japan is backing dam and highway projects in Brazil and the Amazon while much of the world is concerned about deterioration of the rain forest.

- Cultivation of eucalyptus in 1920 square kilometers in Thailand to provide wood chips for Japanese paper and pulp.

- Japan is working on a geothermal energy project.

- Japan exports their most polluting industries to developing countries. Mitsubishi Kasei Corp. is involved in a lawsuit with Malaysian villagers over radioactive waste from a plant that is claimed to have killed a number of children. Japan stopped importing the ore in 1972 because it was too costly to refine it in Japan.

- Since the early 1980s, Japan, Korea, and Taiwan have been sending 700 or more fishing vessels equipped with monofilament net that forms a 30-foot wall stretching for 20 to 35 miles. Squid, fish, seabirds, and dolphins get caught in the net. It has been charged that these nets are also taking salmon and steelhead trout. It's been called the strip mining of the sea.

On the positive side, MITI is encouraging research for new technologies to counter environmental problems including replacements for CFCs,

---

[13]West Germany takes logs only from sustainable exporters.

alternative fuel engines for autos and more powerful solar batteries.[14] Mitsubishi is building a demonstration clean pulp mill in Alberta. The $1.3 billion project on the Athabasca River will set the standard for future mills and mill renovations.

In April 1992, preceding the UN Earth Conference in Rio, Japan called on the developed nations to begin a fund for environmental clean up. In May 1992 Tokyo hosted the CITES Conference.

One hundred firms have joined the government's *New Earth 21* campaign with the goal to create a government-industry partnership to foster new technology to combat global warming and ozone layer depletion. It is a 100-year plan. Hitachi's lab has 94 researchers and a budget of about $15.9 million (¥1.8 billion). Some work on very long-term projects such as developing an algae to transform carbon dioxide into carbohydrates through photosynthesis. Another is to develop a way to pump carbon dioxide onto the ocean floor. Another project is to producing hydrogen for energy more cheaply using microbes and seaweed. Firms are developing integrated systems that both minimize waste and find markets for the recycled waste. Nippon Steel is converting coal ash to zeolite a mineral for water purification. A consortium of firms is trying to convert sulfur and nitrogen oxides (culprits in acid rain) into ammonium sulfate and ammonium nitrate, fertilizers.

CHANGING GENDER ROLES

Nearly half, 47.7%, of Japanese married women in major cities work outside the home, either full- or part-time. Their average salary for full time work is 60% that of men. Most are working to contribute to family finances, but some are trying to accumulate savings or simply to have more of their own money to spend. They are concerned about health and the future quality of life.[15] The number of women in administrative positions has doubled to 48,000 in ten years (to 1987) due to the growing number of women who wish to work permanently. Female workers accounted for 40% of the labor force, about 60.8 million compared to 37% in 1975. Of 750 career diplomats, 20 are women; only three of those are married. Less than 1% of management workers are women. Only 10% of students in law and economics are women.

There are a number of indicators of the tensions of change:

---

[14]*Business Week.*

[15]A survey of newspaper readership found that women's primary interest in newspaper reading was getting more information on the consumption tax. They are interested in family-oriented and regional news. Some 82.4% said they read newspapers for 36.1 minutes a day.

- Women are enjoying economic independence and are postponing marriage. On the other side, 90% of single men want to marry as they fear that lack of marriage will affect their promotion. Single men are finding it more difficult to marry. The Japanese ideal that the man be 3 to 5 years older than wife limits the choices.

- Matchmakers are growing in popularity. However, men must be educated to become aware of the modern women's interests and not expect a traditional housewife. Women are asking for companionship and to be able to continue working to enjoy high quality of life. Also with lower population growth, more men are first sons and expected to inherit their father's business and most women do not want to live with their husband's parents.

- Sexist ads are common in Japan. Many large firms including JAL, Suntory, Central Japan Railway and Victor Co. of Japan have calendars with nude women. JR East Co. has an ad for ski vacations shows a cartoon skier skiing between a woman's bikini-clad breasts. But there is more of an outcry against these.

- Brides are imported from Asia to meet the shortage of women willing to live in rural areas. It costs about ¥3 million for each match. Many came from Sri Lanka (2–3,000) and they are very isolated. (It costs more to buy a car or tractor than a bride). Now women from the Philippines, Taiwan and other Asian countries are filling the role of economic underclass.

- Though the number of women candidates for the Diet has varied all the way up to 85, the number elected has never exceeded ten. The International Group for the Study of Women is headed by a man. Recognition from men has improved the chances of getting funding for the group.

- The first sexual harassment case has gone to court in Fukuoka. A woman claims she was forced to resign her job and is seeking ¥3.7 million from a publishing company. Lawyers at the Second Bar Association held a phone-in and heard 137 complaints from women. About 40% were from women forced to have sexual relations with their bosses at work.

DEMOGRAPHICS

The demographics indicate a significant population shift to the ranks of the retired (see Figure 1.1. and 11.2.) Their number is already growing more than 3% each year. Many of the new retirees will continue working, at least part-time, to maintain and build their fortunes and to establish enough wealth for their children to induce them to care for them in their declining years. This bodes well for a continually declining savings rate.

In 1995, workers aged 20 to 29 will begin to decline, while the elderly will continue to grow (dropping from 18.9 million in 1995 to 18.5 million in 2005). By 2013, Japan's total population will begin to decline from a peak of 163 million. Those over 65 will reach a peak of 23.6% of the population in 2020 and increase to 24.1% in 2045. The average age of women at marriage has risen from 24.2 in 1972 to 25.7 in 1988. The total fertility rate has fallen to 1.66 from 2.0 in 1975.

Figure 11.2
Estimated Growth of *Dependent* Population to Workers Aged 15 to 64

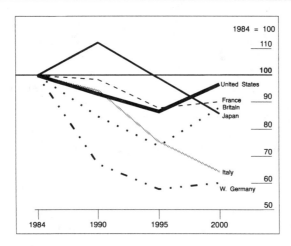

Source: *The Economist.*

THE JAPANESE ECONOMY IN THE LONG TERM

While the economic prospects for Japan look bright, changes are in progress that should make one more cautious about the long-term outlook. Let us look at some of the key factors likely to shape that future.

Japan moved quickly to its current position as the world's top creditor nation with its massive positive trade balances and huge savings rates. The government had to run deficits and borrow huge sums to avoid a recession with these savings rates and low domestic consumption after investment needs slowed. As we saw in Chapter 2, the large savings rates were, among

other things, linked to the high land and house prices as the top goal of the
majority of families is to save enough to buy their own house.   The
economic and governmental emphasis is changing, leading to more
domestic consumption, greater leisure and travel, and a somewhat less
intense work ethic. They are beginning to improve the transportation and
living infrastructure in Japan.

The move from a savings-export economy to one with a consumption
emphasis was officially recommended by the Mayekawa report of April
1986 commissioned to study "economic structural adjustments for the
promotion of international harmony." The IMF forecasts that by 2000 Japan
will be spending a fifth of its GDP on social welfare, versus a seventh now.
The pension and medical care growth rates are expected to be especially
high, as shown in Table 11.4. Europe and all developed countries will also
be spending more because of aging populations.

Some Japanese will emigrate to locales such as Hawaii, California, and
other parts of the U.S., Australia, and other countries where their large
wealth will give them a more comfortable western lifestyle. Those who
emigrate are not the elite who are doing well in Japan but those whose lives
will be substantially improved by the move. A typical example is a 46-year-
old electronics engineer who emigrated to Brisbane, Australia, from Gifu
Prefecture in 1982. He said: "sending all three children to universities,
especially to private ones, which was not financially possible for an ordinary
worker in a rural town like me."

Slowly the Japanese are spending more time away from Japan. There
will not be a mass exodus as, for example, there may be from Hong Kong
before 1997 when England turns the crown colony over to China, especially
in light of the summer 1989 massacres. But the trend will accelerate in areas
where the Japanese population and service infrastructure are well
established. In 1988 total emigration was still minuscule. Some 1,638 went
to the U.S., 497 to Australia, 341 to Canada, and a hundred or so more to
South America and other locales.

Table 11.4
Japan's Social Expenditure, Percent of GNP

		Projections		
	1980	2000	2010	2025
Medical Care	4.8	6.2	7.2	8.4
Pensions	4.2	10.4	14.3	15.3
Education	5.1	4.0	4.3	3.8
Unemplyment	3.0	0.3	0.3	0.3
Family benefits	1.0	1.0	1.0	1.0
Total	15.4	21.9	27.1	28.8

Source: IMF Occasional Paper 47

THE CONSUMER SOCIETY

The U.S. over-consumption arises from a number of factors but easy credit and interest deductibility are major ingredients. Japan was basically a cash society until the early 1990s. With the low crime rates, people feel comfortable carrying wads of ¥10,000 notes to pay for dinner, food, and clothing.

But the credit card economy in Japan is now getting into full swing. The Seibu/Saison group, behind its innovative leader Seiji Tsutsumi, issued six million cards in only a few years but by 1992 there were 166 million. Sixty percent were held by those in their twenties who are increasingly willing to be consumers. Credit cards, consumer loans, and easy cash advances up to ¥300,000 on credit cards will greatly expand consumption. It's simply easier to spend with a credit card than with cash. Although there is widespread use of cash machines to pay bills and purchase prepaid cards, such as those for the phone, the big use will soon be in credit cards. About ¥200 billion was charged on these cards in 1989.

The image of the Japanese as savers is no longer valid. By March 1991, consumer debt excluding mortgages totaled ¥67 trillion ($475 billion) or ¥445,000 per household, about the same share of annual disposable income as in the U.S. (17% in Japan, 18% in U.S.). Much of this is on credit cards and defaults are increasing. The 11 city banks have ¥800 billion in bad consumer loans. Personal bankruptcies are growing and were expected to almost double in the two years since 1990. The stigma to bankruptcy is high with job loss likely for a salaried worker who declares bankruptcy.

GROWING COMPETITION

A further problem for Japan is the increased competition from Korea, Taiwan, Hong Kong, Singapore, Thailand, and other Asian countries. They have lower wage rates and are aggressive exporters. Traditionally, they have linked their currencies to the dollar, so their advantage over Japan rose every time the dollar fell. With the dollar close to bottom, they have moved to link their currencies to the yen, which will maintain their advantage, and when the yen falls, they will increase their exports to Japan.

The trade imbalance will probably correct itself by the early to mid-1990s, and the flow of funds to Japan for goods will likely greatly diminish. This could be countered by a large U.S. deficit on the service account for massive dividends on stocks, coupons on bonds, interest on debt, rents on hotels and offices. Already the trade balance is stabilizing; it fell by 20% in 1988. Moreover, in volume terms, the drop in Japanese exports and rise in imports has been large, but this shift is masked by the falling dollar. Import volume was up over 20% in the year ended March 1988, and exports fell slightly. With overseas investments in plant and equipment in the auto and electronics industries, exports likely will drop sharply in the future.

GOVERNMENT SPENDING

In the late 1990s, the demand for cash by the government to cover its costs with declining revenue will greatly increase. Government borrowing will sharply increase. Massive investments abroad and the predicted $150 to $200 billion net foreign reserves will be a large stockpile to draw on but interest rates and inflation are likely to rise because of the higher demand for funds. Steps can and will be taken to moderate this increase, but the discount rate may not be able to remain at its low of 3.75% indefinitely. The interest rate rise will be devastating for stock and land prices. By then, land prices will have risen far above current levels in nominal, and likely in real terms, especially outside central Tokyo, central Osaka, and other places that even now are vastly overpriced. The vastly overpriced yen will drop in a gradual fashion over an extended and extremely volatile period.

We have argued elsewhere in the book that the Japanese and their government consult frequently and are able to envision trends which they attempt to plan for. In 1990–92, they tried to let the air out of the land and stock market bubbles gradually while maintaining a productive real economy.

President Ronald Reagan retired as an extraordinarily popular president. During his era, despite all the rhetoric about the strong economic expansion, the U.S. changed from a huge creditor nation to a huge debtor nation. In Japan, such a performance would not be popular.

STOCK MARKET

There may be great volatility in the stock market as we have seen already in 1990–92. A replay of the 1986 and 1987 U.S. volatility era is a strong possibility. By then there will be an incredible array of sophisticated banking and financial instruments: options, futures, bank accounts linked to the stock market, portfolio insurance, and other risk-shifting dynamic strategies. These instruments will be commonplace by then, but they do lead to a more risky environment. If there is a giant crash, some will blame these instruments. But, more than likely, as Roll (1988, 1989) found for the October 1987 worldwide stock market crash, it will not be these institutional arrangements that cause the crash; indeed, they may well moderate it. The crash more likely will be caused by excessive volatility and excessively high valuations. Ziemba (1992) has a discussion of the October 1987 crash; see also Bose (1988) and Metz (1988).

What we have had in 1990–92 is a gradual decline with volatile price movements. In the 1949 to 1989 growth period when the NSA rose to over 220 times its initial value, there were twenty declines of 10% or more and nine declines of 20% or more, some of which were in the 50% range. There were six declines of 10% or more in 1990–92 (see Table 5.4). What does this bode for the future investment in Japan? The near term looks nervous for the stock market and the yen likely will not move out of the 110 to 150 range until the corner is turned on the U.S. trade deficit. To be on the safe side, hedging against the yen rise, which provides a 4 to 5% cushion in the futures markets and some sort of portfolio insurance scheme, are recommended.

Once the U.S. trade deficit narrows to about $6 to $8 billion per month, the trend probably will be set. If and when it falls and stays significantly below $5 billion per month, Japanese investments will probably be much more risky. However, Japanese companies will have vast holdings in the U.S. If trade narrows, the U.S. will need to export more than it imports to pay service flows on investment. Some major bifurcation lies ahead, and we are very reluctant to prejudge Japan. We must always remember that Japan has been very adaptable, moving into fluctuating exchange rates, two OPEC oil crises, and a yen revaluation, and it's still taking the lead in a number of major technologies.

THE CHALLENGES FOR COMPETITIVE STRATEGY

Any discussion of competitive strategy today must consider the role of Japanese industry on global markets. The Japanese are helping redefine the multinational into a true global company. Peter Drucker, writing in the *Wall Street Journal* in 1986, suggested that most multinationals are structured on an obsolete model of a parent company with daughters in which all the major decisions about investment are made at headquarters. R&D is done in, by, and for the parent market. In other aspects, the daughters are autonomous and the attempt was to make them fit in the locality and act as profit centers.

Japanese management has had an impact on those countries in which it operates. For example, it has revived the British auto industry. Nissan has given the Newcastle plant sole global responsibility for the 5-door hatchback and they have plans to export to 30 countries. An agreement Toyota signed with the 700,000 person Amalgamated Engineering Union does away with *demarcation* or work considered to belong to other trades, thus improving their flexibility. The average Japanese plant takes 16.8 hours to weld, paint and assemble a car while a typical European plant takes 35 to 55 hours. The Nissan plant at Sunderland is the most efficient in Europe and almost as productive as Japanese plants in Japan.

Japan has an understanding of the need for system-wide decisions and attempts to integrate their regional investment decisions. They have avoided the ideal that each unit operate as an independent profit center. When the Japanese move production into other regions, they try to avoid the trap of inefficient production in small-scale integrated plants in each market by negotiating agreements that will assure that components produced in the region will all be considered local production by each of the countries involved.

In finance, too, local decision making exposes firms to foreign exchange risk and interest risk and hampers the ability to match cash flows with debt. The Japanese, however, treat the world market the way American companies treat the U.S. market. Funds earned in one place have been invested elsewhere according to payoff expectations. Drucker sees that, counter to the centralization of decision making, future R&D must be based where the people are—both the scientists and the consumers. He cites IBM as an example of a company that has transnationalized research rather than keeping it based at home. Increasingly, the Japanese firms are also doing this.

Harvard Professor Michael Porter believes Japanese businesses have enough momentum to continue their success through the 1990s. Beyond the year 2000, they will be faced with challenges requiring them to rethink their direction and goals. They now face the challenge (along with the U.S. and Europe) to work on the structure for the 21st century. Porter considers four main challenges: competitive advantage, globalization, alliances, and diversification. We can consider each of these in light of what we have seen about Japan and speculate about the future.

According to Porter, *competitive advantage* is gained either by lower cost or by differentiation to provide a unique product and or superior value that commands a premium price. Japan's historic advantage was based on labor costs. Through the 1970s and 1980s they were faced with a succession of challenges to this low-cost strategy (high energy costs, rising labor costs, new lower-cost countries, and the yen shock). They adapted by shifting their focus to quality. Porter suggests that success in this transition now requires them to reassess their product lines and continually ensure there is an appropriate linkage back to the mission/definition of the company. He predicts there may be a rise of mergers and acquisitions as business units are realigned. However, the Japanese attitude toward spawning new business units to maintain employment may give them a continued advantage of flexibility and adaptability.

Porter also notes that Japanese firms were early to compete globally. They turned to exports when their local market became saturated and as opportunities opened. The yen shock beginning in the fall of 1985 was fortunate because it encouraged them to go global and to establish foreign production. But globalization introduces new risks that will need to be dealt with. One special risk is the tearing of community within the firm. Foreign operations attempt to be autonomous and independent. Foreign managers, aware of the unique aspects of each market, will want to make independent decision on product design, manufacturing and raw material acquisitions. Japan's success has been that it has operated in context, understanding its workers, markets, and production. The challenge will be whether it can operate globally with the same good sense and enable local managers to make informed local decisions.

Alliances, according to Porter, are a transitional strategy and they, too, bring new challenges to Japanese management. In the U.S., the typical belief is that a company cannot be successful unless it controls all the skills and resources necessary for business. This is why firms that do outside sourcing often produce some of the parts themselves, thus creating distrust and uncertainty. Japanese companies have used alliances well, integrating suppliers into their production processes, but they will be challenged to be able to make them work in the global context.

Diversification is a potential Achilles heel for the Japanese firm. The speed of possible growth tempts and they may have already succumbed. Porter studied U.S. acquisitions over a 30-year period and found more than half had been divested within 3 to 4 years and this understates the problem. Diversification into unrelated products in a portfolio approach may appear to lower risk, but actually increases risk. A firm finds it is producing products it does not understand and cannot manage. To learn, the firm neglects its main lines of business. This has been at the heart of the deterioration of U.S. management, innovation productivity and Japan must be careful to retreat from it (see Schwartz, 1989).

Japanese companies historically had diversified in a unique way: internally, from scratch, into clearly related areas. Noritake is a good example of the Japanese approach encompassing mass production, custom, museum quality custom pieces as well as the new industrial ceramics. The Japanese have a knack of diversifying and maintaining a company mission that encompasses the new business and thus often makes diversification work. They let separate products maintain their separateness and are noninterfering so again it works. This follows perhaps from the Japanese tradition of forming loose associations among different firms in networked groupings. Canon has moved from camera technology to copiers and laser printers and now to personal computers. Sony moved from one electronics product to another. Not only were products related in production technologies or distribution, but also the employees were often from the parent. The firm did not face the problems of integrating independent companies into the parent corporate culture. Japan's experience is different from that of the U.S. and Europe, which proceeded via acquisitions often in unrelated areas.

The proper role of government varies over the development process. When the economy is focused upon low cost and standardized products as Japan was in the 1950s, the government has more leverage than in the current period of sophisticated R&D. The Japanese government policy has shifted, but most Western observers are five to ten years out of date. The government can accelerate the process of change by stimulating the demand for goods as it did when in making faxed documents legal.

Japan has succeeded because it responds well to chance events which are powerful in bringing about change—events like the oil price and *endaka* (high yen) shocks. In modern times, it is nations without raw materials that have innovated. Even raw materials are changing, for example, ceramics are replacing steel. The Japanese have an image of this. They use the Chinese character for *problem* which combines the characters for *danger* and *opportunity·*

Japanese companies' goals—long-term oriented, lifetime employment, commitment to employees—have been consistent with improving the nation's economy. These goals will need attention. After achieving success, firms, industries and nations begin to rest. Workers do not want to work as hard and want an easy life. Much of the criticism that Japan has directed at the U.S. is reflective of some of the tensions in Japan for change.

Already capital markets, and financial goals are changing. There is more trading of shares, institutional investors are buying and selling, not just buying and holding. Changes in the tax laws will also reduce the incentive for long-term gains versus ordinary income.

In an interview on Japanese television, the management expert Tom Peters gave his vision of the future of the world economy and competition. It is that of the gazelle that can move quickly though it is not only speed but shiftiness that may be the best measure of strength for the future. He suggested as a measure of corporate viability the ability to look different in six months. John Young, the energetic and innovative president of Hewlitt Packard lends support to this. He characterized HP as both old and new; it is 50 years old but constantly changing. At any time, more than 50% of its products are less than 3 years old. Jacobs (1984) suggested that the measure of health of a city or economy should relate to the number of new tasks created.

The byword is constant innovation. This is easier in Japan where 75% of R&D goes to process improvement compared to the U.S. with 75% in products. In both Japan and Germany, engineers live where things happen. Innovation is messy, passionate, it requires empowering independent bands of people with the mandate to be irreverent, to be experimenters, not experts.

Young recognized the similarities and differences with Japanese management. HP has had a joint venture in Japan for 25 years and has learned from Japan. The health of the employee is central to both. However differences center around the individual: in the U.S. workers are independent and free spirited and want freedom of expression. So HP links incentives to individual output. The company also focuses on retraining, using junior colleges and other courses.

A balance between individual expression and efficiency of the team will be important.

Motorola made a comeback by using and improving upon Japanese techniques. It strove to increase market share, upgrade quality, constantly improved manufacturing to cut costs and put lots of money into R&D, training and capital. It eliminated its not-invented-here bias and became a supporter of consortiums for R&D and has been forging alliances abroad. In 1987, Motorola made an alliance with Toshiba and reentered the D-RAM market and has recently signed an agreement with IBM. Yet it adds to this with U.S. strengths in marketing and software. Motorola is now first in the U.S. in semiconductors and number four worldwide. Its chips sales in Japan increased 70% in 1988. It has a broad line but particular strength in microprocessors and memory chips and is a leader in electronics for the auto industry. Its cellular phone is a big success.

Much of the manufacturing competitiveness has come from the Six Sigma quality system implemented by CEO George Fisher. Six Sigma is quality control at a rate of 3.4 per million, which it hopes to attain by 1992. Companywide defects have already fallen from 3,000 per million in 1983 to 200 in 1989. Education and training is stressed. Even bonuses are pegged to quality gains and have averaged 3% of the payroll. Managers have even bought those Japanese *daruma* dolls and wished for Six Sigma. Barriers between divisions are being bridged to produce new and better products. Electronics and cellular communications together designed a secure phone. Motorola has also dramatically improved turnaround time: for one product it now takes three days from order to shipment when 18 months ago it took 30 days.

Business Week reports on Motorola's success in attaining the contract to supply Canon's EOS 35mm camera's microprocessor. It was *netsui* or passion that won the day. Motorola let Canon know how much Canon mattered to them. It tailored the required chip and also invented two other key components.

Other firms are learning to mesh the best of Japan with the best of the U.S. *Business Week* calls the result smart factories.[16] The B-2 computer model is intricate and detailed, allowing Northrop Corp. to bypass a mock up and all but 3% of the parts (probably 30,000 in total) fit perfectly the first time. Previously, the best it had achieved was 50%! Westinghouse Electric installed in General Dynamics Corp.'s plant a flexible manufacturing system that oversees a cluster of machine tools and robots and has succeeded in attaining 100% quality. Boeing will use a new software expert system for production scheduling of helicopters. DEC is saving $135 milion a year from automation. HP uses an expert system to track down defects in disk drives, it does the job in 30 seconds versus up to three days in the past.

THE PREDICTABLE LIFE IS CHANGING

Traditional Japanese arts are being transformed for the modern age. There are electronically activated stage settings in Kabuki and new free form ikebana. Japan has the capacity to change and yet maintain its traditions.

Lifetime employment is more a state of mind than a system. Under lifetime employment expectations, the employee was tied to the firm and

---

[16]Smart factories: America's turn, *BusinessWeek* May 8, 1989.

was willing to make sacrifices. In 1986, 87% of companies practiced lifetime employment. The system started in the late 19th century when companies found themselves competing for skilled labor. For most college graduates, getting a job does not mean practicing a profession but joining a company. Due to meager public retirement benefits, lifetime employment ties a person to the company. A report from Asahi Mutual Life Insurance Co. estimates the costs in terms of lifetime earnings from changing jobs. A job change at 25 reduces income 14%, at 30, 21% and at 35, 16%.

Lifetime employment is being cut in half. Professor Masumi Tsuda surveyed Japanese firms and found that only a third of the companies expressed the desire to maintain their employees until retirement; many believe senior workers are too expensive. Fully 65% expect that lifetime employment will end soon. Trends include offering early retirement and sending older employees to affiliated companies. Even employees in their 40s and 50s have been driven from their companies. A number of the trends we have already discussed are behind the change: Technological innovations including office automation are reducing the need for workers. Changing patterns of consumption from mass production to small segmented markets are requiring manufacturers to take greater risks, making it hard for older employees to keep up. Workers need more adaptable and transferable skills that are less company specific. We have seen this already in the area of finance.

More Japanese are choosing part-time work. Part-time work in Japan can really be full-time but is not on the company permanent employment track. Now 12% of the work force (5.3 million workers) are temporary or part-time compared with 5% a decade ago). This is perhaps as many as 18% if one counts those who work more than 35 hours per week. Women are 72% of those working less than 35 hours. Nissan is using part-timers in the back office and encouraging full-timers to drum up sales door to door. Toyota sees more urban seasonal workers on assembly lines for half the year. Asahi Breweries has hired more than 2,000 housewives to supplement its 700-member sales force. Fuji Bank employs 1,500 middle-aged housewives as part-time sales staff to counter the bank's focus on corporate customers. Fifty-eight percent of Daiei's employees are part-time.

The booming economy means that there are 113 job offers for every 100 workers. Bridgestone Corp. has set up a subsidiary to recruit temporary workers for other companies. It will be interesting to see if the two classes of workers can be combined effectively. The trend reflects a more relaxed attitude toward life and job.

Corporate loyalty is fading. In 1987, 2.7 million people or 4.4% of the work force changed jobs which is up 80% from five years ago. This reflects a labor shortage in Japan with the jobless rate at 2.6%. Vacancies to applicants in 1989 were at the highest since 1974 and firms have had difficulty hiring as many recruits as they want. The ratio of job offers to applicants rose in 1988 from 0.62 to 1.12 and for part-timers 1.53 to 3.48. The percentage of those with lifetime employment guarantees slipped from the 40% of the past, with both a shift in corporate structure away from traditional industries and a shift in preferences and willingness to take more risk.

Nascent job mobility makes it easier for foreign companies to hire experienced workers. Lotus Development hired a former Sony marketer, LSI Logic a NEC manager, and both Daimler Benz and BMW hired former Toyota executives. Japanese companies are hiring more mid-career people. At Sony mid-career hires in 1987 accounted for 13% of the new college graduates hired. A survey found that 79% had hired experienced workers in the recent year (versus 36% in 1984).

A survey of recent college graduates suggests that 60% may job switch. Meanwhile Japanese companies are encouraging senior employees to retire early, indicating another weakening of lifetime guarantees.

More college graduates are going freelance. About 14% or 50,000 graduates this year intend neither to look for an employer nor to continue their studies. They join about 1 million freelancers. Women are benefiting from the growth of new professions including stylists for TV commercials, announcers at trade fairs, makeup and coiffure consultants, food advisors, and jewelry, and interior design specialists. Men are working as photographers, copywriters, and designers.

A survey conducted in September 1988 concerned new business strategies and their effects on workers. Some 89.5% of respondents ordered workers to affiliates or subsidiaries. Due to diversifying during the past three years, consumer demands, fully 57.6% had branched into new business fields including firms in banking, insurance, energy, chemicals, textiles, steel, shipbuilders, railway operators, and machinery. Some 71.2% had created new sections or restructured old ones.

Nissan, though cutting steel mill jobs, recruited mid-career engineers and specialists for its diversification. Kirin Breweries hires mid-career marketing managers. In a survey of 338 companies, 79% had hired experienced workers in 1987 compared to 36% in 1984.

The large companies did more hiring in 1990. Most had hired fewer people since the yen rose sharply. Toyota planned to hire 1,200 university and college graduates, up 30% from this year and 2,150 high school graduates up 40%. Nippon Steel, which diversified into electronics, and four other steel companies reported a shortage of workers. They too had cut their work force when the yen rose in 1985. Canon planned to increase the number of graduates hired by 30%. In the service sector, financial institutions complained of shortages. Seibu planned to hire more foreigners to cope with the shortage.

The wealth and opportunity in Japan is attracting a flood of foreign workers. This has ramifications for the structure of the labor market and the communitarian approach to economic management that has existed in Japan. These workers will need to be integrated into the social fabric and treated as permanent residents. In speaking to the problems, the *Japan Economic Journal* quotes Yasunaga Kakuta, the head of the community association in Toshima, a ward of Tokyo:

> I have gotten accustomed to white people on television or in magazines, but not to Asian nationals. I feel scared sometimes. Here, there is big tension between Japanese and foreign residents.

Foreigners from 64 countries are registered in Toshima, making up 6% of the population of the ward. The workers include Vietnamese, Filipinos, Bangladeshis, Indians, Sri Lankans, and South Americans (mostly from Brazil which has a large Japanese community). Many hold *three k* jobs: *kitanai*, *kitsui* and *kiken* or dirty, heavy, and dangerous. In 1988, a total of 941,000 foreigners were registered; about two-thirds are Korean. A survey of firms in Osaka found that 30% are willing to accept unskilled foreigners, of these 7.5% hoped to hire unskilled worked immediately. Nearly 40% of the firms admitted to a labor shortage, particularly those in construction, metal, and transportation industries. In May 1989, 31 business failures were due to labor shortages. The firms that failed averaged about seven employees and went bankrupt owing on average ¥115 million. Ten were located in the Kinki region of Honshu and nine in Kanto.

The problems of fitting the foreigners into the community begin at a very simple level. We might say they are not networked. In Toshima, the Chinese have not learned to sort their garbage and are noisy at night. Many landlords are asking real estate agents not to show apartments to foreigners because the cultural differences and lack of references makes it hard to know who is a good *gaijin*. The workers fill a labor shortage faced especially by small businesses and manufacturing, but the general population is opposed to the influx.

However Japan's labor structure and lifetime employment are defined, and even as those change, the Japanese firm has gained from the longer term commitment to labor. Lifetime employment has given Japan a distinct advantage in maintaining its adaptability and flexibility. This is one of the paradoxes that Japan highlights. We in the West believe adaptability comes from mobility and the freedom of workers to move to new jobs as well as the freedom of firms to fire and hire without regard for a long-term work force. But it is in creating the structure of mutual commitment that Japan has been able to adapt and adopt new technologies without resistance from its work force.

In a sense, the Japanese have capitalized labor in much the same way that a farmer capitalizes cows. The workers become part of the fixed costs of doing business. This means the operating costs are lower and reflect only the cost of materials that truly cannot be avoided, so the decision to produce will be made at a lower price than if all labor costs were considered variable and labor could be fired at will. Also because of the longer term nature of employment, the firm is more willing to invest in training and continual upgrading of the work force. The negative side of this is a higher breakeven level of output, but this is countered by having a substantial portion of the income in the form of bonuses paid only if the firm is doing well. This is an important way in which the Japanese have redefined the context of economic decision making. North America should learn what it can from this, and Japan should tread carefully in changing it.

THE FUTURE

The opening up of Japan is putting pressure on the social web. Banks and finance companies pay much more for new entrants than do industrial companies. And the bonuses they pay are higher. Typically about one-third of one's salary is in the form of twice annual bonuses that historically varied with how well the company did. Now, the successful finance companies are doing well and offering large employment incentives. There are other perks that make it hard to compare; the older industrial companies provide access to subsidized housing, while the finance companies are newer and less likely to have access to housing. For a few years now the top college graduates were drawn into the finance sector. Finance doesn't produce anything but money; the time horizons are shorter and the investment less. One knows sooner whether a strategy has paid off. So it may be harder to argue that seniority matters much or that long-term loyalty is important. Thus there is more pressure to reward individuals with higher pay and fast advancement. When money is the only product, money talks!

The financial restructuring of Japan will impart important changes into the future. Much of the description of Japanese finance can begin with noting how tightly controlled it was before the 1970s. This must always be mentioned in association with the drive for development with one's own funds and production resources. It was what enabled the Japanese to advance.

It is also important to remember that the stocks in Japan were not issued to raise money, but were largely used to create social mutual interdependence. A small share of the stocks are on the market, and these determine market value. But this market value holds only on the limited base. Once all stocks are salable (i.e., alienable) then head for the hills, the price may come tumbling down! The same is true of land.

To sustain the Japanese economy requires maintaining the camaraderie. All stockholders know they will lose face if they sell their comrade's shares or even borrow on them for short positions. This is not empty face saving, as we in the West see it, but it is a true feeling that each needs the other. It is not markets that lend stability to Japan, it is the social fabric.

Will Japan be stable in the future? This is hard to say. As long as the whole fabric stays together, it has many mutually supporting webs. Like a weaving, it appears strong and stable, and is very serviceable. But also like a weaving, if you pull a thread, the whole fabric weakens and begins to unravel. The thread that is most threatening is the thread of finance. If it is pulled too hard, the fabric itself may unravel.

REFERENCES

Adler, Michael, and Bruce Lehmann (1983) Deviations from Purchasing Power Parity in the Long Run. *Journal of Finance 38*: 1471-87.

Altman, Edward J. and Yoshiki Minowa (1989) Analyzing Risks and Returns and Potential Interest in the U.S. High Yield Corporate Debt Market for Japanese Investors. *Japan and the World Economy 13*: 163-86.

Amaya, Nashiro (1988) The Japanese Economy in Transition: Optimistic about the short term; pessimistic about the long term. *Japan and the World Economy 1*: 101-111.

Ando, Albert and Alan J. Auerbach (1990) The Cost of Capital in Japan: Recent Evidence and Further Results. *Journal of the Japanese and International Economies 4*: 323-350.

Aron, Paul H. (1981) Are Japanese P/E Multiples Too High? New York: Daiwa Securities of America.

Aron, Paul H. (1988a) Japanese P/E Ratios and Accountancy: Rhetoric and Reality, Daiwa Securities America Paul Aron Report 32, August 29.

Aron, Paul H. (1988b) Japanese P/E Multiples: The Shaping of a Tradition, Daiwa Securities America Paul Aron Report 33, August 31.

Aron, Paul H. (1989a) Japanese P/E Multiples: The Tradition Continues, Daiwa Securities America Paul Aron Report 35, October 23.

Aron, Paul H. (1989b) Japanese Non-Life Insurance Companies Final Analysis & Report, Daiwa Securities America Paul Aron Report 37, December 29.

Asako, K., M. Kuninori, T. Inoue, and H. Murase (1989) Tochi hyoka to tobin no q: Multiple q no keisoku (Land evaluation and Tobin's q: a measurement of multiple q) *Economics Today 10* (Japan Development Bank, Tokyo).

Bailey, Warren and William T. Ziemba (1991) An Introduction to Japanese Stock Index Options in Ziemba, Bailey and Hamao (1991).

Balassa, Bela and Marcus Noland (1988) *Japan in the World Economy*. Washington, D.C.: Institute for International Economics.

Bank of Japan (1987) *Comparative Economics Statistics*.

Bank of Japan, Statistics Department (1966) *Hundred Years Statistics of the Japanese Economy*. Tokyo.

Bergsten, C. Fred and William R. Cline (1985) *The United States-Japan Economic Problem*. Washington, D.C.: Institute for International Economics.

Blume, Marchall E. and Donald B. Keim (1987) Risk and Return Characteristics of Lower Grade Bonds. *Financial Analysts Journal 43*: 26-33.

Boone, P. (1989) High Land Values in Japan: Is the Archipelago Worth Eleven Trillion Dollars? Mimeo, Dept. of Economics, Harvard University.

Bose, Mihir (1988) *Crash.* London: Bloomsbury.

Brenner, Menachem, Marti G. Subrahmanyam, and Jun Uno (1989) Stock Index Futures Arbitrage in Japanese Markets. *Japan and the World Economy 1:* 303-330.

Brenner, Menachem, Marti G. Subrahmanyam, and Jun Uno (1990a) Arbitrage Opportunities in Japanese Stock and Futures Markets. *Financial Analysts Journal 46:* 14-24.

Brenner, Menachem, Marti G. Subrahmanyam, and Jun Uno (1990b) The Volatility of the Japanese Stock Indices: Evidence from the Cash and Futures Markets. Mimeo.

Brown, Christie (1988) How to Short Japan. *Forbes.* June 27, 288-289.

Buell, Barbara, Neil Gross, Charles Gaffney, The Myth of Japan's Middle Class. *Business Week,* August 29, 1988, pp. 30-33.

Burnstein, Daniel (1988) *Yen!* New York: Simon & Schuster.

Campbell, John Y. and Yasushi Hamao (1988) Predictable Bond and Stock Returns in the U.S. and Japan: A Study of Long-Term Capital Market Integration. Mimeo, University of California, San Diego.

Canaway, Hugh (1990) Land Prices in Japan: No Cause for Alarm. Baring Securities, May.

Chan, K.C. and G. Andrew Karolyi (1991) The Volatility of the Japanese Stock Market: Evidence from 1977 to 1990 in Ziemba, Bailey and Hamao (1991).

Christopher, Robert (1988) *Second to None: American Companies in Japan.* Fawcett-Columbine.

Christopher, Robert C. (1983) *The Japanese Mind: The Goliath Explained.* New York: Simon & Schuster.

Clark, Rodney (1979) *The Japanese Company.* Tokyo: Charles E. Tuttle.

Credit Suisse First Boston (1988) *The SCFB Guide to the Yen Bond Markets.* Chicago: Probus Publishing.

Cults, R. L. (1990) Power from the ground up: Japan's land bubble. *Harvard Business Review (May-June):* 164-172.

Cutler, David M., James M. Poterba and Lawrence H. Summers (1989) What Moves Stock Prices? *Journal of Portfolio Management 15 (Spring):* 4-12.

Daiwa Secruities Company Ltd (1989) Net Asset Value Special Report: New Asset Value of 450 Companies and Q-ratio Rankings. *Investment Monthly* (November) 17-69.

Darrough, Masako and Trevor Harris (1991) Do Management Forecasts of Earnings Affect Stock Prices in Japan? in Ziemba, Bailey and Hamao (1991).

Dornbusch, Rudiger (1987) Dollars, Debts and Deficits. Cambridge: MIT Press.

Dornbusch, Rudiger (1988) Exchange Rates and Inflation. Cambridge: MIT Press.

Drucker, Peter F. (1985) *Innovation and Entrepreneurship.* New York: Harper & Row.

Drysdale, Peter (1989) Australian-Japan Research Center Data on Investment in Australia, Australia National University, Canberra.

Economic Planning Agency (1988) *Japan in the Year 2000,* Tokyo.

Economist (1988) Japan compared: pity the poor Japanese, December 24.

Elton, Edwin J. and Martin J. Gruber, eds. (1989) *Japanese Financial Markets*. New York: Harper and Row.

Ernst, Dieter (1987) U.S.-Japanese competition and the worldwide restructuring of the electronics industry: a European view in Henderson and Castells (1987).

Fallows, James (1989) Containing Japan. *Atlantic Monthly* (May).

Fama, Eugene F. and G. William Schwert (1977) Asset Returns and Inflation. *Journal of Financial Economics*, November, 115-146.

Fingleton, E. (1990) Japan's Other Capital Market Hits a Bunker. *Institutional Investor (April)*.

Flack, S. (1990) The land of the setting property values. *Forbes (April 30)*.

Frankel, Jeffrey A. (1989) Japanese Finance: A Survey. National Bureau of Economic Research Working Paper No. 3156.

French, Kenneth R. and James Poterba (1990) Japanese and U.S. Cross-Border Common Stock Investments. *Journal of the Japanese and International Economics 4*: 476-493.

French, Kenneth R. and James M. Poterba (1991) Were Japanese stock prices too high? *Journal of Financial Economics. 29*: 337-363.

Friedland, Jonathan (1988) Controlled Collapse. *Far Eastern Economic Review*, October 13.

Goldsmith, Raymond W. (1983) *The Financial Development of Japan, 1868-1977*. New Haven: Yale University Press.

Gregory, Gene (1989) Pickens prescription: hard pill to swallow. *Japan Times*, May 8.

Grossman, Stanford J. (1988) An Analysis of the Implications for Stock and Futures Price Volatility of Program Trading and Dynamic Hedging Strategies. *Journal of Business 61*: 278-298.

Gyourko, J and B.B. Keim (1990) The risk and return characteristics of stock market-based real estate indices. Mimeo, Wharton School, University of Pennsylvania.

Hakansson, Nils H. (1990) Asset Allocation via Supershares, presentation at Berkeley Program in Finance in Asia Seminar, Tokyo, June.

Hamada, Koichi, Kazumasa Iwata, Giorgio Basevi and Paul Krugman (1989) On the International Capital Ownership Pattern at the Turn of the Twenty-First Century. *European Economic Review 33*: 1055-1085.

Hamao, Yasushi (1989) Japanese Stocks, Bonds and Inflation (SBI) 1973-1987. *Journal of Portfolio Management 15* , Winter: 20-26.

Hamao, Yasushi and Roger F. Ibbotson (1989) *The Stocks, Bonds and Inflation (SBI) Japan Yearbook*. Ibbotson Associates.

Hamao, Yasushi, Ronald W. Masulis and Victor Ng (1990) Correlations in Price Changes and Volatility Across International Stock Markets. *Review of Financial Studies 3*: 281-307.

Hardouvelis, Gikas and Steve Peristani (1989) Do Margin Requirements Matter? Evidence from U.S. and Japanese Stock Markets. *FRBNY Quarterly Review*: 16-35.

Hawken, Paul (1987) *Growing a Business*. New York: Simon and Schuster.

Hayashi, Fumio and Tohru Inoue (1989) The Relation between Firm Growth and Q with Multiple Capital Inputs: Theory and Evidence. Mimeo, University of Pennsylvania.

Healey, Derek T. (1989) Japanese Private and Public Capital Outflows and Asian Economic Development in the 1980s. Mimeo, Department of Economics, University of Adelaide.

Higgins, R. C. (1985) Introduction to Japanese Finance: Markets, Institutions and Firms. *Journal of Financial and Quantitative Analysis 20*: 169-172.

Hodder, James E. (1986) Evaluation of Manufacturing Investments: A Comparison of U.S. and Japanese Practices. *Financial Management*, Spring 1986, 17-24.

Hodder, James E. (1991) The Cost of Capital for Industrial Firms in the U.S. and Japan in Ziemba, Bailey and Hamao (1991).

Hodder, James E. and A. E. Tschoegl (1985) Some Aspect of Japanese Corporate Finance. *Journal of Financial and Quantitative Analysis 20*: 173-191.

Hoshi, Takeo and Anil Kashyap (1990) Evidence on Q and Investment for Japanese Firms. *Journal of Japanese and International Economies,* forthcoming.

Hoshi, Takeo, Anil Kashyap and David Scharfstein (1990) Corporate Structure, Liquidity, and Investment: Evidence from Japanese Industrial Groups. *Quarterly Journal of Economics,* forthcoming

Hounshell, D. A. (1988) The same old principles in the new manufacturing. *Harvard Business Review (Nov-Dec)*: 54-61.

Ibbotson and Associates (1992) Stocks, Bonds, Bills and Inflation: 1926-91, Chicago, Illinois.

Ishizumi, Kanji (1988) *Acquiring Japanese Companies.* Tokyo: The Japan Times, Ltd.

Ito, Takatoshi (1988) Japan's Structural Adjustment: The Land/Housing Problem and External Balances. Mimeo, Hitsosubashi University.

Ito, Takatoshi (1990) *The Japanese Economy.* Cambridge: MIT Press, forthcoming.

Ito, Takatoshi and V.V. Roley (1987) News from the U.S. and Japan: Which Moves the Yen/Dollar Exchange Rate? *Journal of Monetary Economics 19:* 255-77.

Jacobs, Jane (1969) *The Economy of Cities.* New York: Vantage Books.

Jacobs, Jane (1984) *Cities and the Wealth of Nations.* New York: Vantage Books.

Japan Securities Research Institute (1988) *Rates of Return on Common Stocks.*

Japan Securities Research Institute (1988) *Report of Japan's Stock Price Level*, Tokyo.

Japan Securities Research Institute (1990) *Securities Market in Japan, 1990.*

Japanese Ministry of Finance and the United State Department of the Treasury, Working Group on Yen/Dollar Exchange Rate Issues (1984) *Report by the Working Group on Yen/Dollar Exchange Rate, Financial and Capital Market Issues to Japanese Minister of Finance Noboru Takeshita (and) U.S. Secretary of the Treasury Donald T. Regan*, Tokyo, May.

Jardine Flemming (1989) Japanese Indices, April.

JETRO (1992) *Nippon Business, Facts and Figures.* Tokyo.

Johnson, Chalmers (1982) *MITI and the Japanese Miracle: The Growth of Industrial Policy, 1925-1975.* Stanford, California: Stanford University Press.

Kagono, Tadao (1986) A Comparison of Management of Japanese and U.S. Companies (in Japanese), Tokyo.

Kahn, Herman (1973) *The Emerging Japanese Superstate.* Harmondsworth, England: Penguin Books.

Kahn, Herman and Thomas Petter (1973) *The Japanese Challenge.* Harmondsworth, England: Penguin Books.

Kang, Hyosuk (1989) Effects of seasoned equity offerings in Korea on sharehlder's wealth in Rhee and Chang.

Kanter, Rosabeth Moss (1989) *When Giants Learn to Dance.* New York: Simon and Schuster.

Keizai Koho Center (1988) *Japan 1988: An International Comparison.* Tokyo: The Japan Times, Ltd.

Keizai Koho Center (1989) *Japan Periodicals,* Japan Institute of Social and Economic Affairs.

Kennedy, Paul (1989) *The Rise and Fall of the Great Powers.* New York, Vintage Books.

Kester, Carl (1991) *Japanese Takeovers: The Global Contest for Corporate Control.* Harvard Business School Press, Boston.

King, Stephen (1991) Is Japanese investment under threat? *James Capel,* December.

Kobayashi, Kaoru (1988) Japanese Corporations Expanding Abroad, in *Top 1500 Japanese Corporations.*

Kobayashi, Takao (1990) The Fundamental Value of Japanese Stocks. Mimeo, University of Tokyo.

Komahashi, Kenichi and Norifumi Tsukada (1991) Land; Banking: SOS. *Tokyo Business Today,* November, 30-38.

Konya and Wakasugi (1987) Tobin's Q and Stock Price. *Securities Research 80.*

Krugman, Paul (1988) Exchange Rates and International Adjustment. *Japan and the World Economy 1:* 63-87.

Krugman, Paul (1989) Persistent Trade Effects of Large Exchange Rate Shocks. *Quarterly Journal of Economics, 104:* 635-654.

Krugman, Paul and Richard Baldwin (1987) The Persistance of the U.S. Trade Deficit. *Brookings Papers on Economic Activity 1:* 1-43.

Kuboi, Takashi (1989) *Business Practices and Taxation in Japan.* Tokyo: The Japan Times, Ltd.

Kurokawa (1988) On the Stock Market Collapse: A View from Tokyo, Speech to the Brookings Institution, March 8.

Lincoln, Edward J. (1988) *Japan, Facing Economic Maturity.* Washington, D.C.: Brookings Institution.

Luskin, Donald L. (1988) *Portfolio Insurance: A Guide to Dynamic Hedging.* New York: John Wiley.

Lynn, Richard (1988) *Educational Achievement in Japan.* MacMillan.

Maidment, Paul (1988) Japanese Finance: The End of an Era. *The Economist.* December, 10.

Mankiw, N.G. and D.N. Weil (1988) The baby boom, the baby bust and the housing market, W.P. No 2794 (December), National Bureau of Economic Research, Cambridge, MA.

Mann, A and Charles Schultze (1988) Savings and investment in the U.S. economy. Mimeo, Brookings Institution. Washington, D.C.

Mansfield, M. (1989) The Century of the Pacific, *Speaking of Japan*, KKC, March.

Marcus, Philip N. (1985) Evidence in Decline in Standards in William J. Johnston, ed., *Education on Trial*, San Francisco, Institute of Contemporary Studies.

Marris, S. (1985) *Deficits and the dollar: the world economy at risk.* Policy Analyses in International Economics #14. Washington, D.C.: Institute for International Economics.

Masato, Numako and Adisak Taveerojkumsri (1989) Mergers and Acquisitions: Japanese Style, term paper in Finance III, University of Tsukuba.

McCraw, Thomas K., ed. (1986) *America versus Japan.* Boston: Harvard Business School Press.

McDonald, Jack (1989) The *Mochiai* Effect: Japanese Corporate Cross-Holdings. *Journal of Portfolio Management* (Fall): 90-94.

McKinnon, Ronald and Kenichi Ohno (1986) Getting the Exchange Rate Right: Insular versus Open Economies. Mimeo, Stanford University.

Metz, Tim (1988) *Black Monday.* New York: William Morrow.

Mikami, Tetriji (1990) Investment Strategy: Convertible Bonds and Equity Warrants, Presentation at Berkeley Program in Finance in Asia Seminar, June.

Modigliani, Franco (1988) Reagan's Economic Policies: A Critique. *Oxford Economic Papers 40*: 397-426.

Modigliani, Franco and André Modigliani (1987) The Growth of the Federal Deficit and the Role of Public Attitudes. *Public Opinion Quarterly 51.*

Morishima, Michio (1982) *Why Has Japan 'Succeeded'? Western Technology and the Japanese Ethos*, Cambridge: Cambridge University Press.

Murphy, R. Taggart (1989) Power without Purpose: The Crisis of Japan's Global Financial Dominance. *Harvard Business Review, Mar-Apr*: 71-83.

Myers, David H. and Saehiko Ujiie (1988) Performance Measurement in Japan: The Coming of Age, Benefits and Compensation, *International, June* 27-33.

Nakamura, Masao and Alice Nakamura (1990) Risk Behavior and the Determinants of Bonus versus Regular Pay in Japan. *Journal of the Japanese and Internatinal Economies,* forthcoming.

Noland, Marcus (1988) Japanese Household Portfolio Allocation Behavior. *Review of Economics and Statistics 70:* 135-139.

Normura Research Institute (1988) *Normura Fact Book*, Tokyo.

Norris, Floyd (1990) Investors Relish Bet against Japan. *New York Times*, January 15, page D4.

Ohno, Kenichi (1986) Estimating Purchasing Power Parities in the 1970s and 80s: The Price Pressure Approach. Mimeo, Stanford University.

Okimoto Daniel I., Takuo Sugano, and Franklin B. Weinstein, eds. (1984) *Competitive Edge: The Semiconductor Industry in the U.S. and Japan.* Stanford, Calif.: Stanford University Press.

Ouchi, William G. (1981) *Theory Z: How American Business Can Meet the Japanese Challenge.* Reading, MA: Addison-Wesley Publishing.

Ouchi, William G. (1984) *The M-Form Society.* Reading, MA: Addison-Wesley Publishing.

Pascale, Richard Tanner and Anthony G. Althos (1981) *The Art of Japanese Management.* New York, Simon and Schuster.

Patrick, Hugh and Henry Rosovsky, eds. (1976) *Asia's New Giant: How the Japanese Economy Works.* Washington, D.C.: Brookings Institution.

Patrick, Hugh and Ryuichiro Tachi, eds. (1986) *Japan and the United States Today: Exchange Rates, Macroeconomic Policies, and Financial Market Innovations.* New York: Center on Japanese Economy and Business, Columbia University.

Petri, Peter A. (1984) *Modeling Japanese-American Trade: A Study of Asymmetric Interdependence.* Cambridge, MA: Harvard University Press.

Pettway, Richard S. and Takeshi Yamada (1986) Mergers in Japan and their Impacts upon Stockholders Wealth. *Financial Management 15*: 43-52.

Pettway, Richard S., Neil W. Sicherman and Takeshi Yamada (1989) Japanese Mergers: Relative Size, Corporate Collectivism, and Shareholders' Wealth, in Rhee and Chang (1989).

Pettway, Richard S., Neil W. Sicherman and Takeshi Yamada (1989) The Market for Corporate Control, the Level of Agency Costs and Corporate Collectivism in Japanese Mergers in Elton and Gruber (1989).

Piore, Michael J. and Charles F. Sabel (1984) *The Second Industrial Divide.* New York: Basic Books.

Philips, George (1989) Warrants: Don't Let Them be Misunderstood. *Global Investor*, April: 21-25.

Pickens, T. Boone (1987) *Boone.* Boston: Houghton Mifflin.

Porter, Michael (1989) NHK television interview.

Prestowitz, Clyde V., Jr. (1988) *Trading Places: How We Allowed Japan to Take the Lead.* New York: Basic Books.

Rachev, S. T. and William T. Ziemba (1992) The Distribution of Golf Course Membership Prices in Japan. Mimeo, University of Califronia, Santa Barbara.

Reich, Robert (1991) *The Work of Nations.* New York: Alfred A. Knopf.

Reischauer, Edwin O. (1977) *The Japanese.* Cambridge, MA: Harvard University Press.

Rhee, S. Ghon and Rosita P. Chang, eds (1989) *Research on Pacific Basin Capital Markets.* North Holland.

Roehl, Tom (1985) Data sources for research in Japanese finance. *Journal of Financial and Quantitative Analysis 20*: 273-276..

Roley, V. Vance (1987) U.S. Money Announcements and Covered Interest Parity: The Case of Japan. *Journal of International Money and Finance 6*: 577-70.

Roll, Richard (1988) The International Crash of 1987, in *Black Monday and the Future of Financial Markets* R. W. Kamphuis, R. C. Kormendi and J. W. H. Watson, eds, Chicago: Dow-Jones Irwin.

Rubinstein, Mark (1987) Derivative Assets Analysis. *Journal of Economic Perspectives, 1:* 73-93.

Sasaki, N. (1981) *Management and Industrial Structure in Japan.* Oxford: Pergamon.

Sato, Ryuzo (1988) The U.S.-Japan Trade Imbalance from the Japanese Perspective, Working Paper No. 2379, National Bureau of Economic Research, Cambridge, Massachusetts.

Schoenfeld, Steven A. (1988) The Coming Explosion of the Japanese Futures Markets, *Intermarket*, September.

Schwartz, Sandra L. (1989) Lessons from Japan on a Craft Approach to Creativity, and Innovation. Mimeo, Presented at the University of Calgary.

Schwartz, Sandra L. and Emily Sion (1992) *Ecos: Toward Enablement and Responsible Management.* Forthcoming.

Senner, Madis (1989) *Japanese Euroderivatives.* London: Euromoney Publications.

Shale, Tony (1989) Too much, too soon in the July/August 1989 issue of *Global Investor.*

Sharpe, William F. and Gordon Alexander (1989) *Investments,* 4th Edition, Englewood Cliffs, NJ: Prentice Hall.

Shaw, Julian, Edward O. Thorp and William T. Ziemba (1992) Convergence to Efficiency of the Nikkei Put Warrant Market of 1989-91. Mimeo, University of British Columbia.

Shibata, Yoko (1991) The mounting anguish of the Japanese banks. *Global Finance,* January, 32-35.

Shigehara, K. (1991) Japan's experience with use of monetary policy and the process of liberalization. *Monetary and Economic Studies 9* (Bank of Japan).

Shoken Toshishintatu Kyokai (1989) Investment Trusts in Japan, 1989, Tokyo Shoken Kaikan, Nihonbashi Kayaba-cho 1-5-8, Chu-ku, Tokyo.

Solnik, Bruno (1991) *International Investments, 2nd Edition.* Reading Mass: Addison-Wesley.

Stone, Douglas and William T. Ziemba (1990) Land and Stock Prices in Japan. Mimeo, University of British Columbia and Frank Russell Company, presented at the Berkeley Program in Finance in Asia, Tokyo, June.

Stone, Douglas and William T. Ziemba (1992a) Land and stock prices in Japan. *Journal of Economic Perspectives,* forthcoming.

Stone, Douglas and William T. Ziemba (1992b) Relationships between land and stock prices in Japan. Mimeo, University of British Columbia.

Stone, P.B. (1969) *Japan Surges Ahead: The Story of An Economic Miracle.* New York: Praeger Publishers.

Suzuki, Yoshio (1988) *The Japanese Financial System.* Oxford: Oxford University Press.

Takagi, Keizo (1989) The Rise of Land Prices in Japan: The Determination Mechanism and the Effect of Taxation System. *Bank of Japan Monetary and Economic Studies* 7: 93-139.

Taylor, James (1985) *Shadows of the Rising Sun*. Tokyo, Charles E. Tuttle Co.

Thurow, Lester (1985) *The Zero Sum Solution*. New York: Simon and Schuster.

Thurow, Lester (1988) America's economy: a formula for recovery. *Financial Executive*, May-June.

Thurow, Lester, ed (1986) *The Management Challenge*. Cambridge: MIT Press.

Tobin, James (1987) *Policies for Prosperity*, edited by Peter M. Jackson, Cambridge: MIT Press.

Tokyo Business Today (1991) The Liberal Democratic Party, October, pp 14-22.

Tokyo Stock Exchange (1992) 1991 Fact Book, 2-1 Nihombashi-Kobuto-cho, Chuo-ku, Tokyo 103.

Toyo Keizai Shimposha (1992) Japan Company Handbook, First and Second Sections, various issues updated quarterly.

Ueda, Kazuo (1990a) Financial deregulation and the demand for money in Japan, in *Financial Sector in Open Economies*, P.Hooper et al, eds.

Ueda, Kazuo (1990b) Are Japanese Stock Prices Too High? *Journal of the Japanese and International Economists* 3: 351-370.

Ueda, Kazuo (1991) A comparative perspective on Japanese monetary policy, NBER conference on Japanese monetary policy.

Van Slyke, Richard (1989) Financial Services: Japan's Next Conquest. *New York Times*, Apr 6.

Viner, Aron (1975) *Modern Japanese Organizations and Decision Making*. Berkeley: University of California Press.

Viner, Aron (1979) *Japan as Number One*. Cambridge MA: Harvard University Press.

Viner, Aron (1987) *Inside Japanese Financial Markets*. Homewood, Illinois: Dow Jones-Irwin and *The Japan Times*.

Viner, Aron (1988) *The Emerging Power of Japanese Money*. Homewood, Illinois: Dow Jones-Irwin and *The Japan Times*.

Visser, Margaret (1986) *Much Depends on Dinner*. Toronto: McClelland and Stewart.

Von Wolferen, Karel (1989) *The Enigma of Japanese Power*. London: MacMillan.

Webber, Alan M. (1989) Yasuhiro Nakasone: The Statesman as CEO (interview), *Harvard Business Review*, Mar-Apr: 84-94.

West, K. (1991) An aggregate demand-aggregate supply analysis of Japanese monetary policy, 1973-1990, presented at the NBER conference on Japanese monetary policy.

Whiting, Robert (1987)*You Gotta have Wa*.

Wood, R. C. (1987) Japan's Economic Masochism. *Forbes*, Sept 21.

Wray, Harry (1989) Japanese Education: Is it Better than American Education? Mimeo, University of Tsukuba.

Young, John (1989) NHK Interview.

Ziemba, William T. (1990) Land and stock prices in Japan, Presentation to the Berkeley Program in Finance in Asia Seminar, June.

Ziemba, William T. (1991a) Cumulative Effects of Fundamental Variables on the Tokyo Stock Exchange: 1979-89, working paper, University of British Columbia.

Ziemba, William T. (1991b) Currency Hedging Strategies for U.S. Investment in Japan and Japanese Investment in the U.S., in Ziemba, Bailey and Hamao, eds.

Ziemba, William T. (1991c) Japanese Security Market Regularities: Monthly, Turn of the Month and Year, Holiday and Golden Week Effects, *Japan and the World Economy 3*: 119-146.

Ziemba, William T. (1991d) The Chicken or the Egg: Land and Stock Prices in Japan, in Ziemba, Bailey and Hamao (1991).

Ziemba, William T. (1993) *Strategies for Making and Keeping Excess Profits in the Stock Market*. New York, William Morrow, forthcoming, spring.

Ziemba, William T. and Donald B. Hausch (1987) *Dr. Z's Beat the Racetrack*. New York, William Morrow.

Ziemba, William T. and Sandra L. Schwartz (1991a) The Growth in the Japanese Stock Market, 1949-90 and Prospects for the Future. *Management and Decision Economics 12*: 183-195.

Ziemba, William T. and Sandra L. Schwartz (1991b) *Invest Japan: The Structure, Performance and Opportunities of the Stock, Bond, and Fund Markets*. Chicago: Probus Publishing.

Ziemba, William T. and Sandra L. Schwartz (1992) *Japanese Futures, Options and Warrant Markets*. Chicago: Probus Publishing.

Ziemba, William T., Warren Bailey and Yasushi Hamao, eds (1991) *Japanese Financial Market Research*. Amsterdam: North Holland.

INDEX

OTHER JAPAN TITLES
FROM PROBUS

Japan Inc.: Global Strategies of Japanese Trading Corporations, Max Eli

The Japanese Bond Markets: An Overview & Analysis, ed. Frank J. Fabozzi

The Japanese Management Mystique: The Reality Behind the Myth, Jon Woronoff

The Pacific Rim Futures and Options Markets: A Comprehensive, Country-by-Country Referrence to the World's Fastest-Growing Financial Markets, Keith K.H. Park & Steven A. Schoenfeld

Unlocking Japan's Markets: Seizing Marketing and Distribution Opportunities in Today's Japan, Michael R. Czinkota & Jon Woronoff

Venture Japan: How Growing Companies Worldwide Can Tap into the Japanese Venture Capital Markets, James W. Borton

FORTHCOMING JAPAN TITLES
FROM PROBUS

The Japanese Distribution System: Opportunities & Obstacles/Structure & Practices, Michael R. Czinkota & Masaaki Kotabe (Fall 1992)

The Japanese Futures, Options, and Warrants Markets: Structure, Perfomance and Opportunities, William T. Ziemba & Sandra L. Schwartz (Spring 1992)

About the Publisher

PROBUS PUBLISHING COMPANY

Probus Publishing Company fills the informational needs of today's business professional by publishing authoritative, quality books on timely and relevant topics, including:

- Investing
- Futures/Options Trading
- Banking
- Finance
- Marketing and Sales
- Manufacturing and Project Management
- Personal Finance, Real Estate, Insurance and Estate Planning
- Entrepreneurship
- Management

Probus books are available at quantity discounts when purchased for business, educational or sales promotional use. For more information, please call the Director, Corporate/Institutional Sales at 1-800-PROBUS-1, or write:

Director, Corporate/Institutional Sales
Probus Publishing Company
1925 N. Clybourn Avenue
Chicago, Illinois 60614
FAX (312) 868-6250